GETTING BUSTED

GETTING BUSTED

PERSONAL EXPERIENCES OF ARREST TRIAL and PRISON
EDITED BY ROSS FIRESTONE

A DOUGLAS BOOK
Distributed by the World Publishing Company

DESIGN: BOB CATO AND IRA FRIEDLANDER

ACKNOWLEDGEMENTS

"Walking the Beat: Advice From an Old-Timer" is reprinted by permission of The World Publishing Company and is from *Walking the Beat* by Gene Radano. Copyright © 1968 by Gene Radano.

"Carmencita in Blue: A Dialogue at Dawn" is reprinted by permission of The Village Voice, Inc. Copyrighted by The Village Voice, Inc. 1968.

"Millbrook Raid: An Eyewitness Report" is reprinted by permission of The East Village Other, Inc.

"Gross Weirdness at the Barricades" is from manuscript and printed by permission of the author. Copyright © 1970 by Terry Southern.

"The Day They Busted the Grateful Dead" is reprinted from *The Pill Versus the Springhill Mine Disaster* by Richard Brautigan. Copyright © 1968 by Richard Brautigan. A Seymour Lawrence Book/Delacorte Press. Used by permission. First published by the Four Seasons Foundation in its Writing series edited by Donald Allen.

"Grandma With Orange Hair" is reprinted by permission of The World Publishing Company and is from *The Armies of the Night* by Norman Mailer. Copyright © 1968 by Norman Mailer.

"The United States of America Vs. Piero Heliczer" is from manuscript and printed by permission of the author.

"Die Nigger Die!" is reprinted from *Die Nigger Die!* by H. Rap Brown. Copyright © 1969 by Lynne Brown and used by permission of the publisher, The Dial Press.

"The Shit Hits the Fan at Columbia" is from *The Strawberry Statement*, by James Simon Kunen. Copyright © 1968, 1969 by

CONTENTS

EDITOR'S PREFACE x

INTRODUCTION by MARTIN GARBUS xi

ONE **ARREST**

Prologue: GENE RADANO, "Walking the Beat: Advice From an Old-Timer" 3

I. **Encounter**

CHARLES WRIGHT, "Carmencita in Blue: A Dialogue at Dawn" 5

ANONYMOUS, "Millbrook Raid: An Eyewitness Report" 6

TERRY SOUTHERN, "Gross Weirdness at the Barricades" 8

RICHARD BRAUTIGAN, "The Day They Busted the Grateful Dead" 15

II. **Confrontation**

NORMAN MAILER, "Grandma With Orange Hair" 17

PIERO HELICZER, "The United States of America Vs. Piero Heliczer" 24

H. RAP BROWN, "Die Nigger Die!" 27

JAMES SIMON KUNEN, "The Shit Hits the Fan at Columbia" 30

JUDITH MALINA, "Last Performance at The Living Theatre Invective" 33

HARVEY ROTTENBERG, "Planted, Burnt, and Busted" 37

GREGORY JOHN-MARTIN-PORTLEY, "For Refusing to Unwalk My Dog August 6, 1965" 43

LESLIE A. FIELDER, "On Being Busted at Fifty" 45

PAUL KRASSNER, "The Diamond Ball" 56

LENNOX RAPHAEL, "The *Che!* Bust" 59

RALPH SCHOENSTEIN, "My Kind of Jail, Chicago Has" 64

III. **Madness**

FRANK REYNOLDS, "Freewheelin Frank" 71

JESSE P. RITTER, JR., "Nightmare in a California Jail" 79

ELDRIDGE CLEAVER, "Affadavit #2: Shoot-Out in Oakland" 85

Epilogue: DOC STANLEY, "Policemanship: A Guide for the Arrested" 95

TWO **TRIAL**

Prologue: BERTOLT BRECHT, "Testimony: The House Committee on Un-American Activities" Presented by Eric Bentley 101

BILLIE HOLIDAY, "Don t Know If I'm Coming or Going" 126
WILHELM REICH, "Four Documents: Response, Decree, Statement, and Proposal" 131
LENNY BRUCE, "My Obscenity Trial" 144
TIMOTHY LEARY, "Episode & Postscript" 168
FRANK BARDACKE, "On Trial With the Oakland Seven" 190
MICHAEL ZWERIN, "One of Them" 205
Epilogue: ABBIE HOFFMAN, "Testimony: United States of America, Plaintiff, vs. David T. Dellinger, et al" 211

THREE PRISON
Prologue: JOHNNY CASH, "Folsom Prison Blues" 229
I. Time
JOHN ROSEVEAR, "The Fourth Mad Wall" 231
DONN PEARCE, "Life-styles: Building Time" 237
JAAKOV KOHN, "Time": Two Interviews 246
II. Inside
BUSBY CROCKETT, "The Prison Trip" 259
BOB KAUFMAN, "Jail Poem" 264
MICHAEL ROSSMAN, "Notes From the County Jail" 264
LAWRENCE FERLINGHETTI, "Santa Rita Journal" 280
JOAN BAEZ, "Notes From Santa Rita" 284
BARBARA DEMING, "Prison Notes" 287
KEN KESEY, "Jail Diary" 291
ABIODUN, "Silent Tears and Prison Noises" 295
PIRI THOMAS, "Sex in the Can" 300
RAY BREMSER, "Penal Madness" 305
HERBERT HUNCKE, "Cuba" and "Dancing in Prison" 308
III. Looking Out
MALCOLM X, "Satan" 311
JULIAN BECK, "Thoughts on the Theatre from Jail: Three Letters to a Friend" 319
DICK GREGORY, "Nigger" 323
JERRY RUBIN, "To My Brothers and Sisters" 325
JOHN SINCLAIR, "A Letter to Leni" 329
IV. Death Row
TRUMAN CAPOTE, "Eight Interviews With the Condemned" 331
CARYL CHESSMAN, "Ex Ungue Leonem" 335
EDGAR SMITH, "Life in the Death House" 339
Epilogue: ETHRIDGE KNIGHT, "He Sees Through Stone" 347

EDITOR'S PREFACE

I would like to acknowledge my indebtedness to some of the people whose help has made this book possible. Ira Cohen was a continuous source of profitable suggestions and good advice. Jaakov Kohn opened the resources of the *East Village Other* to me with his characteristic generosity. Mary Higgins of the Wilhelm Reich Infant Trust Fund placed at my disposal important documents by Wilhelm Reich. Terry Southern allowed me to record a little known aspect of the events at Chicago during the Democratic National Convention of 1968. Martin Garbus gave me numerous suggestions and took the trouble to write his perceptive introduction to the book. Gerd Stern and Saul Gottlieb both helped me locate material I would otherwise have missed. And in the formation and development of the basic idea of this book, the sensitive judgment of Alan Douglas was of incalculable benefit.

ROSS FIRESTONE

Introduction
MARTIN GARBUS

Former Associate Director of the
American Civil Liberties Union

"Getting busted" is no longer an experience primarily limited to the inhabitants of the ghetto. When fifteen million Americans, young and old, use drugs, and even more feel that the country's laws are not worth obeying; when it is not uncommon to be stopped and frisked in the streets or even have your house intruded into, it is only a matter of time until the judicial glue binding the country together becomes unstuck.

John Sinclair, a White Panther, receives a sentence of ten years for possession of marijuana. Timothy Leary gets an equivalent amount of time. And Lenny Bruce is hounded to an early death. Selective enforcement of the laws is not uncommon. The government's unlawful use of the legal process was known and felt long before the trial of the Chicago 8. What is new is that the mass arrests and intolerable jail sentences are finally becoming visible to the middle class because it is now they, and their children, who are being put into the jails they used to think were reserved for some other sort of citizenry. The arrest and jailing experience now provides a common bond for the white radical, the militant black, the student pot smoker, and those traditionally repudiated as criminal.

The way in which people are abused by the law cannot be made clear merely be examining the arrest and jail statistics. This book, because it allows the victims to tell it as it has been for them, conveys the grotesque misuse of law so common today in this country. The first person narratives show that Allen Ginsberg's prophecy in *Howl* that some of the best minds of his generation were being institutionalized and destroyed and Lenny Bruce's remark that "in the Halls of Justice, the only justice is in the halls" are perhaps truer today than when they were first uttered some years ago.

The prosecution and persecution of many of the men and women in this book have taught some of us who should have known it before that the illegitimacy of any legal system must in the long run be a force towards its change. The law contributes to the larger revolution and reform within the system because it is so out of touch with the people whose will it allegedly serves. For example, the arrest and conviction of Timothy Leary, the media appointed representative of the drug culture, played a part in teaching the country that drug users come not only from minority groups in the ghettos, but from Middle America as well. As one prominent citizen put it at the time of the 1966 arrest of Timothy Leary in Millbrook, New York: "When they got Leary I felt they got one of us. He's middle class, and I am undeniably so. For the first time I saw drug laws as affecting my own life and the lives of my children."

There is still at least one area of the law strictly reserved for the poor and unschooled and despised. The members of the middle class are virtually granted immunity from the intolerable death penalty. Today the number of people in the Death House throughout the fifty states reaches over five hundred—the largest number in this nation's history. San Quentin has recently built eighteen additional condemned cells to help house those 84 souls who wait down the corridor from California's apple green death chamber. The pain of waiting for months and years in a condemned cell for a death that is certain to come is something we need to have told to us in the first person, and this book has done that.

Yet however gross the inequities of the legal system are, I still believe it is the best forum we have for the confrontation between those in and out of power. In the courtroom the balance is as nearly equal as it can be. And it is the courtroom spectacle that often reveals to the public what has always been there by exposing the system as seen by its victims. The novelty of the experience for the rest of us suggests something important about the callous disregard "we" have reserved for "them."

Each criminal case tried in this country is entitled "The People vs." a named defendant. This is misleading. More often than not, "The People" are represented by the defendant-writers in this book: H. Rap Brown, a university professor, or a Chicago 8 defendant. The ones initiating the prosecution represent government estranged from the people.

As lawyer and friend to many of the men in this book, I have shared some of the described experiences. I have been as frustrated as they have because no one knew what was happening to the receivers of the state's justice. Ross Firestone's book is important because it makes the reader share a pain that has been too long kept private.

ARREST

PROLOGUE
ENCOUNTER
CONFRONTATION
MADNESS
EPILOGUE

PROLOGUE
GENE RADANO

Walking the Beat:
Advice from an Old-Timer

"There are a lot of ways to use your nightstick, kid. If you see a fight on your post first thing to do is to drop your stick to the pavement. I'll make a lot of noise. By the time you get there the two parties usually will have made a hasty peace. A man carries a stick doesn't mean he has to use it only one way. But, thank God, there are still cops with courage enough to use a stick in the way some people find objectionable. There's a time for that too. Why: 'cause he uses a stick he's a sadist? They want him to use his hands! . . . Do you think you can whip everyone on your beat with your bare hands? Then you ought to be fighting on television! . . . It's not the Marquis of Queensbury rules that work out there: remember that. So common sense: a smart cop uses his stick. When necessary! These days a civilian has trouble walking the streets. Without those cops the bums wouldn't even make room for *anybody*. They'd push everyone in the gutter. . . . Sadists? How many of those college-graduate citizens—who do all the squawking about humanity—how many of them ever had to deal with a mob? They never even heard what a mob sounds like! Yet they want to sit and judge us! Everybody wants to judge us these days! And they'll judge you too when the time comes. What the hell do they know about a mob? No bastard knows anything except the poor cop whose ass is on the line. A mob is the ugliest animal in the world! You just try to quiet them by quoting something out of a book. They'd run over you like a herd of cattle! And you haven't got time to wait for the Supreme Court to make a decision. You only got five seconds to decide whether to run like a dog or stand up like a cop. Five seconds: you, God, a mob and no reference books. So you hold the club short and you hit the first son-of-a-bitch on the head—bang! three stitches! If the bastard keeps coming—bang! three more stitches! And that makes you a fascist! For weeks they'll argue whether you did or didn't use too much force! For weeks! And you only had five seconds! . . . I say the cop who stands up to the bums does more for law and order than a roomful of judges. I once shot it out with two bums. On a stickup. I killed them. Whenever I go by where they used to live their friends mutter under their breaths. But they make room! They make room! And they'll make room for you too till you show them they don't have to."

ENCOUNTER
CHARLES WRIGHT

Carmencita in Blue:
A Dialogue at Dawn

Personally, my encounters with "Carmencita in blue" (that's what I heard the fuzz called on Clinton Street) have been brief, innocent, painless. I'm like, clean. No weapons or hard stuff. But I'm always in the street. From Beekman Place to the Bowery to Brooklyn and back again. I am only an innocent traveler through this uptight island of concrete and corruption. But my dialogue with two of New York's finest at five in the morning sounds a little like a scene out of Bill Burrough's police state.

Stoned, feeling surprisingly good, walking down Broadway, below 14th Street. Less than a block away, I spot this cat on the opposite side of the street. There's something about his movements. Something isn't kosher. He crosses over to my side of the street and eases into a dark store entrance. But it so happens that this is where I turn the corner. We are on the same side of the street. He's in the door of his corner which faces Broadway and I'm turning my corner, going west, picking up a little speed.

And who comes cruising along but "Carmencita in blue." Just tooling along like two men who are out for a good day's hunt in the country.

The squad car pulls over to the curb and I go to meet them. The driver looks pleasant, is young, blond: "Do you have any ID?"

"No. Some son of a bitch stole my passport and I wish you'd find the schmuck."

"Where do you live?"

"Down the street. I'm sure I can find something that will verify who I am."

A brief silence. Calm as an opium head, I'm casually leaning against the squad car, smiling at the driver.

"Are you the good guys or the bad guys? You see I'm out to save the city from corruption, like you guys. I'm working on my sainthood this year."

The cop sitting next to the driver takes off his cap and runs his hand through his dark straight hair which is combed back from his forehead. His nose is shaped exactly like a hawk's.

"He's too much." Hawk Nose said.

"Jesus," I lamented. "Are you guys stoned or am I stoned?"

Blondie liked that one. He was getting his jollies off and so was Charles Wright.

Then Hawk Nose came on with: "We're looking for somebody. We wanna bust somebody's balls."

There was a touch of cold reality in his voice.

Equally real, I replied: "Well, if you bust my balls, you'd better leave me on the sidewalk."

Blondie was still smiling and made a playful lunge for his gun or what I hoped was a playful lunge.

Hawk Nose, still in his tough, cop shitting bag, is visibly irritated.

"There was a robbery a few minutes ago," he said, "and you fit the description of the guy. Height, weight, and everything."

Everything meant color. And for a second I had a high fantasy of someone trying to masquerade as me. I started to tell them about the cat in the store entrance. But he didn't look like me and had probably disappeared anyway.

So I stood up straight and waited for the next line.

It was a long time coming, no doubt they were turning different endings over in their mind.

"You'd better not do anything," Hawk Nose warned, "or else we'll lock your ass up."

"Good morning," I said, smiling.

And two of New York's finest rode off into the lambent dawn, the street lamps dazzlingly white like paranoid ghosts, under a wide, uncommitted sky.

ANONYMOUS

Millbrook Raid:
An Eyewitness Report

Sunday morning, April 17, 1966, approximately one forty-five. Six candles burning in the alcove in the third floor room where I am stretched out on a mattress reading the I Ching. Question: How do I avoid game behavior?

The door crashes open. A strong light is thrown in my face. A man in jeans, jacket and cap shouts, "Don't move! Stay where you are!" I know it is the police, having thought of this possibility. A man's home is his castle, is it not? Were I my Scotch-Irish grandfather, an un-uniformed intruder would be shot in-

6

stantly. I shrug and ask for a cigarette. "You've got enough to smoke, don't you?" comes back the sarcastic reply.

Under such circumstances, one simply continues to read the I Ching.

Two or three other men come into the room and mill about for a few moments. One says belligerently, "What you got those candles burning for?" I shrug again. I don't explain that there is no electric outlet in this corner, no light source for reading other than flame.

A tall man in trench coat and cowboy hat comes into the room. "Get your pants on and come downstairs," he says. I get up. "Who are you? What kind of work do you do?" he asks. "I'm a teacher and writer," I reply, showing him an article of mine in Spanish, accompanied by my picture. This seems to calm him down. Perhaps he is afraid of offending someone with "credentials." "I would think a writer and teacher would want more luxurious surroundings," he says gesturing toward the sparsely furnished room. "Writers and teachers are simple people," I counter. "This is quite enough for my taste."

"The writers and teachers I know aren't simple people!" he intones ominously. He leaves the room. I feel sorry for him. I later find out he is Sheriff Quinlan.

I get dressed and go downstairs. I stand around on the second floor landing for some time, while the other guests are routed out of bed. A girl friend of mine from out of town, visiting Castalia for the weekend, is taken into a bathroom by a kindly police matron, disrobed, and searched. I wonder why none of the men are stripped and searched.

Later she is sitting on the floor, leaning against the wall, when three policemen bully their way past and knock a huge framed picture off the wall. It smashes into my friend's face, cutting her lip badly. She bleeds and one of the guests, a medical doctor, comforts her and treats her lip. Later she has a headache and wants an aspirin. We go upstairs to get some Bufferin she has in her purse. As she takes out the bottle, a policeman comes into the room and takes the tablets away from her for "analysis." We go downstairs again. The police matron looks at us and says, "I've got a headache, too. It must be a sympathy headache."

The District Attorney, well dressed, like The New Breed, tie clasped by a tiny silver sixgun, asks me to come into a room with him. Inside, he takes out a pad of paper and asks me my name, age, and address. He wants to know why I am visiting Dr. Leary. I say I am interested in his theories. He asks what his theories are. I reply that they are all in published form and that I prefer not to help the D.A. get out of doing his homework. He seems taken aback and lets me go.

My friend is taken downstairs for interrogation. She is forced to sit at a table with a bright light shining in her face. Several policemen blast her belligerently with rapid-fire questions: "Who are you? Where did you come from? Who brought you here? Why did you come here? Did you have intercourse here? You may be guilty of violating the Mann Act, did you know that? Did you come here for immoral acts? Do you take dope?" My friend is insulted and says, "You are very rude!" When she comes back upstairs she is angry, indignant, upset. "The nerve! How can they get away with this violation!"

From time to time Sheriff Quinlan can be heard saying to guests, "What's a nice person like you doing at a dump like this?" I go downstairs for coffee. The good Sheriff is thumbing through some books. I go up to him, put my hands on his shoulders, look deeply into his eyes and say, "What's a nice person like you doing at a place like this?" He avoids my eyes, stammers, mumbles, "I might ask you the same question." I smile and cock my head, "I'm here because I'm a nice person."

On my way back from the kitchen I see a huge policeman looking at some books. "Christ, this stuff scares me," he says as if to himself. Another officer says, "Well, why don't you go outside and find Joe?" The policeman, armed with club and gun, says, "Not me. I'm not going outside by myself. It's too scary." I feel sad and a wave of futility comes over me. The most gentle people I have ever encountered are guests at Castalia. A six-foot-three, two-hundred pound policeman armed with club and gun is afraid of them. God help him.

TERRY SOUTHERN

Gross Weirdness at the Barricades

Verbatim Transcript of a Recorded Conversation (2/12/70)

This was at night. It was in Chicago, on Monday, August 25th, 1968—at the beginning of the Democratic Convention—and I was sitting in Lincoln Park with Burroughs and Genet. We had come to do a piece for a magazine, and this was our first evening in town.

The kids, thousands of kids who had travelled from all over, to support McCarthy and protest the war, had no place to sleep. They'd asked permission to sleep in the Park, but the grotesque one — "Pig Prick Daley," as he was known (even to his most loyal hood-aides) — had stoutly forbade it, and, in fact, had declared a midnight curfew for the Park. Well, we got there a little before midnight, and it was still full of people. It was a sort of summer-night picnic atmosphere — a few campfires and singing and guitar playing and nothing at all disturbing or boisterous. A really pleasant scene.

On the other side of the park were the cops, lined up as far as you could see — about six or seven hundred of them in their helmets, and carrying gas-masks. They had a sound-truck with a megaphone and a p.a. system, and they kept making these announcements, saying, "All right. We're going to clear the park in five minutes and bla-bla-bla." And we were sitting on the grass by a barricade that had been built out of benches and tables and trashcans — you know, things you might find in a park — anyway, we were sitting there, and this barricade obscured our view of the cops, who were standing about fifty yards away.

So they kept making these announcements over the loud-speaker, and finally they did one that sounded pretty convincing, like *"Okay, this is it. We are moving in."* And so Burroughs and I stood up to see if it was just more bullshit, or if they actually *were* coming in. And when we stood up, the first thing we saw was this squad car that was just very slowly moving along the barricade. We hadn't noticed it before, because we were sitting down, and it was on the other side of the barricade. So now I'm watching the squad car for a minute, when suddenly a guy stood up, ten or twelve feet away from me — a sort of young guy in a T-shirt, and with short crewcut hair and denim pants. And in his hand he's got a big piece of brick, like *half* a brick, and he steps past the end of the barricade, and throws it right against the windshield — you know, *smash! shatter!*

Well, then the shit hits the fan — if one may coin — smoke-bombs, tear-gas, police-charge . . . the whole store. It was chaos-time in panic-ville. Some of the most vicious police brutality of the whole week occured during the next fifteen or twenty minutes . . . or hour, actually, because then it went on, after we were out of the park; they kept charging up and down the streets — like they're supposed to be clearing the streets, but then when people would take refuge in a hallway, they would run into the hallway, yelling "get the hell outta here!" and club them out into the street again. They had freaked out completely, on blood. For an example of their extreme weirdness, clock this little vignette. When the proverbial S. hit the F., we — Burroughs, Genet, and yours truly — moved out at a spritely pace, along with Dick Seaver — of Grove Press editorial fame — and John Berendt — of *Esquire* mag, for whom we were doing the article . . . running, falling, choking, blindly stumbling our way across the park—and this provided, at least in retrospect, our first glimpse of the cops' sadistic and swine-like perversity, namely, the fact that they consistently fired the tear-gas cannisters *beyond the crowd in the direction they were running,* forcing them to run *through* the gas, instead of simply *away* from it. For the moment, however, when we finally reached the street, we were dumbell enough to believe we were safe—since, presumably, the idea had been to get us *out of the park,* and now we *were* out.

We kept walking though because tear-gas was drifting around even here, making it very uncomfortable, and we started along one of the side streets. About a third of the way down the block, we heard a lot of yelling behind us, and looked around to see people running towards us, being chased and beaten by the cops. We were fairly quick to follow suit, but hadn't got far before the same thing happened from the opposite direction—two boys of about eighteen, running towards us, one with his shirt torn off and the other with blood streaming down the side of his face. "Look out," they yelled, "they're coming!" In short, they were closing in from both ends of the block. Everyone began frantically trying to get into the hallways of the apartment buildings on the street. We crowded into one, along with four or five other people, making about ten in all, including two semi-hysterical women— this was in the part where the mailboxes are, the door beyond that being locked (we pressed all the doorbells, but no response), so we huddled there hoping they would pass us by, but being completely unnerved by the yells, curses, and screams as they rousted people out of the hallways nearby, getting closer by the minute, until there they were, five of them, charging up the steps —faces twisted with a hatred and rage seen only in second-rate horror films.

It's weird, the sort of minutiae you will recall from a scene like that. One of the first things that struck me (aside from a club) was the *image of the charge*—the fact that the *second* man was wearing sergeant stripes, whereas the first man wasn't wearing any. This seemed to jibe with the cinematic tradition of the 'officer leading the charge', so I accepted that notion—this is all happening in a split-second, you dig—and I looked at his shoulder and his collar for some indication of rank, finding none . . . and it was then I also dug that neither he nor the sergeant, nor in fact any of them were wearing *badges*. So the movie version wasn't valid, the guy leading the charge (with a sergeant behind him) *wasn't* an officer . . . he wasn't even a private-first-class. What he was, was a freaked-out, gung-ho, criminaltype asshole, and they had given him his head ("go, man, go!") just for kicks.

The two of them charged in—luckily there wasn't room for

more—screaming . . . and that's the word, not 'shouting' or 'yelling', but *screaming*: "OKAY, YOU COMMIE COCK-SUCKERS! *MOVE IT!*" and flailing insanely with their clubs ("night-*sticks*," bullshit, those are *clubs*). It was one of those desperate-panic-fright moments when your reflex is to yell "Help, police!", and then the sickening flash of nightmare-truth: "My god, it *is* the fucking Police!" Fortunately, again—if one may look on the positive side—the place was so crowded that they couldn't get much of a swing going, or it could have been considerably more tragic than comic. As it was, we were crouching—*cowering*, the more apt word—hands and arms overhead to ward off the blows . . . when suddenly I thought of *Genet*. Genet was a kind of special responsibility, to everyone concerned—in the first place, he's about sixty-seven years old, five-feet-two (*and* eyes of blue, natch), speaks not a word of English, and, worse still, had entered the country without a passport—due to his lengthy, albeit groovy, criminal record. *En tout cas*, I suddenly thought of him, and looked up—just in time to see the sergeant raising his club over Genet's head. Then a really extraordinary thing happened: Genet, instead of ducking—reflexively or otherwise—raised his eyes to the sergeant, then lifted his hands in a classic Gallic, and/or Jewish-type, or even your so-called "saint-like" gesture . . . as though to say, very softly, ". . . don't be afraid," or in words of late great groove and gas, L. Buck-oh-roonie: "Everything *coo-oo-oo-oolh*, baby." And then, dig, this terrible, sick, pig-type cop is nailed—or somehow touched otherwise—by Genet's strange, incomprehensible . . . *innocence*—and, just like in a freeze-frame, the club stops abruptly, and the cop turns away, 'aachh,' as in fucking *disgust*, but at the same time falling apart, like *unnerved*, you know?

Well . . . they hustled us out to the street, shoving, prodding, the whole roust-bit, and very forceful. We get to the street, it looks like an ex-battlefield, with people stretched out on the sidewalk and in the street, others sitting, head-in-hands style, or sobbing hysterically, or walking around in shock. Ten feet away, a cop was holding a kid by his shirt which was half torn off, and clubbing him. The kid was pleading, in a tearful, but very reasonable-sounding voice: *"What do you want me to do?"* The cop screamed at him: "I'll show you what you can do, you little cocksucker!" and swung harder. "Little cocksucker," by the way—and, more specifically, "little *Commie* cocksucker"—was the expression of highest incidence (by the Pigmen) throughout the week. The kid finally jerked away, leaving the rest of his shirt behind.

At the end of the block now, towards the park, was a paddy-wagon, and we were being gradually herded in that direction,

11

when suddenly a cop came running by, followed by three or four others. He was carrying a walkie-talkie, and apparently he *was* an officer because he yelled at the sergeant: "Come on—Smitty and his boys have got a bunch of 'em cornered down here!" So they immediately left us, only one of them bothering to say: "So long, creeps!" but another one, as he took off at a run—and I'm pretty sure it was the guy who had led the charge—actually gave a cowboy whoop, and yelled: "*Fresh meat, here I come!*" The whole thing had a weird sort of bacchanal-of-violence atmosphere —so much so that, later, when I first learned about My Lai 4, I understood exactly how it happened.

Well, about four days after that, on Thursday, I was in this march that Dick Gregory was leading. The idea had been to march to Convention Hall, but the Pig Prick said, "No way." So then it was like we were just going to go over to Dick Gregory's house—of all places—about 8,000 people strolling over to Dick's . . . presumably just to fall by and hang out for a while, I mean that's how absurd it had become. Anyway, having been denied the parade-permit, we had to stay on the sidewalk—which was just as well, since the street itself was accomodating a division of National Guard, with tanks, half-tracks, flame-throwers, grenade-launchers, their whole store.

So we were walking on the sidewalk about six abreast, and everything was cool and orderly, except that in the line ahead of us there were a couple of guys who looked very much out of place. One of them was wearing a Notre Dame sweatshirt, and they both had crewcut hair, and they were sort of six-foot-two athlete-looking guys, either bootcamp types or football-squad types—that was the physical impression you got. And they were *juiced*—talking loud, making lewdie remarks about some of the girls in the procession, like "Hey, get a load of *that!*" "How'd you like to dip into *that*!?!" You know, American Legion time. And we were walking through a certain part of town, kind of a ghetto section, and a lot of people were leaning out windows watching—and so every once in a while, one of these guys would yell at them, "Up yours, amigo!" Very low cats. One of the things they did, they noticed a couple of guys taking a leak— but you know, sort of discreet, in a vacant lot—and they started yelling, "Hey, look at the *pissers*! Look at the *pissers*!" Really, the worst cornball asshole-type guys you can imagine.

Anyway, next to me on the other side of me was a woman, a middle-aged lady, and she noticed I was watching these guys. And I had seen her around before—she's apparently very active—and she said, "Do you know who those guys are?" I said, "No." She said, "They're cops—they're with the Chicago Police Department."

And just then, a couple of marshalls—parade marshalls—came by, and she pointed to the two guys, and so the marshalls copped, doing a strong recognition—take, and said, "Okay, *out*." And the two guys didn't protest at all, just looked chagrined, like "oops, we've blown it again," and split. So it turns out that they are well known undercover-agents—and, as is very often the case, incompetent buffoons, which, of course, is quite reassuring . . . except that when they dropped out, they passed right in front of me, and I recognized this one guy—the guy with the white T-shirt—as the guy who had thrown the brick through the windshield of the squad car.

So, the point of all this is that the authorities in Chicago—principally, the incredible Pig Prick Man, presumably on orders from MacBird himself—did not merely *create an atmosphere conducive to violence*, they were capable of actually *instigating the violence* if it didn't happen otherwise.

This was the testimony I tried to get across at the trial. Kunstler and I had gone over it carefully, as one does—I mean, you do go over these things. And he'd said, "Well, they're not going to let you say it." But I didn't believe it—because you just can't believe how weird and surreal that trial scene was until you actually experienced it. Reading about it—reading that the judge was eccentric or that he was prejudiced or even insane was really not enough. You had to actually be there. What's the expression—"seeing is believing"?

And so, sure enough, that's what happened: "Objection sustained." "Objection sustained." All the way through—on the outlandish ruse that it was "hearsay." And there I was, just trying to get across the basic fact that this guy was known—by the woman and by the two marshalls—to be a cop, *and* that I could positively identify him as the guy who threw the brick through the windshield—triggering all the violence (totally *one-sided* violence though it was) of that evening. And you simply could not get it in, so finally I had to just sort of blurt it out: "*He was a police provocateur!*" "Objection." And "sustained." And so they strike it from the record. Fantastic. More than anything else it was all like something out of Gilbert and Sullivan.

Kunstler, however, said he was able to use it in his summation, but the jury, well . . . the thing that really shook me up ("democratic-process" style) was that a jury, *any* jury of twelve people, could sit there for that long—four months? four and a half months?—and not get a sense of the grooviness, not to mention innocence, of the defendants, and a sense of the dignity and the integrity of the defense counsel, both in such vivid contrast to the sickening corruption of the two prosecutors, and the grotesque absurdity and flagrant bias of the Mad Dog Judge. And yet they found them *guilty*. Scarywise, that's some *very heavy shit*.

So the *provocateur* phenomonen was never entered into the record, except insomuch as Kunstler could use it in his summation. He said he was able to make good use of it, because at one point the State had a prosecution-witness who was an *admitted* undercover cop—not an admitted *provocateur*, natch, just your common fink—type cop disguised as a hippy, testifying as to certain inflamatory statements he had heard the defendants make. Then, on a hunch, Kunstler said to him: "Now you were at the barricades on Monday night when it started. Do you recall seeing someone throw a brick through the windshield of a squad car?" He said, "Yeah, I did." And Kunstler said, "What did he look like?" And he said, "Well, he was a young man. He was about . . . bla-bla-bla." And he went on to describe this same guy. Kunstler said: "Was he wearing a white T-shirt?" "Yeah." "Did he have crew-cut hair?" "Yeah, that's right. White T-shirt and crew-cut hair."

So he had gotten a prosecution witness to corroborate what the defense witness had said. He had gotten two separate and identical descriptions of a guy who threw a brick through the windshield of a police car. And then, when this same guy is also identified as a member of the police force . . . well, I mean, when confronted with something so blatant and cynical, you'd think it would cause a huge "TILT" to flash inside the court and jury's collective skull—that, of course, presumes you're being tried by your *peers*. But if you happen to draw—and it is perhaps less improbable than you might think—*twelve morons* and a *maniac* . . . later.

RICHARD BRAUTIGAN

The Day They Busted The Grateful Dead

The day they busted the Grateful Dead
rain stormed against San Francisco
like hot swampy scissors cutting Justice
into the evil clothes that alligators wear.

The day they busted the Grateful Dead
was like a flight of winged alligators
carefully measuring marble with black
    rubber telescopes.

The day they busted the Grateful Dead
turned like the wet breath of alligators
blowing up balloons the size of the
    Hall of Justice.

Confrontation
NORMAN MAILER

Grandma
With Orange Hair

There was not much to see through the canvas arch of the vehicle. A view of a service road they passed along, a little bumping, a bit of swaying—in two minutes they arrived at the next stop. It was the southwest wall of the Pentagon, so much was obvious, for the sun shone brightly here.

Probably they were at the rear of a large mess hall or cafeteria, since a loading platform extended for a considerable distance to either side of where the truck had come in. There were MPs and Marshals on the platform, maybe twenty or thirty, as many again in the back-up area where they had come in. At a long desk at the base of the loading platform, the prisoners were being booked. Each had a Marshal beside him. It was quiet and orderly. The Nazi was standing next to Mailer, but now neither looked at the other. It was indeed all over. The Nazi looked quietly spent, almost gentle—as if the outbursts had been his duty, but duty done, he was just a man again—no need to fight.

They took Mailer's name, having trouble with the spelling again. He was now certain it was not trivial harassment but simple unfamiliarity. The clerk, a stout Marshal with the sort of face that belonged to a cigar, worked carefully at his sheets. The questions were routine—name, address, why arrested—but he entered them with a slow-moving pen which spoke of bureaucratic sacraments taken up, and records set down in perpetuity.

When this was over, Mailer was led by the Marshal who had first arrested him over to the open door of a sort of school bus painted olive-drab. There was, however, a delay in boarding it, and the Marshal said, "I'm sorry, Mr. Mailer, we have to wait here for a minute to get your number."

"I don't mind."

They were being particularly polite with each other. Mailer had a clear opportunity to look again at this Marshal's face; the *vibrations* of the arrest now utterly discharged, he had an agreeable face indeed, quiet, honest, not unintelligent, not unhumorous. And he talked with the pleasant clipped integrity of a West Virginia accent. Mailer was going to ask him if he came from West Virginia, then out of some random modesty about putting too intensive a question and being wrong, he said instead, "May I ask your name?" It was as one might have expected, a name like Tompkins or Hudkins. "May I ask which state you're from, Marshal?"

"It's West Virginia, Mr. Mailer."

"My wife and I had a young lady work for us once who came from West Virginia. Your accent is similar to hers."

"Is that a fact?"

"Yes, I was wondering if you might be related. There's a suggestion of family resemblance." He mentioned the name. No relation.

Now the necessary paper was delivered to the Marshal. He signed it, and Mailer could board the bus. He had been given the number 10. He was the tenth man arrested at the Pentagon.

"Well, goodbye, Mr. Mailer. Nice talking to you."

"Yes."

Perhaps they were troubled partisans. Or did each wish to show the other that the enemy possessed good manners?

No, thought Mailer, it was ritual. At the moment of the arrest, cop and criminal knew each other better than mates, or at least knew some special *piece* of each other better than mates, yes an arrest was carnal. Not sexual, carnal — of the meat, strangers took purchase of each other's meat. Then came the reciprocal tendency to be pleasant. Beneath all those structures advertised as majestic in law and order there was this small carnal secret which the partners of a bust could share. It was tasty to chat afterward, all sly pleasures present that the secret was concealed. Mailer thought of a paragraph he had written once about police — it had probably acted upon him as much as anything else to first imagine his movie. Now his mind remembered the approximate sense of the paragraph, which actually (indulging Mailer's desire to be quoted) went exactly like this:

> . . . they contain explosive contradictions within themselves. Supposed to be law-enforcers, they tend to conceive of themselves as the law. They are more responsible than the average man, they are more infantile. They are attached umbilically to the concept of honesty, they are profoundly corrupt. They possess more physical courage than the average man, they are unconscionable bullies; they serve the truth, they are psychopathic liars . . . their work is authoritarian, they are cynical, and finally if something in their hearts is deeply idealistic, they are also bloated with greed. There is no human creation so contradictory, so finally enigmatic, as the character of the average cop . . .

Yes, and without an arrest, he would never have known that this very nice Marshal from West Virginia, with his good American face and pleasant manners and agreeable accent, had also a full quiver of sadism and a clammy sweat of possession as he put the arm on you. But indeed, what knowledge had the Marshal of him?

Inside the bus, at the rear of the aisle, was a locked cage and three or four protesters were enclosed there; jailed within their jailing. They greeted him with jeers, cat-calls, hellos, requests for cigarettes, water—after the first impact, it was not ill-spirited. "Hey, look," said one of the kids behind the bars, "they got older people in with us too."

"What time does this bus leave for Plainfield?" Mailer asked. The laughter came back. It was going to be all right. He could hear them whispering.

"You Norman Mailer?" asked one.

"Yes."

"Hey, great. Listen, man, we got to talk."

"I hope we don't have too much time." More laughter. He was beginning to feel good for the first time since his arrest. "What did you gentlemen do to be given such honor?" asked Mailer with a wave at their cage.

"We're the ones who were resisting arrest."

"Did you resist it much?"

"Are you kidding?" said one dark-haired gloomy thin young pirate with a large Armenian mustache and a bloodied hand-kerchief on his head, "if we put our hands in front of our face to keep from being beaten to death, they said we were resisting." Hoots and jeers at the fell accuracy of this.

"Well, did you all just sit there and take it?"

"I got in a couple of good shots at my Marshal," said one of the kids. It was hard to tell if he was lying. Something about their incarceration in the cage made it difficult to separate them, or perhaps it was that they seemed part of a team, of a musical group—the Monsters, or the Freaks, or the Caged Kissers—they had not known each other an hour ago, but the cage did the work of making them an ensemble.

The rest of the bus was slowly filling. Mailer had first taken a seat next to a young minister wearing his collar, and they chatted not unhappily for a few minutes, and then both crossed the aisle to sit on the side of the bus which looked out on the loading plat-form and the table where they had been booked. From these seats, Mailer had a view of the Marshals and MPs outside, of new arrests arriving in trucks, and of the prisoners coming into the bus, one by one, every couple of minutes. After a while, he realized the bus would not move until it was filled, and this, short of massive new arrests, would take at least an hour.

It was not disagreeable waiting. Each new prisoner was obliged to make an entrance like an actor coming on stage for his first appearance: since prisoners in transit are an enforced audience, new entrance automatically becomes theater. Some new men sauntered on the bus, some bowed to the faces in the aisle, some grinned, some scowled and sat down immediately: one or two principled pacifists practicing total non-cooperation were dragged off the 2½-ton trucks, bumped along the ground, tugged over to the bus, and thrown in by the Marshals. Bleeding a little, looking dazed, the three or four young men who arrived by this route were applauded with something not unlike the enthusiasm a good turn gets in a music hall. Handsome young boys got on the bus, and slovenly oafs, hippies, and walking wounded. One boy had a pant leg soaked in blood. A fat sad fellow with a huge black beard now boarded; a trim and skinny kid who looked like he played minor league shortstop took a seat; a Japanese boy, androgynous in appearance, told a few prisoners around him that none of the Marshals had been able to decide if he was a boy or a girl, so they had not known—for he would not tell them— whether a Marshal or a Matron should search him. This was quickly taken up with pleasure and repeated down the bus.

Outside, a truck would arrive every five or ten minutes and some boys and girls would dismount and go to the base of the loading platform to be booked, the boys to enter the bus, the girls to go off to another bus. Still no sign of Lowell or Mac- donald. Mailer kept hoping they would appear in the next haul of prisoners. After a while he began to study the Marshals.

Their faces were considerably worse than he had expected. He had had the fortune to be arrested by a man who was incon- testably one of the pleasanter Marshals on duty at the Pentagon, he had next met what must be the toughest Marshal in the place— the two had given him a false spectrum. The gang of Marshals now studied outside the bus were enough to firm up any fading loyalty to his own cause: they had the kind of faces which belong to the bad guys in a Western. Some were fat, some were too thin, but nearly all seemed to have those subtle anomalies of the body which come often to men from small towns who have inherited strong features, but end up, by their own measure, in failure. Some would have powerful chests, but abrupt paunches, the skinny ones would have a knob in the shoulder, or a hitch in their gait, their foreheads would have odd cleaving wrinkles, so that one man might look as if an ax had struck him between the eyes, another paid tithe to ten parallel deep lines rising in ridges above his eyebrows. The faces of all too many had a low cunning mixed with a stroke of rectitude: if the mouth was slack, the nose was straight and severe; should the lips be tight, the nostrils showed an outsize greed. Many of them looked to be ex-First Sergeants, for they liked to stand with the heels of their hands on the top of their hips, or they had that way of walking, belly forward, which a man will promote when he is in comfortable circumstances with himself and packing a revolver in a belt holster. The toes turn out; the belly struts. They were older men than he might have expected, some in their late thirties, more in their forties, a few looked to be over fifty, but then that may have been why they were here to receive prisoners rather than out on the line—in any case they emitted a collective spirit which, to his mind, spoke of little which was good, for their eyes were blank and dull, that familiar small-town cast of eye which speaks of apathy rising to fanaticism only to subside in apathy again. (Mailer had wondered more than once at that curious demand of small-town life which leaves something good and bright in the eyes of some, and is so deadening for others—it was his impression that people in small towns had eyes which were generally livelier or emptier than the more concentrated look of city vision.) These Marshals had the dead eye and sour cigar, that sly shuffle of propriety and rut which so often comes out in a small-town sheriff as patriotism and the sweet stink of a crooked dollar. Small-town sheriffs sidled over to a crooked collar like a High Episcopalian hooked on a closet queen. If one could find the irredeemable madness of America (for we are a nation where weeds will breed in the gilding tank) it was in those late afternoon race track faces coming into the neon lights of the parimutuel windows, or those early morning hollows in the eye of the soul in places like Vegas where the fevers of America go livid in the hum of the night, and Grandmother, the church-goer, orange hair burning bright now crooned over the One-Arm Bandit, pocketbook open, driving those half-dollars home, home to the slot.

"Madame, we are burning children in Vietnam."

"Boy, you just go get yourself lost. Grandma's about ready for a kiss from the jackpot."

The burned child is brought into the gaming hall on her hospital bed.

"Madame, regard our act in Vietnam."

"I hit! I hit! Hot deedy, I hit. Why, you poor burned child—you just brought me luck. Here, honey, here's a lucky half-dollar in reward. And listen sugar, tell the nurse to change your sheets. Those sheets sure do stink. I hope you ain't got gangrene. Hee hee, hee hee. I get a supreme pleasure mixing with gooks in Vegas."

One did not have to look for who would work in the concentration camps and the liquidation centers—the garrison would be filled with applicants from the pages of a hundred American novels, from *Day of the Locust* and *Naked Lunch* and *The Magic*

Christian, one could enlist half the Marshals outside this bus, simple, honest, hard-working government law-enforcement agents, yeah! There was something at loose now in American life, the poet's beast slinking to the marketplace. The country had always been wild. It had always been harsh and hard, it had always had a fever—when life in one American town grew insupportable, one could travel, the fever to travel was in the American blood, so said all, but now the fever had left the blood, it was in the cells, the cells traveled, and the cells were as insane as Grandma with orange hair. The small towns were disappearing in the bypasses and the supermarkets and the shopping centers, the small town in America was losing its sense of the knuckle, the herb, and the root, the walking sticks were no longer cut from trees, nor were they cured, the schools did not have crazy old teachers now but teaching aids, and in the libraries, *National Geographic* gave way to *TV Guide.* Enough of the old walled town had once remained in the American small town for gnomes and dwarfs and knaves and churls (yes, and owls and elves and crickets) to live in the constellated cities of the spiders below the eaves in the old leaning barn which—for all one knew—had been a secret ear to the fevers of the small town, message center for the inhuman dreams which passed through the town at night in sleep and came to tell their insane tale of the old barbarian lust to slaughter villages and drink their blood, yes who knew which ghosts, and which crickets, with which spider would commune—which prayers and whose witch's curses would travel those subterranean trails of the natural kingdom about the town, who knows which fevers were forged in such communion and returned on the blood to the seed, it was an era when the message came by the wind and not by the wire (for the town gossip began to go mad when the telephone tuned its buds to the tip of her tongue) the American small town grew out of itself, and grew out of itself again and again, harmony between communication and the wind, between lives and ghosts, insanity, the solemn reaches of nature where insanity could learn melancholy (and madness some measure of modesty) had all been lost now, lost to the American small town. It had grown out of itself again and again, its cells traveled, worked for government, found security through wars in foreign lands, and the nightmares which passed on the winds in the old small towns now traveled on the nozzle tip of the flame thrower, no dreams now of barbarian lusts, slaughtered villages, battles of blood, no, nor any need for them—technology had driven insanity out of the wind and out of the attic, and out of all the lost primitive places: one had to find now wherever fever, force, and machines could come together, in Vegas, at the race track, in pro football, race riots for the Negro, suburban orgies—none of it was enough—one had to find it in Vietnam; that was where the small town had gone to get its kicks.

That was on the faces of the Marshals. It was a great deal to read on the limited evidence before him, but he had known these faces before—they were not so different from the cramped, mean, stern, brave, florid, bestial, brutish, narrow, calculating, incurious, hardy, wily, leathery, simple, good, stingy, small-town faces he had once been familiar with in his outfit overseas, all those Texans from all those small towns, it was if he could tell—as at a college reunion—the difference these more than twenty years had made. If it were legitimate to read the change in American character by the change in the faces of one's classmates, then he could look at these Marshals like men he had known in the Army, but now revisited, and something had gone out of them, something had come in. If there was a common unattractive element to the Southern small-town face, it was in that painful pinch between their stinginess and their greed. No excess of love seemed ever to come off a poor white Southerner, no fats, no riches, no sweets, just the avidity for such wealth. But there had been sadness attached to this in the old days, a sorrow; in the pinch of their cheeks was the kind of abnegation and loneliness which spoke of what was tender and what was lost forever. So they had dignity. Now the hollows in their faces spoke of men who were rabid and toothless, the tenderness had turned corrosive, the abnegation had been replaced by hate, dull hate, cloud banks of hate, the hatred of failures who had not lost their greed. So he was reminded of a probability he had encountered before: that, nuclear bombs all at hand, the true war party of America was in all the small towns, even as the peace parties had to collect in the cities and the suburbs. Nuclear warfare was dividing the nation. The day of power for the small-town mind was approaching—who else would be left when atomic war was done would reason the small-town mind, and in measure to the depth of their personal failure, would love Vietnam, for Vietnam was the secret hope of a bigger war, and that bigger war might yet clear the air of races, faces, in fact—technologies—all that alienation they could not try to comprehend.

It was not a happy meditation. Among the soldiers he had known, there was the chance to talk. He did not see many faces here who would ever talk. Cheers. They were dragging a girl out of one of the trucks now. Pale-skinned, with light brown hair, no lipstick, dungarees, she had that unhappy color which came from too many trips to marijuana garden. Nonetheless, she waved to her boyfriend while being dragged along the ground. He was eventually dragged into their bus.

Mailer began to chat with the young clergyman. His name was

John Boyle, and he was Presbyterian Chaplain at Yale. The number of his arrest was nine. They joked about this—he had beaten Mailer to the Bench. Actually he had seen the Protagonist get arrested, had followed to see if he were being treated properly (a sign of Mailer's age, a proper sign of status!) was turned back with assurances, wandered behind Pentagon lines, and in the course of protesting the arrest of a demonstrator, was apprehended himself (although the Marshal had wanted to release him when he saw his collar).

"Well," said Mailer, "at least we have low numbers."

"Do you think that will mean much?"

"We should be the first to get out."

From where he sat in the bus, he could see square vertical columns back of the loading platform, columns reminiscent of Egyptian architecture: Mailer now had a rumination about the nature of Egyptian architecture and its relation to the Pentagon, those ultra-excremental forms of ancient Egyptian architecture, those petrified excrements of the tomb and the underground chambers here at the Pentagon, but he was not an Egyptologist, no sir, and the connection eluded him. He must pursue it later. Something there. But the rumination running down, we may quickly leave his thoughts.

PIERO HELICZER

The United States Of America Versus Piero Heliczer

I saw a friend of mine jack martin being tortured on the floor of the lobby of the bway central hotel by some very husky looking goons in loud hawaiian sport shirts, and irene nolan, an old friend of mine who was doing the box office at this function held by one arm and pushed around evidently in pain and distress by a tall young man in a blue suit. I knew that she had just had an operation at saint vincents hospital to remove some large pieces of glass from her backside and that the stitches had just been removed and the wound not yet healed and that any struggle on her part was likely to open and distort the wound. I therefore not knowing what else to do, attempted to distract the tall young mans attention whose back was turned to me by kicking him as he was walking away, i do not know if my kick reached him because two other men jumped on me from behind twisting my arm and pushing me into the ground. I became very cowardly then because the pain was unexpectedly painful and cried. I was also very afraid of what would happen at the hands of people to whom i had already begged for mercy with no result other than to have my arm twisted higher and hear a stream of insulting talk. We were put into a car and left there whereupon Miss Nolan got out and ran a good way before being caught and brought back by another young man in a striped sport shirt. I also got out of the car, again hoping to distract these men and help her to get away. When we were back in the car, uniformed police officers finally showed up and the first thing they told these men was to let us out of the car whereupon the uniformed police officers were shown badges. This is the first time I personally even got so much as a glimpse of a badge. We were then taken to the fifth precinct police station. My left wrist was handcuffed so tightly that the circulation was stopped, and another gentlemean also in a blue suit with black curly hair and dark glasses was seated at my left and twisting my collar tightly from behind. He wd not say a word, whenever I asked him if he couldnt loosen the handcuff a little he just twisted my collar the harder saying nothing. At one point I was amazed to find that he was no longer twisting my collar but had slipped his hand inside and was sort of caressing my neck and shoulder in some kind of homosexual advance, but at that point nothing seemed very suprising. At the police station, I saw Jack Smith seated in a chair and offering no resistance brutally beaten by a man I later learned to be a Detective Imp of the fifth precinct, he gave him continuous body blows with both of his elbows and forearms from behind which looked like some kind of karate or judo and I was told this was so it would show no marks or bruises. I was shocked that this was done in the presence of so many people, including several uniformed policemen. A police sergeant said that the Gestapo hadn't done a good enough job on me or I wouldnt be there. We were then transferred to Federal prison. I felt actually relieved to be out of the arresting officers' hands, and glad to be able to go to sleep. My wrist and left arm were very stiff and swollen the next morning and I had a cut on my wrist from the handcuff, but my wrists were handcuffed behind me even though even the slightest movement or jerk hurt me considerably and i was forced to remain handcuffed in this way when standing before the commissioner, and also fingerprinted three times which hurt excruciatingly, even though i repeatedly begged them not to handcuff me that i would go quietly and that it hurt me to be fingerprinted. During my week in prison, I was not able to work very well and had to take whirlpool baths twice a day for my left wrist. I still have a small scar below the root of my thumb from the handcuffs.

During the time between August 11 until now, the normal course of my life was greatly disrupted by having to show up in Federal Court several times, by having to raise bail, several times we had to show up for no reason just to hear that the trial would be postponed again and again. Having never been arrested or imprisoned before, the whole thing became too much for me emotionally, and began to remind me of the only other similar time in my life, the period just before the end of the war in Italy, when, playing in the hospital garden with my little brother Bobby, I noticed men in dark blue suits and sunglasses pointing us out and looking at us over the hedge. One or more uniformed *carabiniere* with a rifle held at attention, stood every moment of the day and night at my mothers' bed side. I knew that when my mother got well we would be taken out and shot. The doctors kept her infection (on the knee where she still has a rather grotesque scar) open so it wouldn't heal, to save her life. We were saved by the Underground's entry into the town.

My father had been cruelly tortured and killed in the meantime.

What really amazes me now, is: How such a thoroughgoing investigation and trial, which lasted three days, and had twelve jurors in the end arguing and shouting until midnight, when they pronounced three of us guilty and the girl Irene Nolan innocent, come out of an attempted kick in the pants, which i still think some people richly deserve. What bothers me, if I can express myself correctly, is that the whole thing was started by Federal narcotics bureau officers, that they have charged us with what they in effect did, and as far as I understand, do commit as part of a long series of social disruption by this department.

I understand that my father in law, who is a respected barrister in London, and mother in law have both been separately questioned in England. I ask why they should have been involved in this at all. And why all this expense! On both sides!

I understand it will cost something like $9,500 for the appeal. We have had to raise bail, and 1,000 dollars for lawyers fees by giving benefits throughout this time; this took up a great deal of our time, which we could no longer give to our creative efforts.

We were not permitted to leave New York during all this time, and I could not go to England to see my wife as I had planned, nor to Antioch or California to give poetry readings and show films. I could not go to Cannes this year nor to the Finnish writers seminar nor to London where I am supposed to show a film in June. I wanted to live in the country in Normandy and write poems and make a film of Joan of Arc and visit Emily Bronte's tomb.

I once imagined my self in a French court at the turn of the century perhaps, perhaps now, asking to say a word to the judge man to man, and whispering into his ear that my attempted kick in the pants was just being *galant*, and that I am very sorry but I do not see how a gentleman could act any different. Maybe say I'd have to do it again. And now I say life is a poem and I do not see how a poet could have acted differently.

H. RAP BROWN

Die Nigger Die!

From the first day I got to Greene County, the honkies tried to run me out. I was driving down to see Mr. Gilmore, this negro cat that was the candidate for sheriff on the Freedom ballot. I was doing about 70 or 80 and there were these honkies picketing this electrical work company. I shot through there and honkies screamed something at me. I threw on the brakes and backed up. Wasn't nobody in the car but me and George Greene and George don't take no shit off white folks, either. And, of course, I had my action with me, a .38. I backed up and said, "What'd you say?" This honky said, "I said don't be coming through here that fast. Don't you see those men over there?" They were over on the other side of the road. I said, "What you the police or something?" "Naw, I just—I say don't be coming through here that fast." I just drove off. I went on down to Mr. Gilmore's. He wasn't at home, so I turned around and went back through there, doing 80 again. I saw the honky and another cracker run and get in his car, but they couldn't catch me. So I turned off to the side of the road and waited for them to pull in behind me. I jumped out and I had my gun with me. And even though he saw my gun, he was going to try and scare me. So I said, "What you want? You trying to catch me?" "I told you not to go through there again," he said. I said, "Who in the fuck are you? If you ain't the police, you ain't got a damned thing to say to me." I was woofing at the chump and George Greene got out the other side of the car. This other cracker, though, who had acted the fool and jumped in the car wasn't saying nothing. He just sat there trembling and smiling.

So the honky says, "You just come through there like that one more time!" I told him, "You better get the fuck from around me. That's what you'd better do, boy." And that's what he did. This kind of thing happens all the time. White folks feel that they just got to chastise Black people. If it had been a white boy, he wouldn't have jumped in his car and gone chasing him. So, I just had to put him in his place.

Just before I left Alabama, I pulled my gun on a sheriff and two deputies. I had gone to see this girl that I'd met in Selma. She was working with the Department of Labor. She traveled in an integrated team and had this white girl with her. They were going to some place called Jackson, Alabama, which is 50 miles from Mobile. I went down to spend a couple of days with her when this white girl was going to New Orleans or somewhere. The white folks in town were already suspicious, 'cause they didn't like the two of them living and working together. I guess the hotel must've had the line tapped, 'cause they knew I was coming. They were trying to lay a trap, as I soon found out, so they would have an excuse to get the two chicks out of the area.

Well, I drove into town carring my riot gun. Had me a riot gun, a .12 gauge that would shoot seven times and chunk bricks for a half hour. You were supposed to plug it. But I wasn't about to.

I went down there and I had brought some rum with me, so we were copping some t.v. and were gon' drink some rum and just party. All of a sudden I heard a key turn in the door. The sister had put the chain on, so when they pushed it, the chain held the door. I looked out the door and saw all these crackers out there. My first reaction was, what the fuck is going on? I jumped up and got my gun.

They had on ordinary clothes and they looked like regular ol' crackers. Then I dug that they had guns and I realized that I was standing right in front of them. So I moved to the side of the door. One of 'em says, "I'm the sheriff." I said. "You got to do better than that." So he put his little badge through the door. "O.K. What you want?" He said, "Open the door." I said, "She-e-it." But the chick kept saying "Open the door, open the door." So I decided to let them in 'cause I had the drop on 'em.

So I closed the door and took the chain off and let them in. I had the gun on 'em, so if they moved, I moved. The sheriff had a camera in his hand and the other cracker had his pistol. I had the drop on 'em and the muthafucka with the pistol eased it down when he saw that. So I'm standing there talkin' to 'em and another pig eased through the door and put a .38 dead to my head. "All right. Drop that muthafucka." That gun was up against my head so hard I could feel the bullet in the chamber. So I figured, Well, solid. That's the way the deal goes down sometimes. "You got me," I said, and I put my shit down. Then he told me I was under arrest.

Well, you know me. By now this was just routine so I said, "Under arrest! For what?" Hell, I could think of forty charges myself. I knew damned well they wasn't gon' let a nigger get the drop on the sheriff and then let him go, but you got to stay on the offensive all the time. "What you mean I'm under arrest? For what, goddammit?" I was woofing like a champ. Well, the muthafucka said I was under arrest for fornication and a violation of prohibition. It was a dry county and we were drinking rum. Then he looked at the riot gun and said, "Also, a violation of the Federal Firearms Act. This gun is too short." I said, "Naw, it ain't too short!" But they arrested me and the sister. It was her first time going to jail and it really upset her. Her first course in being a sho-nuf nigger. I was impressed at the way she maintained herself and I wondered how many other sisters in situations similar to ours would be as together as she was. (The test will come.)

They took us to the jail, which was about 17 miles away. When we got there I found out that they knew who I was, who I worked for and what time I'd left Selma. The camera had been brought over to take pictures, for evidence. They thought we were screwing and they were going to take pictures for the trial, or for their wives—one of the two. Fornication (screwing) is against the law. If they really tried to enforce that law, there'd be a revolution tomorrow. But to even have laws like that shows how messed up white people are. This country is probably the only country in the world with a law against screwing.

The charges against the sister were eventually dropped. The government provided her defense, and me, well, I had to defend myself. This was not my first time having to do this, and, although I have never won a case, I was ready. My defense was sound, too sound. After the conviction, the judge said since I knew so much about law, he was going to give me some time to study. The only way I finally got out of that was that my main man, Howard Moore, SNCC attorney in Atlanta, came and bought me for $200 and brought me back to outside slavery.

JAMES SIMON KUNEN

The Shit Hits The Fan At Columbia

Monday, April 29: The Majority Coalition (read: jocks) have cordoned off Low and are trying to starve the demonstrators out. We decided to break the blockade. We plan tactics on a blackboard and go, shaking hands with those staying behind as though we might not be back. There are thirty of us with three cartons of food. We march around Low, making our presence known. Spontaneously, and at the wrong tactical place, the blacks in front jump into the jock line. I go charging through the gap with my box of grapefruit and quickly become upon the ground or, more accurately, on top of two layers of people and beneath two. I manage to throw three grapefruit, two of which make it. Then I become back where I started. Some blood is visible on both sides. Back at Math, some of our people say that the jocks they were fighting had handcuffs on their belts. Band-Aided noses abound and are a mark of distinction. We discuss alternative plans for feeding Low and someone suggests blockading the jocks — "If they run out of beer they're through." In the meantime, we can see hundreds of green armbands (for amnesty) throwing food up to the Low windows. We decide on a rope-and-pulley system between a tree and the Low windows, but there is some question about how to get the line up to the people in Low without the jocks grabbing it. When one kid suggests tying an end to a broom handle and throwing it like a harpoon, John (Outside Agitator) suggests we train a bird. A helicopter has already been looked into by Strike Central, but the FAA won't allow it. Finally we agree on shooting in a leader line with a bow and arrow.

A girl and myself are dispatched to get a bow. We go to the roof of the Barnard Library where the phys. ed. archery range is. We are in the midst of discovering how incredibly locked the cabinet is when a guard comes out on the roof. We crouch. He walks right past us. It would be just like TV were I not so preoccupied with it being just like TV. After ten minutes he finds us. The girl laughs coyly and alleged that oh, we just came up to spend the night. I am rather taken with the idea, but the guard is unmoved and demands our I.D.'s. This is our first bust. Our second bust, the real one, begins to take shape at 2:30 A.M. We hear over WBAI that there are busloads of TPF (Tactical Police Force, Gestapo) at 156th and at 125th and that patrol

30

cars are arriving from all precincts with four helmeted cops per auto. I am unimpressed. So many times now we've been going to be busted. It just doesn't touch me anymore. I assume that the cops are there to keep the Mau Maus out.

A girl comes up to me with some paper towels. Take these, she says, so you can wipe the vaseline (slows tear-gas penetration) off your face when you're in jail. I haven't got vaseline on my face. I am thinking that vaseline is a big petroleum interest, probably makes napalm, and anyway it's too greasy. I hear over the walky-talky that Hamilton has been busted and that the sundial people are moving to Low and Fayerweather to obstruct the police. I put vaseline on my face. I also put vaseline on my hands and arms and legs above the socks and a cigarette filter in each nostril and carefully refold my plastic-bag gas mask so I'll be able to put it on quickly with the holes at the back of my head so my hair will absorb the gas and I'll be able to breath long enough to cool the cannister with a CO_2 fire extinguisher and pick it up with my asbestos gloves and throw it back at the cops. Someone tells me that he can't get busted or he'll miss his shrink again.

I take my place with seven others at the front barricade. All along the stairs our people are lined up, ready to hole up in the many lockable-from-within rooms on the three floors above me. We sing "We Shall Not Be Moved" and realize that something is ending. The cops arrive. The officer bullhorns us: "On behalf of the Trustees of Columbia University and with the authority vested in me . . ." That's as far as he is able to get, as we answer his question and all others with our commune motto—"Up against the wall, motherfuckers." We can't hold the barricade because the doors open out and the cops simply pull the stuff out. They have to cut through ropes and hoses and it takes them fifteen minutes before they can come through. All the while they're not more than thirty feet from me, but all I can do is watch their green-helmeted heads working. I shine a light in their eyes but Tom tells me not to and he's head of the defense committee so I stop.

At 4:00 A.M. the cops come in. The eight of us sit down on the stairs (which we've made slippery with green soap and water) and lock arms. The big cop says "Don't make it hard for us or you're gonna get hurt." We do not move. We want to make it clear that the police have to step over more than chairs to get our people out. They pull us apart and carry us out, stacking us like cord wood under a tree. The press is here so we are not beaten. As I sit under the tree I can see kids looking down at us from every window in the building. We exchange the "V" sign. The police will have to ax every door to get them out of those offices. They do. Tom Hayden is out now. He yells "Keep the radio on!

31

Peking will instruct you!" When they have sixty of us they take us to the paddy wagons at mid-campus. I want to make them carry us, but the consensus is that it's a long, dark walk and we'll be killed if we don't cooperate, so I walk. At the paddy wagons there are at least a thousand people cheering us and chanting "Strike! Strike! Strike!" We are loaded in a wagon and the doors shut. John tells a story about how a cop grabbed the cop that grabbed him and then said "Excuse me." We all laugh raucously to show an indomitable spirit and freak out the cops outside.

We are taken to the 24th precinct to be booked. "Up against the wall," we are told. I can't get over how they really do use the term. We turn and lean on the wall with our hands high, because that's what we've seen in the movies. We are told to can that shit and sit down. Booking takes two hours. Lieutenant Dave Bender is the plainclothesman in charge. He seems sternly unhappy that college turns out people like us. He asks John if he thinks he could be a policeman and John says no; he doesn't think he's cut out for it.

We are allowed three calls each. A fat officer makes them for us and he is a really funny and good man. He is only mildly displeased when he is duped into calling Dial-a-Demonstration. He expresses interest in meeting a girl named Janice when three of us give him her number, one as his sister, one as his girlfriend, and one as his ex-wife.

We go downstairs to await transportation to court. A TPF man comes in escorting Angus Davis, who was on the sixth floor of Math and refused to walk down. He has been dragged down four flights of marble stairs and kicked and clubbed all the way. A two-inch square patch of his hair has been pulled out. Ben, Outside Agitator, yells, "You're pretty brave when you've got that club." The officer comes over and dares him to say that again. He says it again. The cop kicks for Ben's groin, but Ben knows karate and blocks it. John says to the cop, "Thank you, you have just proved Ben's point." This is sufficiently subtle not to further arouse the cop, and he leaves. A caged bus takes us all the way downtown to the Tombs (the courthouse). The kid beside me keeps asking me what bridge is this and what building is that. Finally he recognizes something and declares that we are going to pass his grandmother's house. I am busy trying to work a cigarette butt through the window grate so that I can litter from a police bus. Arriving, we drive right into the building; a garage door clamps down behind us.

Our combs and keys are confiscated so that we won't be able to commit suicide. In the elevator to the cells a white cop tells us we look like a fine bunch of men — we ought to be put on the front lines in Vietnam. Someone says that Vietnam is here, now. As we get out I look at the black cop running the elevator for some sort of reaction. He says "Keep the faith."

He said "Keep the faith," I say, and everyone is pleased. We walk by five empty cells and then are jammed into one. Thirty-four of us in a 12x15 room. We haven't slept in twenty-four hours and there isn't even space for all of us to sit down at one time.

Some of our cellmates are from Avery. They tell us how they were handcuffed and dragged downstairs on their stomachs. Their shirts are bloody.

After a couple of hours we start to perk up. We bang and shout until a guard comes, and then tell him that the door seems to be stuck. Someone screams "All right, all right, I'll talk." It is pointed out that you don't need tickets to get to policemen's balls. We sing folk songs and "The Star-Spangled Banner." They allowed one of us to bring in a recorder and he plays Israeli folk music.

A court officer comes and calls a name. "He left," we say. Finally he finds the right list.

We are arraigned before a judge. The Outsiders are afraid they will be held for bail, but they are released on their own recognizance, like the rest of us, except they have some form of loitering charge tacked on to the standard second-degree criminal trespassing.

Back at school I eat in a restaurant full of police. As audibly as possible I compose a poem entitled "Ode to the TPF." It extolls the beauty or rich wood billies, the sheen of handcuffs, the feel of a boot on your face.

Meeting a cellmate, I extend my hand to him and he slaps it. I have to remember that—handslaps, not shakes, in the Revolution.

JUDITH MALINA

Last Performance at
The Living Theatre Invective

Where were we when the lights went out?
We were there
Where we belonged
With our feet on the ground

And our heads in our hearts
And our hearts to your ears.
Where you were dear everybody,
Where the lights blaze on the dark nights when the
    lights
Go on.

Ralph, Ralph what are you doing out there?
We were in there because the only honorable place
For an honorable woman, I said, in a dishonorable
Society is inside listening to the different drummer
Who was at this moment banging on the garbage pails
Drumming it out, drumming it in, HELP SAVE
    THE . . .

I saw thee once in the dreams of climbing over the
    rooves
And on those city rooves thou wast a fearful bastud,
but not now when in all the dark theatres of the
    world
There's a small rim of spill under some leeko light
Saying Peace, while under the earlobes
Of the taxcollectors small bugs crawl crying love me,
    love me.
They are, as it is said, bugged; so are we all,
All bugged:

Mister I gave your outfit one hundred thousand
    dollars and
Lotsa promises to pay, and last week
When there wasn't enough
For the workers and the lovers
I gave you one hundred bucks of their hard-earned
Right out of their shabby smellysweet pockets
And why are you carrying away my little chair?

You are on the wrong side I said to them
Come over to the good guys and he trembled with
    terror
As he carried away the worthless miniature of the
Eiffel Tower a token of award and esteem from
The people of France now locked up on West
    Houston Street
Locked up in the Tax Bureau behind the formidable
Atomic Energy Commission Offices. Because you see

The Living Theatre (God save its mark) is not the
    only

Federal Property
On which we have put
Our Holy Asses
That they think
Is theirs.

We sit where we will,
And where we stand
That ground is free.

The jailor bullied Jenny and I said Lady
Under our feet is free ground
And what you build around us
And call it your jail
Lady that's your hang up
And I'm too happy to do anything but help you.

Shut up she said

Prisoner number everybody requests permission
To abolish the white lines.

Hey baby prisoner number all requests nothing
Everything is his already.

See, like they said: You can't put on your play
And we said: We are putting on our play
And they said We'll lock you up
And we said OK

But now we are putting on our play.

Played children's games on the roof.

I saw thee thou of my heart's delight
Lowering the ladders
For the people to climb upwards
Into their wherever out of their dark
Into our light.

Charged like the Unicorn enraged
Frighting the fuzz
Tossed him out on his ear
I sat on the black man's good hand
Bouncing my sex on him
Till he, opening the door, thought I would jump
Said I would go limp
Hanging from the second storey window
Reaching down to pull him up
While the cops grabbed the ladder out
From under him Julian shouting Don't let the cops

Bully You because You are free,
While Ken the author stood amazed at the beauty
      he had made
And poor Mr. Keenan not talking to us
Because he had gotten to know us so well
And now he had to shut us down.
Down?
Never we soared and will soar and still soar
      because
even if Warren Finnerty played with a patch on
      his eye
and Mark Duffy wore a beard and Michael had a
sick knee and everybody wildly enthusiastic and
      Tom
Lillard climbing down on his belly from the roof
      and
right under the cops' feet and Bob Bates up the
      ladder
and Steve Thompson saying let's sit down and
      Miriam
who knows how to be staunch in the face of
      great suffering
a great beauty forever and Jenny and Tedi
      and the friends
of the real world gathered together like the few
      and the
many forever settling time with their children's
      games of
living in the real world and the living theatre
      which plays
every night
everywhere
where it will take
more than the USA
to shut it down
Shut it up,
Shut it in,
Shut it out.

But the dumb bunnies
Hung up by their ties and shirts
Cried You can't. You can't. You can't.
Not duty whispered low
But the muse sang out
Up the ladders,
In the windows,

Over the roof,
Suddenly on went the lights:

Then we acted out the prison
Where nobody was freer
Than those rare beauties
Because nobody could be so free
That the author cried
Because it was all true
And the doubt of the writer
That the words are true
Was rubbed out as it happened
Because it happened as truth happens
In joy and children's games
With the final scene yet to be played
In the boring courtroom
With the wrong men in charge
Strangling themselves
With their drippy ties
And the judge's robes
Hiding his nakedness.

I suggest that everybody take all their clothes off.
And we will have a perpetual summer.
But if we get cold
We'll make mad love to all the men
Of the Internal Revenue Service
And they'll no longer serve false gods
and everybody will come over to the side of
     everybody.
I suggest an overthrow of all governments by love.
I suggest direct action:
Ergo: Fuck the USA

HARVEY ROTTENBERG

Planted, Burnt, And Busted

After moving far and fast for two weeks, anywhere we could
cook a meal felt good, even the motel in Seattle.

The dinner dishes were done. My old lady was lounging around
in a pair of sheer tights, reading. I was into a yoga pamphlet

titled "How You Can Speak With God." The room was permeated by a feeling of well being and peace that comes as a great home-cooked meal is digested in silent contemplation.

The door rattled. I went to check it out, putting down flashes of paranoia. "Can't be thieves," I thought. "They're making too much noise."

The door flew back. Three men in shoddy overcoats surged in, obnoxiously pushing snub-nosed revolvers before them.

The muscles of their faces were knotted by the tension of anticipation. They probably were out in the hallway for quite a while, hyping themselves to come through the narrow door. They obviously feared for their lives. Buy they must enjoy the feeling or they would find a less dangerous line of work.

"Police," one ejaculated perfunctorily. But his body was still hard-on tense. And his gun jerked in tiny spasms, as he flicked his glassy eyes around the room.

They were all wound like spring steel, really wired.

"Don't move," one spat.

"Sit there," his partner ordered, eyeing my chick's crotch through her tights.

"I told you not to move," the first one menaced us, as we went to sit down.

Two more cops rushed in. We could hear them start to throw things around in the bedroom. They were gentle with the motel's property, buy not very considerate of ours.

Another cop appeared at the patio door, struggling with the outside lock. We were surrounded, just like in the movies. Much later, I speculated that had I been armed and violently inclined, I would have been able to kill all three of the cops who pushed through the narrow door, after the noise they made preceding their entrance, only to be shot myself trying to escape the room.

I moved to let the cop in from the patio, but stopped when one of the heaters leveled his gun at my belly. Just like in the movies, but the gun was real. It looked more solid, more real than anything else in this little drama.

"That's not where we're at," I told him, nodding at the gun.

Apparently all the propaganda about long hairs and peace and love had reached him. Or perhaps he was sensitive enough to realize that the place reeked of peaceful vibes until he and his cronies barged in.

He became embarrassed, it seemed, at having threatened me with the gun. He seemed almost surprised to follow my glance to his hand and find a hunk of deadly metal there. And, as if woken from a dream, he jerkingly holstered his weapon.

The lesson rang home. When dealing with the police, get them to holster their weapons as soon as possible. When a man holds a gun on another, he is totally captured by the idea that violent death is imminent. Even if the idea is obviously false, the gun is strong enough as a symbol to warp his perception to the point where his judgment is affected. And both the holder of the gun and the person at whom it is pointed may begin to deal with each other unaware of what the realities of the situation really are.

The tension relaxed as each of the cops came to the realization that there would be no violent resistance. There was a visible pause in the drama, as they holstered their guns and rechanneled their thoughts from the death-violence groove into relief-release-power grooves.

Some felt the release so strongly that they became manic, chatty, and started to riff with us in overly-familiar terms as they rummaged through the rooms like school kids turned loose in an abandoned house.

When I realized how quickly the moods of these policemen changed, I re-enforced within me the determination to remain calm, as much in control of the situation as was possible. I asked if they had a warrant. They told me I'd see it later.

Let them throw our stuff around all they want, I remember thinking smugly. They may be hip to me. But the pad is clean. Everything is cool. You guys have blown a big bust by arriving a day early.

I was so sure everything would be OK that I found myself rapping about yoga to one of the cops who had caught the title of the pamphlet I still held in my hand.

One of the cops emerged from the bedroom and beckoned to the man in charge of the raid. They disappeared back into the room. I flashed on the litter of small bills, totalling over $1,000, on the dresser top. But before I could move to protect my bread, the cop who was gleefully emptying my old lady's purse in the kitchenette squealed.

"Yours?" he asked. The tiny beaded bag looked strangely out of proportion dangling from his sausage fingers.

"It's mine," she admitted before I could tell her to keep her mouth shut.

"This yours, too?" the cop inquired, producing a microscopic piece of hash and part of an orange tab.

She looked like a kid who had been caught at some mischief —sort of I-guess-you-caught-me-but-isn't-it-cute? But this was no indulgent parent questioning her. It was the Man.

"You are under arrest," he told her. Blah, blah, blah, and anything you say may be used against you.

That was a drag. But she insisted on carrying, even after I

warned her to cool it while I was heavy into my dealing changes. Now she knew why, I thought self-righteously.

Still, it was all cool. There was the money in the bedroom and over a thousand hits of sunshine stashed elsewhere in town. I would be able to bail her out and get a lawyer the next day. We were planning to stay in the Northwest for a few seasons, anyway. My tight-assed smugness disappeared quickly. One of the detectives came out of the bedroom, pulling two lids from his coat pocket. "We found these under the mattress," he said sincerely, as if trying to establish the veracity of his lying words by enunciating them clearly and concisely. "You are under arrest for violation of the Uniform Narcotics Act, etc., etc."

I was really naive. I had really thought that a whole mob of narcs, apparently informed about my activities, were going to crash into my rooms with drawn guns, search them, and just go away if they failed to turn up any incriminating evidence. How foolish.

The sight of this agent of the law, this trusted civil servant, whose word would stand against mine in any court, whipping the evidence out of his pocket in my plain view, really struck me.

Until that point I tried to project the attitude of calm, polite self-assurance that experience had taught me was the correct way to deal with petty bureaucrats and traffic cops.

But the sight of this harrassed little man, forced to bring along his own evidence even after being tipped to my activities by informers, was too much.

I almost laughed out loud, but felt constrained to merely grin and shake my head.

He was enraged that I found his antics humorous. He rushed across the room and locked eyes with me. A mistake, since I remained calmly smiling down into his eyes, though he stuck his face as aggressively close to mine as his limited stature would allow. Considering that I stood a full head taller than he, he looked quite the fool.

"You, you, weirdo, New York ugly. What are you looking at with your buggy eyes," he spewed. He was really trying to get me to blow my cool and swing at him, and this was the best he could come up with.

It still blows my mind that he thought his school girl epithets would lure me into playing his game and maybe getting hit on or shot.

Another detective interrupted our little showdown by crisply snapping, "Would you like to make a statement?" The tension broke immediately to return to routine.

Suddenly, I remembered the money on the dresser. They had not mentioned that it was being held as evidence. I wanted to be sure I had it or it was accounted for when we left for jail.

But again I was being naive. "What money?" the cops who searched the bedroom chorused. The cops who had not been in the bedroom exchanged covert glances. So I announced there was over $1,000, consoled that the money would now be split so many ways that each cop, in essence, would be merely a petty thief.

Now they were anxious to move the routine along. Again, they asked if I would make a statement. Did they really expect me to cooperate, I asked, after they had planted and robbed me?

I told them that if we were under arrest we would like to be booked as soon as possible, so we could start arranging for lawyers and bail.

The name-calling cop snapped back that I shouldn't tell them how to run their business.

But I insisted. It's safer in a cell with a bunch of drunks than in a motel room with armed detectives. Once you're arrested, get to jail as quickly as you can.

After enough time elapsed to show me that they, not I, was making the decision to leave, they told us to move out. I had to remind them that my old lady was only half dressed though most of them had earlier made a point of ogling her ass through the transparent material of her tights. Sometimes cops will ignore the most obvious facts of your rights and comforts. They must be reminded calmly in a way that is impossible to construe as resisting arrest.

The cop who manacled us put the cuffs on loosely. "It's the rules," he apologized so the others would not overhear. This was the same policeman who was embarrassed at having threatened me with his gun. He also seemed very uncomfortable when his buddy flipped out and was genuinely interested when we were rapping about yoga. It appeared that not all cops had surrendered all vestiges of their humanity when they were issued their guns.

But then another cop threatened to tighten the cuffs until they cut off my circulation if I didn't shut up and stop trying to reassure my old lady that everything was going to be all right.

At the station they put us in separate glass cages and refused to allow us to use the bathroom. Instead, the brave law enforcement agents gathered around a nearby desk and made "wee wee" jokes while playing with their guns.

Then the police led five other people I had been hanging with into the station, handcuffed. Apparently they had it in their minds that they were breaking up a big dope ring. It was not very comforting to be caught up in their hallucination.

The police had come down as heavy as they could short of

brutality. On the tip of an informer whom I would never face, even in court, I had been planted, burnt, and busted. Half the people I knew in Seattle were also busted.

But although I wasn't certain of it, and from time to time became overcome by doubt, I knew the inequities in the system would work in my favor. The thought of those unfortunates who were caught on the wrong side of the inequalities in our system often caused concern. But I was glad to be able to take advantage of points in my favor.

I cut my hair and shaved my beard, aware that my Negro cell mates could not disguise themselves so easily. But then there I was a white, middle class, first offender with a college education. I had friends in New York and Seattle raising money for bail and lawyers.

Even though I spent two weeks in jail, and the guards liked to roust us out of bed at weird hours to inspect our cells and assholes, it was all cool.

A sweet old lady judge dropped our bail from $6,000 to less than $1,000. She was impressed that my old lady had been a teacher and social worker in Harlem and that I had been among other things a newspaper reporter. I got the impression that she thought the jails were too barbarous for us, but not for some other type of people. I wasn't about to argue.

Our friends sent us a beautiful, hip, young lawyer. And again, though relieved, I was disgusted because I needed an intermediary to guide me through the labyrinth of our court system. I went along, though, terribly uptight that I couldn't speak for myself and hope to escape a jail term.

In the end the whole thing was set up before we went to court — our plea, the sentence, even the terms of our probation.

We pled guilty. The prosecutor got his conviction. In return he recommended we be put on probation for six months, after which the charges would be dropped.

The court trip had so little to do with the arrest that at times I was sure they were completely unconnected. But that's how it went down. I learned that doing time teaches lessons much more important than any I learned in college. But if you have to stand up and make a plea before a judge, a college education counts. Like Dylan sang, "He's a clean cut kid/ and he went to college too."

GREGORY JOHN-MARTIN-PORTLEY

For Refusing to Unwalk My Dog August 6, 1965

Busted
still on probation
from the last time beaten.
Me rubber ball head
worrying not on its own
but friend and dog
arrested with
objection.
Don't say FASCIST
too loud
hear?
Second day
NIGHT:
100 Center Street
graduated from Brooklyn.

Up behind courtroom sequences
If I am hungry enough
Orange cold tea
Stale peanut butter gone rancid
with jelly.

Papers, fingerprinted papers:
"You! Here!"
"You! Your name! (?)"
"Animal, Your hoof!"
"Bend over let's look up your ass!"
(I'm inclined to be suspicious)
I grub doctor pill dispenser's
STELAZINE.

Papers, yellow, blue, white;
Lined, black-spotted, dotted.
Fingers
Wrenched
from wrist to grease
Grease (black label) won't come off.
Scrub, water wash soap
seatless toilets
sand paper for asses

sticks linty strands
like used condoms wet.
Cardboard metal beds.

Loss to night
Inside wander back and forth
i can't explain why t.v. doesn't interest me
i haggle with imagination's freedom,
playing cards with spades,
by the white of my eyes gone patsy
to rhymes of desertion
from tanned bars of detention.

I gave friend John my socks
it's cold at night
the metal's hard
he's lost his job
tomorrow we'll be handcuffed again
in a sad kind of friendship
after we're acquitted he'll regret.

Half staring through pebbled glass at grey
THROUGH THE GLASS IT IS ALWAYS ONE GREY
    DULL
NO BLUE
NEVER BRIGHTENED
SELDOM DULLER
FLOATING SOMEWHERE IN A DRYING DROP
OF PEBBLED
STALE
COME
. . . THAT IS THE VISION

Outside is stolen from the criminal
I dream one night: I escape.
(My shirtsleeve torn
swings on the strength of the bar
an eye-popped face
my tongue hanging fat
and black
sticking in the official faces)

Waiting on
tomorrow's man with handcuffs
chained to John's loyal objection
his wrist and helpless West Coast
bail-jumping fear
up to the steel-quilted
clanging elevator.

LESLIE A. FIEDLER

On Being Busted at Fifty

"*Az m'lebt, m' lebt alles*," my grandfather began telling me when *he* was fifty and presumably thought me old enough to understand, "if you live long enough, you live through everything." And, I suppose, justice being as imperfectly practiced as it is in our world, one could consider getting arrested as inevitable a function of aging as getting cancer. But some people I know would have to reach 150 at least before falling afoul of the law, and others have sat in their first cell by sixteen or seventeen: so there must be some other, more specific reason why I find myself charged with a misdemeanor just past the half-century mark of my life.

Where did it all begin, I keep asking myself, where did it really start—back beyond the moment those six or eight or ten improbable cops came charging into my house, without having knocked, of course, but screaming as they came (for the record, the first of their endless lies), "We knocked! We knocked!"; and producing only five minutes later, after considerable altercation, the warrant sworn out by a homeless, lost girl on whom my wife and daughter had been wasting concern and advice for over a year. It seems to me that the actual beginning must have been, *was* the moment I got up before the Women's Club (an organization of faculty wives and other females variously connected with the State University of New York at Buffalo) to speak to them of the freedom and responsibility of the teacher.

I have no record of the occasion (was it a year ago, two?), can remember no precise dates or names or faces—but I do recall the horrified hush with which my not very daring but, I hope, elegantly turned commonplaces were received. I spoke of the ironies of our current situation in which a broad range of political dissent is tolerated from teachers, but in which no similar latitude is granted them in expressing opinions about changing stanadrds in respect to sex and drugs. I invoked, I think, the names of Leo Koch (fired out of the University of Illinois) and Timothy Leary (dropped from the faculty at Harvard, I reminded my ladies) and ended by insisting that the primary responsibility of the teacher is to be free, to provide a model of freedom for the young.

Needless to say, tea and cakes were served afterward, and one or two members of the Program Committee tried hard to make conversation with me as I gallantly sipped at the former and politely refused the latter. But there was a growing space around me no matter how hard they tried, a kind of opening *cordon sanitaire* that kept reminding me of a picture which used to hang in my grade-school classrooms, of Cataline left alone on the benches of the Roman Senate after his exposure by Cicero. That evening there were phone calls rather drastically reinterpreting my remarks (I had, it was asserted by one especially agitated source, advocated free love and "pot" for fourteen-year-olds), as well as—for the very first time—voices suggesting that maybe there was something anomalous about permitting one with my opinions to teach in the State University.

It was then, I suspect, that my departmental chairman as well as some officials in the loftier reaches of Administration began receiving hostile letters about me—not many in number, I would judge, but impassioned in tone. Still, though this constituted a kind of prelude, it all might have come to nothing had I not then accepted an invitation to speak to the High School Teachers of English in Arlington, Virginia, at the end of January of this year. It was an intelligent and responsive group to whom I tried to talk as candidly as I could about the absurdity of teaching literature, i.e., teaching a special kind of pleasure under conditions of mutual distrust and according to an outmoded curriculum.

I said many things both in my initial presentation and in response to a considerable stack of written questions about what students should be asked to read in high school (essentially, I said, mythological material from Homer to Shakespeare, and similar stuff from the twentieth century, which they themselves prefer, e.g., J. R. R. Tolkien's *Fellowship of the Ring*); what they should *not* be asked to read (such old standards as *Silas Marner* and *Ivanhoe,* such splendid but currently irrelevant poets as Spenser and Milton, plus the stuffier verse entertainers of the nineteenth century like, say, Tennyson); and what the teachers themselves ought to be reading to have some sense of the group they are theoretically addressing (the obvious New Gurus: Buckminster Fuller, N. O. Brown, Marshal McLuhan, Timothy Leary, etc.).

A reporter for the Washington *Post* was present and moved enough to do a feature piece (marred by minor inaccuracies and odd conjunctions born in his mind rather than in mine) headed: Cool It On Milton, Teachers Advised, which became, as the article was reprinted throughout the country: Author: Study Leary, not Milton. And under an even more misleading rubric (English Teachers Told to Study Leary) the story appeared on the front page of Buffalo's morning newspaper, a journal dedicated to scaring itself and its readers about where the modern world is going, largely—I would gather—to keep mail from the Far Right rolling in. Such readers may not ever have read either Milton or Leary, but they know which is the honorific and which the dirty word. It was at this point, at any rate, that the notion of me as a "corrupter of the young" seems to have taken hold in Western New York at least — spreading as far as the State Legislature, in which a member arose within a couple of weeks (representing, as I recall, the Hornell District) to ask why my presence was being tolerated in a publicly supported institution of higher learning.

I did not at first pay much attention to all this, nor to the fact that in a pamphlet on pornography, prepared by the same body of New York lawmakers, the cover of a nudist magazine advertising the reprint of a review I had once done of that unexpectedly amusing movie, *The Immoral Mr. Tease*, had been given a prominent position. On the one hand, the small local furor had got lost in the overwhelming response the garbled version of what I had said in Arlington brought from all over the country — offers to publish my remarks in publications ranging from *Fact* to the *Catholic World*, invitations to run seminars for grade-school teachers, and pleas to join such organizations as America's Rugged Individualists Spirtualistic Entity (ARISE) and the Friends of Meher Baba. On the other hand, I had come more and more to think of what I had to say about young people and where they were (all that had begun with my immensely ambivalent and much misunderstood article on "The New Mutants" in *Partisan Review*) as being directed *not* to the young at all.

To be sure, in spite of their publicly announced contempt for the opinions of the aging, those under thirty desperately desire reassurance and confirmation from those beyond that magical boundary; but it is weakness in them which makes them ask it — and I had resolved not to respond. No, it seemed to me that it was to my own peers that I had to speak, to explain, to interpret — translating for the benefit of teachers what their students were saying in an incomprehensible tongue, deciphering for parents what their children were muttering in a code they trusted their parents to break. What did I have to tell the young about themselves (about Shakespeare or Dante or even Melville and Faulkner I could talk with special authority, but that is quite another matter) which I had not learned from them? One of the things I had learned — something I might have remembered from the *Apology* but did not — is that the young cannot, will not, be "corrupted" or "saved" by anyone except themselves. Out of my own ambivalence, my own fear, my own hopes and misgivings before a generation more generous and desperate and religious than my own, it seemed to me I could make a kind of sense—at least what might be made to seem "sense" to those in whose definition of that term I myself had been brainwashed.

But I found an adult community more terrified than myself, more terrified even than I had then guessed, of the gap between themselves and the young; and therefore pitifully eager to find some simple explanation of it all, something with which they could deal, if not by themselves, at least with the aid of courts and cops. "Dope" was the simple explanation, the simple word they had found (meaning by "dope" the currently fashionable psychedelics, especially marijuana); and once that was licked, the gap would be closed, the misunderstandings solved, the mutual offense mitigated. For such a Utopian solution, a few arrests on charges of possession and selling, a few not-quite-kosher searches and seizures would be a small enough price to pay.

Meanwhile, however, some among the young (and a few out of the older generations as well) had begun to propagandize in favor of changing the laws against marijuana, or at least of investigating the facts with a view toward changing those laws; and this seemed to the simple-minded enemies of the young a new and even greater cause for consternation. To legalize pot would be, it appeared to them, to legalize long hair and scraggly beards for young men, new sexual mores for young women, Indian head-bands and beads and incense for everyone: to sanction indiscriminate love in place of regulated aggression, hedonism in place of puritanism, the contemplative life in place of the active one. And everyone knew what that meant! At this point, the fight against marijuana with the aid of the police and strategic lies began to be transformed into *a fight against the freedom of expression* (though only in the case of those interested in changing the marijuana laws, to be sure) employing the same weapons.

At this point precisely—it was in March of this year—I became Faculty Adviser to LEMAR, an officially recognized student organization on the campus at Buffalo, dedicated to employing all possible legal means to make the regulations on the consumption of marijuana no more stringent than those on alcohol—and which, incidentally, asked all of its members to sign a pledge not to possess or use pot. I was asked to assume the job, I gather, in large part because I was notoriously "clean," i.e., it was widely known that I (and my wife as well) did not and had never smoked marijuana. Though this may have been in the minds of some of the students who approached me a purely strategic reason for their choice, it seemed to me a principled reason for accepting the position. I would, given the circumstances, be able to fight for the legalization of "grass" not in order to indulge a private pleasure, but in order to extend freedom for everyone. Besides, the situation struck me as intolerable, with exactly the same discrepancy between the actual practice of a community (in this case the subsociety of those under thirty) and the laws which presumably regulated it, as had prevailed in respect to alcohol during the late Twenties.

The same considerations which had led to the repeal of Prohibition early in the following decade seemed to me to demand a change in the laws controlling the consumption of marijuana in 1967. Certainly I felt this with special urgency as one committed to limiting rather than extending or preserving the possibilities of alienation, hypocrisy, and lawlessness for the young. Moreover, I was convinced that if the University could not provide a forum for the calm and rational discussion of the real issues involved, the debate about the legalization of marijuana would continue on the same depressing level of hysteria and sensationalism on which it had begun. Finally, even if I had disagreed totally with its aims, I would have become faculty adviser to any intellectually respectable group that found as much difficulty as LEMAR was apparently having in persuading someone to take on the responsibility.

As a matter of fact, it depressed and baffled me that a score of applicants for the post of faculty adviser had not already stepped forward; though the student leaders of the organization explained to me that there was real cause for fear on the part of reluctant faculty members that sanctions might in fact be taken against them. *But what sanctions*, I asked in my innocence, *could possibly be taken?* A few anonymous letters to the President of the University calling for dismissal? Another indignant "editorial" on TV or in the press? I began to learn soon enough and in an odd way, when an application I was making for an insurance policy was turned down, though my health was fine and my credit good. The letter from the life insurance company was vague and discreet: "like to be able to grant every request . . . not always possible . . . many factors must be taken into consideration . . . I am sorry indeed . . . ." But private conversations with people involved made it quite clear that at the moment of associating myself with LEMAR I had become to the pious underwriters a "moral risk," unworthy of being insured.

While I was considering whether my civil rights had in fact been infringed, and whether I should make an appeal to the American Civil Liberties Union — the local head of the narcotics squad (a man more vain and ambitious than articulate) had been attempting to argue down the students in public debates organized by LEMAR, and had ended in baffled rage, crying out, according to the student head of LEMAR who was his interlocuter: "Don't worry kid — when we get you LEMAR guys, it's gonna be

on something bigger than a little pot-possession," and "Yeah
—there are some of those professors out at U.B.—bearded beat-
nik Communists. I wouldn't want any of my kids to go out there,
but that's all right—they'll be gotten rid of."

The issues are clearly drawn—*not* criminal issues at all in the first
instance, but differences of opinion and style felt to be critical
enough to be settled by police methods, even if this requires
manufacturing a case. After all, what other way is there to cope
with an enemy who is bearded (i.e., contemptuous of convention
and probably cleanliness as well), and "beat" (i.e., dangerously
abberant), and a Communist (i.e., convinced of ideas more liberal
than those of the speaker), and—worst of all—a professor (i.e.
too smart for his own good, too big for his britches, etc., etc.).
Indeed, the case against one bearded professor at least was being
"prepared" for quite a while. The statements quoted above were
made on April 18 and April 20, and on April 29, the day of the
arrest, a spokesman for the police was reported as having said
that for ten days my house, watched off and on for "months,"
had been under "twenty-four-hour surveillance"—a scrutiny
rewarded (according to police statements in the press) by the
observation of "many persons, mostly young, going in and
out. . . ." All of which seems scarcely remarkable in a household with six children, each equipped with the customary number
of friends.

What is remarkable is to live under "surveillance," a situation
in which privacy ceases to exist and any respect for the person
and his privileges yields to a desire to "get rid of" someone with
dangerous ideas. Slowly I had become aware of the fact that my
phone kept fading in and out because it was probably being
tapped; that those cars turning around in nearby driveways or
parked strategically so that their occupants could peer in my
windows, though unmarked, belonged to the police; that the
"bread van" haunting our neighborhood contained cops; and that
at least one "friend" of my children was a spy.

It was the police themselves who had released to the press (the
unseemly desire for publicity overcoming discretion and reti-
cence) the news that this "friend," a seventeen-year-old girl
with a talent for lies, had been coming in and out of our house
with a two-way radio—picking up all conversations within her
range, no matter how private, and whether conducted by members of my household or casual visitors. She had the habit of disappearing and reappearing with a set of unconvincing and con-
tradictory stories about what exactly had happened to her (she
had been in the hospital for a V.D. cure; she had been in jail;
she had been confined to an insane asylum; she had been beaten

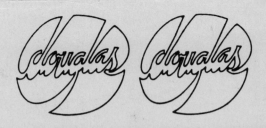

DOUGLAS BOOK CORPORATION
535 West 112th Street
New York, N.Y. 10019

Review Copy

TITLE GETTING BUSTED

AUTHOR Ross Firestone, Ed.

PRICE $5.95 (cloth); $2.45 (paper)

PUB. DATE September 22, 1971
Kindly send us two clippings
of your review of this book.

PUB. DATE   September 22, 1971
Kindly send us two clippings
of your review of this book.

up by incensed old associates)—but always she seemed so lost and homeless and eager for someone to show some signs of concern that it seemed impossible ever to turn her out. For me, the high point—the moment of ultimate indignity—in the whole proceedings came at my last Passover Seder when, just after I had spoken the traditional lines inviting all who were hungry to come in and eat, the "friend" had entered, bearing (we now know) her little electronic listening device, to drink our wine and share our unleavened bread.

The ironies are archetypal to the point of obviousness (one of my sons claims we were thirteen at table, but this I refuse to admit to myself), embarrassingly so. I prefer to reflect on the cops at their listening post (in the bread van?) hearing the ancient prayers: "Not in one generation alone have they risen against us, but in every generation. . . . This year we are slaves, next year we shall be free!" I cannot resist reporting, however, that at the end of the evening, the electronically equipped "friend" said to me breathlessly, "Oh, Professor, thank you. This is only the second religious ceremony I ever attended in my life." (My wife has told me since that the first was the lighting of Channukah candles at our house.)

Fair enough, then, that the first really vile note I received after my arrest and the garbled accounts of it in the local newspapers (made worse by a baseless reference to "trafficking in drugs" in the initial release from the University concerning my case) should have struck an anti-Semitic note, reading, "You goddamned Jews will do anything for money." Though I had not really been aware of the fact, anti-Semitism was already in the air and directed toward the University of which I was a member. (Hate mail from an organization calling itself MAM, or more fully, *Mothers Against Myerson*, had already begun to refer to Martin Myerson, the President of our University, as "that Red Jew from Berkeley"). It was all there, ready to be released: hostility to the young, fear of education and distrust of the educated, anti-Semitism, anti-Negroism, hatred for "reds" and "pinkos," panic before those who dressed differently, wore their hair longer, or—worst of all—dissented from current received ideas.

I should have been prepared by my experiences only a few weeks before the police invasion of my home, by some of the responses I got over the telephone when I had agreed to explain the nature and purposes of LEMAR and to comment generally on the culture of the young over one of those three-hour question-and-answer radio programs which appear to bring out all the worst in all the worst elements in any community. The tone of the whole thing was set by the letter of invitation in which the conductor of the program ended by saying that he could not understand why a man so often quoted by *Time-Life* would agree to act as faculty adviser to LEMAR, or in his terms "would willingly take up the posture of Pied Piper to those young louts. . . ."

Still I was not merely distressed but *astonished* when, just as I was recovering from being mugged, fingerprinted, misquoted, and televised, I received an anonymous letter purporting to be from "a group of Central Park neighbors," which began by assuring me that I and my children were "condemned to a ghetto life," went on to refer to their Negro friends (two of whom were also arrested after the police broke into my house) as "the colored, thieving and prostituting for a ratish living . . ."; and concluded: "If Myerson doesn't dispose of you and you leave our neighborhood in a reasonable length of time be assured of total harassment. . . " What such "total harassment" involves has teased my imagination—though I begin to have a clue or two, since having received only recently a notice that our homeowner's insurance policy was being canceled out of hand (in the extralegal world of the insurance companies, all men are presumed guilty until proven innocent), which would mean—unless we can replace it—the loss of our mortgage.

In this context of abject fear and pitiful hatred, the actual arrest, the charges, the legal maneuvering and courtroom appearances seem of minor importance, however annoying and time-consuming they may be. The elements of enticement, entrapment, planting of "evidence," etc., involved in "the well-prepared case" of the police will be revealed if and when the matter comes to trial (it is now adjourned until September 5), and the charges against my wife and me, my children and their friends are, as they must be, dismissed. Meanwhile it seems proper and appropriate only to repeat a couple of paragraphs from a letter I wrote to *Time* after they had published an account of the events which seemed to me to verge on slander, a correction which they shortened and slightly altered:

> When the police recently broke into my home in Buffalo, after weeks of unseemly surveillance, they did not discover—as your columns erroneously reported—anything remotely resembling a "pot-and-hashish party." They found rather my wife, my oldest son, my daughter-in-law and me at the point of setting out for the movies, and another son plus two friends at widely scattered places in a large and rambling house. That second son—absurdly charged with "possession of marijuana" —far from indulging in some wild orgy, happened to be in the process of taking a bath.
>
> The context of your article suggested that university students may have been involved in the events; this is untrue. It further seemed to imply that I was smoking pot. This is also without basis in fact. Neither my wife no I has ever used or

possessed an illegal drug, nor are we charged with this even in the case manufactured by the police. What we are accused of is "maintaining a premise"—i.e., keeping up the mortgage payments and maintaining in good repair our home in which other people are alleged to have been in possession of marijuana.

Beyond this legal considerations forbid my going at the moment, though I suppose two items could be added without indiscretion. First, I was initially surprised and pleased that the cops did not tear my first-floor study apart after they had crashed in on me: I attribute their unlooked-for courtesy either to a lurking respect for professors (they were only really rough—as could have been predicted—with the two Negro boys in the house at the time), or to their being unnerved at finding themselves for once in so grand a neighborhood (one of them could not help exclaiming in awe, "You can bet this is the biggest house I ever seen!"). But I have learned since, alas, that their whole "search" of the premises was a perfunctory sham—except on the third floor, where their young agent had been sent in an hour before the bust to leave a "little present" of marijuana, and where, she had assured them (exiting just five minutes before), it safely reposed. And second, the movie we were headed for was *Casino Royale*—a spy and pursuit film which, for obvious reasons, we have felt no need to see since.

I do not mean to say that even the courtroom is not penetrated by the hysteria that affects the community; at our original arraignment, for instance, a respectable judge was disturbed enough to lose all sense of decorum and to lecture those attending the proceedings (quite as if he were speaking over the heads of a group of condemned criminals) on the folly of considering a university a place where one learns "through the sweat of marijuana smoke. . . . They are taught this is not habit-forming. The records indicate otherwise." There is, finally, little doubt that agencies entrusted with law-enforcement have in Buffalo become instrumental in creating an atmosphere in which not only I, but my wife and children are persecuted and chivvied (largely for the simple fault of being *my* wife and children), my whole life at home and at school harried—quite as if we were all living in a Nazi or Communist totalitarian state supervised by Thought Police.

Even my children's friends have had to pay for their friendship, as the police have diligently tried to shore up their shaky case. One of them, as a matter of fact, was arrested before the 29th of April in the company of the same teeny-bopper spy who swore out our warrant; though it remains unclear whether this was a rehearsal for her, or the occasion of recruiting her for "police work." Since our arrest, there have been a couple more: one of a girl who plays in the same rock-and-roll group as my youngest son—the most shameless frame-up of all, in which, according to her story, the police simply broke down her door, walked in the middle of her living room, plunked down a packet of marijuana on a table, and looking up with a smirk, said, "Hey, see what we found!" More publicized was the second, which involved the arrest in their farmhouse home of what the police called "the operator of an electronic-psychedelic nightclub" and his wife—along with two of my sons and my daughter-in-law who had just come to call.

Quite as interesting to the cops as a "loose substance which will be analyzed to determine if it is marijuana, and several tablets and pills which will also be analyzed" were such other dangerous materials, which they confiscated along with them, as a pack of Tarot cards, some jars of macrobiotic foods, and "a lot of psychedelic literature," i.e., several copies of a volume of short stories written by "the operator of an electronic-psychedelic nightclub." The local press found even more intriguing and, apparently, damning the exotic furniture of the place (" . . . there were mattresses on the floor, there were short-legget [sic] tables . . . candles were burning and there was incense in the room . . . ") and the garb worn by those arrested ("a long white cotton robe . . . a kimono . . . a black and white mini-skirt with black net stockings . . . "hippie-type" sportswear, including tight-fitting denim trousers . . ."). That the "tight-fitting denim trousers" were nothing more nor less than garden-variety blue jeans the magic word "psychedelic" concealed from the titillated readers of the *Courier-Express*; and the adjective "hippie-type" glossed it for others less literate but equally convinced that all who dress differently from themselves are guilty even though ultimately found innocent—*especially* guilty if devious enough to convince the courts that they are less insidious than their clothes declare them.

Yet this is not the whole story; for everywhere there is a growing sense (especially as the police in their desperation grow more and more outrageous) that not I and my family, but the police themselves and those backward elements in the community, whose panic and prejudice they strive vainly to enforce, are on trial. The ill-advised remarks of the police court judge at my arraignment, for instance, brought an immediate rebuke and an appeal to the local Bar Association for "appropriate action" from a professor of Law who happened to be present. And my own University has stood by me with a sense that not only my personal freedom but the very atmosphere of freedom on which learning depends is imperiled.

When there was some talk at an earlier stage of the game of "suspending" me pending an investigation, my own department served notice that they would meet no classes unless I could meet mine; the Student Senate voted to strike in sympathy if the need arose, and the Graduate Students Association seconded them. In the end, the President of the University announced that, "on the advice of the Executive Committee of the Faculty of Arts and Sciences and after consultation with the State University attorneys and Chancellor Samuel B. Gould," *no* action against me was warranted. The ground for this decision was, he indicated, "the American heritage of fair play in which a man is considered innocent until proved otherwise"; and for the ground as well as the decision, he won the overwhelming support and admiration of his faculty — some of whom, however, were prepared to go just a little further and insist on the principle advocated by the American Association of University Professors: "Violations of the civil or criminal law may subject the faculty member to civilian sanctions, but this fact is irrelevant to the academic community unless the infraction also violates academic standards. . . ."

Meanwhile, letters, phone calls, and telegrams had been pouring in to both President Myerson and me (for the first forty hours after my arrest I received not a single hostile or malicious message) from the faculties of America's great colleges and from many schools abroad — all expressing solidarity and the conviction that at stake was the future of a major university and of higher education as well as my personal fate. Even in Buffalo itself I have begun to sense of late a considerable shift of opinion in my favor — not merely on the part of other teachers and those professionals closest to us, like clergymen and psychiatrists, but from every sector of the population; as it becomes clearer and clearer that the unendurably vague charge of "maintaining a premise" (what high school or university would not fall under it?) has been invented to justify the malicious persecution of dissenting opinion.

Needless to say, my awareness of this growing support lifts up my sagging spirits. I have no taste for martyrdom; I do not know how to find pleasure in suffering even for the best of causes; and I find it harder and harder to laugh at even the most truly comic aspects of my situation. But if the Keystone Comedy being played out around me can be turned into an educational venture (education being, hopefully, an antidote to fear itself) which will persuade the most abjectly prejudiced that everyone, even a college professor advocating a change in the law, is entitled to full freedom of speech — then the shameless invasion of my privacy, the vindictive harassment of my family, and the (perhaps inevitable) misrepresentation of all of us in the press will have been worth enduring.

PAUL KRASSNER

The Diamond Ball

My lawyer just phoned and said that the District Attorney will dismiss the case if I say I was present at the demonstration as a journalist.

I can't resort to that cop-out.

Actually, I was present neither as a reporter nor a protester. You see, I moonlight as a part-time rapist and, quite coincidentally, was on my way to Central Park to report for work to my supervisor (who, incidentally, started mugging purely as a hobby, ended up organizing a union, became foreman and the rest is geography) when I got stuck in the middle of this crowd which was successfully picketing some wooden barriers and all of a sudden the police proceeded to push us in a northerly direction.

Afraid for our skulls, we cooperated. But there was a red light. *Cross at the green and not in between,* I remembered. I turned around and shouted to the officers: "There are cars coming! We have to wait!"

The police then conspired with the demonstrators to disrupt traffic on 59th Street. When we got across, they began gently swinging their clubs.

A policeman kept plucking at my elbow. "Where do you want me to go?" I asked. He pretended he was acting in "Persona" and said nothing. "You're not *arresting* me, are you?" He repeated nothing. "What am I charged with?" He remained mute as he led me to the paddy wagon.

We were frisked for weapons and taken to 100 Center Street, our home away from home. Night court. We didn't even bother going to a local precinct first. For this particular occasion, the middleman had been eliminated. Along with due process.

We were not told what our rights were. Those we were already familiar with — such as the right to make a telephone call — were denied. What I really wanted to do was call Eartha Kitt.

We were all asked if we used "junk." Personally, I use only the finest stuff on the market.

Polaroid cameras were in the arsenal, and we each had our photo taken standing side by side with the arresting officer. "Hey," I whispered to mine, "where we gonna go after the prom?"

Meanwhile, the demonstration was continuing.

Moviegoers coming out of the Paris Theatre, where the film version of Camus' *The Stranger* was appropriately first-running in New York City, were treated on this evening of January 24th to a second feature: an outdoor ritual ballet staged in front of the plush Plaza Hotel by a winter stock company of protesters and policemen.

Inside, the Diamond Ball was gathering moss.

"Protest the Festival of the Vultures," announced a leaflet sponsored by a dozen organizations ranging from the Pageant Players, a street theatre troupe, to the Bertrand Russell Peace Foundation, and including BAND, or Blacks Against Negative Dying. "What is a vulture? A vulture lives off death. It gets its nourishment from dying flesh!"

The Diamond Ball was a fund-raising ploy for the Institute of International Education, which proudly admits that: "Many corporations have benefited from the Institute's wide experience and counsel" as they "have expanded their direct foreign investments by 60 per cent in a decade—to $40 billion at the end of 1963."

The past five years have been a race between the symbiotic escalations of their dollar involvement and their human detachment.

Among the guest vultures:

Charles W. Engelhard, largest U.S. investor in South African slave labor diamond mines, largest slumlord in Newark, and one of the largest contributors to the Democratic Party. Lyndon Johnson took him along to Australia after the death of Prime Minister Holt as a combination political advisor and swimming instructor.

Nelson Rockefeller, who ran for governor to counteract guilt by association with his family, which owns Chase Manhattan Bank (a heavy investor in South Africa), McDonnell-Douglas Aircraft (the stock shoots up as the planes get shot down), RCA-NBC (electronics-radio-TV manipulation), Standard Oil (supplier of oil for the planes that get shot down, importing 1.6 million barrels a day from Mideast oil fields).

Roger Lewis, President of General Dynamics, major recipient of defense contracts, enjoying a 30 per cent increase in profits during the 1965–66 period of the Vietnam war alone.

George D. Woods, predecessor to Robert McNamara at the World Bank, chief U.S. weapon for the financial penetration and domination of foreign countries and economies.

Hubert H. Humphrey, retired druggist.

Before he arrived at nine p.m., the police had forced the demonstration to evolve into mobile tactics, a portion of which found itself at Rockefeller Center where an outdoor ice-skating party was being sponsored by Kennedy-for-President fans. Some of them were hauled in by police too. After all, a banner's a banner.

Meanwhile, I still didn't know what I was being charged with. As it turned out, of the 30-odd persons arrested, most were charged with the legal cover-all, "Disorderly Conduct," including a group dressed as Keystone cops and clubbing each other, a performance which inspired the Real Fuzz to join in, using actual nightsticks.

Keith Lampe of the New York Workshop in Non-Violence had obtained a peddler's license. He wasn't arrested but lost two brand-new unsharpened pencils in the fracas.

Ben Morea of Black Mask tried to rescue someone who was conducting an involuntary investigation of police brutality and was charged with interfering with an arrest. The helmet he was wearing got cracked in the process.

Tom Neumann of the East Side Service Organization arrived swathed in blood-soaked bandages. As a gesture of obeisance to the great god Public Relations he was not arrested.

The demonstrators who were arrested were all white, except for one Negro who was in whiteface and, together with a pair of girls in theatrical makeup, was accused of masquerading without a license, a charge generally reserved for Indians and transvestites.

The regular criminals, though, were virtually all black or Spanish-speaking. The officer in charge had a pad of pink slips —literally, receipts for each man put in the cell—and police would make little jokes like, "No tickee, no prisoner."

It was indeed like a Chinese laundry, complete with the separation of white wash and colored wash.

I was the first demonstrator to be called by the court clerk, and when my name was announced, many of the spectators applauded. It was kind of embarrassing. The judge ordered: "Clear the courtroom!" And—with total equality—out went friends of demonstrators, relatives of criminals, and those who had come there as a Cheap Date satori.

I finally found out the specific charge against me: "Loud and boisterous conduct, and refusing to move when told to by an officer." I was released without bail until my trial.

We were lucky. At a West Coast demonstration, prisoners had been clubbed, tossed in the paddy wagon, sprayed with Mace, and taken for a careening ride.

All I got was Excedrin headache #42.

LENNOX RAPHAEL

THE CHE! BUST

Excerpt from a brief from the District Attorney's Office, New York City, April 1, 1969:

> "The instant suit arose from the performance of a play entitled *Che!* in New York County. Plantiff Raphael is author of the play, while the remaining plaintiffs are the actors, actresses, director, and other persons[1] associated with its production. The play opened on March 22, 1969, after having given public previews for a week. On March 24, 1969, the Honorable Amos S. Basel, a judge of the Criminal Court of the City of New York, attended a performance. At its conclusion, after the audience had left, Judge Basel signed arrest warrants for those associated with the performance. Plaintiffs were thereupon arrested. They were arraigned on the complaint of Deputy Inspector Pine, and were released in $500 bond.
>
> The complaints in the Criminal Court charged plaintiffs with various violations of the New York Penal Law. Specifically it was charged that acts of consensual sodomy and public lewdness were committed by members of the cast during an obscene performance and that the plaintiffs conspired to commit those crimes."

Fine show. Remember, we opened with our original Son of King Kong, David, and David was so right for it, he burned his baby burn into the Sister of Mercy, and the first night when the Son of Kong said Make me Yours I had to squeeze my heels from crying, he was so good, the way he used to do it. Of course, there are different ways of doing it, dimensions of the position (the lotus for example is a love position, God above), David moved his shoulders correctly; in his arms the Sister of Mercy, under the

[1] The ten arrested were: Larry Bercowitz, who played Che; Paul Georgiou (President); Jeanne Baretich (Mayfang, angelspy); Mary Anne Shelley (Sister of Mercy); John Kornhauser (Chili Billy, Son of King Kong); Don McAdams (Breakstone Fearless); Ed Wood, director; Sait Müneyyarci, costume designer; Jimmy Sullivan, usher; and playwright Lennox Raphael.

watchful-envious eyes of Breakstone Fearless, she comes to life, chimes into Kong's disprotected innocence. His orgasms were majestic & flowed freely thru theatre like messengers from a glorious rage. The cops loved to watch him do it to the Sister of Mercy; they loved him adorably. They spoke of him everywhere. At the Police Academy they fought over visions of his name, envied his empress. Go skin diving today. Everybody wanted to play Kong. O come all ye Kongsters; OK. They wanted to be shady, and all they got was over the ocean. The ape in all of us became gorilla. "That ape," one of the cops said, "that f*ng ape can really hit her hard . . . ha . . . ha. Some people have all the luck in the world."

So Kong spread joy. So much. And joy turned to sadness in repose.

But Kong is Kong. David's father was sick somewhere warm Bahamas or Miami & wanted David near. He stayed however till Our Big Opening Night of ten-gallon champagne bottles and extravagant kisses. And the Opening was David's strife as he stepped lightly into the Sister of Mercy like Tom Paine reborn a stranger in this strange land. The house was packed. Our friends breathed heavy tremulous & wild into laughter and strobes dancing in the eyes of the Vice Squad. The Squad flew in out of nowhere, about ten men and two women & the poor judge, Basel was his name, who, so entranced by the Sister's ingenious wiggle, the President's efflusive majesty, Che's definitions, and May-fang's devious wickedness, saw no redeeming social values, not even the Sister of Mercy (so a few days later he received a letter: dear sir, enclosed three tickets good for any showing of *Che!* you must come; let us know when you come; shout: you must understand, sir, with so much killing so much hate & vengeance galloping in our veins, redeeming social values are hard to come by: and we have tried. there is one point where the President says I love to f*k cows, which is a beautiful historical line & we have searched for a spotted cow, a polkadotted wonder to graze in the seduction chambers readied for the President's rape of Che. we want a beautiful cow, a virgin cow; and we must have 13 watermelons. socially redeeming ones; so tell us dearly when you're coming and we shall have the chambers ready with sweet spices and all the values that choke you to satisfaction and notice, the President said, notice the gentle verve of my voice. Hot wax.)

Needless to say (but one must continue somehow) this letter pained him very much. He gasped. He tugged at the collar of his Van Heusen, he read the letter again; he saw it plainly, the President and Che in bed and Mayfang erect and watchful thru eyes of the gun dream kisses floating in the air restless & blue. The judge pulled back. Wondered whether the first kiss redeemed the second, or the third more relevant to his mind already made up of course before he set foot in the Free Store Theatre to jack off in our dreams & will to do a beautiful thing for nobody's mind, he should have read *Portnoy's Complaint* before coming. He held back his eyes. The President has this massive energizer friboltvroom, and the judge stared it down for a minute, a few seconds more perhaps, in all his years on the bench, he had never seen such a demanding presence, his trepidation trembled. The President's authority was beyond the pale of redemption. The judge laughed. You must not seek to understand this laughter. Its laughingness points the way, the judge laughed into Mayfang's scouring crotch of gold, said to himself this thing here is really too much look at this young man he should have his sandblaster covered for god's sake this is a hell of a thing to let happen in a moral society. Belief leads to innocence, and innocence to corruption of the spontaneous. The judge crossed his legs to illuminate various perspectives, and Mayfang said, You're jive.

And our judge winced when Mayfang her wicked self pingled Che against the wall in an effort to dismantle his beauty. He could make neither head nor tail of it, but he laughed sometimes when he laughed his face settled and he'd look around to see the other faces, but he was still free, nobody (but I shouldn't write this, because the Vice Brigade was inside the theatre right there in the President's office having a damn good time (don't blame them) and sneaking chuckly looks at our judge. A judge does his job. Our judge moved away from Mayfang, he watched Mr. Mayfang seek her innocence in the debris of the President's lust, how she climbed into him with generous alchemy. She knows how much the President wants Che, this sexy Latin thing shining in the ideological moonlight; and much more than that, because interpretations of the lie are further from the truth Climb over their frothing loins. Desire being illusion, and illusion without desiring a frivolous respite from loneliness. Pardon my awkward vision of the judge's eyes. ·

After the bust, which came at the end of the performance (the police being extremely charitable in matters sexual), the judge's eyes rushed into my face. I stood at the front slidedoor thruout the show, and there was the judge right below me, and I was so happy, I happied for him, he was enjoying himself so much. Really, this judge is guilty of entrapment; we were entrapped by the wanton joy of release in his eyes; but it doesn't matter; there are two sides to each man: redemption & self; and if we didn't redeem his social values, we still took care of his loins for a few minutes, and that's enough. The artist can't afford to be too greedy in times of sensual disaster. *Che!* is no less socially redeeming than a Kennedy ½ dollar or the Statue of Liberty. But I didn't say this to the judge.

He saw the show, he says he left the show after the President killed Che, walked to the sidewalk, hands leafed before him, and signed the arrest warrants; and we were under arrest, ten of us, even King Kong, John Kornhauser, who replaced David, and Jimmy, 16, who ran the mimeo and helped us keep the place clean for the judge. They walked right in, stormed out our weeks of toil to the dressing-room & shagged You're under ARREST!!!!!!!

Incredible, being busted, why? They wouldn't tell us right away, not read out the charges before the inquisition, but I started wondering who cared? Here we are ten of us on our little trip-association with the holiness of everything unrotten of the body, and some expert perverts call this going too far; but any port for a storm, babe. LITTLE BEDLAMS. Phone calls. For God's sake, someone shouted at Inspector Pine, Our Man In Sexualia, don't lay your filthy hands on the President's authority. I know why you guys trying to arrest him want to take him down to the edge of the moat and blow up his sensuality with a Harley Davidson pump, my God, have a heart, you're mugging us in the back, you sonofalawman. But the Inspector wasn't listening, his mind traveling far away and wide to the complications of *Che!* that he was in search of the Vicelords, the war was wide open & breathing heavily, they searched for grass, scag, snatch, and the President's highly dubious contraceptives. Took our director's iron tablets.

The Department was up against the wall, for a change, and everything had to be right for this big one, BUST OUT like Wall Street peep-pervs and their horde of subway diffusions; so they had been watching us from the start, reading our beautiful notices how they were pissed-off to the john. Different folks, different strokes: sure they fought among themselves for tickets as to who should see Che dabble in the Sister of Mercy's innocence, everybody whispering in the Police Academy is it true they really f*k like nobody's business, yes, man, over&over again they do it every night they feel like it and you should see the President, man, he's a motherf*kr. Lots were cast dreams swapped, and there's tremendous goodwill in this redeeming circle.

Night after night they came. Even those who couldn't get in on the detail. Everybody came. We take care of our trips, Mayfang warned. Come to me naked but bring me the real you. Our judge somehow failed to appreciate the dialectical immensity involved in going down, how it's like sharing a Spring Coke with someone. "There is, in fact, no way back either to the wolf or to the child." (Hesse) and our Judge fought to restrain his impatience. Uphill-fight. They spent almost (conservatively speaking) one thousand dollars on tickets, and thousands upon thousands more in manpower and spying equipment. They came in with their latest electronic ears. They recorded our speeches, night after night they came to entrap us with their enjoyment.

And our backers! The Communist Party had the FBI and we had the DA & over twenty-five thousand policemen, lining up to see this beautiful show like *I Am Curious* (blue)! Piled us into paddywagons & straight to the ninth precinct on Fifth Street, Deputy Inspector Fink's palace; but Fink wasn't in; this was perhaps bigger than Fink; and only Richard kept his cool, and sent hello words to the Florida Decency Rally. Now all the cops wanting free tickets, but they take our scripts our reservations book, and, this being the unkindest cut of all, Mayfang's plastic penis & balls; balls of fire and pillar of light; they took these things unto themselves and researched (?) the presentation of their case against us even as we sought to enjoin them from further harassing our loins.

The police bought us pizza, went outside in the dark night with their fragile noses and brought us three large pizzas, and several cups of coke as we held them at bay with promises. They were so beautiful as they scrambled for the promises of our eyes, but later, after we had been fingerprinted etcetera bull, we were led to the dungeon and forced to spend the night there in the freeze. Somebody brought me a jonah-cig which threw me out on the sands of serenity; and, suddenly, fingers still showing signs of fingerprinting mess, it was morning, vibrant, go skin diving today, babe, and we were handcuffed, look-out here come the Vicers, make way for our revenge, they hustled us to the courthouse; women in separate chambers, searched us in the Centre Street Detention Center, all the correction officers easing up to us for tickets. Only the bums weren't interested.

Our Judge was aware of all these strange vibes coming our way. All the cops, all the correction officers, they were curious. Everybody wanting to know who did the f*king. Body found/ Easter Sunday called off. We said everybody got a piece, and we took care of extracurricular declensions of the flesh during rehearsals. We erected desires, Sir Judge.

In the cell we waited our turn hours. The bums were the only ones holy, they lay on the cold floor and begged for wine.

"Come here," one said, "I want to buy a liquor store."

We laughed.

"Im sick," he called to the officer, "PUT ME IN BED WITH A NURSE."

He was inside for "imitating a human being."

Which (always) hurts.

"Every time I visit my father, he gives me a sandwich wrapped in a road map," he said, knowing the laugh.

We knew the laughter too. The show must go on. Viceroy's good taste *never* quits.

Climax.

RALPH SCHOENSTEIN

My Kind of Jail, Chicago Has

On the first night of that study in surrealism called the Democratic Convention, I did a TV salute to Mayor Daley, the last in style of mayors going back to Hague, Crump, and Borgia. On ABC's "Evening News," I said:

People are wondering why the Convention is so festive, why there's a smile on the face of every trooper and the birdies are singing on the old barbed wire fence . . .

Mayor Daley has worked hard at this Convention to please everyone from Lyndon Johnson to General Westmoreland. With the sure hand of a genial host, he has barred live television from the streets and roofs because he's well aware how TV fosters violence . . .

A certain lunatic fringe of liberals, Negroes, Czechoslovakians, and anchor men says that Daley has suppressed freedom in Chicago just because he has stopped all outdoor meetings, parades, TV remotes, and sleeping in parks. But he has made the trains run on time. And he's a great foe of unemployment. He's already given out 60,000 jobs—to the finest friends and fence builders around . . .

An hour after this broadcast, I was at the ABC studios in the Amphitheatre, where I'd put on the cap and pants of an usher to guard Gore Vidal against the adolescent abuse of William Buckley. Suddenly, I was arrested by two Chicago cops for "criminal trespassing and impersonating an officer," charges that required soaring imagination, for I had shown the cops my press credential while a network executive explained my role. If I *had* been impersonating an officer, I deserved to close in New Haven: I was wearing a blue button-down shirt, the kind you'd find only on the night watchman at Brooks Brothers. In spite of their two-figure IQ's, the cops surely knew that my mission was journalistic because they also saw my fully accredited photographer, Jill Krementz. Nevertheless, they grabbed us both. A captain named Reilly did a particularly inspired job of grabbing Jill, searching major areas of her blouse for concealed weapons.

"Tell that guy to *stop* it," she whispered as we were being led away.

"Maybe he's in love," I said. "Look, just stay calm till I can remember the Supreme Court ruling on feeling photographers."

After we'd been questioned for almost two hours, Jill was released and I was led from the hall by a sergeant named Radzicki. To make sure that I didn't slip away through the sewer system, he guided me with a firm hand on my kidney. I was receiving the world's longest rabbit punch.

"You know, you can be tough and have manners *too*," I finally said, the Amy Vanderbilt of custody. "I'd hate to have to write your review board."

But this was clearly a bluff: a Chicago police review board is the second cop that hits you.

"You TV guys are really a bunch o' wiseguys," he said.

"You mean for trying to cover the convention," I said.

As he moved me out of the hall like a billiard ball, I was heartened by the thought that I had a perfect defense: the only sincere impersonation of a Chicago cop could be given in the Menninger Clinic.

In the stenchy darkness outside the Amphitheatre, Radzicki shoved me into a police car that held two other cops in blue helmets, one a lieutenant. Not only was I honored by the pinch itself, for the best people were being arrested, but I was also deeply flattered to draw more than just an enlisted man. And so we rode off in the night, off to make me the first man booked on a charge of disorderly writing, while the radio was reporting the fury of the pacifists, who were coming at the cops with concealed flowers and deadly folk songs.

"Where you from, Mr. Bernstein?" said the lieutenant, managing to read a good half of my ABC badge.

"Oh, somewhere back East," I said neatly avoiding the trap of having my birthplace used against me.

Just before midnight, we reached police headquarters on State Street. Radzicki got out first and opened the door for me, a sign that perhaps my little lecture had done some good.

"You got cuffs?" said the lieutenant.

I felt a surge of excitement, for I had never been handcuffed, except by paying the rent; but my captors finally decided that any two of them would be able to take me up, especially now that they'd worn down my kidneys.

While entering the elevator that said FOR PRISONERS ONLY, I was suddenly aware that I was going to jail. I had often felt a vague yen to go to jail, usually when my daughters were romping on my desk, for many writers had worked nicely there; and now, as I approached the desk sergeant on the 11th floor, I was exhilarated to think of what Dostoevsky had produced in stir.

While Radzicki filled out an arrest form, the desk sergeant said, "Take everything out of your pockets and put it up here."

The whole gang seemed happy as I dropped my cash and Kleenex, but their faces fell when I added the gold container of Max Factor Erace.

"What the hell is *this?*" said one of the cops. "Fag *and* reporter?"

"It's TV makeup," I said. "You guys would know that if you ever watched Frank Reynolds instead of Bugs Bunny."

And then I sensed that perhaps I'd gone too far, especially since I didn't have a lawyer.

"I wanna call a lawyer," I said, and they pointed to a pay phone on the wall near a row of cells.

Luckily, I knew a lawyer who was out for the convention, although his representation might have its drawbacks since he wasn't licensed to practice in Illinois. However, his specialty was theatrical contracts, so he'd be just the man for the charge of impersonating an officer.

"It's very fashionable to be arrested out here tonight," he said.

"I know," I told him. "I always like to be up with the style setters. In fact, these charges set a style of their own. It's not easy to be booked for criminal trespassing in your own studio."

"Well, just sit still. I'll be right down to bail you out."

Back at the desk, Sergeant Radzicki was having some trouble with his arrest form. Suddenly, I almost liked him, for he looked the way *I'd* always looked in the last ten minutes of a geology exam.

"I'm just never sure how to say it," he told another cop as he pondered the prose of his charges. It was an essay question and he was a man who needed true-false.

After I'd signed a receipt for my money, pencil, and Kleenex, another cop searched me with the kind of pats that he must have considered a favor to a man who carried Max Factor. And then, just as I was leaving the desk, Tom Hayden, head of the young protesters, was brought in. He had a cleanly shaved face, an open white shirt, and pressed khakis—an appearance that moved one cop to say, "Here comes another animal." With quick efficiency, Hayden took the change from his pockets and put it on the desk. He knew the routine better than Radzicki.

"That's a pretty famous man," I told a cop, "and a damn good one."

"So why the hell don't he stay home where he belongs?"

"Because he happens to be fighting for the country's soul."

"Now *who* told you crap like that? You think these stupid kids really *believe* this stuff? It's just a big party."

"Do *you* go to a party to have your head cracked?" I said, aware that his head *did* need some rearranging.

After failing as Hayden's press agent, I was taken for finger-printing.

"Gee," said the cop after making my first impressions, "you have almost no fingerprints. They're very faint."

With a pang of regret, I thought of all the fruitful years that I could have spent in crime. What Bonnie and Clyde would have given for my nearly anonymous hands.

While I was washing off the ink under a sign that said IS YOUR WEAPON EXPOSED?, about ten Yippies came in, some in beards and all in clothes. If this was a party, they were all party poops, for they walked to the desk in silent dignity. One of them was holding a handkerchief on what was more than an Excedrin headache.

"Look at 'em," said a cop with disgust. "They're all on LSD."

It was the voice of the department's drug authority. To me, the boys looked bright-eyed, which set them apart from the cops. For a moment, I stood beside them, for they were jungle junkies to the cops but the conscience of America to me. I was proud to be booked with them and sorry that my own charge involved not their principle but a piece of Gilbert and Sullivan. When they were finally taken to a cell, they continued to flout society by quietly discussing McCarthy while counting bail money.

The thrill of being fingerprinted paled when a cop then led me to a big black camera that faced a white wall. Hanging a sign around my neck that carried the date and a number, he said, "You better take off your glasses."

"But without the glasses," I said, "it isn't *me*. You're just making it tough for yourself to grab me in the future."

I figured that such cooperation might cut my sentence a bit.

"No," he said thoughtfully, "I like you better with 'em off."

He was trying to be as creative as my charges.

After taking a full face and a profile shot, he removed the packet, waited half a minute, and peeled off the prints.

"Gee," I said, "just like the commercial. And they're lovely.

Look, this may be a bit out of line, but do you think I could get a few eight-by-ten's? The ABC publicity shots aren't nearly as good. I mean, maybe you could run off a few for the post office and let me have 'em."

"Now *you* know I couldn't do that. You can't copy a *Polaroid.* Say, what's the charge on you, anyway?"

"Participating in TV coverage."

"Sure, I *knew* you wasn't one o' *them.*" He looked towards the cell full of Yippies. "Goddamn animals."

The animals had just started singing "We Shall Overcome," but it *was* a vicious rendition.

When another cop started leading me towards a cell, I knew The Moment had come. I wasn't taken to the Yippies but around the corner to an empty block. The copy unlocked the door, I walked in, and he closed it behind me. After several seconds, I was struck by the realization that I couldn't get out. And my nerves further tightened when I remembered that these cops had already protected the peace by beating up some newsmen on the streets. So what would they do to me in *private?* They had even clubbed High Hefner, for whom I'd written stories. And now I had visions of their coming to my cell and torturing me by dangling *Playboy* centerfolds.

The lack of freedom in jail is surely a problem, but an even bigger one is the fact that there's nothing to *do* there. Since I had no pencil, books or magazines, I decided to read my wallet; but my driver's license lacked a certain narrative power, so at last I got up and began exploring my cell in Gun City. It was definitely nothing for *Better Homes and Gardens:* just two wooden bunks, a sink, and a toilet bowl with no seat, hardly a spur to regularity.

I finally did discover some reading matter: the walls. There was one couplet that said

2, 4, 6, 8,

CHICAGO IS A POLICE STATE

Had I a pencil, I would've added

10, 12 AND 14

WHO'S GOT THE LAWYER FOR SCHOENSTEIN

The opposite wall was devoted to prose, such as this flash of eloquence:

I WAS ARRESTED FOR HAVING A PIG ON THE SIDEWALK

So my cell had been used by Pegasus' campaign manager. And near this political memoir was another thought about government, a comment on Mayor Daley's eating habits, which hardly included his full diet.

Just below this analysis was a half-done game of boxes, a

game that I'd often played with my daughter Jill. You needed two to play and it might be hours before I got another reporter as a roommate. Looking at the boxes, I started thinking of Jill, whose favorite song was called "I Wanna Be Free." The version was by the Monkees and now her Daddy was in the hands of the apes.

After exhausting the entertainment value of the walls, I sat down on the wooden bed and began making notes with the point of my tie clip on some paper that hadn't been taken from me. Thinking of Oscar Wilde, I started to write "The Ballad of the Cook County Can."

THIS PLACE STINKS. THE BATHROOM BOWL NEEDS AJAX.
THE COPS ARE CRETINS.

It needed work, of course, but the epic theme was there. I was just rhyming moon and goon when a cop came and opened the cell. I walked joyously to a screen door, where my lawyer was waiting on the other side.

"These charges are *ridiculous*," I told him.

"I know," he said, "but for some reason, your case has gone all the way up to Daley."

"You mean all the way *down* to Daley."

"Just be patient. I'll have you out as soon as I can."

"Right *now* would be a wonderful time."

"No, you can't be bailed till your fingerprints clear Washington. I'm afraid it might take an hour or two."

When I returned to the cell, I was scared for the first time. Daley's office had surely seen my TV salute; and on top of that, I pictured what would happen when the FBI got my fingerprints. The agents would be sore about getting a faint set on such a busy night; and when they saw that the prints belonged to a man who hadn't held a job in thirteen years, I'd be moved to Joliet.

It was just 3 a.m. when I stopped writing my ballad and decided to try for sleep. Putting my folded jacket under the back of my head, I lay down on the super posture-pedic bed and closed my eyes. When the overhead fluorescent light came pouring through the lids, I held my forearm over my face. I now had darkness, but that bed would've given insomnia to an encephalitic Hindu; so when a cop passed by, I couldn't resist saying, "Hey, don't you guys have any *mattresses?*"

"You know what would happen to mattresses in this place?" he said. "They'd tear 'em up and stuff 'em down their throats."

"Look, speaking of that, I haven't eaten in 12 hours. Have you got a cracker machine around or something?"

He smiled and walked away.

Angrily, I picked up my tie clip and made some notes so the case would be easier for Abe Fortas when it reached him. Just then, a Yippie passed the cell.

"Why'd they pick you up?" I cried, no longer weighing my words. "For hanging around with a reporter?"

"Peace, brother," he said with a smile.

"You better watch that kinda talk."

The other Yippies had stopped singing and now their cell was silent; but from a cell nearby an old man was singing in the style of Aretha Franklin, who'd shown the convention how the National Anthem had come up the river from New Orleans. He sang for many minutes, a mournful dirge that was perfectly fitting for this great Chicago burial of the Bill of Rights.

It was almost 4:30 a.m. when my cell opened again and I was taken into a courtroom where my lawyer, a judge, and two clerks awaited.

"I had to spread a little money around," the lawyer whispered, "so just apologize for what you did and pretend you're coming back for trial."

"But the charges don't make any *sense*," I said.

"*Look*, Dreyfus, it's a *fix*. You're just here because you didn't give them your photographer's pictures. One nice thing about Daley's gang: they may drag you to jail for no reason, but once you're here it's crooked enough so you can get right out."

And so I stood before the judge and apologized for my theatrics and my criminal trespassing. Then he grimly told me the date when I'd have to return for trial. Even though I knew that it was all make believe, I still felt a chill, for a return to Chicago would have been worse than a first trip to hell.

After my lawyer and the clerk had exchanged a handshake full of more than manners, I was finally released, five hours after my arrest and nearly three hours after the cell door had closed behind me. I went down in the elevator and out into the streets of Chicago. Chicago, city of big shoulders and little minds. Chicago, where I'd spent more time in jail than Al Capone.

MADNESS
FRANK REYNOLDS

Freewheelin Frank

After the ski trip to Tahoe and after a day of sleep at home in Frisco, I woke in the evening. Everything was very still, as it always seems after and during LSD. We had a bar at this time which we all went to in the evenings. It was Charley's Geneva Club just across the county line in San Mateo. I decided to go there to see who was around and know what was happening. In Charley's Geneva Club there is a long bar and at the end of it a separate small cafe counter, and there's a pool table in the middle of the floor surrounded by tables and chairs. On the wall are large photos of the San Francisco Seals, the ice hockey team. For a normal Hell's Angel bar it's very clean and well kept.

As I entered the bar I noticed there were several Hell's Angels present, along with various customers old and new. I first saw Andy, a Frisco Hell's Angel, chewing on an unlit cigar that stuck out about a foot in front of him, as he swore boisterously and slopped his Lucky Lager on the floor. "The motherfuckers are going to try to draft me tomorrow!" He then caught sight of me as I entered and saw his huge giantlike stance, with the look of a reincarnation of a German officer here to make things right where they failed before; he shouted out, "HAYYYYY, LITTLE FRANK!"

I said, "What the hell was it I heard you say? About goin to war in Viet Nam?" And the same time I laughed, and said, "They're sure to lose the war if they take you."

He said, "Every motherfucker is goin to lose if they take me tomorrow."

I said, "What's this all about, anyway?"

He said, "YEAHHH, I got a letter this morning when I woke up. What a fuckin bummer!"

I said, "You can't go in no fuckin Army, you're already in one."

He said, "You're goddam right, and I'm going to stay in it."

A game of pool was going on, other members stood around waiting for their turn, for revenge with the eight ball. After a couple of beers, and a shot of red wine, I became bored and I was tired so I decided to go home. Tomorrow night would be the meeting and I had to catch up on the minutes. I told Lovely Larry and George, "I got to split, I got minutes to catch up on."

71

Before leaving, I promised Andy I'd be with him at seven o'clock in the morning to meet the bus which is supposed to take him away to the Army and reassured him, "I know they'll never take you—they never have taken any of us when we went over to the draft board together and let em know who we was." His eyes looked as though they appreciated the confidence. I then turned and walked out the door, and swung my right leg over my chopper and kicked it over. And at the same time I noticed a black and white squad car wheel around the corner a block up the street.

In the back of my mind there was no fear as the squad car disappeared. So I roared out across the double yellow line, leaving Charley's Geneva Club behind, in the shifting roars as I went through my gears heading for the county line, San Francisco bound. The air was clean and breezy as it ripped around my ears. I felt it was airing out my mind after coming down from acid and Tahoe. The thought still flashes through my mind of how *Freewheelin* I really felt at that time. I had won some money also while we were on the ski trip. Everything was just one-hundred-percent groovy! As I leaned my head to the right, the sun was already down, and darkness was about. I glanced at Lovely Larry's house where his family lived and his young sister, who I had just met for the first time this night—in her maiden-like value I left her behind at the bar. I remember laughing to myself as I thought of her, that it didn't really matter, for I'd pick her up on the next round and guard her with all values. She had hair of gold dust, with freckles sprayed in the right places upon her face and cheeks. Her mouth I knew would taste of honey. It was so good to dream of this as I rode on.

Then out of the blackness of the night there was a flash of red light, followed by the echoing sound of a siren, which roared into my ears like thunder. I'd just turned the throttle on to a full twist getting ready to hear my pipes back off when this uproaring sound blurted in at all angles. It had startled me so much that I just held onto the throttle wide-open. My bike felt as if it was lifting right off of the ground for it was already in fourth gear, as I roared up the Geneva straight stretch crossing the county line of San Francisco. As I checked my rear-view mirror, all I could see was a red flashing ball of fire, along with a siren, which had to be a Daly City heat of San Mateo County: the one who had wheeled around the corner when I was mounting my bike. I knew in my mind he'd been laying for me. My iron horse in its thunder said: Let's get home and get those minutes done. We got no time to be signing tickets. There was a red light up above, as I came screamin into the intersection. I geared down, tires burning, and I laid a beautiful right hand turn. Now on Moscow

Street I was heading towards McLaren Park. The houses, all in their peaklike roofs — something one would see on the streets of a German village — flashed by. The roar of the siren echoed in my ears. The man was still on my tail. I started flipping lefts and rights and circling blocks but my calculations were wrong. At times the scream of his tires was keeping time with mine as we rounded the corners in hairpin style. What a magnificent driver this man must be at the wheel of this car! If I had given him more credit at the start I would have lost him by going into McLaren Park with its tiny dirt trails. But now it was like a crossword puzzle between he and I. My engine was winding hard in third gear. Dropping into second — back into third — the blocks weren't long enough to ever reach fourth. What a victory I would soon have — I was telling myself: a magnificent display of horsemanship in the era of Hell's Angels. As I crossed through Excelsior and it came to an end with the freeway crossing in front of me, the newness of its divided roads and merging on ramps confused my mind. I found myself going around and around the same block trying to find a way out. I started to become violently angry. After wheeling a corner and gaining a lead of half a block on the squad car, I jammed the brakes on and U-turned onto the sidewalk, with my lights out and my engine still running as the squad car wheeled the corner. By the law of averages I had lost him this time. But it seemed as though he had a built-in radar in his mind . . . And along with it I heard screams of sirens in the not too far distance approaching the area which we were encoved in.

I knew then I had to make a break. I chose to cross the freeway over an overpass rather than go onto it. I knew I could outmaneuver the squad cars — but at high speed they would catch me. As I crossed over the overpass, the cars on the freeway beneath me whistled and screamed. My mind was in a complete turmoil. The taillights of the cars were like the flashing red lights on the squad cars.

Everything flashed red and screamed. I don't even want to talk about it. I could no longer calculate. Up above me I saw the flashing red lights of two squad cars as they whistled through an intersection in front of me. The district I was now entering was St. Mary's Park. BLAST IT! *All it has is dead-end streets!* I felt as though I were a wounded gladiator with a broken sword as I screamed through St. Mary's Park. At one time there was a loud screeching of brakes as two squad cars almost collided head-on in an intersection behind me. Everywhere I looked I saw squad cars. And I didn't know HOW IN THE HELL TO GET OUT OF ST. MARY'S PARK! The only thing that delayed the kill in the cops' favor was the small twisted area in which they had to drive their squad cars. But they knew it was over for me as well as I did. A solo police motorcycle was now on my heels. Gearing down, we were both gearing down to keep from getting off in the twisted corners. I had lost the cars when someone had double-parked in one of the main thoroughfares through St. Mary's Park. Thoroughfares are like cow trails there. Fate was against me. If there had not been a solo motorcycle cop at that time on the scene, I would have had the odds in my favor, for the person who had left the car double-parked in the street left only room enough for a motorcycle to pass through. This brought the squad cars to a screeching halt — one of them slamming into the rear of the parked car. At this time I could not remember where I was or what was happening to me. My bones ached from the strain of the long duel. And then I turned my last corner. In front of me was another dead-end street. In the pitch blackness of night, enlightened only by street lamps, which were very dim, as I came into the dead-end street, I knew it was over. My bike howled — it too was a complete overrun . . . miscalculated . . . chaos.

I knew I did not have the energy to come out of the dead-end street and try to go on through a victory in motion.

I heard the bike cop behind me swearing loudly. At the same time a squad car burst up behind me as if he were trying to knock me down. To keep from getting hit I drove straight onto a lawn where the street lamp gave what little light there was. I could hear the cursing and swearing in a steady roar as I brought my iron to a halt.

I raised my right arm high into the air, trying to signal a surrender. I remember saying, "You win! You win . . ." trying to show what gallant feeling was left, for it's hard when you lose. But the words barely got out as I was jerked by several different hooklike hands that groped — the kind that fear the simplest of beings, but live and thrive to kill a cripple. I was grabbed by the neck, the throat, the hand, the arm, the foot, as a half dozen of those blue-bellied bastards pawed and cursed for what they were tryin to present as revenge on someone for offending or breaking the law. I don't think these punks ever were in a street fight when they were kids. They were probably too chickenshit to get away from thinking about someday being a cop. Anyway, there they were, at least a half dozen of them, slapping handcuffs, swinging their nightsticks, kicking with their boots of shiny leather, and howling as though they were in a real man-to-man battle. As I lay face down on the ground, one cop wrenched the handcuffs on with his foot in my back. My forehead caught a boot. I could hear snickers by now. These cats were probably the descendants of the ones who burned witches.

Several times I was picked up by the handcuffs and raised into the air and dropped face first onto the pavement. I could not protect my face because my hands were handcuffed behind me. I heard one cop say, "KILL THAT SON OF A BITCH!"

I kept wondering why I hadn't gone unconscious. It must have had to do with the acid, the LSD, because otherwise I should have gone unconscious when dropped onto the pavement face first. I remember taking all of the slams on the left side of my face. Each time I hit the pavement gushes of blood surged through my brain in a technicolor-like feeling. The pain was so intense and so great — it was pain I never had imagined before or ever heard described.

I was then lifted to my feet and shoved into the back seat of a squad car. As my head stopped swirling I saw people coming out of the houses. I saw a bike cop leaning over my bike as it lay on its side, where it had fallen when they jerked me from it before I could put the kickstand down. In the insanity of mind, I remember screaming when seeing my bike, "OHHHHHHHHHH, BIKE!" as if he too had been kicked and stomped as he lay on his side motionless.

People were standing around in a circle gawking at me and my bike as though we were animals in a zoo. My eyes were swelling shut. I could not see too clearly, everything was blurry. But my mind started burning with hate as I saw the cops! Everywhere there were cops! Motorcycle cops! Blue uniforms! I knew that I wanted to kill each and every one of them, and then stand up before the world and say: *I did it! Each and every one of them! I did it. I killed them. Wife or no wife, baby or no baby, I killed the cops who were trying to kill me and bike!* This flashed through my mind in the purest and deepest and richest most real of hatred.

One of the blue uniforms approached the door of the squad car I was encased in. I was screaming in the inside — I knew I could not be heard. As the door opened the sound rushed out like a crack of thunder as it met the voices screaming and mocking at me.

I yelled out as hard as I could, at the top of my lungs as the cop grabbed for me to take me to the paddy wagon, "YOU DIRTY ROTTEN COCKSUCKING, MOTHERFUCK-ING, ROTTEN MOTHERFUCKIN BASTARDS!!! YOU KICKED THE SHIT OUT OF ME AND BIKE!" I over-heard one telling a bystander, "He's bleeding pretty bad, he got off his bike as he come in this driveway."

Again I yelled, "YOU LYING MOTHERFUCKIN SONS OF BITCHES! I'LL KILL YOU HEARTLESS BAS-TARDS!!"

Two more cops jerked at my collar, twisting my wrists, shaking and trembling, all three of them tryin to make a front as they took me to the paddy wagon in the darkness, as dark as their black hearts. They modified their viciousness into a phony act of lead-the-prisoner-away-who-hates-everyone, who-wants-to-kill-all-the-good-people. God would have to rearrange the structure of each of their souls before He would ever consider forgiving them for what they did there and what they represent in this manner.

When they got me inside the paddy wagon the cursing started again and the slapping of leather as it kicked into my ribs and at the back of my head. One stomped at my groin over and over and over. Lucky that his connection was not good, or the Police Department of San Francisco today would all be freaks — I'd see to it. I hate them! Today I hate them. Today I curse them as I cursed them then, as they stomped and swore as I lay motionless, hoping they would stop kicking. And there was one bastard who kept jerking the handcuffs. My wrists felt as if they had swollen as big as my waist, my hands felt like acid was all over them, and they burned like fire. I'll never forget that one voice that said, *"The bastard is still breathin!"*

The paddy wagon rolled up to Alameda General Emergency Hospital where I was taken and had the cuts in my head stitched. The doctor and the nurse must have been leftovers of warmed-over death, of the German Nazi doctors who butchered humans! To find out whatever the hell it was like to be evil. They had no mercy. I asked them to have the cops release the handcuffs a little bit. My hands were numb, I told them. The nurse looked behind my back and said, "They are turning blue." The doctor must have been deaf, for his morguelike face never even flickered a reaction. I was then taken to the Ingleside precinct substation of this cesspool of cops.

During what must have been a change of shift, the cops mingled and milled around me. The whole room we were standing in was full of these men in blue suits with badges — all staring at me, acting as if I was another wounded dog that had been taken off the streets and brought into the dog pound. The pain was so intense inside my mind from the beating I'd just had that I felt like biting them, as they stared at me, for the handcuffs were still holding my hands behind my back.

As I was brought to the booking desk, I looked up at the sergeant. He was typing away on a typewriter and he turned around and his face looked just like a dog's — they all looked like dogs. He had a pair of glasses on that hung over a large nose, and his cheeks hung down like those of a boxer dog. It is hard to describe such an ugly face. All had scowls on their faces: they all looked hungry for human flesh.

I tried to bite one of them. I went right into his face tryin to bite him on the nose—he jumped back and got away as I growled. It was a roar like that of a mighty cat beast in a pit of hungry dogs. As the cop jumped back, I heard this other dog with sergeant's stripes on his arms say to another one off in the corner: "YOU'VE BEATEN THIS MAN INSANE—GET HIM OUT OF HERE!"

The man at the typewriter then turned away, there were no more questions asked. I then remember two Daly City police officers coming into the room and taking me away in their car.

They drove me to Daly City in the Daly City police car that had chased me originally. There was a cop there that run something down like: "This guy wouldn't even make a sad disciple." He too was trying to spit and mock at me. I, in turn, remember saying, "Yeah, you bet, we both didn't go to the same Sunday school, did we?" At that the cop looked baffled in his square face. As I stood in the Daly City police station, waiting to be booked for drunken driving, they finally took off the handcuffs and let me stand free to get my picture taken, and there, for the first time, one cop took a little mercy on me as he fingerprinted my hands that were so mangled and cut and swollen from the handcuffs. My shirt had spots of dried blood where it had streaked when it ran and splashed up and down my shirt. I remember looking at a mirror once and saw that I looked as though I had been used to mop up the pools of blood in a slaughterhouse after the day's chore of killing was over. Fingerprinting took a long time but finally it was finished.

I remember, as I stood before the booking desk in the San Francisco station, the song flashed through my mind, "It's Alright Ma (I'm Only Bleeding)." I was so wound up from acid I quoted the song out loud as I stood there for all the cops to hear.

"My eyes collide head-on with stuffed graveyards
False Gods, I scuff at pettiness which plays so rough
Walk upside down inside handcuffs
Kick my legs to crash it off
Say O.K., I've had enough."

I said this right in front of the face of the cop that was standing next to me trying to make me quote to a typewriter. I was so mad I defied the presence of these cops prying into my mind.

I remember the cell door clanging shut on me as I fell upon the cot. I asked the cop again when I could make a call to arrange bail. He said he'd call me in a few minutes. I let my head slam against the bed as I fell back. As the cop's footsteps echoed away I remember laughing savagely and madly into the night of quietness. I felt as though I had been locked away in an insane asylum for the night. I rose up off the bed and lit my last cigarette with my last match—*that* I remember. I stood up and paced the floor madly waiting for the chance to make the phone call. By this time my eyes were both swollen shut.

It still wasn't two o'clock, when the bars close, so I phoned back to Charley's Geneva Club. Frank, the bartender, answered the phone, and I asked for any of the Hell's Angels who might be there. I soon heard Lovely Larry's voice on the other end of the phone. He was still laughing in his wine. Then he picked up the vibrations of my voice and the condition I was in. He stopped abruptly on the phone, saying to the other Angels in the bar: "FRANK'S BEEN FUCKED OVER BY THE HEAT!" He then reassured me they'd make bail immediately, so I felt very good as I hung up the phone and was led back to the cell through a narrow hallway. It seemed like it was going down all the time. It was all twisted and angled due to the condition of my mind. I couldn't help but laugh from time to time hysterical-like because of the acid. The acid was still highly twisting my mind in a magnetic-like way. Everything becomes larger, mainly one's body, hands, anything that you think or feel with seems to swell. The cop looked up in the air as I was laughing madly and said, "WOWWWWW! LET'S GET THIS GUY BACK IN-SIDE!"

I was not releasd on bail because I entered a plea of guilty on going to court the next morning. I was supposed to have entered a plea of not guilty and have bail set. As I stood up before the judge in his blue cloak and heard the charge read off by some fucking clerk, I remember saying, "I'll plead guilty to the charge, your honor, but I'd like to know why I was brutally beaten by San Francisco police officers upon surrendering."

The judge, in turn, repeated, "That is beyond my jurisdiction. I will sentence you to *six months* under the care of a doctor. When I receive his report, I will then determine how much of the six months you will do. In the meantime his report will determine blah blah . . ."

He was kidding! I had six months to do! I didn't find out till later that I should have plead not guilty. Anyway it did not matter—I was fucked up. I kind of felt like I needed to punish myself for losing the battle and the chase. I wanted everybody to get off my fucking back and quit asking me questions. It didn't even occur to me at the time to wonder why I was in this San Mateo court and not in a San Francisco court where I'd been caught.

The earth is Hell and on it there are Hell's Angels.

JESSE P. RITTER, JR.

Nightmare in a California Jail

When I moved my family to San Francisco last year to teach in the English department at San Francisco State College, I did so with misgivings. I knew that the educational atmosphere in California was far from tranquil — Governor Reagan was waging virtual war against student protesters, and the political polarization between the left and the right could only be described in terms of paranoia. Through the year, my fears were confirmed as I witnessed student and faculty strikes, bombings, brawls, police assaults, mass arrests. But none of those events — brutal as they were — prepared me for the nightmare that followed my recent chance arrest this spring in Berkeley. Overnight that experience, which can be verified by many reliable witnesses, turned a father of five, veteran of the Korean war, and law-abiding citizen into a bitter man.

On Thursday morning, May 22, I left San Francisco State College with four other teachers to drive to Berkeley. We were beginning work on an environmental art project one of the teachers was directing. We planned to borrow a sailboat from a couple I knew in Berkeley and dump a small amount of nontoxic dye in the bay water at strategic points to observe the action of the currents.

We arrived in Berkeley about noon. After a pleasant lunch and a trip to buy supplies for the sail we walked toward Shattuck on Addison Street. There we were to meet my friend's wife, Nora.

The city of Berkeley was then in something like a state of siege because of the People's Park issue. On the streets, under the command of Alameda County Sheriff Frank Madigan, was a vast force of National Guard troops, county sheriffs, San Francisco Tactical Squad units. Madigan had authorized use of shotguns against demonstrators. One man had already been killed, and many others wounded. Demonstrators, workers, and onlookers trapped in a plaza on the University of California campus had been sprayed from a helicopter with a virulent form of tear gas currently being used in Vietnam. To protest, approximately 2,000 students had now begun a spontaneous march from the University campus through downtown Berkeley.

We could see a concentration of National Guard troops, policemen and citizens several blocks east of us. I described what Nora looked like to the others and we stopped at the southwest corner of Shattuck and Addison to scan the crowd for her. We decided not to go any farther because we saw soldiers, police, and people both to the east and south of us. The National Guard troops nearest us were climbing into trucks and moving out. Small groups of people on each corner of the intersection watched the troops; others walked casually on the sidewalks.

Berkeley policemen and Alameda County deputies began moving our way. An officer leading four or five others approached our group of 12 to 15 people and said, "Let's move out; clear the area!" Everyone on our corner obediently started walking away. Suddenly, a Berkeley policeman ran in front of us, spread his arms and shouted, "Stay where you are!" Behind us, two other policemen kept repeating, "Keep moving, clear out of here!" We said we were leaving, and at this point a Berkeley police sergeant approached and began pointing to various people in our group, saying, "Get that one, that one, that one."

An officer snapped handcuffs on me and joined me with the cuffs to a protesting youngster. I asked if we were under arrest and the officer said yes—we were charged with blocking traffic. We were not allowed to talk to the policemen after that. The sergeant who had us arrested taunted us, using obscenities and accusing us of being revolutionaries, rock-throwers, and hippies. Those not fingered by the sergeant continued down the street and were not apprehended. While we were being herded into the paddy wagon, however, officers continued to arrest people at random—mostly young people, and particularly those with long hair, mustaches, sideburns. Three of the teachers with me were arrested; our fifth companion was not, and he immediately began calling friends and relatives to arrange our release.

Nineteen of us—17 men and two women—were packed into a paddy wagon. I was never able to identify myself or state my business; indeed, the policemen threatened anyone who talked at all. We sat in the wagon for about 20 minutes, then it backed up the street a block, where we were transferred to a large bus. We were all being taken to "Santa Rita," a place I had never heard of.

During the 45-minute ride our feelings were reinforced that it had been an indiscriminate bust. Aboard were students with books and notepads who had been on their way to and from classes at the University. There was a U.S. mailman (with long hair), still carrying his bag of mail, and a resident psychiatrist who had stepped outside his hospital for a short walk during a 30-minute break. Others included several young divinity students and five medical observers—young men in white smocks with red crosses—who had accompanied the student march down Shattuck Avenue. The police blew it, I thought. They went too far this time. Most of us will be released when we get to wherever we're going.

The bus stopped inside the Santa Rita Rehabilitation Center and Prison Farm, an institution run by Alameda County. Prison guards who work under the jurisdiction of County Sheriff Madigan now took charge of us. We heard repeated orders through the frosted bus windows: "Unload single file and march. Anybody talks and he'll get a club up the butt!" As we filed off the bus the sight that greeted us was from a World War II movie — shabby wooden barracks, barbed-wire fences, rickety watch towers, and rows of men lying face down in an asphalt-paved compound. We were marched into the compound and ordered to lie prone in rows. Those who looked around or stumbled or didn't move fast enough were prodded and hit with clubs. Frequently, men were dragged out of the marching lines and forced to kneel while being struck. The guards shouted and screamed, often giving conflicting commands and clubbing those unable to obey them. Our chief source of terror was not so much the beatings as the wild hysteria that had seized many of the guards. They walked up and down our rows of flattened men, striking upraised hands with clubs, striking us on the soles of our feet with clubs to make us lie in even rows. We were told we would be shot if we tried to escape. We were cursed continuously; we were called dope users, revolutionaries, filthy long-hairs. We would, they shouted, be taught such a lesson that we would never again cause trouble. All of us were identified as political troublemakers. No attempt was made to distinguish us by age, nature of charges, or physical condition. Periodically we were ordered to turn our heads to the left or right. I experienced severe leg cramps and sharp twinges of pain from an arthritic elbow. From time to time we were forced to close up ranks by crawling across the asphalt, which was covered with sharp gravel. Those accused of speaking or looking around or moving slightly were dragged out and forced to kneel with their hands behind them in a separate group. Some remained kneeling for hours. There were some 300 men on the ground.

After a few of us asked to use the rest rooms (and were abused for it), guards began allowing small groups to go. At times, the guards said, "You'll have to wait another half hour." One kid near me identified himself as a diabetic in the rest room and was cruelly beaten.

This savage parody of prison discipline had an obvious psychology behind it. Humiliate the prisoners totally from the beginning so they will obey orders and accept punishment without resistance. Of course, we weren't prisoners — *we were simply being held for booking*!

During the time I was lying in the compound, from approximately 4 until 8:30 p.m., new arrestees were brought in and forced to lie in rows. It was cold when the sun went down, and men around me were shivering. At 8 we were allowed to stand and exercise in place for a few minutes. We then lay back down on our faces. They had taken our names when we were first arrested, and about every 20 minutes a guard would call out some names in alphabetical order. At 8:30 my name was called along with seven others, and we were taken into an adjoining barracks for booking.

Here we experienced new refinements. We were forced to sit in single file on the floor, knees together, while a squat, dark-haired guard waving a blackjack shouted that if we didn't do exactly as he said he would beat us until we couldn't walk. He had us face the wall, spread our legs, and place our hands high on the wall. We then turned and threw our jackets, belts and the contents of our pockets into a pile. During this procedure, the squat guard struck prisoners in the back, stomach, face, and legs with his fist or the blackjack. He struck me four times with the blackjack during the booking process—either for not having my heels tightly together or for not clasping my hands in front of me. He assaulted one of us—a very young boy with long hair—by slugging him with his fist and then grabbing the boy's hair and slamming his face into the wall. Later, in the barracks, we saw that the boy's left eye had swollen badly and he could barely open his jaw.

After the booking and fingerprinting, we again had to sit on the floor with legs drawn up, heels together. We were then lined up and marched to Barracks B across the street. The guard in charge treated us firmly but decently, telling us that while we were in the barracks we could get together and talk, plan our bail procedures and wait our turn to use the telephone. He repeated what other guards had told us in the compound—that the regular prisoners were outraged at us because we were trouble-makers, because we were responsible for the regular inmates' missing movies and other privileges. The inmates would beat us terribly, and the guards couldn't prevent it. We would be turned over to "hardened criminals and sex perverts."

At about 11:30, four lawyers from the People's Park Defense Committee appeared in the barracks. They told us they were trying to arrange bail procedures for as many people as possible, but they lacked funds and organizations for rapid release. We filled out forms giving information about our families and personal legal arrangements. We later were told that many of these forms were destroyed by prison guards who claimed they were "messages." At no time during our detention did anyone in my barracks have an opportunity to make a telephone call to relatives or lawyers.

During the night we were taunted and threatened by different prison guards. We left in small groups all through the night to have photos taken—I went in a group at 2:45 a.m. Few of us slept.

At 4:30 a.m., the door crashed open and three guards moved among the bunks rousting out people with curses, threats, and blows. We were going to eat, they said, and we would eat what we took or it would be "shoved in your faces." Under continual threats, we were marched to the mess hall. Breakfast was Corn Chex and milk (no sugar), half-cooked prunes, white bread, and artificial marmalade. We sat packed at the tables, ordered not to move or talk. Five men were dragged from their seats and forced to kneel before an empty table for such things as "looking around," "talking" or "moving." They were not allowed to eat. One boy was forced to lean his head on a post while the guards beat on the post. His nose began bleeding. Guards would prod him, pull him off the post and strike him, or kick his feet back farther until he was leaning at a severe angle to the post, his head and neck bearing the full weight of his body. After about 15 minutes of quivering spasmodically, the boy collapsed to the floor. Two guards dragged him over to the empty table and made him kneel, still twitching, with the others. After we finished eating, we were forced to kneel on the floor in columns of two and wait for about 15 minutes before being marched back to the barracks.

At 6 a.m. a new guard, a small man with reddish-blond hair on his neck, came into the barracks, yelling, "I had a good night's sleep and I feel like KILLING!" He announced that he was now in total control of us and said he needed a "boss" in the barracks. He grabbed my bunkmate, Professor Gary Oberbillig, by the shirt and dragged him out to the center of the floor. "Get out here," he said. "You're big; you want to take me? Come on, let's go outside. Want to go outside?" He then instructed Oberbillig that he, Oberbillig, was the "barracks boss" and was to "beat the——! out of anybody who don't do right!"

At 7:30 a guard came in and read off a list of names. We lined up and marched outside into the street, where several other guards spent approximately 30 minutes giving us military marching commands, making those who did not execute the commands smartly do calisthenics. (Ironically, not one of them was able to give an accurate "about-face" command, and our ragged "about-face" maneuvers enraged them.) We marched at double-time, forced to yell "WE LOVE THE BLUE MEANIES!"

The guards were proud of this idea: I overheard one tell another, "Say, we've gotta do that Blue Meanies bit some more." We marched to what appeared to be the receiving center of the prison, where we were put in open-screen cells already occupied by new arrestees. It was here that we learned we would be released soon. While we waited in the cells, several men were dragged out and beaten in our presence and told that they were on the way to further beatings and a stay in the "quiet room."

My three companions and I were finally processed for release on bail by 8:30 a.m., Friday, May 23, nearly 18 hours after our arrest. All released prisoners had to catch rides out of the main gate, a distance of a half mile, with outgoing bail bondsmen.

The first thing I learned facedown on the Santa Rita asphalt was that I could make it without begging or breaking. This felt good; it was enough strength to counter the fears engendered by the heavy blue-black guards' shoes slowly crunching by my eyes six inches away. *But to be put to these tests in America!*

At a press conference, Alameda County Sheriff Frank Madigan admitted there had been "irregularities" at Santa Rita on that Thursday. He put the responsibility on his guards. Many of the deputies assigned there, he said, are young Vietnam war veterans and "they have a feeling that these people should be treated like Vietcong."

On July 2 Madigan suspended 10 of his officers at Santa Rita for "violating civil service and/or departmental rules" in handling the mass arrests. The officers, all of whom were told they had the right to appeal (only four chose to do so), included the commander, his two immediate assistants and a sergeant. By July 9, charges against all the people who had been arrested—a total of 480—had been dropped by the court.

Still, several hundred young men and women came out of Santa Rita believing there is no middle ground anymore—nowhere to stand to reconcile the growing polarities of our political lives. I am haunted by the bitterness brought forth by such assaults on our humaneness and human rights. When in the history of man have prisons and guards ever rooted out the ideas in which men really believe?

ELDRIDGE CLEAVER

Affidavit # 2:
Shoot-Out In Oakland

While dictating his "Requiem for Nonviolence" in the Ramparts *office in San Francisco, Cleaver got a telephone call and drove over to Oakland, leaving the essay in the middle of a sentence. A few hours later he was arrested in the aftermath of the shoot-out with the Oakland police and sent to Vacaville Prison. He wrote Affidavit # 2 there as his account of the Oakland incident.*

I think that the so-called shoot-out on 28th Street was the direct result of frantic attempts by the Oakland Police Department to sabotage the Black Community Barbecue Picnic, which the Black Panther Party had set up for April 7th in DeFremery Park. The shoot-out occurred the night before the scheduled picnic. We had been advertising the barbecue picnic over the radio (KDIA & KSOL) and we had leafleted the community very heavily and put up many posters, inviting the community to come out and share in the picnic. Also, members of the Black Panther Party had been driving all over East and West Oakland in a sound truck, for a week, telling the people about the picnic and inviting them to come out.

The barbecue picnic was a fund raiser for the Black Panther Party Campaign Fund and for the Huey P. Newton Defense Fund. We were uptight for funds for both of these operations. We were running three candidates for public office: Huey P. Newton for Congress in the 7th Congressional District of Alameda County; Bobby Seale for the 17th Assembly District seat in Alameda County; and Kathleen Cleaver for the 18th Assembly District seat in San Francisco. These campaigns were being run on less than a shoestring, and we came up with the idea of the barbecue picnic hoping to raise a little money. And, of course, there was a constant need of funds for Huey's defense.

We knew that the Oakland Police Department was against the picnic because at first they tried to block clearance when we sought it from the park authorities to hold the picnic at De-Fremery Park. They failed in that, but they did succeed in getting the park authorities to impose a lot of ridiculous and crippling rules upon us, such as no speeches at the park, no sound equipment, no passing out of campaign literature, etc. Also, there was constant harassment of the brothers and sisters who were operating the sound truck, and members of the Oakland Police Department had been very active in tearing down the posters we put up to advertise the picnic, just as they had been tearing down the posters we put up to advertise Huey and Bobby's political campaigns. Oakland police were also stopping and harassing party members whom they observed putting up these posters or passing out leaflets. We had invested about $300 in the picnic, so we were anxious for it to come off successfully and without incident.

We had noticed that whenever we staged a large fund-raising event, the Oakland police would move, first, to try to prevent it from happening; then, failing that, they would arrest a lot of party members and drain off whatever money was raised because we would then have to bail these party members out of jail and there were legal fees. We became very aware of this. This became very clear to us when we staged the Huey P. Newton Birthday Benefit Rally at the Oakland Auditorium on February 17. At first the Oakland police tried to refuse us the use of the auditorium on the grounds that such a rally would be a public nuisance and create a dangerous situation. We had to get Attorney John George to go down with us and threaten Mr. Luddekke, who operates the auditorium for the City of Oakland, with a civil suit, before they backed up and agreed to allow us the use of the facility. Even so, within a week after the rally, the Oakland Police Department and the Berkeley Police Department arrested a total of sixteen members of our party, including the notorious incident in which our Chairman, Bobby Seale, and his wife Artie were dragged from their bed in the wee hours of the morning and charged with conspiracy to commit murder. There was a lot of public outcry against the police for this blatant harassment and frameup and that charge was quickly dropped. But what a lot of people don't understand is that it was also very expensive to us. Even though the ridiculous charge was dropped, the real purpose of the cops was achieved successfully: to drain away our funds through exorbitant bails and legal fees.

So, in staging the barbecue picnic, we had this experience in mind, and we had cautioned all party members to be on their best behavior in order to avoid any incidents with the police that would provide a pretext for arrest.

Here I have to bring up the name of Captain McCarthy of the Oakland Police Department, because he is one of the chief instigators within the OPD against the Black Panther Party and he has a special grudge against me. When we were making the preliminary arrangements for the rally at the Oakland Auditorium,

Mr. Luddekke kept urging us to get in touch with a Sergeant White of the OPD to discuss matters of security with him. Such a discussion seemed disgusting to us at first so we avoided it, but as the date of the rally drew nearer it was clear that it would be best if the matter were dealt with, so on either February 16th, or 17th, I can't remember which, I called the number given me by Mr. Luddekke, talked to Sergeant White, and made an appointment to meet with him to discuss the subject of security at the auditorium during the rally.

Another member of the Black Panther Party, Mr. Emory Douglass, who is our Revolutionary Artist, accompanied me to this meeting, which was held at the headquarters of the Oakland Police Department. When we arrived there, we were met in the lobby by Sergeant White, who took us in to talk to a Captain McCarthy. Entering the room where Captain McCarthy was waiting, Sergeant White introduced us. Captain McCarthy stuck out his big ham of a hand to shake mine. I declined, to which the captain responded: "What's the matter, you too good to shake my hand or something?"

I replied: "In view of the present relationship between your organization and mine, I think that our shaking hands would be out of order."

The captain stared into my eyes. His were cold and murder blue, and his fat neck, stuffed inside his shirt and choked with his tie, turned red, the color creeping all the way up from his adam's apple to his face and I could see that it took an effort, or a sense of a more urgent interest, to keep him from throwing us out of his office. I made a mental note then to stay out of this pig's way because he was not likely either to forgive or forget me.

Two months later, this captain, backed up by a phalanx of Oakland cops with shotguns levelled at the ready, tried to kick down the door to St. Augustine's Church on 27th and West Street in Oakland and terrorized one of our meetings. On this raid, the captain brought with him and his pigs a white priest and a black preacher, and he used them to try to cool down Reverend Neil, whose church it was and who would not be cooled down by the pious entreaties of the captain's anointed accomplices. This occurred on April 3, three days before this same captain, this time with an army of pigs, directed the murderous attack upon members of the Black Panther Party in which one party member, Bobby Hutton, was viciously and wantonly shot to death by racist pigs who had long lain in wait for a chance to shed the blood of the Black Panthers.

On the night the pigs murdered Little Bobby, we had all been very busy making last minute arrangements for the barbecue picnic scheduled for the next day. The Brother who owns the Soul Food restaurant next to our office at 41st and Grove Street in Oakland was cooking the meat for us and we were running sisters back and forth between the restaurant, the stores, and David Hilliard's house at 34th and Magnolia Street where we were assembling the supplies for the next day.

The cops had been following our cars around all day long. During the day, several different cop cars, at different times, had parked directly across the street from our office and made no secret of the fact that they were watching us, with ugly pig scowls on their faces, that look that says to a black man, "I don't like you, nigger, and I'm watching you, just waiting for one false move." Increasingly, the cops had been following me around so much that I had learned to ignore them and to go on about my business as though they did not even exist.

A white man in Berkeley, who sympathized with the work that our party was doing and who wanted to help us out, called us up one day and said that he had read in our paper that we needed transportation badly and offered to give us two cars. I know that we got one of the promised cars, a white Ford several years old but in good shape, but I do not know if we ever got the other. This was a big help to us but also a headache, because the car had a Florida license plate and none of the brothers liked to drive it because you would invariably be stopped by the cops, particularly when driving through Oakland, and they would use the Florida license plate as a pretext for stopping the car. It took only a few days for the word to get around amongst the Oakland cops that the Panthers had a white Ford with a Florida license plate, and from then on the car was marked. For this reason, I took the responsibility of using the car most of the time because I had what is considered good I.D.—driver's license, draft card, Social Security card, and a variety of press cards from my job at *Ramparts* magazine. I even had one press card issued to me by the United Nations, guaranteed to slow down the already sluggish mental processes of a pig cop, especially a dumb Oakland pig. Several brothers had been stopped driving this car and the cops put them through all kinds of changes: "Are you from Florida? How long have you been in California?" Once an Oakland cop stopped me in this car, and when he asked me whose car it was I told him that a white man from Florida had given it to the Black Panther Party. This seemed to make him very mad, and he said: "You expect me to believe that story? No white man in his right mind would give the Black Panthers a car."

"Maybe this white man is crazy," I said to him.

Anyway, that's why I started using this car more frequently than any of the others we had available to the party.

It is a rule of our party that no well known member of the party is to be out on the Oakland streets at night unless accompanied by two or more other people, because we felt that if the Oakland cops ever caught one of us alone like that there was a chance that such a one might be killed and there would be only racist pig cops for witnesses: Verdict of the Coroner's Inquest, "Justifiable Homicide." Period. After the way they tried to murder our leader, Minister of Defense Huey P. Newton, we were not taking any chances. So on the night of April 6, the car I was driving was being followed by two carloads of Panthers and I was on my way to David Hilliard's house at 34th and Magnolia. In the car with me were David Hilliard, Wendell Wade, and John Scott, all members of the Black Panther Party.

We were only a few blocks away from David's house when, all of a sudden, I was overcome by an irresistible urge, a necessity, to urinate, and so I turned off the brightly lighted street we were on (I think it was 30th Street, but I'm not sure, not being overly familiar with the area), pulled to the curb, stopped the car, got out and started relieving myself. The two Panther cars following us pulled up behind to wait. While I was in the middle of this call of nature, a car came around the corner from the direction that we ourselves had come, and I found myself in danger of being embarrassed, I thought, by a passing car. So I cut off the flow, then, and awkwardly hurried around to the other side of the car, to the sidewalk, to finish what had already been started and what was most difficult to stop—I recall that I did soil my trousers somewhat. But this car, instead of passing, stopped, and a spotlight from it was turned on and beamed my way. I could see it was the cops, two of them. They got out of the car and stood there, not leaving the car, each standing just outside. One of them shouted, "Hey, you, walk out into the middle of the street with your hands up, quick!"

For the second time, I had to deal with a ticklish situation and I was so close to the end that I could not resist finishing. I shouted back to the cops, "O.K., O.K.!" I turned, trying to zip up my fly and get out into the middle of the street. Common sense told me that I'd best have my hands up by the time I cleared the front of my car. But before I cleared, the cop on the passenger side of his car started shouting and firing his gun, and then the other cop started shooting. I am not sure they were shooting at me because the lights from their car were shining brightly at me, blocking my vision. But the explosions from their guns sounded right in my face and so, startled, I dove for cover in front of my car. The Panthers in the other two cars started yelling at the cops and honking their horns and getting out of their cars, and the brothers who were in my car scrambled out of the passenger side.

Above my head, the windshield of my car shattered and I

looked behind me. There was another cop car at the other end of the street, from which shots were also being fired at us. In fact, shots seemed to be coming from everywhere; it sounded like the entire block had erupted with gunfire. It took only a split second to see that they had us in a cross fire, so I shouted to the brothers, "Scatter! Let's get out of here!" Our best bet, it was clear, was to make it across the street and that's where we headed. As we started across, one of the Panthers, Warren Wells, got hit and let out an agonized yelp of pain as he fell to the ground. I dove for the pavement, in about the middle of the street, with bullets ricocheting off the pavement all around me and whizzing past my head. I was being fired at from several different directions and for the second time within the space of a few minutes I could taste death on my tongue. But I kept crawling across the street as fast as I could and I truthfully didn't know whether I had been hit or not, whether I was dead or dying. I was hurting all over from scraping against the pavement and I was still being shot at. I saw a couple of Panthers run between two houses and got to my feet and followed them. A cop with a shotgun was running after me, shooting. I didn't have a gun but I wished that I had! (O, how I wish that I had!!!)

As I ran between those two houses, I saw a Panther climbing over what looked like a fence. I hit it just as soon as he was over, only to find out, as I climbed up, that it was some sort of a shed and I was on top of it and the cop behind me was still shooting at me with the shotgun. I dove off and onto the ground on the other side, landing on top of Bobby Hutton. Before I had recovered from the jolt of my leap, I was wishing that I had never come over the top of that shed, that I had stayed there to face that cop with that blazing shotgun, because little Bobby and I were boxed in. The shed at our backs spanned the space between the houses on either side of us, and although the area in front of us was clear all the way out to the street, we could not budge from that little nook because the street was filled with cops and they were pumping shots at us as though shooting was about to go out of style. In the dark, I could not see that Little Bobby had a rifle, until it started to bark, producing a miraculous effect: the cops, cowardly pigs from their flat feet to their thick heads, all ran for cover. The few seconds that this gave us allowed us to find a door into the basement of the house to our right, and we dove inside. We were just in time to escape a murderous fusillade of shots that scoured the tiny area we had just abandoned.

But if jumping over the shed had been like going from the frying pan into the fire, entering that house defies description. The walls were like tissue paper and the pigs were shooting through them from all four sides at once. It was like being the Indians in all the cowboy movies I had ever seen. What saved us for the moment was an eighteen-inch-high cement foundation running around the cellar at the base of the wall. We lay down flat against the floor while the bullets ripped through the walls. This unrelenting fire went on for about half an hour, and then it stopped and the pigs started lobbing in tear gas. While the gas was being pumped in through the windows, Little Bobby and I took the opportunity to fortify the walls with whatever we could lay our hands on: furniture, tin cans, cardboard boxes — it was hopeless but we tried it anyway. While I was standing up trying to move a thick board over against the wall, I was struck in the chest by a tear gas cannister fired through a window. It knocked me down and almost out. Little Bobby, weak from the gas, was coughing and choking, but he took all my clothes off in an effort to locate a wound in the dark, patting me down for the moist feel of blood.

The pigs started shooting again and we had to hit the deck. The material we had stacked along the wall was blown away by what sounded like machine gun fire. We decided to stay in there and choke to death if necessary rather than walk out into a hail of bullets. Above the din of gunfire, we could hear the voices of people yelling at the cops to stop shooting, calling them murderers and all kinds of names, and this gave us the strength and the hope to hang on. The tear gas was not as hard to endure as I had imagined it to be. My lungs were on fire, nose and eyes burning, but after a while I couldn't feel anything. Once Little Bobby told me he was about to pass out. He did, but he came to before long, and the two of us lay there counting the minutes and ducking the bullets that were too numerous to count. One of the shots found my leg and my foot with an impact so painful and heavy that I was sure I no longer had two legs. But it didn't seem to matter because I was also sure that it was only a matter of seconds before one of the bullets found a more vital spot. In my mind, I was actually saying goodbye to the world and I was sure that Little Bobby was doing the same thing. Lying there pinned down like that, there was nothing else to do. If there was I couldn't think of it. I said goodbye to my wife, and an image of her dancing for me, as I had watched her do so many times before, floated past my mind's eye, and I reached out to touch her, to kiss her goodbye with my fingers. Then my mind seemed to dwell on crowds of people, masses of people, millions of people, as though the whole human race, all the men and women who had ever lived, seemed to present themselves to my view. I saw images of parades, crowd scenes in auditoriums. I remembered the people at the rally in the Oakland Auditorium, the surging, twisting sea of people at the Peace and Freedom Party Convention at the Richmond Auditorium; these two events somehow coupled in my mind. I saw throngs of students at Merritt College, at San Francisco State College, and at UC Berkeley, and then I heard Little Bobby ask me, "What are we going to do?"

I felt an impotent rage at myself because all I could tell him was to keep his head down, that head with its beautiful black face which I would watch a little later, again powerless, as the mad dogs outside blasted him into eternity. Was it in cold blood? It was in the coldest of blood. It was murder. MURDER! And that must never be forgotten: the Oakland Police Department MURDERED Little Bobby, and they cannot have that as a victory. Every pig on that murderous police force is guilty of murdering Little Bobby; and lying, hypocritical Chief Gains is Murderer No. 1. And we must all swear by Little Bobby's blood that we will not rest until Chief Gains is brought to justice, either in the courts or in the streets; and until the bloodthirsty troops of the Oakland Police Department no longer exist in the role of an occupying army with its boots on the neck of the black community, with its guns aimed at the black community's head, an evil force with its sword of terror thrust into the heart of the black community. That's what Little Bobby would ask you to do, Brothers and Sisters, put an end to the terror—by any means necessary. All he asks, all Huey asks, all I ask, is what Che Guevara asked:

> *Wherever Death may surprise us*
> *It will be welcome, provided that*
> *This, our battle cry, reach some*
> *Receptive ear; that another hand*
> *Reach out to pick up the gun, that*
> *Other fighting men come forward*
> *To intone our funeral dirge*
> *To the staccato of machine gun fire*
> *And new cries of battle and victory.*

The rest of the story is madness, pain, and humiliation at the hands of the Pigs. They shot firebombs into the cellar, turning it into a raging inferno, and we could not stand the heat, could not breathe the hot air with lungs already raw from the tear gas. We had to get out of there, to flee from certain death to face whatever awaited us outside. I called out to the Pigs and told them that we were coming out. They said to throw out the guns. I was lying beneath a window, so Little Bobby passed me the rifle and I threw it outside, still lying on my back. Then Little Bobby helped me to my feet and we tumbled through the door. There were pigs in the windows above us in the house next door, with guns pointed at us. They told us not to move, to raise our hands. This we did, and an army of pigs ran up from the street. They started kicking and cursing us, but we were already beyond any pain, beyond feeling. The pigs told us to stand up. Little Bobby helped me to my feet. The pigs pointed to a squad car parked in the middle of the street and told us to run to it. I told them that I couldn't run. Then they snatched Little Bobby away from me and shoved him forward, telling him to run to the car. It was a sickening sight. Little Bobby, coughing and choking on the night air that was burning his lungs as my own were burning from the tear gas, stumbled forward as best he could, and after he had traveled about ten yards the pigs cut loose on him with their guns, and then they turned to me. But before they could get into anything, the black people in the neighborhood who had been drawn to the site by the gunfire and commotion began yelling at them, calling the pigs murderers, telling them to leave me alone. And a face I will never forget, the face of the captain with the murder blue eyes, loomed up.

"Where are you wounded?" he asked me.

I pointed out my wound to him. The Pig of Pigs looked down at my wound, raised his foot and stomped on the wound.

"Get him out of here," he told the other pigs, and they took me away.

Why am I alive? While at Highland Hospital, a pig said to me: "You ain't going to be at no barbecue picnic tomorrow. You the barbecue now!" Why did Little Bobby die? It was not a miracle, it just happened that way. I know my duty. Having been spared my life, I don't want it. I give it back to our struggle. Eldridge Cleaver died in that house on 28th Street, with Little Bobby, and what's left is force: fuel for the fire that will rage across the face of this racist country and either purge it of its evil or turn it into ashes. I say this for Little Bobby, for Eldridge Cleaver who died that night, for every black man, woman, and child who ever died here in Babylon, and I say it to racist America, that if every voice of dissent is silenced by your guns, by your courts, by your gas chambers, by your money, you will know, that as long as the ghost of Eldridge Cleaver is afoot, you have an ENEMY in your midst.

EPILOGUE
DOC STANLEY

Policemanship:
A Guide for the Arrested

Your life and future depend on how you handle yourself in your contacts with the police. If you handle yourself poorly, you will go to jail, be subjected to police harassment, get beaten up or perhaps even killed. If you handle yourself well, you will be permitted to continue your life as a free citizen. Policemanship is perhaps the most important art one can learn in contemporary America.

The first, prime, ultimate thing to remember in dealing with police officers is RESPECT. RESPECT is the key. If you treat police officers with respect, you will have less trouble in your relations with the police than if you do not. If you cause or permit a police officer to feel that you do not respect him or his department, you may be beaten up, arrested roughly, or shot.

It should be borne in mind that respect is often confused with fear in the minds of some policemen. Thus a citizen who does not present a conservative middle class fear-respect attitude when being engaged in conversation by police is apt to be bullied and tested in order to determine his level of hostility to authority. If an individual protests his treatment, police officers have been known to bait him into a violent outburst which justifies the use of force and restraint in investigations. Provocative testing of individuals from minority groups has been held to be a major cause of the violent demonstrations among such groups.

Police officers are also touchy about being called by diminutive, pejorative, or slang names. Address all policemen as "officer," "Sergeant," "sir," or by their title if they are higher ranking officers. Do not under any circumstances use terms like "copper," "fuzz," "nabs" or any other appellation which could be interpreted to indicate disrespect.

In talking with police in the street or in public places, look them in the eye and smile. Keep your hands in sight and make no rapid or fast moves. If you have occasion to reach into one of your pockets or into your purse, inform the officer that you wish to do so and ask his permission before you begin to move. "May I get my wallet out of my back pocket, please. Sir?" is a good form to use when asked for identification by a policeman. Stand at attention with your hands in the air when talking with a policeman after he has accepted your identification.

In all conversations with police officers it is safe to assume that at the time of the conversation you are in fact under arrest. The officer believes this and in case he feels it necessary to shoot you, he will testify that you resisted arrest and thus justify his action. Therefore, keep your hands up, speak in polite tones, and don't make any sudden moves, unless you want to get beaten up or die on the spot.

Keep conversation with police officers to a minimum. Anything you may say will be used against you. There is no such thing as friendly conversation with a policeman. Any question he may ask or any information you may volunteer is part of his investigation.

Establish the fact that you are under arrest as quickly as possible in any encounter with policemen. Ask "Am I under arrest?" The officer must answer this question. If he answers "Yes," then ask him to transport you to the police station at once. Ask him to open the door of the police car and get in. Never, under any circumstances, offer the slightest resistance to arrest.

Welcome arrest, be happy about it, get to jail as fast as you can. The faster you get to jail, the faster you will get out and the less chance you give a police officer to beat or shoot you the better off you are. In this day and age it is rare for prisoners and arrestees to be beaten once they arrive at the station house or police headquarters. If any beating or shooting is to occur, it will be in the street or in the police car on the way to the lockup. If you are in the hands of the police, get this part of the process over with as fast as you can in order to minimize the danger to your person.

You are entitled to the advice of a lawyer at ALL times in your dealings with the police. Under NO circumstances should you attempt to explain to police ANYTHING without the aid of your lawyer. Refuse to talk to police interrogators when your lawyer is not present. You are entitled to three phone calls at PUBLIC EXPENSE. Demand your calls and refuse to talk to police until you have contacted your lawyer. Do what he tells you—no more, no less.

Tell the policemen you expect to be called Mr., Mrs. or Miss, but don't argue about it. Tell them you would like the name and badge numbers of the officers, and write them down. Tell them your lawyer said to do so, and always carry an attorney's card to show to the police.

If the police want to search, ask for their search warrant. Tell them, "You don't have my permission but I won't stop you." Say this whether you have anything to hide or not. While the search is on, say nothing except, "I'm innocent and I can't say anything until my lawyer gets here."

If you are arrested say you want to know the charge. They have 24 hours to book you.

If, on the other hand, when you ask "Am I under arrest?", the officer answers "No," then thank him for his time and tell him, "I decline to discuss my private lawful business with police officers. Excuse me, sir," and wait until he drives away. Do not walk away from the police car—LET THE CAR PULL AWAY FIRST.

If the officer attempts to question you as to why you are continuing to stand by the police car after you have declined to discuss your private lawful business with the police, tell him that you are waiting for him to leave first. If you begin to walk away before the officer leaves the scene of the contact, he may shoot you and later claim that you were resisting arrest. You won't be there to contradict him, as you will probably be dead. LET THE OFFICER LEAVE FIRST! This is very important.

A particular problem with the police is often experienced by persons who suffer chronic physical disabilities. Persons requiring medication should carry printed cards signed by a physician testifying to their condition.

Don't take "friendly" advice from officers, or discuss your case with other prisoners. Only your own lawyer is looking out for you. Ask for a chemical drunk test, if it's a drunk charge arrest.

It's all right to sign a traffic ticket. You don't admit anything by signing. But once you sign, appear in court or pay the bail to prevent a warrant from being issued.

Juveniles are entitled to a lawyer from the very beginning.

In short, remember to stay calm, don't resist physically, don't talk, and know how you can reach a lawyer in a hurry.

PROLOGUE
EPILOGUE
TRIAL

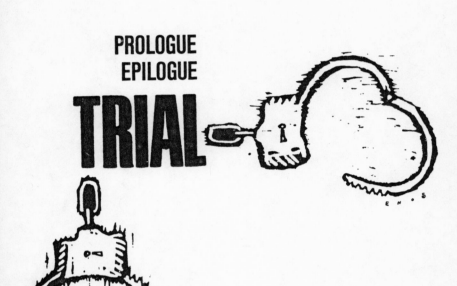

PROLOGUE
BERTOLT BRECHT

Testimony:
The House Committee on Un-American Activities

Presented by ERIC BENTLEY

The House Committee on Un-American Activities takes down all that is said in its public hearings, and the Government Printing Office in Washington reprints the transcript. What follows comes from a section of the Committee's records, 549 pages long, entitled: Hearings Regarding The Communist Infiltration Of The Motion Picture Industry. *Although these hearings were not tape-recorded on the spot, they were broadcast, and the broadcasts were subject to reproduction by, shall we say?, private entrepreneurs. I came upon such a privately-made sound recording and brought it out as an album on the Folkways label in 1963 with my own spoken comments. These comments are reproduced here with a few corrections and additions. Anyone who wishes to explore the topic further will want to consult both the record album and the book* Thirty Years of Treason *as edited by me, Viking Press, 1970.*

Eric Bentley, 1970.

Between the 20th and the 30th of October, 1947, the Committee on Un-American Activities of the House of Representatives held some "hearings regarding the Communist infiltration of the motion picture industry."

The Chairman of the Committee was J. Parnell Thomas of New Jersey, and among its members were several men who either were or would later be famous, such as Richard M. Nixon of California, Karl E. Mundt of South Dakota, and John Rankin of Mississippi.

Among the witnesses called during that ten-day period were: Jack L. Warner, Louis B. Mayer, Ayn Rand, Adolph Menjou, Robert Taylor, Robert Montgomery, Ronald Reagan, Gary Cooper, Walt Disney, John Howard Lawson, Dalton Trumbo, Albert Maltz, Alvah Bessie, Samuel Ornitz, Herbert Biberman, Emmet Lavery, Edward Dmytryk, Adrian Scott, Dore Schary, Ring Lardner Jr., and Lester Cole.

101

*"We have subpenaed witnesses," Mr. Thomas said, "repre-
senting both sides of the question," and the testimony turned
out to be chiefly of two kinds. One group of witnesses spoke
against Communism and named persons in Hollywood whom
they regarded as Communists. The other group invoked the
First Amendment, and maintained that the investigation was
improper. The second group—the "Hollywood Ten"—would
later get jail sentences for contempt of Congress. But one or
two witnesses stood outside both the groups. Dore Schary is an
example. Another is Emmet Lavery, who stated a social philosophy close to that of Pope John XXIII's encyclicals of the nineteen sixties.*

*The witness who stood furthest apart from the others was
Bertolt Brecht, whose testimony follows.*

*The scene of this Brechtian tragi-comedy is the crowded
Caucus Room of the old House Office Building, Washington,
D.C. The date is October 30th, 1947.*

*Present are only three members of the Committee: Parnell
Thomas, John McDowell of Pennsylvania, and Richard B. Vail
of Illinois. With them is Robert E. Stripling, chief investigator.
Bertolt Brecht is accompanied by two attorneys (Bartley Crum
and Robert W. Kenny) who were helping all the "unfriendly"
witnesses.*

MR. STRIPLING: Mr. Berthold* Brecht.

THE CHAIRMAN: Mr. Brecht, will you stand, please, and raise
your right hand?

Do you solemnly swear the testimony you are about to give is
the truth, the whole truth, and nothing but the truth, so help you
God?

MR. BRECHT: I do.

THE CHAIRMAN: Sit down, please.

**TESTIMONY OF BERTHOLD BRECHT (ACCOMPANIED BY COUNSEL, MR.
KENNY AND MR. CRUM)**

MR. STRIPLING: Mr. Brecht, will you please state your full
name and present address for the record, please? Speak into
the microphone.

MR. BRECHT: My name is Berthold Brecht. I am living at 34
West Seventy-third Street, New York. I was born in Augsburg,
Germany, February 10, 1898.

MR. STRIPLING: Mr. Brecht, the committee has a—

THE CHAIRMAN: What was that date again?

MR. STRIPLING: Would you give the date again?

*Sic! The correct spelling is "Bertolt."

THE CHAIRMAN: Tenth of February 1898.

MR. MCDOWELL: 1898?

MR. BRECHT: 1898.

MR. STRIPLING: Mr. Chairman, the committee has here an interpreter, if you desire the use of an interpreter.

MR. CRUM: Would you like an interpreter?

THE CHAIRMAN: Do you desire an interpreter?

MR. BRECHT: Yes.

THE CHAIRMAN: Mr. Interpreter, will you stand and raise your right hand, please?

Mr. Interpreter, do you solemnly swear you will diligently and correctly translate from English into German all questions which may be propounded to this witness and as diligently and correctly translate from German into English all answers made by him, so help you God?

MR. BAUMGARDT: I do.

THE CHAIRMAN: Sit down.

(Mr. David Baumgardt was seated beside the witness as interpreter.)

MR. STRIPLING: Would you identify yourself for the record, please, sir?

MR. BAUMGARDT: David Baumgardt.

MR. STRIPLING: Where are you employed, Mr. Baumgardt?

MR. BAUMGARDT: In the Library of Congress.

MR. BRECHT: Mr. Chairman, may I read a statement in English?

THE CHAIRMAN: Yes; but has the chief investigator completed his investigation of both the interpreter and the witness?

MR. STRIPLING: No, sir; I have not.

Now, would you speak into the microphone, Mr. Baumgardt? Are you employed in the Congressional Library?

MR. BAUMGARDT: I am employed in the Congressional Library, yes.

MR. STRIPLING: What is your position in the Congressional Library?

MR. BAUMGARDT: Consultant of philosophy of the Library of Congress.

MR. STRIPLING: Now, Mr. Brecht, will you state to the committee whether or not you are a citizen of the United States?

MR. BRECHT: I am not a citizen of the United States; I have only my first papers.

MR. STRIPLING: When did you acquire your first papers?

MR. BRECHT: In 1941 when I came to the country.

MR. STRIPLING: When did you arrive in the United States?

MR. BRECHT: May I find out exactly? I arrived July 21 at San Pedro.

MR. STRIPLING: July 21, 1941?

MR. BRECHT: That is right.

MR. STRIPLING: At San Pedro, Calif.?

MR. BRECHT: Yes.

MR. STRIPLING: You were born in Augsburg, Bavaria, Germany, on February 10, 1888: is that correct?

MR.BRECHT: Yes.

MR. STRIPLING: I am reading from the immigration records—

MR. CRUM: I think, Mr. Stripling, it was 1898.

MR. BRECHT: 1898.

MR. STRIPLING: I beg your pardon.

MR. CRUM: I think the witness tried to say 1898.

MR. STRIPLING: I want to know whether the immigration records are correct on that. Is it '88 or '98?

MR. BRECHT: '98.

MR. STRIPLING: Were you issued a quota immigration visa by the American vice consul on May 3, 1941, at Helsinki, Finland?

MR. BRECHT: That is correct.

MR. STRIPLING: And you entered this country on that visa?

MR. BRECHT: Yes.

MR. STRIPLING: Where had you resided prior to going to Helsinki, Finland?

MR. BRECHT: May I read my statement? In that statement—

THE CHAIRMAN: First, Mr. Brecht, we are trying to identify you. The identification won't be very long.

MR. BRECHT: I had to leave Germany in 1933, in February, when Hitler took power. Then I went to Denmark but when war seemed imminent in '39 I had to leave for Sweden, Stockholm. I remained there for 1 year and then Hitler invaded Norway and Denmark and I had to leave Sweden and I went to Finland, there to wait for my visa for the United States.

MR. STRIPLING: Now, Mr. Brecht, what is your occupation?

MR. BRECHT: I am a playwright and a poet.

MR. STRIPLING: A playwright and a poet?

MR. BRECHT: Yes.

MR. STRIPLING: Where are you presently employed?

MR. BRECHT: I am not employed.

MR. STRIPLING: Were you ever employed in the motion-picture industry?

MR. BRECHT: Yes; I—yes. I sold a story to a Hollywood firm, *Hangmen Also Die*, but I did not write the screenplay myself. I am not a professional screenplay writer. I wrote another story for a Hollywood firm but that story was not produced.

BENTLEY: *Credit for the screenplay of* Hangmen Also Die *went to John Wexley.*

MR. STRIPLING: *Hangmen Also Die*—whom did you sell to, what studio?

MR. BRECHT: That was to, I think, an independent firm, Pressburger at United Artists.

MR. STRIPLING: United Artists?

MR. BRECHT: Yes.

MR. STRIPLING: When did you sell the play to United Artists?

MR. BRECHT: The story—I don't remember exactly, maybe around '43 or '44; I don't remember, quite.

MR. STRIPLING: And what other studios have you sold material to?

MR. BRECHT: No other studio. Besides the last story I spoke of I wrote for Enterprise Studios.

MR. STRIPLING: Are you familiar with Hanns Eisler? Do you know Johannes Eisler?

MR. BRECHT: Yes.

BENTLEY: *With this it becomes clear that Bertolt Brecht's presence in Washington had less to do with American writers from Hollywood than with an even more celebrated case. In September, 1947, the German Communist Gerhart Eisler had been brought before the Committee. J. Edgar Hoover had reported that he had been the representative of the Communist International to the Communist Party of the U.S.A. Eisler's sister, Ruth Fischer, denounced him before the Committee as a leading agent of the Russian secret police. "I regard him as a most dangerous terrorist," she said. ". . . I consider Eisler the perfect terrorist type . . . conditioned to hand over to the GPU his child, his sister, his closest friend." There followed a lengthy questioning by the Committee of the composer Hanns Eisler, brother of Gerhart and Ruth. The Hanns Eisler material in the Committee's printed records fills more than 200 pages. It also only narrowly missed creating the biggest national scandal since the Teapot Dome Scandals, for it was made to seem possible that Mrs. Eleanor Roosevelt's name was involved in conspiracy. She had had something to do with getting Hanns Eisler a visa, and Hanns Eisler had had a great deal to do with the international Communist movement. The published transcript is illustrated with photographs showing Eisler leading Russian children in song, Eisler giving the clenched-fist salute, and what not. Well, one name that was bound to come up was that of Bertolt Brecht, whose words Hanns Eisler had often set to music. The Committee had a complete translation made of the Brecht-Eisler oratorio* The Measures Taken *and wrote it into the record. Gerhart Eisler was convicted of contempt of Congress and of passport violations. Hanns Eisler, having been arrested, was out on bond awaiting a hearing on a deportation order. It was at this interesting point in time that Mr. Stripling put the question: how long have you known Johannes Eisler?*

MR. STRIPLING: How long have you known Johannes Eisler?

MR. BRECHT: I think since the middle of the Twenties, 20 years or so.

MR. STRIPLING: Have you collaborated with him on a number of works?

MR. BRECHT: Yes.

MR. STRIPLING: Mr. Brecht, are you a member of the Communist Party or have you ever been a member of the Communist Party?

MR. BRECHT: May I read my statement? I will answer this question but may I read my statement?

MR. STRIPLING: Would you submit your statement to the chairman?

MR. BRECHT: Yes.

THE CHAIRMAN: All right, let's see the statement.

(Mr. Brecht hands the statement to the chairman.)

BENTLEY: *Parnell Thomas looked over the statement and made the following comment.*

THE CHAIRMAN: Mr. Brecht, the committee has carefully gone over the statement. It is a very interesting story of German life but it is not at all pertinent to this inquiry. Therefore, we do not care to have you read the statement.

BENTLEY: *The statement Brecht was not allowed to read was as follows.*

I was born in Augsburg, Germany, the son of an industrialist, and studied natural sciences and philosophy at the universities of Munich and Berlin. At the age of twenty, when participating in the war as a member of the medical corps, I wrote a ballad which the Hitler government used fifteen years later as reason for my expatriation. The poem *Der Tote Soldat* (*The Dead Soldier*) attacked the war and those wanting to prolong it.

I became a playwright. For a time, Germany seemed to be on the path of democracy. There was freedom of speech and of artistic expression.

In the second half of the 1920's, however, the old reactionary militarist forces began to regain strength.

I was then at the height of my career as a playwright, my play *Dreigroschenoper* being produced all over Europe. There were productions of plays of mine at Berlin, Munich, Paris, Vienna, Tokio, Prague, Milano, Kopenhagen, Stockholm, Budapest, Warschau, Helsinki, Moscow, Oslow, Amsterdam, Zurich, Buckarest, Sofia, Brussels, London, New York, Rio de Janeiro, etc. But in Germany voices could already be heard demanding that free artistic expression and free speech should be silenced. Humanist, socialist, even Christian ideas were called "undeutsch" (un-German), a word which I hardly can think of without Hitler's wolfish intonation. At the same time, the cultural and political institutions of the people were violently attacked.

The Weimar Republic, whatever its faults had been, had a powerful slogan, accepted by the best writers and all kinds of artists: DIE KUNST DEM VOLKE (ART BELONGS TO THE PEOPLE). The German workers, their interest in art and literature being very great indeed, formed a highly important part of the general public of readers and theatre-goers. Their sufferings in a devastating depression which more and more threatened their cultural standards, the impudence and growing power of the old militarist, feudal, imperialist gang alarmed us. I started writing some poems, songs and plays reflecting the feelings of the people and attacking their enemies who now openly marched under the swastika of Adolf Hitler.

The persecutions in the field of culture increased gradually. Famous painters, publishers, and distinguished magazine editors were persecuted. At the universities, political witch hunts were staged, and campaigns were waged against motion pictures such as *All Quiet on the Western Front*.

These, of course, were only preparations for more drastic measures still to come. When Hitler seized power, painters were forbidden to paint, publishing houses and film studios were taken over by the Nazi party. But even these strokes against the cultural life of the German people were only the beginning. They were designed and executed as a spiritual preparation for total war which is the total enemy of culture. The war finished it all up. The German people now have to live without roofs over their heads, without sufficient nourishment, without soap, without the very foundations of culture.

At the beginning, only a very few people were capable of seeing the connection between the reactionary restrictions on the field of culture and the ultimate assaults upon the physical life of a people itself. The efforts of the democratic, anti-militarist forces, of which those in the cultural field were, of course, only a modest part, then proved to be weak altogether; Hitler took over. I had to leave Germany in February, 1933, the day after the Reichstag fire. A veritable exodus of writers and artists began of a kind such as the world had never seen before. . . . I settled down in Denmark and dedicated my total literary production from that time on to the fight against Naziism, writing plays and poetry.

Some poems were smuggled into the Third Reich, and Danish Naziism, supported by Hitler's embassy, soon began to demand my deportation. Of course, the Danish government refused. But in 1939 when war seemed imminent, I left with my family for Sweden, invited by Swedish senators and the Lord Mayor of Stockholm. I could remain only one year. Hitler invaded Denmark and Norway.

We continued our flight northward, to Finland, there to wait for immigration visas to the U.S.A. Hitler's troops followed. Finland was full of Nazi divisions when we left for the United States in 1941. We crossed the USSR by the Siberian Express, which carried German, Austrian, Czechoslovakian refugees. Ten days after our leaving Vladivostok aboard a Swedish ship, Hitler invaded the USSR. During the voyage, the ship loaded copra at Manila. Some months later, Hitler's allies invaded that island. We applied for American citizenship (first papers) on the day after Pearl Harbor.

I suppose that some poems and plays of mine, written during this period of the fight against Hitler, have moved the Un-American Activities Committee to subpoena me.

My activities, even those against Hitler, have always been purely literary activities of a strictly independent nature. As a guest of the United States, I refrained from political activities concerning this country even in a literary form. By the way, I am not a screen writer, Hollywood used only one story of mine for a picture showing the Nazi savageries in Prague. I am not aware of any influence which I could have exercised in the movie industry whether political or artistic.

Being called before the Un-American Activities Committee, however, I feel free for the first time to say a few words about American matters: looking back at my experiences as a playwright and a poet in the Europe of the last two decades, I wish to say that the great American people would lose much and risk much if they allowed anybody to restrict free competition of ideas in cultural fields, or to interfere with art which must be free in order to be art. We are living in a dangerous world. Our state of civilization is such that mankind already is capable of becoming enormously wealthy but, as a whole, is still poverty-ridden. Great wars have been suffered, greater ones are imminent, we are told. One of them might well wipe out mankind, as a whole. We might be the last generation of the specimen man on this earth.

The ideas about how to make use of the new capabilities of production have not been developed much since the days when the horse had to do what man could not do. Do you not think that, in such a predicament, every new idea should be examined carefully and freely? Art can present clear and even make nobler such ideas.

BENTLEY: *The German original of Brecht's statement did not appear in print until long a er the English had appeared both in Gordan Kahn's* Hollywoo on Trial *(1948) and my record album (1963). Reading the original, one discovers that the translation has errors in it. On the other hand, it contains one sentence which has been edited out of the German—the sentence in which Brecht mentions having taken out American citizenship papers.*

MR. STRIPLING: Mr. Brecht, before we go on with the questions, I would like to put into the record the subpena which was served upon you on September 19, calling for your appearance before the committee. You are here in response to a subpena, are you not?

108

MR. BRECHT: Yes.

MR. STRIPLING: Now, I will repeat the original question. Are you now or have you ever been a member of the Communist Party of any country?

MR. BRECHT: Mr. Chairman, I have heard my colleagues when they considered this question not as proper, but I am a guest in this country and do not want to enter into any legal arguments, so I will answer your question fully as well I can.

I was not a member or am not a member of any Communist Party.

THE CHAIRMAN: Your answer is, then, that you have never been a member of the Communist Party?

MR. BRECHT: That is correct.

MR. STRIPLING: You were not a member of the Communist Party in Germany?

MR. BRECHT: No; I was not.

MR. STRIPLING: Mr. Brecht, is it true that you have written a number of very revolutionary poems, plays, and other writings?

MR. BRECHT: I have written a number of poems and songs and plays in the fight against Hitler and, of course, they can be considered, therefore, as revolutionary because I, of course, was for the overthrow of that government.

THE CHAIRMAN: Mr. Stripling, we are not interested in any works that he might have written advocating the overthrow of Germany or the government there.

MR. STRIPLING: Yes; I understand.

Well, from an examination of the works which Mr. Brecht has written, particularly in collaboration with Mr. Hanns Eisler, he seems to be a person of international importance to the Communist revolutionary movement.

Now, Mr. Brecht, is it true or do you know whether or not you have written articles which have appeared in publications in the Soviet zone of Germany within the past few months?

MR. BRECHT: No; I do not remember to have written such articles. I have not seen any of them printed. I have not written any such articles just now. I write very few articles, if any.

MR. STRIPLING: I have here, Mr. Chairman, a document which I will hand to the translator and ask him to identify it for the committee and to refer to an article which appears on page 72.

MR. BRECHT: May I speak to that publication?

MR. STRIPLING: I beg your pardon?

MR. BRECHT: May I explain this publication?

MR. STRIPLING: Yes. Will you identify the publication?

MR. BRECHT: Oh, yes. That is not an article, that is a scene out of a play I wrote in, I think, 1937 or 1938 in Denmark. The play is called *Private Life of the Master Race*, and this scene is one of the scenes out of this play about a Jewish woman in Berlin in the year of '36 or '37. It was, I see, printed in this magazine *Ost und West.*

BENTLEY: *And in fact* The Private Life of the Master Race *had been presented in New York in '45, complete with "The Jewish Wife" scene.*

MR. STRIPLING: Mr. Translator, would you translate the frontispiece of the magazine, please?

MR. BAUMGARDT: "East and West, Contributions to Cultural and Political Questions of the Time, edited by Alfred Kantorowicz, Berlin, July 1947, first year of publication enterprise."

BENTLEY: *Kantorowicz was a Communist or Communist sympathizer at that time. In 1956 he was to break with the Communists and flee from East to West Germany.*

MR. STRIPLING: Mr. Brecht, do you know the gentleman who is the editor of the publication whose name was just read?

MR. BRECHT: Yes; I know him from Berlin, and I met him in New York again.

MR. STRIPLING: Do you know him to be a member of the Communist Party of Germany.

MR. BRECHT: When I met him in Germany I think he was a journalist on the Ullstein Press. That is not a Communist—was not a Communist—there were no Communist Party papers so I do not know exactly whether he was a member of the Communist Party of Germany.

MR. STRIPLING: You don't know whether he was a member of the Communist Party or not?

MR. BRECHT: I don't know, no; I don't know.

MR. STRIPLING: In 1930 did you, with Hanns Eisler, write a play entitled, *Die Massnahme*?

MR. BRECHT: *Die Massnahme.*

MR. STRIPLING: Did you write such a play?

MR. BRECHT: Yes; yes.

MR. STRIPLING: Would you explain to the committee the theme of that play—what it dealt with?

MR. BRECHT: Yes; I will try to.

MR. STRIPLING: First, explain what the title means.

MR. BRECHT: *Die Massnahme means (speaking in German).*

MR. BAUMGARDT: Measures to be taken, or steps to be taken—measures.

MR. STRIPLING: Could it mean disciplinary measures?

MR. BAUMGARDT: No; not disciplinary measures; no. It means measures to be taken.

MR. MCDOWELL: Speak into the microphone.

MR. BAUMGARDT: It means only measures or steps to be taken.

MR. STRIPLING: All right. You tell the committee now, Mr. Brecht—

MR. BRECHT: Yes.

MR. STRIPLING (*continuing*): What this play dealt with.

MR. BRECHT: Yes. This play is the adaptation of an old religious Japanese play and is called No Play, and follows quite closely this old story which shows the devotion for an ideal until death.

MR. STRIPLING: What was that ideal, Mr. Brecht?

MR. BRECHT: The idea in the old play was a religious idea. This young people—

MR. STRIPLING: Didn't it have to do with the Communist Party?

MR. BRECHT: Yes.

MR. STRIPLING: And discipline within the Communist Party?

MR. BRECHT: Yes, yes; it is a new play, an adaptation. It had as a background the Russia-China of the years 1918 or 1919, or so. There some Communist agitators went to a sort of no man's land between the Russia which then was not a state and had no real—

MR. STRIPLING: Mr. Brecht, may I interrupt you? Would you consider the play to be pro-Communist or anti-Communist, or would it take a neutral position regarding Communists?

MR. BRECHT: No; I would say—you see, literature has the right and the duty to give to the public the ideas of the time. Now, in this play—of course, I wrote about 20 plays, but in this play I tried to express the feelings and the ideas of the German workers who then fought against Hitler. I also formulated in an artistic—

MR. STRIPLING: Fighting against Hitler, did you say?

MR. BRECHT: Yes.

MR. STRIPLING: Written in 1930?

MR. BRECHT: Yes, yes; oh, yes. That fight started in 1923.

MR. STRIPLING: You say it is about China, though; it has nothing to do with Germany?

MR. BRECHT: No, it had nothing to do about it.

MR. STRIPLING: Let me read this to you.

MR. BRECHT: Yes.

MR. STRIPLING: Throughout the play reference is made to the theories and teachings of Lenin, the A, B, C of Communism and other Communist classics, and the activities of the Chinese

Communist Party in general. The following are excerpts from the play:

"THE FOUR AGITATORS: We came from Moscow as agitators, we were to travel to the city of Mukden to start propaganda and to create, in the factories, the Chinese Party. We were to report to party headquarters closest to the border and to requisition a guide. There, in the anteroom, a young comrade came toward us and spoke of the nature of our mission. We are repeating the conversation.

"THE YOUNG COMRADE: I am the secretary of the party headquarters which is the last toward the border. My heart is beating for the revolution. The witnessing of wrongdoing drove me into the lines of the fighters. Man must help man. I am for freedom. I believe in mankind. And I am for the rules of the Communist Party which fights for the classless society against exploitation and ignorance.

"THE THREE AGITATORS: We come from Moscow.

"THE YOUNG COMRADE: The two of us have to defend a revolution here. Surely you have a letter to us from the central committee which tells us what to do?

"THE THREE AGITATORS: So it is. We bring you nothing. But across the border to Mukden, we bring to the Chinese workers the teachings of the classics and of the propagandists: The ABC of communism: to the ignorant, the truth about their situation: to the oppressed, class consciousness; and to the class conscious, the experience of the revolution. From you we shall requisition an automobile and a guide.

"THE FOUR AGITATORS: We went as Chinese to Mukden—four men and a woman—to spread propaganda and to create the Chinese Party through the teachings of the classics and of the propagandists—the ABC of communism; to bring truth to the ignorant about their situation; the oppressed class conscious, and class conscious, the experience of the revolution.

"THE YOUNG COMRADE: The individual has two, the party has a thousand eyes. The party sees seven states. The party has many hours. The party cannot be destroyed, for it fights with the methods of the classics which are drawn from the knowledge of reality and are destined to be changed in that the teachings spread through the masses. Who, however, is the party? Is it sitting in a house with telephones? Are its thoughts secret, its revolutions unknown? Who is it? It is all of us. We are the party. You and I and all of you—all of us. In your suite it is, Comrade, and in your head it thinks: wherever I live there is its home and where you are attacked there it fights."

BENTLEY: *The translation is close enough to the German: it is Mr. Stripling's way of reading that makes it hard to follow. He says "suite" for "suit," "class-conscious" for "class consciousness," "it is" for "is it," and so on. He also skips from page to page without saying so. Sometimes he even doubles back without saying so. Let me refer anyone who wishes to read* The Measures Taken *properly to the full text as now published by the Grove Press. The point here is that Stripling had quizzed*

Hanns Eisler on The Measures Taken *a month earlier and that Eisler said the play* was *about the murder of a Communist by three other Communists and that the title* could *be translated* The Disciplinary Measure.

MR. STRIPLING: Now, Mr. Brecht, will you tell the committee whether or not one of the characters in this play was murdered by his comrade because it was in the best interest of the party, of the Communist Party; is that true?

MR. BRECHT: No, it is not quite according to the story.

MR. STRIPLING: Because he would not bow to discipline he was murdered by his comrades, isn't that true?

MR. BRECHT: No; it is not really in it. You will find when you read it carefully, like in the old Japanese play where other ideas were at stake, this young man who died was convinced that he had done damage to the mission he believed in and he agreed to that and he was about ready to die in order not to make greater such damage. So, he asks his comrades to help him, and all of them together help him to die. He jumps into an abyss and they lead him tenderly to that abyss, and that is the story.

THE CHAIRMAN: I gather from your remarks, from your answer, that he was just killed, he was not murdered?

MR. BRECHT: He wanted to die.

THE CHAIRMAN: So they kill him?

MR. BRECHT: No; they did not kill him—not in this story. He killed himself. They supported him, but of course they had told him it were better when he disappeared, for him and them and the cause he also believed in.

BENTLEY: *Brecht would seem to be speaking here not of* The Measures Taken, *but of* Der Jasager, He who says yes, *another play of his that is derived from the same No play as* The Measures Taken. *No one will ever know whether Brecht's memory was playing him tricks, or whether he wanted to lead Mr. Thomas a dance.*

MR. STRIPLING: Mr. Brecht, could you tell the committee how many times you have been to Moscow?

MR. BRECHT: Yes. I was invited to Moscow two times.

MR. STRIPLING: Who invited you?

MR. BRECHT: The first time I was invited by the Volks [voks] Organization for Cultural Exchange. I was invited to show a picture, a documentary picture I had helped to make in Berlin.

MR. STRIPLING: What was the name of that picture?

MR. BRECHT: The name—it is the name of a suburb of Berlin, Kuhle Wampe.

BENTLEY: *The picture was shown in the U.S. under the title* Wither Germany? *Ernst Busch was a leading actor in it, and it had a score by Hanns Eisler. The Brecht-Eisler "Solidarity Song," to be mentioned shortly by Stripling, was sung in the picture.*

MR. STRIPLING: While you were in Moscow, did you meet Sergi Tretyakov — S-e-r-g-i T-r-e-t-y-a-k-o-v; Tretyakov?

MR. BRECHT: Tretyakov; yes. That is a Russian playwright.

MR. STRIPLING: A writer?

MR. BRECHT: Yes.

BENTLEY: *Sergei Tretyakov was indeed a Russian playwright and quite a famous one. He wrote* Roar China, *which the Theatre Guild produced in New York in 1930. It is ironical that the article cited by Stripling appeared in a Moscow magazine as late as 1937, for, two years after that, Stalin had Tretyakov shot as an enemy of the people. Brecht had written, but not published, a poem about Tretyakov's death.*

MR. BRECHT: He translated some of my poems and, I think one play.

MR. STRIPLING: Mr. Chairman, the International Literature No. 5, 1937, published by the State Literary Art Publishing House in Moscow, had an article by Sergi Tretyakov, leading Soviet writer, on an interview he had with Mr. Brecht. On page 60, it states: He is quoting Mr. Brecht —

> "I was a member of the Augsburg Revolutionary Committee," Brecht continued. "Nearby, in Munich, Leviné raised the banner of Soviet power. Augsburg lived in the reflected glow of Munich. The hospital was the only military unit in the town. It elected me to the revolutionary committee. I still remember Georg Brem and the Polish Bolshevik Olshevsky. We did not boast a single Red guardsman. We didn't have time to issue a single decree or nationalize a single bank or close a church. In 2 days General Epp's troops came to town on their way to Munich. One of the members of the revolutionary committee hid at my house until he managed to escape."
>
> He wrote *Drum at Night* [*Drums in the Night, Ed*]. This work contained echoes of the revolution. The drums of revolt persistently summon the man who has gone home. But the man prefers quiet peace of his hearthside.
>
> The work was a scathing satire on those who had deserted the revolution and toasted themselves at their fireplaces. One should recall that Kapp launched his drive on Christmas Eve, calculating that many Red guardsmen would have left their detachments for the family Christmas trees.
>
> His play, *Die Massnahme*, the first of Brecht's plays on a Communist theme, is arranged like a court where the charac-

ters try to justify themselves for having killed a comrade, and judges, who at the same time represent the audience, summarize the events and reach a verdict.

When he visited in Moscow in 1932, Brecht told me his plan to organize a theater in Berlin which would reenact the most interesting court trials in the history of mankind.

Brecht conceived the idea of writing a play about the terrorist tricks resorted to by the landowners in order to peg the price of grain. But this requires a knowledge of economics. The study of economics brought Brecht to Marx and Lenin, whose works became an invaluable part of his library.

Brecht studies and quotes Lenin as a great thinker and as a great master of prose.

The traditional drama portrays the struggle of class instincts. Brecht demands that the struggle of class instincts be replaced by the struggle of social consciousness, of social convictions. He maintains that the situation must not only be felt, but explained—crystallized into the idea which will overturn the world.

Do you recall that interview, Mr. Brecht?

MR. BRECHT: No. (*Laughter.*) It must have been written 20 years ago or so.

MR. STRIPLING: I will show you the magazine, Mr. Brecht.

MR. BRECHT: Yes. I do not recall there was an interview. (*Book handed to the witness.*) I do not recall—Mr. Stripling, I do not recall the interview in exact. I think it is a more or less journalistic summary of talks or discussions about many things.

BENTLEY: *Brecht was right. And Stripling omitted to say that this was all explained in the article itself. Stripling also did not bother to explain that he did not read straight on in the article but made omissions ad lib. The German version, in print today (1970) in a Reclam volume,* Erinnerungen an Brecht, *is quite a bit different. In the just-quoted excerpts, for example, the names Georg Brem and Olshevsky do not occur but, instead, the single name Wajciechowsky.*

MR. STRIPLING: Yes. Have many of your writings been based upon the philosophy of Lenin and Marx?

MR. BRECHT: No; I don't think that is quite correct but, of course, I studied, had to study as a playwright who wrote historical plays. I, of course, had to study Marx's ideas about history. I do not think intelligent plays today can be written without such study. Also, history written now is vitally influenced by the studies of Marx about history.

MR. STRIPLING: Mr. Brecht, since you have been in the United States, have you attended any Communist Party meetings?

MR. BRECHT: No; I don't think so.

MR. STRIPLING: You don't think so?

MR. BRECHT: No.

THE CHAIRMAN: Well, aren't you certain?

MR. BRECHT: No—I am certain; yes.

THE CHAIRMAN: You are certain you have never been to Communist Party meetings?

MR. BRECHT: Yes; I think so. I am here 6 years—I am here those—I do not think so, I do not think that I attended political meetings.

THE CHAIRMAN: No; never mind the political meetings, but have you attended any Communist meetings in the United States?

MR. BRECHT: I do not think so; no.

THE CHAIRMAN: You are certain?

MR. BRECHT: I think I am certain.

THE CHAIRMAN: You think you are certain?

MR. BRECHT: Yes; I have not attended such meetings, in my opinion.

MR. STRIPLING: Mr. Brecht, have you, since you have been in the United States, have you met with any officials of the Soviet Government?

MR. BRECHT: Yes, yes. In Hollywood I was invited, sometimes three or four times, to the Soviet consulate with, of course, many other writers.

MR. STRIPLING: What others?

MR. BRECHT: With other writers and artists and actors who they gave some receptions at special Soviet [speaking in German]—

MR. BAUMGARDT: Festivities.

MR. BRECHT: Festivities.

MR. STRIPLING: Did any of the officials of the Soviet Government ever come and visit you?

MR. BRECHT: I don't think so.

MR. STRIPLING: Didn't Gregory Kheifets visit you on April 14, 1943, vice consul of the Soviet Government? You know Gregory Kheifets, don't you?

MR. BRECHT: Gregory Kheifets?

THE CHAIRMAN: Watch out on this one.

MR. BRECHT: I don't remember that name, but I might know him; yes.

BENTLEY: *Gregory Kheifets was a Soviet vice consul in San Francisco. Eisler seems to have been questioned about him in executive session by a subcommittee of the HUAC that went out to California in the spring of 1947. Later, on the same day as Bertolt Brecht appeared in Washington, a Committee investi-*

gator, Louis J. Russell, would claim to have linked Gregory Kheifetz, through intermediaries, to J. Robert Oppenheimer. One could say with some reason that the whole Oppenheimer Case dates from here.

MR. BRECHT: I don't remember—

MR. STRIPLING: Did he come and visit you on April 14, 1943?

MR. BRECHT: It is quite possible.

MR. STRIPLING: And again on April 27, and again on June 16, 1944?

MR. BRECHT: That is quite possible, yes; that somebody—I don't know. I don't remember the name, but that somebody, some of the cultural attachés—

MR. STRIPLING: Cultural attachés.

MR. BRECHT: Yes.

THE CHAIRMAN: Spell the name.

MR. STRIPLING: Gregory, G-r-e-g-o-r-y Kheifets, K-h-e-i-f-e-t-s. I will spell the last name again, K-h-e-i-f-e-t-s.

MR. BRECHT: Kheifets?

MR. STRIPLING: Yes. Do you remember Mr. Kheifets?

MR. BRECHT: I don't remember the name, but it is quite possible. But I remember that from the—I think from the—yes, from the consulate, from the Russian consulate some people visited me, but not only this man, but also I think the consul once, but I don't remember his name either.

MR. STRIPLING: What was the nature of his business?

MR. BRECHT: He—it must have been about my literary connections with German writers. Some of them are friends of mine.

MR. STRIPLING: German writers?

MR. BRECHT: Yes; in Moscow.

MR. STRIPLING: In Moscow?

MR. BRECHT: Yes. And there appeared in the Staats Verlag the Sergei Tretyakov translations of my plays, for instance, *The Private Life of the Master Race*, *A Penny for the Poor*, and poems, and so on.

MR. STRIPLING: Did Gerhart Eisler ever visit you, not Hanns, but Gerhart?

MR. BRECHT: Yes; I met Gerhart Eisler, too. He is a brother of Hanns, and he visited me with Hanns and then three or four times without Hanns.

MR. STRIPLING: Could you tell us in what year he visited you? Wasn't it the same year that Mr. Kheifets visited you?

MR. BRECHT: I do not know, but there is no connection I can see.

MR. STRIPLING: Do you recall him visiting you on January 17, 1944?

MR. BRECHT: No; I do not recall such date, but he might have visited me on such date.

MR. STRIPLING: Where did he visit you?

MR. BRECHT: He used to ask for his brother, who, as I told you, is an old friend of mine, and we played some games of chess, too, and we spoke about politics.

MR. STRIPLING: About politics?

MR. BRECHT: Yes.

THE CHAIRMAN: What was the last answer? I didn't get the last answer.

MR. STRIPLING: They spoke about politics.

In any of your conversations with Gerhart Eisler, did you discuss the German Communist movement?

MR. BRECHT: Yes.

MR. STRIPLING: In Germany?

MR. BRECHT: Yes; we spoke about, of course, German politics. He is a specialist in that, he is a politician.

MR. STRIPLING: He is a politician?

MR. BRECHT: Yes; he, of course, knew very much more than I knew about the situation in Germany.

MR. STRIPLING: Mr. Brecht, can you tell the committee, when you entered this country, did you make a statement to the Immigration Service concerning your past affiliations?

MR. BRECHT: I don't remember to have made such a statement, but I think I made the usual statements that I did not want to or did not intend to overthrow the American Government. I might have been asked whether I belonged to the Communist Party, I don't remember to have been asked, but I would have answered what I have told you, that I was not. That is what I remember.

MR. STRIPLING: Did they ask you whether or not you had ever been a member of the Communist Party?

MR. BRECHT: I don't remember.

MR. STRIPLING: Did they ask you whether or not you had ever been to the Soviet?

MR. BRECHT: I think they asked me, yes; and I told them.

MR. STRIPLING: Did they question you about your writings?

MR. BRECHT: No; not as I remember, no; they did not. I don't remember any discussion about literature.

MR. STRIPLING: Now, you stated you sold the book, the story, *Hangmen Also Die*, to United Artists; is that correct?

MR. BRECHT: Yes; to an independent firm; yes.

MR. STRIPLING: Did Hanns Eisler do the background music for *Hangmen Also Die*?

MR. BRECHT: Yes; he did.

MR. STRIPLING: Do you recall who starred in that picture?

118

MR. BRECHT: No; I do not.

MR. STRIPLING: You don't even remember who played the leading role in the picture?

MR. BRECHT: I think Brian Donlevy played it.

MR. STRIPLING: Do you remember any of the other actors or actresses who were in it?

MR. BRECHT: No; I do not. You see, I had not very much to do with the filmization itself. I wrote the story and then to the script writers some advice about the background of Nazis, Nazism in Czechoslovakia, so I had nothing to do with the actors.

THE CHAIRMAN: Mr. Stripling, can we hurry this along? We have a very heavy schedule this afternoon.

MR. STRIPLING: Yes.

Now, Mr. Brecht, since you have been in the United States have you contributed articles to any Communist publications in the United States?

MR. BRECHT: I don't think so; no.

MR. STRIPLING: Are you familiar with the magazine *New Masses*?

MR. BRECHT: No.

MR. STRIPLING: You never heard of it?

MR. BRECHT: Yes; of course.

MR. STRIPLING: Did you ever contribute anything to it?

MR. BRECHT: No.

MR. STRIPLING: Did they ever publish any of your work?

MR. BRECHT: That I do not know. They might have published some translation of a poem, but I had no direct connection with it, nor did I send them anything.

BENTLEY: *I believe that Brecht's answer is truthful: search in* The New Masses *files does not turn up anything by him. It seems that he sent* The New Masses *a letter in 1935 protesting against the Theatre Union's production of his play* The Mother *but that* The New Masses *did not print this letter. "In Praise of Learning," which Mr. Stripling is about to mention, is a song from* The Mother, *and it was often sung by itself, as for example on an American phonograph record of the Thirties issued under the label of Timely Recording Company, sung by the New Singers, with Marc Blitzstein at the piano. The line which will be debated reads in German: "du musst die Fuehrung uebernehmen," which means: "you must take over the leadership." The translation which Brecht is about to object to is actually rather close to the original.*

MR. STRIPLING: Did you collaborate with Hanns Eisler on the song "In Praise of Learning"?

MR. BRECHT: Yes; I collaborated. I wrote that song and he only wrote the music.

MR. STRIPLING: You wrote the song?

MR. BRECHT: I wrote the song.

MR. STRIPLING: Would you recite to the committee the words of that song?

MR. BRECHT: Yes; I would. May I point out that song comes from another adaptation I made of Gorky's play, *Mother*. In this song a Russian worker woman addresses all the poor people.

MR. STRIPLING: It was produced in this country, wasn't it?

MR. BRECHT: Yes. '35, New York.

MR. STRIPLING: Now, I will read the words and aks you if this is the one.

MR. BRECHT: Please.

MR. STRIPLING: (*reading*):

> Learn now the simple truth, you for whom the time has
> come at last; it is not too late.
> Learn now the ABC. It is not enough but learn it still.
> Fear not, be not downhearted. Again you must learn the
> lesson, you must be ready to take over—

MR. BRECHT: No, excuse me, that is the wrong translation. That is not right.(*Laughter*) Just one second, and I will give you the correct text.

MR. STRIPLING: That is not a correct translation?

MR. BRECHT: That is not correct, no; that is not the meaning. It is not very beautiful, but I am not speaking about that.

MR. STRIPLING: What does it mean? I have here a portion of *The People*, which was issued by the Communist Party of the United States, published by the Workers' Library Publishers. Page 24 says:

> In praise of learning, by Bert Brecht; music by Hanns
> Eisler.

It says here:

> You must be ready to take over; learn it.
> Men on the dole, learn it; men in the prisons, learn it;
> women in the kitchen, learn it; men of 65, learn it. You must
> be ready to take over—

and goes right on through. That is the core of it—

> You must be ready to take over.

MR. BRECHT: Mr. Stripling, maybe his translation—

MR. BAUMGARDT: The correct translation would be, "You must take the lead."

THE CHAIRMAN: "You must take the lead"?

MR. BAUMGARDT: "The lead." It definitely says, "The lead." It is not "You must take over." The translation is not a literal translation of the German.

MR. STRIPLING: Well, Mr. Brecht, as it has been published in these publications of the Communist Party, then, if that is incorrect, what did you mean?

MR. BRECHT: I don't remember never—I never got that book myself. I must not have been in the country when it was published. I think it was published as a song, one of the songs Eisler had written the music to. I did not give any permission to publish it. I don't see—I think I have never saw the translation.

MR. STRIPLING: Do you have the words there before you?

MR. BRECHT: In German, yes.

MR. STRIPLING: Of the song?

MR. BRECHT: Oh, yes; in the book.

MR. STRIPLING: Not in the original.

MR. BRECHT: In the German book.

MR. STRIPLING: It goes on:

> You must be ready to take over; you must be ready to take over. Don't hesitate to ask questions, stay in there. Don't hesitate to ask questions, comrade—

MR. BRECHT: Why not let him translate from the German, word for word?

MR. BAUMGARDT: I think you are mainly interested in this translation which comes from—

THE CHAIRMAN: I cannot understand the interpreter any more than I can the witness.

MR. BAUMGARDT: Mr. Chairman, I apologize. I shall make use of this.

THE CHAIRMAN: Just speak in that microphone and maybe we can make out.

MR. BAUMGARDT: The last line of all three verses is correctly to be translated: "You must take over the lead," and not "You must take over." "You must take the lead," would be the best, most correct, most accurate translation.

MR. STRIPLING: Mr. Brecht, did you ever make application to join the Communist Party?

MR. BRECHT: I do not understand the question. Did I make—

MR. STRIPLING: Have you ever made application to join the Communist Party?

MR. BRECHT: No, no, no, no, no, never.

MR. STRIPLING: Mr. Chairman, we have here—

MR. BRECHT: I was an independent writer and wanted to be an independent writer and I point that out and also theoretically, I think, it was the best for me not to join any party whatever. And all these things you read here were not only written for the German Communists, but they were also written for workers of any other kind; Social Democrat workers were in these performances; so were Catholic workers from Catholic unions; so were workers which never had been in a party or didn't want to go into a party.

THE CHAIRMAN: Mr. Brecht, did Gerhart Eisler ever ask you to join the Communist Party?

MR. BRECHT: No, no.

THE CHAIRMAN: Did Hanns Eisler ever ask you to join the Communist Party?

MR. BRECHT: No; he did not. I think they considered me just as a writer who wanted to write and do as he saw it, but not as a political figure.

THE CHAIRMAN: Do you recall anyone ever having asked you to join the Communist Party?

MR. BRECHT: Some people might have suggested it to me, but then I found out that it was not my business.

THE CHAIRMAN: Who were those people who asked you to join the Communist Party?

MR. BRECHT: Oh, readers.

THE CHAIRMAN: Who?

MR. BRECHT: Readers of my poems or people from the audiences. You mean — there was never an official approach to me to publish —

THE CHAIRMAN: Some people did ask you to join the Communist Party.

MR. KENNY: In Germany. (*Aside to witness.*)

MR. BRECHT: In Germany, you mean in Germany?

THE CHAIRMAN: No; I mean in the United States.

MR. BRECHT: No, no, no.

THE CHAIRMAN: He is doing all right. He is doing much better than many other witnesses you have brought here.

Do you recall whether anyone in the United States ever asked you to join the Communist Party?

MR. BRECHT: No; I don't.

THE CHAIRMAN: Mr. McDowell, do you have any questions?

MR. MCDOWELL: No; no questions.

THE CHAIRMAN: Mr. Vail?

MR. VAIL: No questions.

THE CHAIRMAN: Mr. Stripling, do you have any more questions?

MR. STRIPLING: I would like to ask Mr. Brecht whether or not he wrote a poem, a song, rather, entitled, "Forward, We've Not Forgotten."

MR. MCDOWELL: "Forward," what?

MR. STRIPLING: Forward, We've Not Forgotten."

MR. BRECHT: I can't think of that. The English title may be the reason.

MR. STRIPLING: Would you translate it for him into German?

BENTLEY: *A literal translation of the German would read: "Forward and do not forget." It is a song well known to German left-wingers, and generally called* Solidaritätslied, *"Solidarity Song." The translation deviates from the German a good deal because the translator is hard up for rhymes and has to fit his words to Eisler's music. This translation, attributed to Henry Jordan, was also put on a disc by Timely Recording Company in the Thirties.*

MR. BRECHT: Oh, now I know; yes.

MR. STRIPLING: You are familiar with the words to that?

MR. BRECHT: Yes.

MR. STRIPLING: Would the committee like me to read that?

THE CHAIRMAN: Yes; without objection, go ahead.

MR. STRIPLING (*reading*):

> Forward, we've not forgotten our strength in the fights we've won;
> No matter what may threaten, forward, not forgotten how strong we are as one;
> Only these our hands now acting, build the road, the walls, the towers. All the world is of our making.
> What of it can we call ours?

The refrain:

> Forward. March on to the tower, through the city, by land the world;
> Forward. Advance it on. Just whose city is the city? Just whose world is the world?
> Forward, we've not forgotten our union in hunger and pain, no matter what may threaten, forward, we've not forgotten.
> We have a world to gain. We shall free the world of shadow; every shop and every room, every road and every meadow.
> All the world will be our own.

Did you write that, Mr. Brecht?

MR. BRECHT: No. I wrote a German poem, but that is very different from this. (*Laughter.*)

MR. STRIPLING: That is all the questions I have. Mr. Chairman.

THE CHAIRMAN: Thank you very much, Mr. Brecht. You are a good example to the witnesses of Mr. Kenny and Mr. Crum.

BENTLEY: *At that Bertolt Brecht left the room, and within a few hours had also left the United States—forever. I personally was not present at this historic encounter. But it had been broadcast, and a year or so later—in his livingroom at Feldmeilen near Zurich—Brecht played me a recording of the broadcast which some friend had put on a disc for him. I can still hear him laughing his dry laugh at the many comic turns in the dialogue. Some of Brecht's friends wished he had pleaded the First Amendment, but he re-iterated in private what he had said on the stand: as a visitor to America, he did not think he should claim the privileges of a citizen. He added that his chief legal adviser, Bartley Crum, advised him to state that he was a Communist. "Nothing can happen to you, since you're not a citizen, and it was the German Party you would have been a member of." "But I wasn't a member." Brecht said he protested. "It makes no difference," Crum is supposed to have argued. "If you say you weren't a member, they'll forge a Party card and get you for perjury." Brecht told me he was unwilling to take this line and preferred to risk telling the truth.*

Possibly the aspersion cast by Crum on the honesty of the Committee will seem unfair. On the other hand, the Committee's chairman did go to jail in 1949, and the charge, in essence, was dishonesty—he had accepted kickbacks from employees.

Even before the final exposure of Parnell Thomas as a fraud, Brecht was embarrassed by the compliment he had received from him—"You are a good example to the witnesses of Mr. Kenny and Mr. Crum." But he gave Thomas and his colleagues credit for one thing. "They weren't as bad as the Nazis," he said. "The Nazis would never have let me smoke. In Washington, they let me have a cigar, and I used it to manufacture pauses with between their questions and my answers."

ADDENDUM.

The two lyrics cited at the end of the Brecht testimony appear above in so garbled a form that the reader may be grateful to see what they were really like. The English texts concerned follow. Another English translation of the same songs is in print today in The Brecht-Eisler Song Book *(Oak Publications).*

In Praise Of Learning

Learn now the simple truth.
You for whom the time has come at last
It is not too late.
Learn now the ABC
It is not enough but learn it still.
Fear not! Be not downhearted!
Begin, you must learn the lesson:
You must be ready to take over.
Learn it, men on the dole!
Learn it, men in the prisons!
Learn it, women in the kitchens!
Learn it, men of sixty five!
You must be ready to take over.
Go back to school again, homeless people!
Just learn all you can, you freezing ones!
Starving, get hold of a book!
Let that be a weapon!
You must be ready to take over.
Don't hesitate to ask questions, comrade.
Don't be persuaded, but prove for yourself:
What you don't learn yourself, you don't know.
Check up the bill, for it's you who must pay it!
Point with your finger to every item!
Say that you want it explained!
You must be ready to take over.

Forward, We've Not Forgotten

Forward, we've not forgotten
Our strength in the fights we have won!
No matter what may threaten
Foward, not forgotten,
How strong we are as one!
Only these our hands now aching
Built the roads, the walls, the towers.
All the world is of our making.
What of it can we call ours?
Forward, march on to power
Through the city, the land, the world.
Forward, advance the hour!
Just whose city is the city?
Just whose world is the world?
Forward, we've not forgotten
Our union in hunger and pain.
No matter what may threaten
Forward, not forgotten,
We have a world to gain.
We shall free the world of shadow
Every shop and every room
Every road and every meadow,
All the world will be our own.
Forward, march on to power

Through the city, the land, the world.
Forward, advance the hour!
Just whose city is the city?
Just whose world is the world?

BILLIE HOLIDAY

Don't Know If I'm Coming Or Going

It was called "The United States of America versus Billie Holiday." And that's just the way it felt.

They brought me into a courtroom in the U.S. District Courthouse at Ninth and Market streets in Philly—only two blocks from the Earle Theatre where it had all begun eleven days before. But those two damn blocks seemed like the Atlantic Ocean. It was Tuesday, May 27, 1947.

Somebody read off the charge: "On or about May 16, 1947, and divers dates theretofore in the Eastern District of Pennsylvania, Billie Holiday did receive, conceal, carry and facilitate the transportation and concealment of . . . drugs . . . fraudulently imported and brought into the United States contrary to law, in violation of Section 174, Title 21, U.S.C.A."

An assistant U.S. district attorney opened. "All right, Billie Holiday," he said. "You are charged with violation of the Narcotics Act and you have been shown a copy of the information and have indicated your desire to waive the presentation of an indictment by the Grand Jury. You are entitled to a lawyer."

"I have none," I said. And that was the truth. I hadn't seen one, talked to one.

"Do you want a lawyer, Miss Holiday?" The D.A. asked.

"No," I answered.

I didn't think there was anyone who would help me. And worse, I had been convinced that nobody *could* help me.

"Then this is a waiver of appointment of counsel if you will sign 'Billie Holiday' on that line."

They shoved me a pink paper to sign and I signed it.

I would have signed anything, no matter what. I hadn't eaten anything for a week. I couldn't even keep water down. Every time I tried to take a nap, some big old officer would come around and wake me up to sign something, make me dress, go to another office.

When it came time for me to appear in court I couldn't even

126

walk. I was in no shape to go before the judge. So they agreed to give me a shot to keep me from getting sick. It turned out to be morphine.

Then the judge spoke up. "Was this woman ever represented by counsel?" he asked.

The district attorney replied, "I had a call today from a man who had been her counsel, and I explained the matter to him and then he returned a call and stated they were not interested in coming down and wanted the matter handled as it is being handled now."

I can read that sentence today and weep. "They were not interested in coming down and wanted the matter handled as it is being handled." In plain English that meant that no one in the world was interested in looking out for me at this point.

If a woman drowns her baby, about the worst thing you can do, she's still got a right to see a lawyer, and I'd help get her one if I could.

I couldn't very well expect the Legal Aid Society to come rushing in to help a chick making a couple thousand a week or more. I knew I was on my own. Glaser had told me this before. "Girl," he said, "this is the best thing that could happen to you."

I needed to go to a hospital and he was telling me the wood-shed would be better.

So they handed me a white paper to sign. "This is a waiver of presentation of an indictment to the Grand Jury, Miss Holiday." They never had it so easy. I signed the second paper. The rest was up to them. I was just a pigeon.

"How do you plead?" said the clerk.

"I would like to plead guilty and be sent to a hospital," I said.

Then the D.A. spoke up. "If Your Honor please, this is a case of a drug addict, but more serious, however, than most of our cases. Miss Holiday is a professional entertainer and among the higher rank as far as income is concerned. She has been in Philadelphia and appeared at the Earle Theatre, where she had a week's engagement; our agents in the Narcotics Bureau were advised from our Chicago office that she was a heroin addict and undoubtedly had heroin on her."

"The Chicago office advised you?" the judge asked.

"That is right," the D.A. replied. "She had previously been in Chicago on an engagement. They checked and found that when she left the Earle Theatre or prepared to leave the Earle Theatre, prior to leaving she had in her possession some capsules . . . and transferred them to a man who was supposed to be her manager, named James Asundio.

"Subsequent to that, while James Asundio and Bennie Tucker were packing the bags, the agents came and identified themselves and told them why they were there, and Asundio said it was his room. They made a search of the room with his permission and found wrapped up a package, wrapped in silk lining, containing some capsules. . . .

"Subsequently, Miss Holiday was apprehended in New York," he went on. "She has given these agents a full and complete statement and came in here last week with the booking agent (Glaser) and expressed a desire to be cured of this addiction. Very unfortunately she has had following her the worst type of parasites and leeches you can think of. We have learned that in the past three years she has earned almost a quarter of a million dollars, but last year it was $56,000 or $57,000, and she doesn't have any of that money.

"These fellows who have been travelling with her," this young D.A. continued melodramatically, "would go out and get these drugs and would pay five and ten dollars and they would charge her one hundred and two hundred dollars for the same amount of drugs. It is our opinion that the best thing that can be done for her would be to put her in a hospital where she will be properly treated and perhaps cured of this addiction."

Then the judge took over. He asked my age, if I was married, how long I'd been separated from my husband, if we had any kids, where he worked, my life story, my show-business history.

He asked me if I didn't know it was "wrong" to have possession of narcotics. What did he expect me to say? I told him I couldn't help it after I started. Then he asked how much I used. When the federal agent Roder told him, the judge wanted to know if this was a large amount. Roder told him it was enough to kill either of them. They wouldn't be dead, they'd be damn high, that's all.

Then he wanted to know how many grains I had started with. Hell, I was no more of a pharmacist than he was. I was sick of grown men getting their kicks out of all this. They had told me if I pleaded guilty they'd send me to a hospital. I was sick and wanted to get there. This wasn't getting anyone anywhere.

I broke in and spoke to the judge. "I'm willing to go to the hospital, Your Honor," I said.

"I know," he said, brushing me off.

"I want the cure," I told him.

"You stand here indicted criminally as a user of narcotics," he said, looking me in the eye. Then the judge and the federal agents got into a long hassle which had nothing to do with me, either. The chief of the Philadelphia bureau stepped up and gave the judge a lecture on how hard they were working and said, "I am only saying very little, if any, good will be served with their indictment and conviction other than her individual interest if we do not get some lead as to the source."

The judge seemed to be saying they were doing me a favor. And he kept talking about an indictment and conviction, but there was nobody there to object.

Then the judge started on me again, asking me where I'd been on tour, who was with me, how much money I made, and where it was. This might have gone on forever except that somebody came in, went into a huddle with the judge. He must have been a probation officer or a social worker or something.

Then the judge lowered the boom.

"I want you to understand, as I intimated at the time of your plea, that you stand here as a criminal defendant, and while your plight is rather pitiful, we have no doubt but that you, having been nine years associated in the theatrical world, pretty well appreciate what is right — and your experiences have been many, I have been led to understand.

"I want you to know you are being committed as a criminal defendant; you are not being sent to a hospital alone primarily for treatment. You will get treatment, but I want you to know you stand convicted as a wrongdoer. Any other wrongdoer who has associated with you is a matter that is not for our consideration now.

"In your imprisonment you are going to find that you are going to get the very best medical treatment which can be accorded to you. That is the beneficial part of the government's position in this case.

"I do not think you have told the whole truth about your addiction at all. . . . Your commitment will depend largely on yourself, that of the supervisor and the government generally, and we hope that within the time limit in which you are to serve you will rehabilitate yourself and return to society a useful individual and take your place in the particular calling which you have chosen and in which you have been successful.

"The sentence of the court is that you undergo imprisonment for a period of one year and one day. The Attorney General will designate the prison in which the incarceration will be made."

It was all over in a matter of minutes; they gave me another shot to keep me from getting sick on the train, and at nine o'clock that night I was in an upper berth on a train headed for the Federal Woman's Reformatory at Alderson, West Virginia, with two big fat white matrons guarding me.

They acted as though they were scared to death of me. When I asked one of them to get me a bottle of beer she gasped and told me it was against regulations. Hell, I had a package of stuff to keep me from getting sick. That was against regulations too. Except nobody wanted to take a chance of letting me get deadly sick on the train. Finally one matron gave up and went and got me one little old bottle of beer.

But the Philadelphia story wasn't over. They started bringing me back from Alderson to Philly to question me and question me. I hated that. They brought me up so often, the girls at the place began to think I was a stool pigeon. And there's no place worse than the Philadelphia jail where they used to keep me. It's worse than Welfare Island, damp all the time, with rats in it big as my chihuahua. There were women there with t.b. and worse, doing life terms for murder and stuff, and I had to eat with them and sleep with them.

When they weren't finding out what they thought I knew, the Treasury agent fixed it so I'd arrive at the Philly jail on Friday night and have to lay over in the hellhole until Monday before I was questioned. Talk about your brainwashings, I've had it.

What made it worse was they brought me up when they tried Jimmy Asundio and again later when they tried Joe Guy. Both of them stood on their legal rights. They had good lawyers, and both of them got off. Jimmy's conviction was reversed by a higher court because the federal agents had come into his room without a warrant. And Joe Guy was acquitted by a jury in a few minutes. They had no case; the judge told them so, and the jury agreed.

I felt like the fool of all time.

People on drugs are sick people. So now we end up with the government chasing sick people like they were criminals, telling doctors they can't help them, prosecuting them because they had some stuff without paying the tax, and sending them to jail.

Imagine if the government chased sick people with diabetes, put a tax on insulin and drove it into the black market, told doctors they couldn't treat them, and then caught them, prosecuted them for not paying their taxes, and then sent them to jail. If we did that, everyone would know we were crazy. Yet we do practically the same thing every day in the week to sick people hooked on drugs. The jails are full and the problem is getting worse every day.

WILHELM REICH

Four Documents:
Response, Decree, Statement, And Proposal

1. Response

February 25th, 1954

The Hon. Judge Clifford
Federal Court House
Portland, Maine
Dear Judge Clifford:

I am taking the liberty of transmitting to you my "Response" to the complaint filed by the Food and Drug Administration regarding the Orgone Energy Accumulator. My "Response" summarizes my standpoint as a natural scientist who deals with matters of basic natural law. It is not in my hands to judge the legal aspects of the matter.

My factual position in the case as well as in the world of science of today does not permit me to enter the case against the Food and Drug Administration, since such action would, in my mind, imply admission of the authority of this special branch of the government to pass judgment on primordial, preatomic cosmic orgone energy.

I, therefore, rest the case in full confidence in your hands.

Sincerely yours,
/s/ Wilhelm Reich, M.D.

RESPONSE
Regarding the Request of the Food and Drug Administration (FDA) to Enjoin the Natural Scientific Activities of Wilhelm Reich, M.D.

In order to clarify the *factual* as well as the *legal* situation concerning the complaint, we must, from the very beginning, distinguish concrete *facts* from *legal procedure* to do justice to the facts.

Technically, legally the US Government has filed suit against the natural scientific work of Wilhelm Reich.

From *History of the Discovery of the Life Energy*, Documentary Supplement No. 3, A-XII-EP, 1954.

Factually, the FDA is NOT "The US Government." It is merely one of its administrative agencies dealing with Foods, Drugs, and Cosmetics. It is not empowered to deal with *Basic Natural Law*.

ORGONOMY (see "Bibliography on the History of Orgonomy") is a branch of BASIC NATURAL SCIENCE. Its central object of research is elucidation of the Basic Natural Law.

Now, in order to bring into line the legal procedure with the above-mentioned facts, the following is submitted:

The common law structure of the United States rests originally on Natural Law. This Natural Law has heretofore been interpreted in various ways of thinking, metaphysically, religiously, mechanistically. It has never, concretely and scientifically, been subjected to natural scientific inquiry based upon a discovery which encompasses the very roots of existence.

The concept of Natural Law as the foundation of a secure way of life, must firmly rest upon the practical concrete functions of LIFE itself. In consequence, a correct life-positive interpretation of Natural Law, the basis of common law, depends on the *factual* elucidation of what Life actually is, how it works, what are its basic functional manifestations. From this basic premise derive the claims of natural scientists to a free, unmolested, unimpeded, natural scientific activity in general and in the exploration of the Life Energy in particular.

The complaint of the FDA is factually intimately interconnected with a basic social issue which, at present, is reverberating in the lives of all of us here and abroad.

Abraham Lincoln once said: "What I do say is that no man is good enough to govern another man without that other's consent. I say this is a leading principle, the sheet anchor of American republicanism."

At this point, I could easily declare "I refuse to be governed in my basic natural research activities by the Food and Drug Administration." But exactly here, in this constitutional right of mine, the basic confusion in the interpretation of Natural and Common Law becomes apparent.

There are conspirators around whose aim it is to destroy human happiness and self-government. Is now the right of the conspirator to ravage humanity the same as my right to free, unimpeded inquiry?

It obviously is NOT THE SAME THING. I shall not try to answer this basic dilemma of American society at the present. I shall only open an approach to this legal and factual dilemma. It has a lot to do with the position of the complainant, trying to enjoin the experimental and theoretical functions of Life in its emotional, educational, social, economic, intellectual and medical implications.

According to natural, and in consequence, American Common Law, no one, no matter who he is, has the power or legal right to enjoin:

> The study and observation of natural phenomena including Life within and without man;
> The communication to others of knowledge of these natural phenomena so rich in the manifestations of an existent, concrete, cosmic Life Energy;
> The stir to mate in all living beings, including our maturing adolescents;
> The emergence of abstractions and final mathematical formulae concerning the natural life force in the universe, and the right to their dissemination among one's fellow men;
> The handling, use and distribution of instruments of basic research in any field, medical, educational, preventive, physical, biological, and in fields which emerge from such basic activities and which, resting on such principles, must by all means remain free.

Attempts such as branding activities and instruments of such kind as "adulterated," in other words as fraud, only characterizes the narrowness of the horizon of the complaint.

No man-made law ever, no matter whether derived from the past or projected into a distant, unforeseeable future, can or should ever be empowered to claim that it is greater than the Natural Law from which it stems and to which it must inevitably return in the eternal rhythm of creation and decline of all things natural. This is valid, no matter whether we speak in terms such as "God," "Natural Law," "Cosmic Primordial Force," "Ether" or "Cosmic Orgone Energy."

The present critical state of international human affairs requires security and safety from nuisance interferences with efforts toward full, honest, determined clarification of man's relationship to nature within and without himself; in other words, his relationship to the Law of Nature. It is not permissible, either morally, legally or factually to force a natural scientist to expose his scientific results and methods of basic research in court. This point is accentuated in a world crisis where biopathic men hold in their hands power over ruined, destitute multitudes.

To appear in court as a *"defendant"* in matters of basic natural research would in itself appear, to say the least, extraordinary. It would require disclosure of evidence in support of the position of the discovery of the Life Energy. Such disclosure, however, would invoke untold complications, and *possibly national disaster.*

Proof of this can be submitted at any time only to a duly *authorized* personality of the US Government in a high, responsible position.

Scientific matters cannot possibly ever be decided upon in court. They can only be clarified by prolonged, faithful bona fide observations in friendly exchange of opinion, never by litigation. The sole purpose of the complainant is to entangle orgonomic basic research in endless, costly legal procedures a la Panmunjon, which will accomplish exactly NOTHING rational or useful to human society.

Inquiry in the realm of Basic Natural Law is *outside the judicial domain*, of this, or ANY OTHER KIND OF SOCIAL ADMINISTRATION ANYWHERE ON THIS GLOBE, IN ANY LAND, NATION OR REGION.

Man's right to know, to learn, to inquire, to make bona fide errors, to investigate human emotions must, by all means, be safe, if the word FREEDOM should ever be more than an empty political slogan.

If painstakingly elaborated and published scientific findings over a period of 30 years could not convince this administration, or will not be able to convince any other social administration of the true nature of the discovery of the Life Energy, no litigation in any court anywhere will ever help to do so.

I, therefore, submit, in the name of truth and justice, that I shall not appear in court as the "defendant" against a plaintiff who by his mere complaint already has shown his ignorance in matters of natural science. I do so at the risk of being, by mistake, fully enjoined in all my activities. Such an injunction would mean practically exactly nothing at all. My discovery of the Life Energy is today widely known nearly all over the globe, in hundreds of institutions, whether acclaimed or cursed. It can no longer be stopped by anyone, no matter what happens to me.

Orgone Energy Accumulators, the *"devices"* designed to concentrate cosmic Orgone Energy, and thus to make it available to further research in medicine, biology and physics, are being built today in many lands, without my knowledge and consent, and even without any royalty payments.

On the basis of these considerations, I submit that the case against Orgonomy be taken out of court completely.

Wilhelm Reich, *M.D.*
Chairman of Basic Research
OF THE WILHELM REICH FOUNDATION

Date: February 22, 1954

134

2. Decree of Injunction

CIVIL ACTION NO. 1056

Plaintiff having filed a Complaint for Injunction herein to enjoin the defendants and others from further alleged violations of the Federal Food, Drug, and Cosmetic Act; and each defendant having been duly served, on February 10, 1954, with a summons and copy of the Complaint; and no defendant having appeared or answered in person or by representative, although the time therefore has expired; and each defendant having been duly served, on February 26, 1954, with a copy of Requests for Admissions; and no defendant having served any answer to said Requests, although the time therefore has expired; and the default of each defendant having been entered herein; and it appearing that the defendants, unless enjoined therefrom, will continue to introduce or cause to be introduced or delivered, or cause to be delivered into interstate commerce orgone energy accumulators, devices within the meaning of the Federal Food, Drug, and Cosmetic Act, 21 U. S. C. 301 et seq, which are misbranded and adulterated, and in violation of 21 U. S. C. 331 (a) and (k); and the Court having been fully advised in the premises;

IT IS HEREBY ORDERED, ADJUDGED, AND DE-CREED that the defendants, THE WILHELM REICH FOUNDATION, WILHELM REICH, and ILSE OLLEN-DORFF and each and all of their officers, agents, servants, employees, attorneys, all corporations, associations, and organizations, and all persons in active concert or participation with them or any of them, be, and they hereby are, perpetually enjoined and restrained from doing any of the following acts, directly or indirectly, in violation of Sections 301(a) or 301(k) of the Federal Food, Drug, and Cosmetic Act (21 U. S. C. 331(a) or (k)) with respect to any orgone energy accumulator device, in any style or model, any and all accessories, components or parts thereof, or any similar device, in any style or model, and any device purported or represented to collect and accumulate the alleged orgone energy:

(1) Introducing or causing to be introduced or delivering or causing to be delivered for introduction into interstate commerce any such article or device which is:

(a) Misbranded within the meaning of Section 502(a) of the Act (21 U. S. C. 352(a)) by reason of any representation or

From the court record, U.S. Court of Appeals for the First Circuit, *Wilhelm Reich, et. al.,* v. U.S.A.

135

suggestion in its labeling which conveys the impression that such article, in any style or model, is an outstanding therapeutic agent, is a preventive of and beneficial for use in any disease or disease condition, is effective in the cure, mitigation, treatment, and prevention of any disease, symptom, or condition; or

(b) Misbranded within the meaning of Section 502 (a) of the Act (21 U. S. C. 352(a)) by reason of any representation or suggestion in its labeling which conveys the impression that the alleged orgone energy exists; or

(c) Misbranded within the meaning of Section 502(a) of the Act (21 U. S. C. 352(a)) by reason of any photographic representation or suggestion with a caption, or otherwise, which conveys the impression that such is an actual photograph depicting the alleged orgone energy or an alleged excited orgone energy field; or

(d) Misbranded within the meaning of Section 502(a) of the Act (21 U. S. C. 352(a)) by reason of any other false or misleading representation or suggestion; or

(e) Adulterated within the meaning of Section 501(c) of the Act (21 U. S. C. 351(c)) in that (1) its strength differs from or its quality falls below that which it purports or is represented to possess or (2) it purports to collect from the atmosphere and accumulate in said device the alleged orgone energy; or

(2) Doing any act or causing any act to be done with respect to any orgone energy accumulator device while such device is held for sale (including rental, or any other disposition) after shipment in interstate commerce which results in said device becoming misbranded or adulterated in any respect; and

IT IS FURTHER ORDERED:

(1) That all orgone energy accumulator devices, and their labeling, which were shipped in interstate commerce and which (a) are on a rental basis, or (b) otherwise owned or controlled by any one of the defendants, or by the defendants, be recalled by the defendants to their place of business at Rangeley, Maine; and

(2) That the devices referred to in (1) immediately above, and their parts, be destroyed by the defendants or, they may be dismantled and the materials from which they were made salvaged after dismantling; and

(3) That the labeling referred to in paragraph (1), just above, except those items for which a specific purchase price was paid by their owners, be destroyed by the defendants; and

(4) That all parts or portions of orgone accumulator devices shipped in interstate commerce and returned to Rangeley, Maine, or elsewhere, and awaiting repair or reshipment be de-

stroyed by the defendants, or, they may be dismantled and the materials from which they were made salvaged after dismantling; and

(5) That all copies of the following items of written, printed, or graphic matter, and their covers, if any, which items have constituted labeling of the article of device, and which contain statements and representations pertaining to the existence of orgone energy, its collection by, and accumulation in, orgone energy accumulators, and the use of such alleged orgone energy by employing said accumulators in the cure, mitigation, treatment, and prevention of disease, symptoms and conditions:

> *The Discovery of the Orgone* by Wilhelm Reich
> Vol I – *The Function of the Orgasm*
> Vol II – *The Cancer Biopathy*
> *The Sexual Revolution* by Wilhelm Reich
> *Ether, God and Devil* by Wilhelm Reich
> *Cosmic Superimposition* by Wilhelm Reich
> *Listen, Little Man* by Wilhelm Reich
> *The Mass Psychology of Fascism* by Wilhelm Reich
> *Character Analysis* by Wilhelm Reich
> *The Murder of Christ* by Wilhelm Reich
> *People in Trouble* by Wilhelm Reich

shall be withheld by the defendants and not again employed as labeling; in the event, however, such statements and representations, and any other allied material, are deleted, such publications may be used by the defendants; and

(6) That all written, printed, and graphic matter containing instructions for the use of any orgone energy accumulator device, instructions for the assembly thereof, all printed, and other announcements and order blanks for the items listed in the paragraph immediately above, all documents, bulletins, pamphlets, journals, and booklets entitled in part, as follows: CATALOGUE SHEET, PHYSICIAN'S REPORT, APPLICATION FOR THE USE OF THE ORGONE ENERGY ACCUMULATOR, ADDITIONAL INFORMATION REGARDING SOFT ORGONE IRRADIATION, ORGONE ENERGY ACCUMULATOR ITS SCIENTIFIC AND MEDICAL USE, ORGONE ENERGY BULLETIN, ORGONE ENERGY EMERGENCY BULLETIN, INTERNATIONAL JOURNAL OF SEX-ECONOMY AND ORGONE RESEARCH, INTERNATIONALE ZEITSCHRUFT FUR ORGONOMIE, EMOTIONAL PLAGUE VERSUS ORGONE BIOPHYSICS, ANNALS OF THE ORGONE INSTITUTE, and ORANUR EXPERIMENT, but not limited to those enumerated, shall be destroyed; and

(7) That the directives and provisions contained in paragraphs (1) to (6) inclusive, above, shall be performed under the supervi-

sion of employees of the Food and Drug Administration, authorized representatives of the Secretary of Health, Education and Welfare; and

(8) That for the purposes of supervision and securing compliance with this decree the defendants shall permit said employees of the Food and Drug Administration, at reasonable times, to have access to and to copy from, all books, ledgers, accounts, correspondence, memoranda, and other records and documents in the possession or under the control of said defendants, including all affiliated persons, corporations, associations, and organizations, at Rangeley, Maine, or elsewhere, relating to any matters contained in this decree. Any such authorized representative of the Secretary shall be permitted to interview officers or employees of any defendant, or any affiliate, regarding any such matters subject to the reasonable convenience of any of said officers or employees of said defendants, or affiliates, but without restraint or interference from any one of said defendants; and

(9) That the defendants refrain from, either directly or indirectly, in violation of said Act, disseminating information pertaining to the assembly, construction, or composition of orgone energy accumulator devices to be employed for therapeutic or prophylactic uses by man or for other animals.

/s/ John D. Clifford, Jr.
United States District Judge
for the District of Maine.

March 19, 1954.
2:45 P.M.

A true copy of original filed at 2:45 P.M. on March 19, 1954.
ATTEST:

/s/ Morris Cox
Clerk, United States District Court

3. Statement to Court and Press in Portland Maine, U.S.A., on July 16, 1955 at the Hearing on "Contempt of Court" Charge Against Wilhelm Reich M.D. and Michael Silvert, M.D.

All I have done in the past and may do in the future is being dictated by my responsibilities as a scientist, as a physician and as a responsible citizen. Permit me to rip open a piece of the IRON CURTAIN that hides the issue here. I am pleading "not guilty," of course. Guilty of contempt of truth and justice are these who have engineered this conflagration on the public scene, guilty of treason are those who have tried to destroy the Discovery of the Life Energy.

The question asked most frequently is: *WHY DID WILHELM REICH NOT APPEAR IN COURT IN MARCH 1954* to defend his case? I would like to tell now why I did not appear in court:

At first I was ready to go to court although it was perfectly clear from the complaint of the FDA that this was a well-set trap to kill my discovery and to get me into jail as a fraudulent person. The decision not to appear in court was made when a lawyer pointed out to me that TRUTH IS NOT THE PRIME OBJECTIVE IN AMERICAN COURT PROCEDURES. What counts, he said, is the process of LITIGATION. The one who litigates better wins. The truth may or may not come forth in these procedures.

The injunction itself proves the point:

a.) It is unconstitutional.

b.) As a fantastic product of sick minds it cannot be carried out.

c.) It gives an agency which supervises Foods, Drugs, and Cosmetics power over experimental basic scientific research. In looking through the nature of the trap I have of course denied, on principle, to both court and government the right to decide on matters of basic natural research. These matters can never be decided by litigation.

Now, I am by my very nature an experimental research man. I like to solve problems and I thrive emotionally on finding truth. When I heard what this lawyer said, my interest in finding out whether his statement was correct far outweighed the risk I took by not appearing in court. Also, at that early phase, though I knew that I was dealing with traitors to Truth and Justice, I was not prepared to meet the malignancy successfully. At that time I could not know that a few months later several hundred traitors would be cleaned out from the Department of Health and Welfare of which the FDA is a branch.

In the meantime a great deal has been found out with the result that I, who have discovered the Life Energy practically, am standing here today accused by traitors of contempt of court. This fact seems to prove the statement correct that only procedure and not the Truth counts in American courts.

However this is not the end of the story: Having found out the mechanisms by means of which truth and justice can lose out in two courts before four judges, having furthermore succeeded in finding the link of this mechanism to the Political Plague that besets our social life everywhere, I am now ready to proceed in public to expose the traitors who have shaken in honest, hardworking men the belief that truth and justice prevail in courts of justice.

I wish to state here briefly that this case is only one link, though a crucial one, in a chain of events precipitated in the USA and abroad by Moscow. They have changed their methods in a very dangerous manner. While they are talking peace and bargain *here*, they are busy there in a quite unsuspected place and with the help of frightened common people, to undermine and finally destroy our trust in each other, our confidence in the workings of decency, our hopes and our lives.

I am looking forward to the opportunity to reveal what I know about this in public. There is much to learn here.

I am proud to have stood my ground so far. What I have done I would do again in a similar situation. No threat of jail can alter here anything. To yield here would mean no less than to abandon Truth to the practices of the "Beria" type hoodlums, no matter whether Russian or American.

4. Proposal

NEW LAWS NEEDED TO RESTRAIN PATHOLOGICAL POWER DRUNKENNESS — PROPOSED BY WILHELM REICH, M.D.

Wisdom gained in clouds
is clouded wisdom —
True wisdom is rooted in
seething reality.

WR 1956.

First: On Lawfulness of Laws

All new laws proclaimed to govern human conduct in a growing and developing planetary society are designed to secure life, liberty and happiness for all. They must be *Lawful* laws. They must not be unlawful laws. Laws must be based on facts, not on opinions; on truth, not on falsehood. Unlawful orders are automatically null and void.

Second: On Wellsprings of Social Existence

Love, Work and Knowledge are the wellsprings of our existence. They are the wellsprings of our life, liberty and happiness with equal justice for all. They shall govern the future planetary social organization.

Third: On Life-Necessary Work

Life-necessary work and *naturally grown interhuman relationships* shall determine the lawfulness of laws, social responsibility and social guidance. Life-necessary work and natural interhuman relationships comprise *Natural Work Democracy*.

Fourth: On Unlawful Laws

Laws and orders which contradict, impede, destroy or otherwise endanger the development of self-determination and violate peaceful development, shall be null and void.

Fifth: On Protection of Truth

Social battles for truthful procedure are lawful battles. Procedures for elimination, evasion, eradication or falsification of factual truth are unlawful.

5-1. Juries, judges, magistrates and other judicial persons or bodies must render their verdicts fully informed on all pertinent facts involved in the case. Verdicts based on untruth, suppression or falsification of evidence are unlawful and intrinsically void.

5-2. Social administrations must not interfere with the search for factual truth and basic new knowledge.

5-3. *Learning is the only authority on Knowledge of the Future.* There are no authorities in undisclosed realms of nature or New Knowledge. Learning and improving ability to find and correct one's own mistakes are, among others, true characteristics of bona fide basic research.

5-4. Scientific tools and publications based on learning and search for new knowledge must never be controlled, censored or in any other way molested by any administrative agency of society. Such acts are unlawful, only perpetrated in dictatorships.

5-5. Bona fide scientists, i.e., men and women engaged in learning and searching for new knowledge, must not be ever dragged into courts of justice for their opinions or be harassed by commercial or political interests of the day.

5-6. The citizen has the constitutional right to ignore complaints against him *IF* he can prove to the satisfaction of the court that:

A. He has informed the court of his reasons for ignoring the complaint;

B. His reasons to ignore the complaint were weighty, based on proof of fraudulent presentations of fact, on motives to complain other than bona fide grievance, on a competitive conspiracy using illegal means, etc.;

C. The Judge has been victimized, misled, or otherwise prejudiced;

D. Responding to the complaint would have meant inevitable undeserved disaster.

"A" in conjunction with either of "B," "C" or "D" constitute sufficient reason lawfully not to appear in court as defendant.

5-7. *Disclosure of scientific information must not be forced* under any circumstances, by anyone or for whatever reasons.

5-8. *New knowledge requires new administrative laws.* Laws applicable in one defined realm cannot be applied in a different realm of social or natural functioning.

5-9. *Judicial errors must be realized and corrected.* They must not be perpetuated to the detriment of justice. Perpetuation of judicial errors for whatever reason is unlawful.

5-10. *Judicial procedures which are shown to hamper truth and fact and run counter to the very meaning of due process of law,* which is to safeguard indivisible factual truth, *are to be revised or abolished.*

a) Judges acting in courts of justice are responsible for the safety of truth and fact from any interference by expediency, negligence, political or commercial interests. Judges are administrators of truth and justice, and nothing else.

b) *There is no excuse whatever for judicial error.* The innocent must not fall prey to faulty procedure. Judges are as law officers subjected to the *Boomerang Law* in case of gross neglect of justice. They shall suffer what they meted out unjustly.

c) Judges are to be appointed on the basis of their judicial expertness, not on any other, political, racial, commercial or similar grounds.

d) Judges may only interpret statutory laws. They may not legislate themselves under our Constitution.

e) Judges must not be beneficiaries or advocates of religious, commercial or political enterprises. Their only realm of functioning is jurisprudence and jurisdiction under the Constitution of the U. S. A., in pursuit of common law decency, truth, fact, above-board activity, absence of deceit, etc.

Sixth: On Enemies of Mankind

Individuals, legal persons, organizations and social groupings which advocate or operate on lines adverse to common natural laws or laws under the Constitution, or I to IV of the "New Law," shall be excluded from determining the course of society.

They may *talk* against work democracy, but they may *not act* against the socially-organized rule of Love, Work and Knowledge. As *ENEMIES OF MANKIND*, they may not be elected to public office. Those lawfully declared to be Enemies of Mankind, if insisting on acts of fiendship against the self-rule of Love, Work and Knowledge, shall be subjected to the Seventh Law.

Seventh: On Boomerang Justice

Officers of the law, officials of a self-governing society and other highly placed responsible citizens (of the Planet Earth) shall be, if necessary, called before courts of justice to answer charges of *"treason to mankind."* If convicted upon *factual* evidence of treason, they shall be subjected to the *BOOMERANG LAW*: They shall suffer themselves whatever they may have planned against the planetary citizens who through safeguarding *Love, Work* and *Knowledge* as the natural foundations of a self-governing social system have secured true justice at the very source of social life.

Eighth: On Striking Obsolete Laws

In order to secure social rational progress and to prevent the development of irrational human adherence to untimely or hampering tradition, statutory laws which are no longer representing or reflecting living, actual reality shall be stricken from the statute books ("Statutory Rape").

Ninth: On Safety of Natural Love

Natural love functions leading up to and expressed in natural courting mating shall be considered *natural functions at the very basis of man's bioenergetic existence*. They shall be protected and secured by special laws. Human activities adverse to this basic natural function shall be prohibited by lawful procedures insofar as they tend to impede or destroy these natural love functions in infants, children, adolescents and grown-ups. Abuse of natural love functions for political, conspiratorial, commercial, pathological (unnatural) and similar purposes is in violation of this law.

Tenth: On Supervision of Unlawfulness of Legal Procedures

A special legislative body in Congress shall be established by way of amendment of the Constitution to constantly survey and supervise judiciary and law enforcement procedures. This committee shall be responsible to the people and their organizations of life-necessary work, not only for security of justice, truth and fact; it shall safeguard the constitutional laws which guarantee the development of society to ever more complete self-government of nations, organizations and responsible citizens.

LENNY BRUCE

My Obscenity Trial

The first time I got arrested for obscenity was in San Francisco.
I used a ten-letter word onstage. Just a word in passing.

"Lenny, I wanna talk to you," the police officer said. "You're
under arrest. That word you said—you can't say that in a public
place. It's against the law to say it and do it."

They said it was a favorite homosexual practice. Now that I
found strange. I don't relate that word to a homosexual practice.
It relates to any contemporary chick I know, or would know, or
would love, or would marry.

Then we get into the patrol wagon, and another police officer
says, "You know, I got a wife and kid . . . "

"I don't wanna hear that crap," I interrupted.

"Whattaya mean?"

"I just don't wanna hear that crap, that's all. Did your wife
ever do that to you?"

"No."

"Did anyone?"

"No."

"Did you ever say the word?"

"No."

"You never said the word one time? Let ye cast the first
stone, man."

"Never."

"How long have you been married?"

"Eighteen years."

"You ever chippied on your wife?"

"Never."

"Never chippied on your wife one time in eighteen years?"

"Never."

"Then I love *you* . . . because you're a spiritual guy, the kind
of husband I would like to have been . . . but if you're lying,
you'll spend some good time in purgatory . . . "

Now we get into court. They swear me in.

THE COP: "Your Honor, he said blah-blah-blah."

THE JUDGE: "He said *blah*-blah-blah! Well, I got grandchil-
dren . . . "

Oh, Christ, there we go again.

"Your Honor," the cop says, "I couldn't believe it, there's a guy on the stage in front of women in a mixed audience, saying blah-blah-blah . . . "

THE DISTRICT ATTORNEY: "Look at him, he's smug! I'm not surprised he said blah-blah-blah . . . "

"He'll probably say blah-blah-blah again, he hasn't learned his lesson . . . "

And then I dug something: they sort of *liked* saying blah-blah-blah.

(*Even* THE BAILIFF:) "What'd he say?"

"He said blah-blah-blah."

"Shut up, you blah-blah-blah."

The actual trial took place in the early part of March 1962. The People of the State of California vs. Lenny Bruce. The jury consisted of four men and eight women. The first witness for the prosecution was James Ryan, the arresting officer. Deputy District Attorney Albert Wollenberg, Jr., examined him.

Q: . . . And on the night of October the fourth did you have any special assignment in regard to [the Jazz Workshop]?

A: I was told by my immediate superior, Sergeant Solden, that he had received a complaint from the night before that the show at this club was of a lewd nature, and that some time during the evening I was to go in and see the show and find out what the complaint was all about . . .

Q: And during the course of his act did any . . . talking about an establishment known as Ann's 440 arise?

A: Yes . . . during this particular episode at the 440 he was talking to some other person, who, as near as I can recall, I think was either his agent or another entertainer. And during this conversation . . . one person said, "I can't work at the 440 because it's overrun with cocksuckers."

Q: . . . Now, after this statement, what then occurred?

A: A little later on in the same show the defendant was talking about the fact that he distrusted ticket takers and the person that handled the money, and that one of these days a man was going to enter the premises and situate himself where he couldn't be seen by the ticket taker, and then he was going to expose himself and on the end of it he was going to have a sign hanging that read, "When We Reach $1500 The Guy In The Front Booth Is Going To Kiss It."

Q: . . . Now, subsequent to the statement about hanging a sign on a person exposed, was there any further conversation by the defendant while giving his performance?

A: Yes. Later in the show he went into some kind of chant where he used a drum, or a cymbal and a drum, for a tempo, and the dialog was supposed to be . . .

MR. BENDICH (*my attorney,* ALBERT BENDICH): I'll object to what the witness infers the conversation or dialog was supposed to import, your Honor. The witness is to testify merely to what he heard.

THE COURT: Sustained.

MR. WOLLENBERG: . . . Can you give us the exact words or what your recollection of those words were?

A: Yes. During that chant he used the words "I'm coming, I'm coming, I'm coming," and . . .

Q: Did he just do it two or three times, "I'm coming, I'm coming, I'm coming"?

A: Well, this one part of the show lasted a matter of a few minutes.

Q: And then was anything else said by the defendant?

A: Then later he said, "Don't come in me. Don't come in me."

Q: Now, did he do this just one or two times?

A: No. As I stated, this lasted for a matter of a few minutes.

Q: Now, as he was saying this, was he using the same voice as he was giving this chant?

A: . . . Well, this particular instance where he was saying "I'm coming, I'm coming," he was talking in a more normal tone of voice. And when he stated, or when he said "Don't come in me. Don't come in me," he used a little higher-pitched voice . . .

Mr. Bendich now cross-examined.

Q: Officer Ryan, would you describe your beat to us, please?

A: . . . It takes in both sides of Broadway from Mason to Battery.

Q: And in the course of your duties, Officer, you have the responsibility and obligation to observe the nature of the shows being put on in the various clubs in this area?

A: Yes, sir, I do.

Q: Would you tell us, Officer, what some of those clubs are? . . . Then I'll ask you some questions about the content of the work that is done there . . .

MR. WOLLENBERG: Well, that's irrelevant and immaterial, if your Honor, please, other than that they are on his beat, the content of the work done there.

MR. BENDICH: We're talking about community standards, your Honor.

THE COURT: [Mr. Wollenberg's objection] overruled. Now, the question is just to name some of the establishments. (*The officer named several night clubs.)*

Q: . . . Now, officer, you testified, I believe, on direct examination that you had a specific assignment with reference to the **Lenny Bruce** performance at the Jazz Workshop, is that correct?

A: That's correct.

Q: Tell us, please, if you will, what your specific assignment was.

A: My assignment was to watch the performance of the show that evening.

Q: What were you looking for?

A: Any lewd conversation or lewd gestures or anything that might constitute an objectionable show.

Q: What were your standards for judging, Officer, whether a show was objectionable or not?

A: Well, any part of the show that would violate any Police or Penal Code sections that we have . . .

MR. BENDICH: . . . [You have previously described] the clubs that are situated upon the beat that you patrol, and among other clubs you listed the Moulin Rouge. . . . And would you be good enough to tell us, Officer Ryan, what the nature of the entertainment material presented in the Moulin Rouge is?

A: Primarily a burlesque-type entertainment.

Q: Strip shows are put on . . . ?

A: That's correct.

Q: And, as a matter of fact, Officer Ryan, there is a housewives' contest put on at the Moulin Rouge with respect to superior talent in stripping, is there not?

a: I don't know if it just encompasses housewives; I know they have an amateur night.

Q: Now, Officer Ryan, will you tell us a little bit about what occurs during amateur night?

A: Well, just what it says, I believe. Girls that have had little or no experience in this type of entertainment are given a chance to try their hand at it.

Q: To try their hand at it, and they try their body a little, too, don't they?

MR. WOLLENBERG: If your Honor please, counsel is argumentative.

THE COURT: Yes. Let us not be facetious, Mr. Bendich.

MR. BENDICH: I will withdraw it. I don't intend to be facetious.

Q: Officer Ryan, will you describe for the ladies and gentlemen of the jury, if you will, please, what the ladies who are engaged in the competition on amateur night do?

MR. WOLLENBERG: If your Honor please, this is irrelevant.

THE COURT: Overruled.

THE WITNESS: Well, they come on the stage and then to the accompaniment of music they do a dance.

MR. BENDICH: And in the course of doing this dance, they take their clothes off, is that correct?

A: Partially, yes.

Q: Now, these are the amateur competitors and performers, is that correct?

A: That's correct.

Q: Tell us, please, if you will, what the professional performers do.

A: Approximately the same thing, with maybe a little more finesse or a little more ability, if there is ability in that line.

Q: And you have witnessed these shows, is that correct, Officer Ryan?

A: I have, yes.

Q: And these are shows which are performed in the presence of mixed audiences, representing persons of both sexes, is that correct?

A: That's true.

Q: Now, Officer Ryan, in the course of your official duties in patrolling your beat you have occasion, I take it, to deal with another club, the name of which is Finocchio's, is that correct?

A: That's true.

Q: And you have had occasion to observe the nature of the performances in Finocchio's, is that true? . . . Would you be good enough, Officer Ryan, to describe to the ladies and gentlemen of the jury what the nature of the entertainment presented in Finocchio's is?

A: Well, the entertainers are female impersonators.

Q: May I ask you to describe for the jury what female impersonators are?

A: A male that dresses as a woman, and the type of show they put on is, I guess, a pretty average show, other than the fact that they are female impersonators. They have songs that they sing, dances that they do, and so forth.

Q: . . . And can you describe the mode of dress, Officer, of the female impersonators in Finocchio's?

A: Well, they wear different types of costumes. Some of them are quite full, and others are . . .

Q: Quite scanty?

A: Not "quite scanty," I wouldn't say, no, but they are more near to what you'd call scanty, yes.

Q: "More near to what you'd call scanty." Well, as a matter

of fact, Officer, isn't it true that men appear in the clothes of women, and let's start up — or should I say, down at the bottom — wearing high-heeled shoes?

MR. WOLLENBERG: Oh, if your Honor please, he's already answered that they're wearing the clothes of women. That covers the subject. We're not trying Finocchio's here today.

MR. BENDICH: We're certainly not trying Finocchio's but we are trying Lenny Bruce on a charge of obscenity, and we have a question of contemporary community standards that has to be established, and I am attempting to have Officer Ryan indicate what the nature of the community standards on his beat are.

THE COURT: . . . Well, ask him to be more specific.

MR. BENDICH: Very well. Will you please be more specific, Officer Ryan, with regard to describing the nature of the scantily dressed female impersonators in terms of their attire.

A: They have all different kinds of costumes. Now, which particular one — I never paid that much attention to it, really.

Q: Well, they appear in black net stockings, do they not?

A: I imagine they do at times.

Q: And they appear in tights, do they not?

A: On occasion, yes.

Q: And they appear wearing brassieres, do they not?

A: That's correct.

Q: I think that's specific enough. . . . Officer Ryan, in the course of your observations of the strip shows in the Moulin Rouge, have you ever had occasion to become sexually stimulated?

A: No, sir.

MR. WOLLENBERG: I'm going to object to this and move to strike the answer as incompetent, irrelevant, and immaterial, if your Honor please.

THE COURT: The answer is in; it may remain.

MR. BENDICH: Were you sexually stimulated when you witnessed Lenny Bruce's performance?

MR. WOLLENBERG: Irrelevant and immaterial, especially as to this officer, your Honor.

THE COURT: Overruled.

THE WITNESS: No, sir.

MR. BENDICH: Did you have any conversation with anyone in the Jazz Workshop on the night that you arrested Mr. Lenny Bruce?

A: No.

Q: Officer Ryan, you're quite familiar with the term "cocksucker" are you not?

A: I have heard it used, yes.

Q: As a matter of fact, Officer Ryan, it was used in the police station on the night that Lenny Bruce was booked there, was it not?

A: No, not to my knowledge.

Q: As a matter of fact, it is frequently used in the police station, is it not?

MR. WOLLENBERG: That's irrelevant and immaterial, if your Honor please. What's used in a police station or in a private conversation between two people is completely different from what's used on a stage in the theater.

THE COURT: Well, a police station, of course, is a public place.

MR. WOLLENBERG: That's correct, your Honor.

THE COURT: As to the police station, the objection is overruled.

MR. BENDICH: You may answer, Officer.

A: Yes, I have heard it used.

Q: Yes, you have heard the term used in a public place known as the police station. Now, Officer Ryan, there is nothing obscene in and of itself about the word "cock," is there?

MR. WOLLENBERG: I'm going to object to this as being irrelevant and immaterial, what this man feels.

THE COURT: Sustained.

MR. BENDICH: Just two last questions, Officer Ryan. You laughed at Lenny Bruce's performance the night that you watched, did you not?

A: No, I didn't.

Q: You didn't have occasion to laugh?

A: No, I didn't.

Q: Did you observe whether the audience was laughing?

A: Yes, I did.

Q: And they were laughing, were they not?

A: At times, yes.

Q: And no one in the audience made any complaint to you, though you were in uniform standing in the club?

A: No one, no.

MR. BENDICH: No further questions.

MR. WOLLENBERG *re-examined the witness.*

Q: Now, Officer, when the word, "cocksucker," was used during the performance, did anybody laugh?

A: Not right at that instant, no.

Q: . . . Now, in Finocchio's, have you ever heard the word "cocksucker" used from the stage?

A: No, sir, I never have.

Q: . . . Now, at the Moulin Rouge, Officer, they do have a comedian as well as a strip show, isn't that right?

A: That's right.

Q: Have you ever heard the comedian at the Moulin Rouge use the term, "cocksucker"?

A: No, sir, never.

Q: Did you have a conversation with the defendant Bruce after his performance?

A: Yes, I did.

Q: And where was that?

A: In front of the Jazz Workshop.

Q: . . . Was that in relation to any of the terms used?

A: Yes, it was.

Q: And what was that?

A: I asked the defendant at that time, "Didn't I hear you use the word 'cocksucker' in your performance? And he says, 'Yes, I did.'"

Later, MR. WOLLENBERG *examined the other police officer,* SERGEANT JAMES SOLDEN.

Q: . . . And did you have occasion while in that area (the Jazz Workshop) to see the defendant Bruce? . . . Did you have a conversation with him?

A: I had a conversation with Mr. Bruce as we led—took him from the Jazz Workshop to the patrol wagon . . . I spoke to Mr. Bruce and said, "Why do you feel that you have to use the word 'cocksucker' to entertain people in a public night spot?" And Mr. Bruce's reply to me, was, "Well there are a lot of cocksuckers around, aren't there? What's wrong with talking about them?"

MR. BENDICH (*opening statement to the jury*): To tell you what it is that I am going to attempt to prove to you in the course of the presentation of the defense case. . . . I am going to prove through the testimony of several witnesses who will take the stand before you, ladies and gentlemen of the jury, that Mr. Bruce gave a performance in the Jazz Workshop on the night of October fourth last year which was a show based on the themes of social criticism, based upon an analysis of various forms of conventional hypocrisy, based upon the technique of satire which is common in the heritage of English letters and, as a matter of fact, in the heritage of world literature. We are going to prove, ladies and gentlemen of the jury, that the nature of Mr. Bruce's performance on the night of October the fourth was in the great tradition of social satire, related intimately to the kind of social satire to be found in the works of such great authors as Aristophanes, Jonathan Swift . . .

MR. WOLLENBERG: I'm going to object. Aristophanes is not testifying here, your Honor, or any other authors, and I'm going to object to that at this time as improper argument.

MR. BENDICH: Your Honor, I didn't say I would call Mr. Aristophanes.

THE COURT: I don't think you could, very well . . .

It seems fitting that the first witness for the defense was RALPH J. GLEASON, *a brilliant jazz critic and columnist for the* San Francisco Chronicle. GLEASON *was my first real supporter, the first one who really went out on a limb for me, to help my career.*

MR. BENDICH *examined him.*

Q: . . . Mr. Gleason, will you describe for us, if you will, please, what the themes of Mr. Bruce's work were during the appearance in the Workshop for which he was arrested?

MR. WOLLENBERG: I will object to just the themes, your Honor. He can give the performance or recite what was said, but the "themes" is ambiguous.

THE COURT: Overruled.

THE WITNESS: The theme of the performance on the night in question was a social criticism of stereotypes and of the hypocrisy of contemporary society. . . . He attempted to demonstrate to the audience a proposition that's familiar to students of semantics, which is that words have been given, in our society, almost a magic meaning that has no relation to the facts, and I think that he tried in the course of this show that evening to demonstrate that there is no harm inherent in words themselves.

Q: . . . How important, if at all, was the theme of semantics with reference to the entire show given on the evening in question?

A: In my opinion, it was very important — vital to it.

Q: And what dominance or predominance, if any, did the theme of semantics occupy with respect to the content of the entire show on the night in question?

A: Well, it occupied an important part in the entire performance, not only in the individual routines, but in the totality of the program.

Q: Yes. Now, with respect to the rest of the program, Mr. Gleason, would you tell us about some of the other themes, and perhaps illustrate something about them if you can, in addition to the theme of semantics which Mr. Bruce worked with?

A: Well, to the best of my recollection there was a portion of the show in which he attempted to show satirically the hypocrisy inherent in the licensing of a ticket taker who had a criminal record for particularly abhorrent criminal acts and demanding a bond on him . . .

MR. GLEASON *was asked to read to the jury an excerpt from an article in* Commonweal, *a Catholic magazine. The article was by* NAT HENTOFF, *who's Jewish, so it doesn't really count.* GLEASON *read:*

"It is in Lenny Bruce—and only in him—that there has emerged a cohesively 'new' comedy of nakedly honest moral rage at the deceptions all down the line in our society. Bruce thinks of himself as an ethical relativist and shares Pirandello's preoccupation with the elusiveness of any absolute, including absolute truth.

"His comedy ranges through religion-in-practice ('What would happen if Christ and Moses appeared one Sunday at Saint Patrick's?'); the ultimate limitations of the white liberal; the night life of the hooker and her view of the day; and his own often scarifying attempts to make sense of his life in a society where the quicksand may lie just underneath the sign that says: 'Take Shelter When the Civilian Defense Alarm Sounds.'

"Bruce, however, does not turn a night club into Savonarola's church. More than any others of the 'new wave,' Bruce is a thoroughly experienced performer, and his relentless challenges to his audience and to himself are intertwined with explosive pantomime, hilarious 'bits,' and an evocative spray of Yiddishisms, Negro and showbusiness argot, and his own operational semantics. Coursing through everything he does, however, is a serious search for values that are more than security blankets. In discussing the film *The Story of Esther Costello*, Bruce tells of the climactic rape scene: 'It's obvious the girl has been violated. . . . She's been deaf and dumb throughout the whole picture . . . All of a sudden she can hear again . . . and she can speak again. So what's the moral?' "

Later—after the judge had pointed something out to the Deputy District Attorney ("Mr. Wollenberg," he said, ". . . your shirttail is out.")—Mr. Gleason was asked to read to the jury a portion of an article by Arthur Gelb in The New York Times.

"The controversial Mr. Bruce, whose third visit to Manhattan this is, is the prize exhibit of the menagerie, and his act is billed 'for adults only.'

Presumably the management wishes to safeguard the dubious innocence of underage New Yorkers against Mr. Bruce's vocabulary, which runs to four-letter words, of which the most printable is Y. M. C. A. But there are probably a good many adults who will find him offensive, less perhaps for his Anglo-Saxon phrases than for his vitriolic attacks on such subjects as facile religion, the medical profession, the law, pseudo-liberalism, and Jack Paar. ('Paar has a God complex. He thinks he can create performers in six days,' Mr. Bruce is apt to confide.)

"Although he seems at times to be doing his utmost to antagonize his audience, Mr. Bruce displays such a patent air of morality beneath the brashness that his lapses in taste are often forgivable.

"The question, though, is whether the kind of derisive shock therapy he administers and the introspective freeform patter in which he indulges are legitimate nightclub fare, as far as the typical customer is concerned.

"It is necessary, before lauding Mr. Bruce for his virtues, to warn the sensitive and the easily shocked that no holds are barred at Basin Street East. Mr. Bruce regards the night-club stage as the 'last frontier' of uninhibited entertainment. He often carries his theories to their naked and personal conclusions and has earned for his pains the sobriquet 'sick.' He is a ferocious man who does not believe in the sanctity of motherhood or the American Medical Association. He even has an unkind word to say for Smokey the Bear. True, Smokey doesn't set forest fires, Mr. Bruce concedes. But he eats Boy Scouts for their hats.

"Mr. Bruce expresses relief at what he sees as a trend of 'people leaving the church and going back to God,' and he has nothing but sneers for what he considers the sanctimonious liberal who preaches but cannot practice genuine integration.

"Being on cozy terms with history and psychology, he can illustrate his point with the example of the early Romans, who thought there was 'something dirty' about Christians. 'Would you want your sister to marry one?'—he has one Roman ask another—and so on, down to the logical conclusions in present-day prejudice.

"At times Mr. Bruce's act, devoid of the running series of staccato jokes that are traditional to the night-club comic, seems like a salvationist lecture; it is biting, sardonic, certainly stimulating and quite often funny—but never in a jovial way. His mocking diatribe rarely elicits a comfortable belly laugh. It requires concentration. But there is much in it to wring a rueful smile and appreciative chuckle. There is even more to evoke a fighting gleam in the eye. There are also spells of total confusion.

"Since Mr. Bruce operates in a spontaneous, stream-of-consciousness fashion a good deal of the time, he is likely to tell you what he's thinking about telling you before he gets around to telling you anything at all . . ."

MR. BENDICH *resumed his line of questioning.*

Q: Mr. Gleason, would you tell us, please, what in your judgment the *predominant* theme of the evening's performance for which Mr. Bruce was arrested was?

A: Well, in a very real sense it's semantics—the search for the ultimate truth that lies beneath the social hypocrisy in which we live. All his performances relate to this.

Q: Mr. Gleason, as an expert in this field, would you charac-

154

terize the performance in question as serious in intent and socially significant?

MR. WOLLENBERG: I will object to this as irrelevant and immaterial.

THE COURT: Overruled.

THE WITNESS: Yes, I would characterize it as serious.

MR. BENDICH: And how would you characterize the social significance, if any, of that performance?

A: Well, I would characterize this performance as being of high social significance, in line with the rest of his performances.

Q: Mr. Gleason, what in your opinion, based upon your professional activity and experience in the field of popular culture, and particularly with reference to humor, what in your opinion is the relation between the humor of Lenny Bruce and that of other contemporary humorists, such as Mort Sahl, Shelley Berman, Mike and Elaine?

MR. WOLLENBERG: That's immaterial, your Honor, what the comparison is between him and any other comedian.

THE COURT: Objection overruled.

THE WITNESS: Mr. Bruce attacks the fundamental structure of society and these other comedians deal with it superficially.

MR. BENDICH: Mr. Gleason, you have already testified that you have seen personally a great many Lenny Bruce performances, and you are also intimately familiar with his recorded works and other comic productions. Has your prurient interest ever been stimulated by any of Mr. Bruce's work?

A: Not in the slightest.

MR. WOLLENBERG: I will object to that as calling for the ultimate issue before this jury.

THE COURT: The objection will be overruled . . . You may answer the question.

THE WITNESS: I have not been excited, my prurient or sexual interest has not been aroused by any of Mr. Bruce's performances.

The complete transcript of my San Francisco trial runs 350 pages. The witnesses — not one of whose sexual interest had ever been aroused by any of my night-club performances — described one after another, what they remembered of my performance on the night in question at the Jazz Workshop, and interpreted its social significance according to his or her own subjectivity.

For example, during the cross-examination, the following dialog ensued between MR. WOLLENBERG *and* LOU GOTTLIEB, *a Ph.D. who's with the Limeliters:*

Q: Doctor, you say you have heard Mr. Bruce in Los Angeles?
A: Yes.

Q: And what was the last remark he makes on leaving the stage in his show in Los Angeles?

A: I must say that Mr. Bruce's last remarks have varied at every performance that I have ever witnessed.

Q: Did he make any reference to eating something in his last remarks in Los Angeles when you heard him perform?

A: No.

Q: . . . Now, Doctor, you say the main theme of Mr. Bruce is to get laughter?

A: That's the professional comedian's duty.

Q: I see. And do you see anything funny in the word "cocksucker"?

A: . . . To answer that question with "Yes" or "No" is impossible, your Honor.

MR. WOLLENBERG: I asked you if you saw anything funny in that word.

THE COURT: You may answer it "Yes" or "No" and then explain your answer.

THE WITNESS: I found it extremely unfunny as presented by Mr. Wollenberg, I must say, but I can also —

THE COURT: All right, wait a minute, wait a minute. I have tolerated a certain amount of activity from the audience because I knew that it is difficult not to react at times, but this is not a show, you are not here to be entertained. Now, if there's any more of this sustained levity, the courtroom will be cleared. And the witness is instructed not to argue with counsel but to answer the questions . . .

THE WITNESS: I do not [see anything funny in that word], but as Mr. Bruce presents his performances he creates a world in which normal dimensions . . . become — how shall I say? Well, they are transmuted into a grotesque panorama of contemporary society, into which he places slices of life, phonographically accurate statements that come out of the show-business world . . . and sometimes the juxtaposition of the generally fantastic frame of reference that he is able to create and the startling intrusion of slices of life in terms of language that is used in these kinds of areas, has extremely comic effect.

Q: . . . Doctor, because an agent uses that term when he talks to his talent, you find nothing wrong with using it in a public place because you're relating a conversation between yourself and your agent? This excuses the use of that term?

A: What excuses the use of that term, Mr. Wollenberg, in my opinion, is its unexpectedness in the fantastic world that is the frame of reference, the world which includes many grotesqueries that Mr. Bruce is able to establish. Then when you get a phonographic reproduction of a snatch of a conversation, I find that this has comic effect very frequently.

Q: Do you mean "phonographic" or "photographic?"

A: "Phonographic." I mean reproducing the actual speech verbatim with the same intonation and same attitudes and everything else that would be characteristic of, let's say, a talent agent of some kind.

Q: I see. In other words, the changing of the words to more — well, we might use genteel — terms, would take everything away from that, is that right?

A: It wouldn't be phonographically accurate. It would lose its real feel; there would be almost no point.

Q. . . . And taking out that word and putting in the word "homosexual" or "fairy," that would take away completely, in your opinion, from this story and make it just completely another one?

A: I must say it would.

Similarly, MR. WOLLENBERG *cross-examined* DR. DON GEIGER, *associate professor and chairman of the department of speech at the University of California in Berkeley; also author of a few books, including* Sound, Sense and Performance of Literature, *as well as several scholarly articles in professional journals.*

Q: . . . And what does the expression "I won't appear there because it's overrun with cocksuckers" infer to you?

A: "I won't go there because it's filled with homosexuals."

Q: I see. And does the word "cocksucker" denote any beauty as distinguished from the word homosexual?

A: I couldn't possibly answer that, I think. That is, you would have to provide a context for it, and then one could answer that. I would say this about it . . . that "homosexual" is a kind of neutral, scientific term which might in a given context itself have a freight of significance or beauty or artistic merit. But it's less likely to than the word "cocksucker," which is closer to colloquial, idiomatic expression.

Later, KENNETH BROWN, *a high school English teacher, testified as to his reaction to the "to come" part of my performance:*

THE WITNESS: The impression is, he was trying to get over a point about society, the inability to love, the inability to perform sexual love in a creative way. The routine then would enter a dialog between a man and a woman and they were having their sexual difficulties at orgasm in bed; at least, one of them was. And one said, "Why can't you come?" And, "Is it because you don't love me? Is it because you can't love me?" And the other one said, "Why, you know me, this is where I'm hung up. I have problems here." And that was enough to give me the impression that—with the other things in context that were going on before and after—that he was talking, dissecting our problems of relating to each other, man and woman. . . Great comics throughout literature have always disguised by comedy, through laughter, through jokes, an underlying theme which is very serious, and perhaps needs laughter because it is also painful . . .

MR. BENDICH: May I ask you this question, Mr. Brown: On the basis of your professional training and experience, do you think that the work of Mr. Bruce as you know it, and in particular the content of Mr. Bruce's performance on the night of October fourth, for which he was arrested, for which he is presently here in this courtroom on trial, bears a relation to the themes and the fashion in which those themes are presented in the works which we have listed here [*Lysistrata* by Aristophanes; *Gargantua and Pantagruel* by Rabelais; *Gulliver's Travels* by Jonathan Swift]?

A: I see a definite relationship, certainly.

Q: Would you state, please, what relationship you see and how you see it?

MR. WOLLENBERG: I think he hasn't qualified as an expert on this, your Honor.

THE COURT: Well, he may state what the relationship is that he sees.

THE WITNESS: These works use often repulsive techniques and vocabulary to make—to insist—that people will look at the whole of things and not just one side. These artists wish not to divide the world in half and say one is good and one is bad and avoid the bad and accept the good, but you must, to be a real and whole person, you must see all of life and see it in a balanced, honest way. I would include Mr. Bruce, certainly, in his intent, and he has success in doing this, as did Rabelais and Swift.

At one point during the trial, a couple of 19-year-old college students were admonished by the judge; they had been distributing the following leaflet outside the courtroom:

WELCOME TO THE FARCE!

Lenny Bruce, one of America's foremost comedians and social critics, is at this moment playing on unwilling part as a straight man in a social comedy put on by the City and County of San Francisco.

Incongruously, in our urbane city, this is a poor provincial farce, insensitively played by some of the city's most shallow actors.

Bruce may be imaginative, but the dull-witted, prudish lines of the police department are not, neither are the old-maidish lyrics of section 311.6 of the California Penal Code,

which in genteel, puritan prose condemns the users of — — —
— — — — and — — — — — — and other common expressions
to play a part in the dreary melodrama of "San Francisco Law
Enforcement."

Really, we are grown up now. With overpopulation, human
misery, and the threat of war increasing, we need rather more
adult performances from society.

You know, and I know, all about the hero's impure thoughts.
We've probably had them ourselves. Making such a fuss isn't
convincing at all—it lacks psychological realism—as do most
attempts to find a scapegoat for sexual guilt feelings.

Forgive Lenny's language. Most of us use it at times; most
of us even use the things and perform the acts considered
unprintable and unspeakable by the authors of (Section 311.6
of the Penal Code of the State of California), though most of
us are not nearly frank enough to say so.

Lenny has better things to do than play in this farce; the
taxpayers have better uses for their money; and the little old
ladies of both sexes who produce it *should* have better amuse-
ments.

With a nostalgic sigh, let's pull down the curtain on *People
vs. Bruce* and its genre; and present a far more interesting
and fruitful play called *Freedom of Speech*. It would do our
jaded ears good.

*The writer and distributor of the leaflet were properly chastised
by the judge. And so the trial continued.*

One of the witnesses for the defense was CLARENCE KNIGHT,
*who had been an assistant district attorney for a couple of years
in Tulare County, California, and was deputy district attorney for
four years in San Mateo, where he evaluated all pornography
cases that were referred to the district attorney's office. He had
passed on "probably between 200 and 250 separate items of
material in regard to the pornographic or nonpornographic
content thereof."*

*As with the others, his prurient interests were not aroused by
my performance at the Jazz Workshop. In fact, he said, while
being cross-examined about the "cocksucker" reference: "In
my opinion, Mr. Wollenberg, it was the funniest thing Mr. Bruce
said that night."*

*Finally, I was called as a witness in my own behalf. I took the
stand, and* MR. BENDICH *examined me.*

Q: Mr. Bruce, Mr. Wollenberg yesterday said [to Dr. Gottlieb]
specifically that you had said, "Eat it." Did you say that?

A: No, I never said that.

Q: What did you say, Mr. Bruce?

A: What did I say when?

159

Q: On the night of October fourth.

MR. WOLLENBERG: There's no testimony that Mr. Wollenberg said that Mr. Bruce said, "Eat it," the night of October fourth, if your Honor please.

THE COURT: The question is: What did he say?

THE WITNESS: I don't mean to be facetious. Mr. Wollenberg said, "Eat it." I said, "Kiss it."

MR. BENDICH: Do you apprehend there is a significant difference between the two phrases, Mr. Bruce?"

A: "Kissing it" and "eating it," yes, sir. Kissing my mother goodbye and eating my mother goodbye, there is a quantity of difference.

Q: Mr. Wollenberg also quoted you as saying, "I'm coming, I'm coming, I'm coming." Did you say that?

A: I never said that.

MR. BENDICH: . . . Mr. Bruce, do you recall using the term "cocksucker"?

A: Yes.

Q: Can you recall accurately now how you used that term?

A: You mean accuracy right on the head—total recall?

Q: Yes, Mr. Bruce.

A: If a "the" and an "an" are changed around, no. I don't have that exact, on-the-head recall. That's impossible; it's impossible. I defy anyone to do it. That's impossible.

Q: Mr. Bruce, if a "the" and an "an" were turned around, as you have put it, would that imply a significant difference in the characterization of what was said that evening?

A: Yes, yes.

Q: Are you saying, Mr. Bruce, that unless your words can be given in exact, accurate, verbatim reproduction, that your meaning cannot be made clear?

THE WITNESS: Yes, that is true. I would like to explain that. The "I am coming, I am coming" reference, which I never said—if we change—

THE COURT: Wait a minute, wait a minute. If you never said it, there's nothing to explain.

THE WITNESS: Whether that is a coming in the Second Coming or a different coming—

THE COURT: Well, you wait until your counsel's next question, now.

MR. BENDICH: Mr. Bruce, in giving your performance on the night of October fourth in the Jazz Workshop, as a consequence of which you suffered an arrest and as a result of which you are presently on trial on the charge of obscenity, did you intend to arouse anybody's prurient interest?

A: No.

There had been a tape recording made of that particular show. I listened to it, and when I came to the first word that San Francisco felt was taboo or a derogatory phrase, I stopped; then I went back about ten minutes before I even started to relate to that word, letting it resolve itself; I did this with the three specific things I was charged with, put them together and the resulting tape was played in court . . . this tape I made to question a father's concept of God who made the child's body but qualified the creativity by stopping it above the kneecaps and resuming it above the Adam's apple, thereby giving lewd connotations to mother's breast that fed us and father's groin that bred us.

Before the tape was played, MR. BENDICH *pointed out to the judge that "there are portions of this tape which are going to evoke laughter in the audience."*

THE COURT: I anticipated you; I was going to give that admonition.

MR. BENDICH: Well, what I was going to ask, your Honor, is whether the audience might not be allowed to respond naturally, given the circumstances that this is an accurate reproduction of a performance which is given at a night club; it's going to evoke comic response, and I believe that it would be asking more than is humanly possible of the persons in this courtroom not to respond humanly, which is to say, by way of laughter.

THE COURT: Well, as I previously remarked, this is not a theater and it is not a show, and I am not going to allow any such thing. I anticipated you this morning, and I was going to and I am now going to admonish the spectators that you are not to treat this as a performance. This is not for your entertainment. There's a very serious question involved here, the right of the People and the right of the defendant. And I admonish you that you are to control yourselves with regard to any emotions that you may feel during the hearing this morning or by the taping and reproduction of this tape. All right, you may proceed.

And the tape was played:

> . . . The hungry i. The hungry i has a Gray Line Tour and American Legion convention. They took all the bricks out and put in Saran Wrap. That's it. And Ferlinghetti is going to the Fairmont.
>
> You know, this was a little snobby for me to work. I just wanted to go back to Ann's. You don't know about that, do you? Do you share that recall with me? It's the first gig I ever worked up here, a place called Ann's 440, which was across the street. And I got a call, and I was working a burlesque gig with Paul Moore in the Valley. That's the cat on the piano

here, which is really strange, seeing him after all these years, and working together.

And the guy says, "There's a place in San Francisco but they've changed the policy."

"Well, what's the policy?"

"Well, I'm not there anymore, that's the main thing."

"Well, what kind of a show is it, man?"

"A bunch of cocksuckers, that's all. A damned fag show."

"Oh. Well, that is a pretty bizarre show. I don't know what I can do in that kind of a show."

"Well, no. It's—we want you to change all that."

"Well—I don't—that's a big gig. I can't just tell them to stop doing it."

Oh, I like you, and if sometimes I take poetic license with you and you are offended—now this is just with semantics, dirty words. Believe me, I'm not profound, this is something that I assume someone must have laid on me, because I do not have an original thought. I am screwed—I speak English—that's it. I was not born in a vacuum. Every thought I have belongs to somebody else. Then I must just take—ding-ding-ding—somewhere.

So I am not placating you by making the following statement. I want to help you if you have a dirty-word problem. There are none, and I'll spell it out logically to you.

Here is a toilet. Specifically—that's all we're concerned with, specifics—if I can tell you a dirty toilet joke, we must have a dirty toilet. That's what we're talking about, a toilet. If we take this toilet and boil it and it's clean, I can never tell you specifically a dirty toilet joke about this toilet. I can tell you a dirty toilet joke in the Milner Hotel, or something like that, but this toilet is a clean toilet now. Obscenity is a human manifestation. This toilet has no central nervous system, no level of consciousness. It is not aware; it is a dumb toilet; it cannot be obscene; it's impossible. If it could be obscene, it could be cranky, it could be a Communist toilet, a traitorous toilet. It can do none of these things. This is a dirty toilet here.

Nobody can offend you by telling you a dirty toilet story. They can offend you because it's trite; you have heard it many, many times.

Now, all of us have had a bad early toilet training—that's why we are hung up with it. All of us at the same time got two zingers—one for the police department and one for the toilet.

"All right, he made a kahkah, call a policeman. All right, OK, all right. Are you going to do that anymore? OK, tell the policeman he doesn't have to come up now."

All right, now we all got "Policeman, policeman, policeman," and we had a few psychotic parents who took it and rubbed it in our face, and those people for the most, if you search it out, are censors. Oh, true, they hate toilets with a passion, man. Do you realize if you got that wrapped around with a toilet, you'd hate it, and anyone who refers to it? It is dirty and uncomfortable to you.

Now, if the bedroom is dirty to you, then you are a true atheist, because if you have any of the mores, superstitions, if anyone in this audience believes that God made his body, and your body is dirty, the fault lies with the manufacturer. It's that cold, Jim, yeah.

You can do anything with the body that God made, and then you want to get definitive and tell me of the parts He made; I don't see that anywhere in any reference to any Bible. Yeah, He made it all; it's all clean or all dirty.

But the ambivalence comes from the religious leaders, who are celibates. The religious leaders are "what *should* be." They say they do not involve themselves with the physical. If we are good, we will be like our rabbi, or our nun, or our priests, and absolve, and finally put down the carnal and stop the race.

Now, dig, this is stranger. Everybody today in the hotel was bugged with Knight and Nixon. Let me tell you the truth. The truth is "what *is*." If "what is" is, you have to sleep eight, ten hours a day, that is the truth. A lie will be: People need no sleep at all. Truth is "what *is*." If every politician from the beginning is crooked, there is no crooked. But if you are concerned with a lie, "what should be"—and "what should be" is a fantasy, a terrible, terrible lie that someone gave the people long ago: This is what *should* be—and no one ever saw what should be, that you don't need any sleep and you can go seven years without sleep, so that all the people were made to measure up to that dirty lie. You know there's no crooked politicians. There's never a lie because there is never a truth.

I sent this agency a letter—they are bonded and you know what that means: anybody who is bonded never steals from you, nor could Earl Long. Ha! If the governor can, then the bond is really—yeah, that's some bond.

Very good. Write the letter. Blah, blah, blah, "I want this," blah, blah, blah, "ticket taker."

Get a letter back, get an answer back, Macon, Georgia:

"Dear Mr. Bruce: Received your letter," blah, blah, blah. "We have ticket sellers, bonded. We charge two-and-a-half dollars per ticket seller per hour. We would have to have some more details," blah, blah, blah, "Sincerely yours, Dean R. Moxie."

Dean R. Moxie . . . Dean R. Moxie . . . Moxie, buddy. Dean R. Moxie, from the Florida criminal correctional institution for the criminally insane, and beat up a spadefed junkie before he was thrown off the police force, and then was arrested for *schtupping* his stepdaughter. Dean R. Moxie. Hmmm.

All right, now, because I have a sense of the ludicrous, I sent him back an answer, Mr. Moxie. Dig, because I mean this is some of the really goodies I had in the letter, you know. He wants to know details.

"Dear Mr. Moxie: It would be useless to go into the definitive, a breakdown of what the duties will be, unless I can be sure that the incidents that have happened in the past will not be reiterated, such as ticket takers I have hired, who claimed they were harassed by customers who wanted their money back, such as the fop in San Jose who is suing me for being stabbed. Claims he was stabbed by an irate customer, and it

was a lie — it was just a manicure scissors, and you couldn't
see it because it was below the eyebrow, and when his eye
was open, you couldn't see it anyway. (So I tell him a lot of
problems like that.) And — oh yes, oh yeah — my father . . .
has been in three mental institutions, and detests the fact that
I am in the industry, and really abhors the fact that I have
been successful economically and has harassed some ticket
sellers, like in Sacramento he stood in line posing as a customer and, lightning flash, grabbed a handful of human feces
and crammed it in the ticket taker's face. And once in Detroit
he posed as a customer and he leaned against the booth so
the ticket seller could not see him, and he was exposing himself, and had a sign hanging from it, saying: 'When We Hit
$1500, The Guy Inside The Booth Is Going to Kiss It.' "

Now, you'd assume Dean R. Moxie, reading the letter,
would just reject that and have enough validity to grab it in
again.

"Dear Mr. Moxie: You know, of course, that if these facts
were to fall into the hands of some yellow journalists, this
would prove a deterrent to my career. So I'm giving you, you
know, my confessor, you know," blah, blah, blah. "Also, this
is not a requisite of a ticket seller, but I was wondering if I
could have a ticket seller who could be more than a ticket seller — a companion."

Really light now. This is really subtle.

"A companion, someone who I could have coffee with,
someone who is not narrow-minded like the — I had a stunning
Danish seaman type in Oregon, who misinterpreted me and
stole my watch."

Ha! Ha, is that heavy?

"Stole my watch. Am hoping to hear from you," blah, blah,
blah, "Lenny Bruce."

OK. Now I send him a booster letter.

"Dear Mr. Moxie: My attorney said I was mad for ever
confessing what has happened to me, you know, so I know
that I can trust you, and I have sent you some cologne."

Ha!

"Sent you some cologne, and I don't know what's happened . . ."

Isn't this beautiful?

"And I don't know what's happened to that naughty post-
man, naughtiest . . ."

Get this phraseology. I hadn't heard, you know. Now I get
an answer from him:

"We cannot insure the incidents that have happened in the
past will not reoccur. A ticket seller that would socialize is out
of the question."

I think this is beautiful.

"And I did not receive any cologne nor do we care for any.
Dean R. Moxie . . ."

(With drum and cymbal accompaniment.)

To is a preposition.
To is a preposition.
Come is a verb.

To is a preposition.
Come is a verb.
To is a preposition.
Come is a verb, the verb intransitive.
To come.
To come.

    I've heard these two words my whole adult life, and as a
kid when I thought I was sleeping.

To come.
To come.
It's been like a big drum solo.
Did you come?
Did you come?
Good.
Did you come good?
Did you come good?
Did you come good?
Did you come good?
Did you come good?
Did you come good?
Did you come good?
I come better with you, sweetheart,
than anyone else
in the whole goddamned world.
I really came so good.
I really came so good 'cause I love you.
I really came so good.
I come better with you sweetheart,
than anyone in the whole world.
I really came so good.
So good.
But don't come in me.
Don't come in me.
Don't come in me, me, me, me, me.
Don't come in me, me, me, me.
Don't come in me.
Don't come in me, me, me.
Don't come in me, me, me.
I can't come.
'Cause you don't love me,
that's why you can't come.
I love you, I just can't come;
that's my hang-up,
I can't come when I'm loaded,
all right?
'Cause you don't love me.
Just what the hell
is the matter with you?
What has that got to do with loving?
I just can't come.

    Now, if anyone in this room or the world finds those two
words decadent, obscene, immoral, amoral, asexual, the words
"to come" really make you feel uncomfortable, if you think I'm

rank for saying it to you, you the beholder think it's rank for listening to it, you probably can't come. And then you're of no
use, because that's the purpose of life, to re-create it.

MR. WOLLENBERG *called me to the witness stand for cross-
examination:*

Q: Mr. Bruce, had you a written script when you gave this
performance?
A: No.
MR. BENDICH: Objected to as irrelevant, your Honor.
THE COURT: The answer is "No"; it may stand.
MR. WOLLENBERG: I have no further questions.
THE COURT: All right, you may step down.
THE WITNESS: Thank you.
MR. BENDICH: The defense rests, your Honor.

The time had come for the judge to instruct the jury:

"The defendant is charged with violating Section 311.6 of the
Penal Code of the State of California, which provides:

Every person who knowingly sings or speaks any obscene
song, ballad, or other words in any public place is guilty of a
misdemeanor.
" 'Obscene' means to the average person, applying contemporary standards, the predominant appeal of the matter, taken as a
whole, is to prurient interest; that is, a shameful or morbid interest in nudity, sex, or excretion which goes substantially beyond
the customary limits of candor in description or representation
of such matters and is matter which is utterly without redeeming
social importance.
"The words 'average person' mean the average adult person
and have no relation to minors. This is not a question of what
you would or would not have children see, hear or read, because
that is beyond the scope of the law in this case and is not to be
discussed or considered by you.
" 'Sex' and 'obscenity' are not synonymous. In order to make
the portrayal of sex obscene, it is necessary that such portrayal
come within the definition given to you, and the portrayal must
be such that its dominant tendency is to deprave or corrupt the
average adult by tending to create a clear and present danger of
antisocial behavior.
"The law does not prohibit the realistic portrayal by an artist of
his subject matter, and the law may not require the author to put
refined language into the mouths of primitive people. The speech

166

of the performer must be considered in relation to its setting and the theme or themes of his production. The use of blasphemy, foul or coarse language, and vulgar behavior does not in and of itself constitute obscenity, although the use of such words may be considered in arriving at a decision concerning the whole of the production.

"To determine whether the performance of the defendant falls within the condemnation of the statute, an evaluation must be made as to whether the performance as a whole had as its dominant theme an appeal to prurient interest. Various factors should be borne in mind when applying this yardstick. These factors include the theme or themes of the performance, the degree of sincerity of purpose evident in it, whether it has artistic merit. If the performance is merely disgusting or revolting, it cannot be obscene, because obscenity contemplates the arousal of sexual desires.

"A performance cannot be considered utterly without redeeming social importance if it has literary, artistic, or esthetic merit, or if it contains ideas, regardless of whether they are unorthodox, controversial, or hateful, or redeeming social importance.

"In the case of certain crimes, it is necessary that in addition to the intended act which characterizes the offense, the act must be accompanied by a specific or particular intent without which such a crime may not be committed. Thus, in the crime charged here, a necessary element is the existence in the mind of the defendant of knowing that the material used in his production on October 4, 1961 was obscene, and that, knowing it to be obscene, he presented such material in a public place.

"The intent with which an act is done in manifested by the circumstances attending the act, the manner in which it is done, the means used, and the discretion of the defendant. In determining whether the defendant had such knowledge, you may consider reviews of his work which were available to him, stating that his performance had artistic merit and contained socially important ideas, or, on the contrary, that his performance did not have any artistic merit and did not contain socially important ideas."

The COURT CLERK *read the verdict:*

"In the Municipal Court of the City and County of San Francisco, State of California; the People of the State of California, Plaintiff, *vs* Lenny Bruce, Defendant; Verdict . . ."

I really started to sweat it out there.

"We, the jury in the above-entitled case, find the defendant not guilty of the offense charged, misdemeanor, to wit: violating Section 311.6 of the Penal Code of the State of California . . ."

"Ladies and gentlemen of the jury, is this your verdict?"

THE JURY: Yes.

THE COURT: All right. Do you desire the jury polled?

MR. WOLLENBERG: No, your Honor.

THE COURT: Would you ask the jury once again if that is their verdict?

THE CLERK: Ladies and gentlemen of the jury, is this your verdict?

THE JURY: Yes.

Isn't that weird!
It's like saying, "Are you sure?"

TIMOTHY LEARY

Episode & Postscript

On December 22, 1965, I was arrested in Laredo, Texas, along with my wife, Rosemary, my daughter, Susan, and my son, Jack, for the possession of less than half an ounce of marijuana. During the subsequent three and a half years, my family and I were engaged in a continuous series of bizarre legal contests with American law-enforcement agencies. I was arrested eight times (potential total prison time—69 years), Jack also eight times Rosemary three times and Susan once—all on charges directly or indirectly connected with the possession of grass. In fairness to all concerned, I do not use the word harassment to describe the pressure police directed toward us, because I suspect that many policemen (certainly those with teenage kids of their own) have felt more than equally harassed by our activities. In addition, we bailed out and defended over 50 of our communal brothers. This involved the aid of 18 lawyers and more than $150,000 in legal costs. The expense to the taxpayer to maintain this long engagement was certainly many times greater.

During this 42-month period, I lived in a curious state of limited physical and political freedom. My body could not leave the country. As a felon on bail, my day-to-day liberty was at the whim of the Federal Department of Justice. What I said and wrote was censored. While my case was in the courts, it did not seem mannerly nor sportsmanlike to talk about what happened in Laredo and afterward. A player can't broadcast his version of the game from the huddle or the side lines while the game is still going on. My version of the great control/pleasure, FBI/LSD, narcs/heads, crewcut/long-hair, turn-off/turn-on, uptight/feel-good contest was also censored by a paradoxical consensus between my lawyers and the Feds. Said the former: "We want to win your case on the law, on the basis of an unconstitutional injustice. We don't want to lose it because your social image deteriorates to that of a bedrugged anarchist."

Along the same censorial lines, in April 1968, a Federal judge in Houston approved a motion by a Federal attorney to revoke my bail and make me begin my 30-year prison sentence on the grounds that my "continual public appearances, particularly at college campuses," made me "a danger to the impressionable minds of youth and a menace to the community." My lawyers kept me out on this one by a last-minute promise that I would not make any public statements advocating that people feel good illegally. Turn off, tune out — and shut up.

There is one basic political struggle dividing mankind, of which economic, racial and military frictions are just superficial symptoms. This basic conflict, recognized (and despaired over) by Sigmund Freud some 50 years ago, is between man's desire to *do* good (as defined by social conditioning) and man's desire to *feel* good. This conflict rages everywhere, in every action of the human being. It manifests itself as psychological conflict, as interpersonal conflict, and as social conflict. Painful duty versus free pleasure. Repressive control versus joyful expression. Social conditioning versus doing what comes naturally, the unconditioned neurological state, being high.

Since Freud, it has become an accepted axiom among psychologists and psychiatrists that society's task is to "manage" the pleasure principle. Modern industrial societies, through the media of parents, teachers — indeed, all adult authority — condition children to become productive, narrowly genital little citizens and to repress any movement in the direction of polymorphous pleasure. We are all familiar with the systems of reward and punishment that accomplish this anti-pleasure social conditioning. Many philosophers and educators have sought a method of suspending these Pavlovian patterns. How can we break the powerful neurological grasp of the frigid mother, or the ghetto, or the Southern bigoted household, or the frightened, mortgage-ridden suburban father? The answer now, in hindsight, seems obvious: You blow your mind.

The phrase blowing your mind, like most of the slang floating up from the underground, is precisely, neurologically accurate. Pleasure is the unconditioned state, the experience of getting high, of getting our of your social mind. While suspension of conditioning often produces intense fear and distress, it happens to be the only source of wholly natural pleasure. If you have never been very "high," you may not know the difference between natural pleasure and learned reward, and you will not know what the unconditioned state is. That positive feeling you get from doing well, doing right, attaining some goal is game reward, not pleasure. Most of the things we like are artificial, learned rewards—the artificial, man-made bell that made Pavlov's dog salivate. Do you call that pleasure? Do you really want the cultivated, trained reward rather than the natural kick?

This issue underlies many of the conflicts of modern politics. In my view, that's what law and order is all about. That's what the racial hassle is all about. That's also what the welfare-aid-poverty scandals are all about: Many middle-class people fear the poor because the poor are seen to be shiftless, lazy, unambitious, and pleasure-seeking, preferring today's kick to tomorrow's sober bank balance. Why should we add to their pleasure our painfully earned material rewards? Many whites dislike blacks for the same reason, except more so. Eldridge Cleaver has written exact and poetic descriptions of white envy of the graceful, rhythmic, natural, turned-on black body. And we all know why many old people envy carefree youth.

From 1961 to the end of 1965, all of my energies were offered to the Marcusian program of bringing about a nonrepressive society. Erotic politics. Hedonic engineering. My own modest contribution was to encourage a large group of young Americans to decondition themselves away from the work-duty ethic by means of psychedelic drugs. I believe that the effect of LSD and marijuana is to suspend learned conditioning, to allow the user to move in the direction of the natural, to get back where he belongs. The psychedelic person inevitably becomes more and more like those three outgroups in our society who live closer to a life of natural fleshly pleasure—the uneducated, the blacks, and the young. (Notice how the hippies have automatically become our white blacks—choosing to live like the lowest economic class, either in ghettos or on remote farms; taking pleasure in doing what comes naturally.

When I speak of this deliberate desire to encourage young persons to sever the conditioned reflexes that tie them to the values of their parents, I am not speaking metaphorically. Our political technique was physiological and our hope was to bring about a visible change in exactly that headquarters where all change must originate—the human brain. The motto "Turn on, tune in, drop out," for example, is a specific psychopharmacological formula: (1) blow your mind with a powerful psychedelic; (2) recondition yourself to rewards and punishments that you select; (3) avoid all institutions based on involuntary reward-punishment conditioning. The aim was to produce the first generation in human history that could choose its own mode of conditioning, react selectively to self-selected rewards and, literally, neurologically *make up its own mind.*

From the standpoint of my small part in this hedonic revolution, it was obvious by the fall of 1965 that the psychedelic point of view was about to become established. Sexual freedom. Erotic honesty. Marijuana merriment. *Eros. Hair.* Head. Kiss. *Screw.* The Who? Rolling Stones. The Fugs. Beyond The Doors. Beyond even Blood Sweat and Tears on the Airplane to Electric Ladyland. In spite of and to the despair of the Law-and-order generation, the young were joyously rejecting the Protestant work ethic and were initiating the leisure-time life of the future. The complex tasks of harnessing electronic-psychedelic energies to the new social structure now could be left to younger and more technically talented prophets, such as the Beatles, Tom O'Horgan, Tiny Tim, Stanley Kubrick, the righteous dealers and the underground alchemists. I nominated John Lennon as my successor and dropped out of the Pied Piper business. Thus, honorably emeriti, Rosemary and I turned ourselves to our long-awaited postretirement projects—to stay high, make love, and write science fiction.

In December 1965, we closed the big house at Millbrook, put rock shrine markers over all the stashes, and started driving to Mexico, where we had rented a house on a beach. This was to be a nostalgic return to our southern neighbor, whose first dollar-earning export was and still is the world's most holy and loving dope. Two years before, we had been deported from Mexico—along with eleven Harvard Ph.D.s, a rabbi, two ministers, the editor of *Gourmet* magazine and three pupil-dilated businessmen—for running a psychedelic commune in a beautiful hotel near Acapulco. As we drove back toward Mexico through Louisiana, I told the family about the final amusing incident of that other trip: Two Mexican secret policemen, who had been assigned to put me on the midnight plane, had to argue violently with Mexican immigration officials, who wouldn't let me leave the country without surrendering my tourist card, which the secret police had confiscated.

We got to Laredo at sundown, drove across the International Bridge and parked in front of the Immigration Building to get our tourist cards. There was a waiting room with benches and a door leading into the government office, which was fully equipped with a long counter and clacking typewriters. I walked to the door and was accosted by a man who had been standing hidden behind the threshold. He broke into a warm, welcoming smile.

"Timoteo!" he cried in joy.

His obvious pleasure provoked a reflex response of affection from me. Here, I thought, is some person I have befriended in the past. But what is his name?

Suddenly, the smile turned official. "Where do you think you are going? Do you remember me. You aren't allowed in Mexico. I know because I am Jorge Garcia, who deported you from Mexico in 1963. You are *persona non grata* in Mexico. *Prohibido.*"

I was still radiating from his warm greeting (Libras thrive on popularity) and pardoned my dear old friend his official excitability. I remembered his pounding the counter in the Mexico City airport in 1963.

"No, Jorge, I have a letter from the Ministry of Gubernacion, saying that we can return as tourists."

Jorge thought for a moment. "Stay right here." He ran through the waiting room and out to the parking lot. I followed and watched him from the door. Jorge jumped into a car and shouted. "I'll be right back."

At this point, a black spider of paranoia started spinning a sticky web around the waiting room of my mind. Until that moment I had prided myself on my complete lack of paranoia. Since my first mind-blowing mushroom session—also in Mexico, in 1960—I had been too busy deciphering cosmic plots, contacting Tibetan masters, and desperately avoiding brain-control conspiracies to worry about such planetary matters as being busted. How could I be arrested? I had not one shred of guilt about what I was doing and, instead, felt the presence of an enormous bank account of karmic virtue. After all, I had, at the most modest appraisal, provided more satori, nirvana, tantric bliss, illumination, heightened pleasure, sensory bliss, and longer lovemaking for more of my fellow men than any Ph.D. in the history of the American Psychological Association. To say the least.

I walked up to Rosemary, Susan, and Jack and whispered: "We're apparently having a little hassle here with the Mexican government. Someone go out to the car and get rid of the grass."

Jack Leary, then 16, nodded and got up. Jack is a super-Libra and routinely deals with the cosmos in a maddeningly superior, deliberate, balanced way. In a crisis, he is the most swift, resourceful dependable person I know. In a couple of minutes he sauntered back, disappeared in the men's room and returned to the bench with a mission-accomplished nod.

172

Good! We're clean.

Then Jorge Garcia reappeared, by this time *mucho* business-like, an ultraconfident official. "No, Señor Timoteo, not is it possible for you to go to Mexico tonight. I must call the capital in the morning to confirm. You must return to the United States now. It will all be different *mañana*."

In retrospect, it is easy to see that we were caught in a B-movie scenario, swept up by some fast-moving current of melodrama beyond our control. If I believed in witchcraft (and, believe me, I do), I would say that we were under some astrological spell, some black- or white-magic manipulation that moved us, unthinking, to the next spot on the duty-pleasure game board.

You see, we didn't actually have to return to the United States and criminal notoriety. Nuevo Laredo, Mexico, is a border town, a transient tourist town. You can make the scene there day and night without papers. We could have checked into a hotel, unpacked our bags, showered and then wandered around the streets, watching the hustlers and the pimps and the tourists, and looked into the gift shops and eaten enchiladas for dinner and slept like free souls and in the morning repacked our bags and returned to the immigration office, got our cards for the interior and proceeded to Yucatán.

But marionette strings pulled us back to the car, which I turned around and steered across the International Bridge. I was nervous, dazed, and unaware of scramblings in the back seat. About halfway across the bridge, I saw a sign saying UNITED STATES CUSTOMS, KEEP RIGHT, and it suddenly dawned on me that even though we hadn't been in Mexico, we would have to pass through the American Customs, just like the VW caravans that wend their way from purple Michoacán, golden Acapulco, green Zacatecas, seedless Guadalajara and the other fabled cities of the southland. My mind flashed alarm: "All the grass is out of the car—right?"

Susan, sitting in the front seat, said, "No, we just found the silver box here."

The car rolled on toward the Customs station. Frantic rummaging in the back seat. The silver box. Can't throw it out the window, blang, bang, metallic flash in the middle of the bridge.

"I hid it," said Susan.

As the Custom's officer walked up. I handed him the unused Mexican papers and started talking first and fast. "We didn't enter Mexico, officer." I expected him to check the papers, nod, salute smartly with an understanding smile and let us pass.

He nodded, all right, and ordered everyone out of the car. He leaned in the front door, reached down and came up with something he held in his fingers.

"What is this seed I found on your car floor?"

In a flash, the car was surrounded by agents. "Remove all the baggage."

"Officer, you must be kidding!" The station wagon was packed with the impedimenta of a three-month expedition. Sacred books, beach and city clothing, theological manuscripts, and scuba-diving equipment.

"Yup. All of it. Out!"

Other tourists passing by the check point quick-glanced at us with virtue's detached, shunning disapproval. I wanted to run after them and shout, "It's all a mistake, really, we're not smugglers! We didn't even get into Mexico!"

Then we were ordered to sit on separate benches in the Customs' office and forbidden to talk to one another. There were no magazines. Not even Muzak. Phone calls brought two more chief inspectors. Interrupted at eight o'clock on Saturday night by duty's call. What had they been doing? Watching TV? Drinking bourbon? Dressing to go out to dinner? Sorry, dear, there's a big bust down at the office.

With a triumphant flourish, an agent came into the waiting room, carrying boxes filled with brown flour. A cluster of fuzz buzzed around. What's this? Pollen dust from Persia's brilliant red flower? Processed in Lebanon labs and converted to brilliant nod-out crystals near Marseilles and smuggled across the Atlantic by swarthy members of the Seafarers Union? No, it's worse. Gentlemen, there is enough organic health food there to get every high school kid in the country to kick the white-bread habit. Headlines and promotions for every agent who helped smash this unadulterated bread network!

We were called, one by one, into small rooms and examined for needle marks. Our pockets were emptied carefully and the dust and tobacco flakes caught in the linings were combed out and neatly folded into envelopes.

I still couldn't believe we were busted, until the chief agent called me into his office and laid the now-familiar mantra on me: "You are entitled to call a lawyer and to refuse to answer my questions. I warn you that anything you say may be used against you when the entire stenographic record of your life is read before the shadowed court of dread Anubis." Or something to that effect.

At that second, I had a minor revelatory experience, a quick, highly detailed view into the future, like a speeded-up newsreel. I could see the headlines — "EX-HARVARD PROF NABBED AS SMUGGLER" — the arraignments, the bails, the indictments, the pleas, the lawyers' offices, the endless legal ratiocinations, the trials, the fund raisings, the rallies, the HANDS OFF TIM LEARY buttons, the appeals, the trite, only partially re-edited scripts of Dreyfus, Socrates, the earliest Christians, Dr. Sam, Alger Hiss, Candy Mossler, and Galileo.

It was immediately obvious to me that I would have to test the constitutionality of the marijuana laws, return from delicious high retirement, come strolling across the turf from the bull pen and spend long years of public hassle until, in the hushed and marbled solemnity of the Supreme Court, nine black-robed Justices whom I would never meet would rule on the right of American citizens to turn on, to get high, to feel good in their homes. I flashed on: three years of barnstorming and old-fashioned sloganeering. *Don't Tread on Me. Let's Fly United. Six Miles High. Turn on, tune in, drop out. Acapulco Gold Means Fine Tobacco. When the punishment evokes more honest horror than the crime, then the law is wrong. Lucy in the Sky with Diamonds. A house cannot stand half uptight and half turned on. Your only hope is dope. With a little help from your friends.*

At that second, I groaned inwardly and then, looking at the agent, I began to laugh. He looked at me curiously.

"Don't you know what you're doing, officer?" I was saying to myself. "You may have just put yourself out of a job. You may have just knocked out the Federal marijuana laws."

I knew at that arresting moment that I couldn't cop a plea, make a deal. "On a plea of guilty, we can get you off, Tim, with a suspended sentence and a few years' probation. After all, it was only half an ounce." But I just couldn't recant, confess, throw myself at the mercy of a well-meaning, sincere Texas judge separated light-years from the folkways of my home.

The trip to the Laredo jail was complicated, because we had to load all our luggage into the cars of the two agents. The inspector possessively patted the hood of our station wagon and said, "This car is now confiscated. Property of the U.S. Government." He grinned. "Too bad. It's brand-new, isn't it?"

I shrugged. "You'll have to discuss all that with the rental agency. The car's only leased."

His face fell in disappointment.

At the jail, under the glare of the naked light bulbs, I kissed Rosemary and made a brave, wavering speech to the family. "Well, beloved, there's not one person in history whom we admire who didn't do his time in the Man's prison. It's all part of our education."

Jack was locked in the second-floor tier with juveniles—all Mexican or black. I was taken to the third-floor tier. The jailer unlocked two barred doors and then directed me down the dark cell row. When I got to the fifth cell, he pressed a button and the metal door creaked open. Metal on metal is the worst sound.

Then, after I entered, the door slid shut. Remote control. *Slam! Clang!* The first time you find yourself in jail is an educational moment for everyone, I guess.

The next morning, the four of us were assembled in the jailer's office. Jack and I were handcuffed together and we were all marched two blocks to the office of the U.S. commissioner. There were photographers and TV cameramen dancing backward in front of us.

The commissioner was stern, relentless, and mainly preoccupied with our financial status. How much cash? How much in the bank? What stocks and bonds? Property? He made Rosemary cry by demanding that she tell her parents to mortgage their house. Bail was set at some startling figure that merciful memory has misplaced. Twenty-five thousand? Back in jail, the efficient machinery of the Laredo marijuana combine took over. The jailer gave me the name of one bail-bondsman. He's the best in town. The bail-bondsman gave me the name of one lawyer. He's the best in town. He'll get your bail reduced. The lawyer was a a nice guy. He sat right down to talk business, radiating that genial self-confidence that only the unjailed can express toward the imprisoned. He was certain we could get bail reduced. He began scribbling on a piece of paper. Let's see; you have $1400 cash. It will cost about $500 for you to fly back to New York and my fee will be $500. That leaves $400 for Joe the bondsman. And with his percentage, le't see, we'll ask for $2500 for you and Rosemary and get the kids out on your guarantee.

Within an hour, we were back in the commissioner's office. This time it was all cordial, as though we had just purchased a new, expensive car and made the down payment and it was just a matter of some paperwork and we'd be behind the wheel and off on our white-Christmas trip back to Millbrook.

The indictments came down in January. Susan and I were charged with three counts: smuggling marijuana, transporting smuggled marijuana, and failure to pay the marijuana tax.

For an overview of the complex, devious strategy the Federal Government used until very recently to enforce its marijuana statutes, the reader is referred to Dr. Joel Fort's "Pot: a Rational Approach" in the October, 1969 issue of *Playboy*. For the purposes of this account, it is enough to note that by the 1960s, the repression of pot smoking had become an enormous law-enforcement industry, providing delightful game rewards to thousands of cops at all levels of government.

Just at the time when civil rights muscle was making it more difficult to harass the "lazy, concupiscent, music-loving black man," a new and even more vulnerable outgroup appeared: the "heads." Psychedelic enthusiasts provided a made-to-order scapegoat for a middle-aged, self-righteous American society. Heads were infuriatingly young and sexy. They were intolerably pleasure-seeking. They were openly skeptical of Johnson City and San Clemente values. And, what was most delightful to the lower-middle-class constabulary, they tended to be bookreading, art-loving college people—the natural enemies of the crew-cut, gun-collecting TV watcher.

I had the opportunity to watch the emergence of this peculiarly American pogrom in some detail. At Laredo, for example, the Customs agents were automatically on the alert for youngsters who showed any signs of deviation from the Joe College model. Young blacks, young long-hairs, kids from Eastern colleges— especially New Yorkers—bookish kids with old cars all came under special scrutiny. "After a while, you get an unerring sense of who is holding marijuana," a border official confided to me after my trial.

Detection of pot smokers was facilitated by the use of Mexican informers, I am here to tell you. For example, some Princeton kids show up on the Nuevo Laredo night-life scene. They are approached by a hustler, who offers them grass. "Sure, that's what we came down here for." The pusher collects his fee, hands over the low-quality weed and then notifies the border patrol, who is waiting the next day. The suspect's baggage is searched, he is stripped, his bare arms examined—sometimes more intimate apertures are probed—and, *voila!*, 20 joints are found hidden in his FM portable radio. During my period of anthropological research in Laredo, I talked to dozens of Northern college kids who were being processed like naughty sausages through Laredo morality mill. The take averaged over $2000 per kid, when you added up the bondsman, the local lawyer, the fine and the confiscated car, not to mention the boon to local innkeepers and restaurants. A tidy little involuntary tourist trade for a sleepy border town.

The disposition of Federal weed cases became a delicate ballet of Sicilian complexity. The kid who was busted on the bridge immediately faced the three familiar charges: smuggling, with a maximum sentence of 20 years and a minimum mandatory of 5 years; transportation, with a maximum of 20 years and a minimum mandatory of 5 (only a Presidential pardon can lower these mandatory terms, and Nixon ain't a head, brother); and the "tax count." This last allowed more leeway—from suspended sentence and probation up to ten long years.

The standard routine was to allow the middle-class offender to plead guilty to the tax count in return for dismissal of the two heavy mandatory raps. There was little choice for the victim. He had to make the deal. If he wanted to go to trial and fight the case, then the Government would not drop the two heavy counts and the defendant was faced with an almost certain and unparolable ten years. Almost certain, because Northerners just didn't win cases in front of a Laredo jury and a Texas judge. It's a very small town, remember, and everyone around the court- house knows everyone who is likely to show up on a jury panel. The Customs officers play bridge with the lawyers and the jury is made up of merchants and housewives who are members of the same church societies. I never saw a Negro on a Laredo jury.

Not to mention the up-front legal helplessness of the American citizen who wanders across the border into his own country's Customs office. An archaic, xeno-phobic paranoia makes all men suspect at any national border. Protections such as search warrants and the idea that there should be reasonable criteria of probable cause for stripping and seizure are jettisoned.

Another pressure toward making the tax-count deal was the fact that the Government did not want to go to trial on grass cases. In the first place, it took time and onerous preparation for the attorneys. And all the arresting agents had to spend a day waiting around court, when they could have been down at the bridge, stripping hippies and protecting the border from hedonic invasion. More important, the Justice Department didn't like to try middle-class Americans on the smuggling and transporting charges, because victory became embarrassingly dangerous. Ten years in the penitentiary for the college kid caught with ten joints. Trouble from the Congressman back home.

It's much easier to bust the Princeton kid, relieve him of his car and $2000, scare him into repentance and send him back to the campus under five years' probation, in familial and academic disgrace, a sorry object lesson for other undergraduates who are tempted to score for their friends. Interestingly enough, most middle-class parents highly approved of this chastising exercise. When Dad flew down to Laredo for the hearing and stood in court next to Junior, his eyes would meet the yes of the judge and an implicit agreement would be sealed. We'll teach Junior a lesson, but we both want to keep him in business school and out of a ten-year rap.

Of course, it all depended on repentance and the remorseful desire to mend your ways. Middle-class kids who acted like ghetto kids—that is, who expressed no guilt, who refused to beg for the chance to go back to school, who suggested that they considered pot smoking acceptable behavior—could be sent up for a discretionary few months until they got the point. Aston- ishingly, many parents encouraged the brief incarceration of their kids, in the hope that they would mend their rebellious ways.

I remember calling a Laredo lawyer who had "defended" a young rock musician from San Francisco who family instructed the lawyer to let him do a year. "We've tried everything else to get him to go back to college, and maybe a little time in a structured military-type environment will knock the nonsense out of him and teach him a trade," the parents said. "At least they'll cut his goddamn hair."

The lawyer was quite blunt with me. "His folks are right. He's a cocky kid. The discipline will do him good."

The Government's most pressing reason for avoiding a vigorously fought marijuana trial was the uneasy knowledge that the Federal weed law was a bizarre monstrosity from the bureaucratic standpoint and unconstitutional from the legal standpoint. Conservative constitutional scholars assured me that the grass laws violated the Fifth Amendment (forbidding self-incrimination, in this case, by being forced to purchase a license for an illegal act), the Eighth Amendment (forbidding cruel and unusual punishment) and the Ninth Amendment (guaranteeing personal freedoms unmentioned in the other amendments).

The only other person who wouldn't make a deal during the four months that I was in and out of Laredo was a brash young hood from Newark. He couldn't cop the tax plea, seek probation, and play it straight for five years. "Are you kidding? All my friends are ex-cons. My office is in a pool hall. How can I work that out with a probation officer?" I told him to make noises about appealing his verdict, which he did, much to the horror of his own Laredo lawyer. On the day he was to go to trial, the Government dropped all charges. His own lawyer shook his head and muttered disapproval.

There are dozens of turned-on young barristers in New York, San Francisco and Los Angeles, but in other parts of the country and, particularly, in Southern border towns, forget it. I am willing to testify under oath that in the state of Texas in 1965, there was no criminal lawyer of repute who would vigorously fight to keep America green.

For two months, I phoned and personally interviewed Texas lawyers who would look at me with the disbelieving curiosity they might exhibit toward a child molester. "Constitutional right to use *narr-cott-ticks*, huh?" What Texas lawyer wants to become known as the man who freed the land for dope addicts? One prospective attorney had me fly down to Houston to spend the day with a psychiatrist, ostensibly because he might testify on my behalf but really to check out the degree of my insanity. That lawyer used to chuckle and make jokes about my nutty LSD-type defense. "First Amendment, ha-ha." His fees were equally lysergic: $5000 an ounce.

We straggled onto the playing court, finally, with a rather weak defense quartet: There were two jolly, Laredo lawyers for whom fighting the grass laws—a tactic that, if successful, would cut down on their regular source of clients—was only slightly less than treasonable. They took the case because I was a likable maniac with some money in a legal defense fund to throw away. They were backed by two young idealistic lawyer friends of mine who had never tried a criminal case before.

In any event, the jury trial was pointless. I freely admitted possession of the offensive half ounce. Our aim was to build up a good record for the appeal. I had to testify that I didn't apply for the tax stamp because I knew I wouldn't get it and further knew that I would be incriminating myself as a grass user. And I had to testify that I had used psychedelic drugs as part of my religion, my profession, and my righteous home life. Drs. Ralph Metzner and Joel Fort argued that grass was less harmful than alcohol. A Hindu monk swore that I had been initiated on the banks of the Ganges into a Bengali sect that used ganga as a sacramental aid to meditation. And a photo of me standing in front of a government-licensed Calcutta Ganga shop with a holy man was submitted as evidence, to the puzzlement of the clerk. Since the jury was bound to come in with a verdict of guilty, precluding courtroom mesmerism and Ciceronian forensic feats on my part, my goals for the trial itself were limited. I decided that the logical step was for me to try to turn on the judge, to get to his mind, to teach him something about the art and science of getting high.

The moment of achievement came during my second day on the stand, when the judge leaned toward me and said, by way of clarification, "What you are saying is that there are several levels of consciousness and taking drugs is like going up an elevator. Different drugs take you to different floors. Is that it?"

"Thank you, your Honor. That is precisely what I was trying to say."

At the end of the trial, when the door to the jury room closed, one of my Laredo lawyers glanced at his watch in a pleased, brisk manner and said, "Well, it will take them five minutes to sit down and light cigarettes. And ten minutes to elect a foreman and read the instructions. And, say, seven minutes to count the votes. They'll be out with the verdict in twenty-two minutes."

And so they were. Practice makes perfect. After the verdict, I was called up before the judge and sentenced to 30 years' imprisonment and a $40,000 fine for the unrepentant crime of possessing less than half an ounce of grass.

The 30-year rap was a noisy buy empty gesture. Lost in the headlines was the fact that the judge had ordered a 90-day period of psychiatric observation in a prison hospital for the criminally insane—a sincere or cynical attempt, I suppose, to imply that I was a madman. After 90 days, I would return for resentencing or, perhaps, for commitment. In any case, it was unlikely that I would be forced to serve more than the minimum mandatory sentence, which would balance out neatly to one year for each dollar's worth of grass in the little silver box.

The sentence caused the expected flap. Press, TV, radio. A seismological revulsion of sympathy and outrage—particularly from foreign lands. A nice television station in Tokyo offered Rosemary and me a two-week guided tour of Japan if we would spend an hour telling our story before the cameras. I was suddenly escalated, thanks to Harvard and Laredo, to a curious role of notoriety somewhere between those of Christine Keeler and Ché Guevara.

The prospect of serving any substantial prison time had never played any part in my mythology. I had no intention of becoming a martyr. Suffering for others was a bad trip 2000 years ago, and we are still trying to undo that miserable blood-guilt mischief. No good cause, and certainly not our jolly crusade for kicks, can be helped by that sadomasochistic dance we call martyrdom.

So the illegal law wouldn't get me. We would get the illegal law first. The appeal was turned over to a dedicated young civil-libertarian lawyer, Joel Finer, then on the faculty of the University of Texas law school. Finer struck off on his own into a jungle of visionary tracts and theological manuscripts and eventually came up with a classic defense of psychedelic religious freedom. A few years too early.

The next step for me was to accept the fact that I had been rudely snatched out of retirement and to try to use the absurdity at Laredo to my advantage. We figured—rightly—that it would take about three years for the case to get to and come down from the Supreme Court. So I had some 30 or 40 months to pitch myself back into the hedonic revolution, to once again take up what I now saw as a grand nationwide psychological and political experiment.

The experiment, which had started at Harvard in 1961, would determine empirically if psychedelic drugs could bring about a reconditioned society. For the test to work, to prove anything, my sample of subjects had to run into the millions. The time limit on it would be the day of the Supreme Court verdict. By the time the decision came down, either the society would be reconditioned or it wouldn't. If it wasn't—if society hadn't changed significantly in the direction of pleasure freedom by 1969—then my own freedom would be forfeit. Rosemary and I would spend the rest of our lives in jail or in exile.

I must confess that I had certain continual misgivings about my new professional duties. By the end of the first year following the arrest, I had become a notorious and noisy agitator for the revolution, which was gathering momentum in all quarters where young people put their heads. Yet I am, by nature, a skeptical, ironic, introspective person with a strong sense of Celtic dignity. Here I was, a scholarly researcher from Harvard with graying sideburns and two teenage children, sitting barefoot and beflowered on a strobe-lit stage, accompanied by sitar and tabla and urging an audience of several thousand theatergoers to "slide together in molecule embrace."

When I would fail to appreciate this faintly ridiculous situation, my friends would be quick to remind me. I remember sitting, profusely made up, under the floodlights of a Hollywood studio and surrounded by a 40-man film crew, listening to Dick Alpert's quizzical, disapproving question, "Timothy, why are you doing this?" I could only reply, "Well, Professor, I'd be delighted to have you take my place."

A political strategy involving neurological changes may seem radical, but you'd better get used to that idea. If drugs change minds—and they do—how long will it be before a totalitarian state not the least bit interested in freedom and pleasure initiates researches where the mind-changing drugs are *not* self-administered? In 1962, we clearly saw that control of mind-changing drugs would be the key political issue in tomorrow's society. *Woodstock.*

December 25, 1979, Washington, D.C.: Top-Secret Memo to School Administrators. Subject: Revised dosage recommendations for socio-pharmacological additives to school lunches.

1. The standard dosage for third-grade students is changed to 30 mg. of Industrin.

2. The addition of anti-conceptionals and anti-aphrodisiacs will now commence in the eighth grade.

3. Uncooperative students from grades one to seven will receive 50 mg. of Docilin daily.

4. Dosages of Intelligen and concentrationols will remain the same, pending results of ongoing research being conducted by the Defense Department.

This may sound like science fiction, but Rosemary and I and our friends have been living in a weird sci-fi world for several years. The point is this: In the politics of the nervous system, the touchstone of freedom is self-administration. My own modest contribution to the free society to come was to persuade the youngsters who will be running things in 2001 that they should instinctively distrust and reject any Governmental control of mind drugs and learn, on their own, the complexities of self-directed reconditioning. *Woodstock.*

The standard liberal cliché about psychedelic drugs is that they should certainly be controlled by the Government but available to authorized, responsible, serious-minded, conscientious, competent researchers. In my visions of the future, just such a plausible prospect becomes the ultimate horror. The last person I want controlling drugs that can change my mind is a serious Government scientist. The only persons who can control the chemicals that change your head are you and your girl. *Woodstock.*

Our educational campaign to proselytize this new political message was effective enough to capture the imagination of a large percentage of our youth and, by 1966, to stimulate an enraged backlash from the custodians of the established order. Anti-psychedelic-drug laws were hurriedly passed and the police offensive escalated. L. B. J. himself added a useful datum to our files when he took the time in his 1968 State of the Union message to denounce LSD by name as one of the many evil forces surrounding the House of White.

The laws and the Presidential denunciations pleased me enormously. The more illegal it was to turn on, the happier I became. The dream of any revolutionary is to find a mode of change that is symbolically effective and psychologically contagious. Picketing? Demonstrations? Marches? Sit-ins? Self-immolations? Hunger strikes? Card burnings? Old stuff! Such familiar revolutionary techniques have become repetitious and stale.

The truth of the matter is that turning on with *illegal* psychedelic drugs is the most powerful revolutionary technique ever developed. Neurological anarchy, and nothing less! By 1966, the taking of a psychedelic drug in the United States, western Europe, Russia, and even Cuba had become a subversive political act directed against the adult establishment. Any person who has turned on in the past few years has had to say to himself and implicitly to Chairman Mao Tse-Nixon-Kosygin, etc.: "I reject Governmental control of my head and my pleasure." The dove-tailed joint of marijuana and the deconditioning sugar cube become the ultimate instruments of political change. *Woodstock.*

And what an infectious, merry revolt! Protesting and demonstrating have undertones of peevish irritation. Such devices have little power to change anyone's mind. I believe that such public acts of defiance simply polarize and harden everyone's previously held attitudes. But the quiet protestant turning on illegally in his home has engaged in several revolutionary actions. In order to score, he has connected himself to an underground of gentle, trustworthy collaborators. Turning on automatically makes the cops and the state your persecutors, a point not to be over-looked these days, when the old-style appeals to stir up the downtrodden no longer cut it. What wouldn't Karl Marx have given for a method guaranteed to convert 75 percent of the aristocratic student body of St. Petersburg University into objects of harassment by the hated Cossacks?

But the greatest revolutionary impact of the psychedelic act is this: The drug itself liberates and anarchizes your nervous system. Unlike the picket sign or the draft card, the drug suspends exactly those socially conditioned reflexes that tie you to the rewards and punishments of the aging system you want to overthrow. Turning on is an ominous threat to any social system. It leads to the smiling dropout. You no longer bother to fight the old system. You just start living in the old society in a new, smiling, conspiratorial style. *Woodstock.*

As this social mutation started to manifest itself, the harassing muscle of the law moved to stop the experiment in general and our activities in particular. The first police raid on Millbrook, in April 1966, introduced us to 24 booted, helmeted, and armed deputies, who entered our bedrooms at Saturday midnight. It was the classic surprise invasion so familiar to nonconforming Russians, fun-loving Greeks, and free Czechs. Now it is happening here in the college dormitories and youth ghettos. The new terror. Anyone who hasn't faced the threat of a night raid by the thought police has been cheated of one of the authentic, classic experiences of our era. The raid on Millbrook and the five-hour ransacking of bedrooms was just the beginning of our testing.

Next started a grand-jury investigation of our home life. All of the members of our commune, including ten-year-old children, were subpoenaed and urged under threat of jail to talk about our domestic affairs. Who sleeps with whom? Who takes dope? Rosemary refused, righteously, on the grounds that the daily life of her family and the spiritual practices of her coreligionists were no business of District Attorney Rosenblatt. She did a month in jail for this.

Then the rousting and harassing on the streets and highways. Many people do not know that to a large group of Americans, the streets are unsafe, a no man's land ventured into only at the risk of harrassment. And not just in the ghetto. As you drive around Southern California, you will notice police cars everywhere. Observe who is being stopped. Keep a tally. Nine out of ten are blacks, Mexicans, or long-haired kids. When we'd drive from Millbrook to New York, it became a game. How many miles before we'd be stopped?
184

This has been another invaluable educational experience. For four years we have had the privilege of sharing, in a small way, the alert, animal sensitivity of the black man in the South, the black man in the North, the freedom-loving Czech, the Jew in Germany. The constant awareness that the armed agents of your uptight, warlike government are hunting *you*.

Then came the blockades around the Millbrook estate. For months, anyone leaving our grounds was likely to be stopped and busted. The young mother bicycling on the road adjoining our land was hauled off for not having identification papers in her shorts. Twenty-five dollars bail for dirty license plates, paid, on the spot or you go to jail. Then there's the exquisitely complex social dilemma provided by the presence of unknown informers in your house. Only after the search-warrant affidavits are made public do you know which of the smiling faces around your dining table last summer was the police spy. Then the lectures scheduled by the student bodies and canceled by the administrations. And the police tails. And more raids. The smashing of our door by officers with John Doe warrants, seeking nonexistent teenage runaways. The incessant demands for bail and for funds for our overworked, routed-out-of-bed-at-midnight lawyers.

The saddest thing was the dropping away of old friends who were attempting to maintain conditioned reward-punishment games in the form of responsible jobs. They were posed with tricky moral dilemmas. If they came to visit us, they were in danger of being stopped and searched, of being caught in a raid, of getting their names on a list.

Gradually, month by month, we found ourselves spending more and more of our time with spiritual outlaws and psychedelic criminals, and less and less time with straights, even grass-smoking straights. We hardly see anyone these days who has not been arrested for political or spiritual crimes. This is a tribal reflex that always occurs in times of social change. It is not a conscious choice.

We lost the trial at Laredo and the second round in the Federal Court of Appeals. Meeting in New Orleans on October 14, 1967, the Fifth Circuit Court upheld the 30-year rap and rejected our claim that the right to get high, the right to worship in the way that got you highest, was guaranteed by the First Amendment. The next recourse was the Supreme Court—highest in the land, we hoped.

At this point, the case was turned over to Robert J. Haft, a securities lawyer known as the Vince Lombardi of Wall Street. His inexperience in constitutional law was matched by the asset that he never loses. Yet, the case looked like a long shot. The Supreme Court grants certiorari in less than one percent of the

185

appeals to it. The First Amendment religious defense seemed more and more lysergic. But just at the time that Haft was preparing his brief, fortune presented us with a gift. The Federal Gambling Tax—which required illegal bookies to purchase a $25 gambling-tax stamp—was held by the Supreme Court to violate the Fifth Amendment. The harassed gambler was clearly being forced by law to buy a license to perform an unlawful act and thus, among other things, mark himself as a pigeon for the police. Self-incrimination.

Therefore, reasoned my lawyer, the marijuana tax must also be unconstitutional. From the standpoint of the conscientious stamp collector, marijuana is a heads-I-win, tails-you-lose gambling game run by the Feds. Again, you are being punished for failing to purchase a Federal tax stamp that would put your name on record as one who intends to commit a felony, according to the law of your state. (In North Dakota, for example, you could get 99 years for trying to use your Federal grass-tax stamp.) The bizarre Treasury Department machinations of 1937, which sought to prohibit marijuana under the guise of a revenue law, were finally coming under rational judicial review.

On May 7, 1968, in Washington, D. C., the highest Court granted certiorari in *Leary vs the U.S. Government.* It agreed to hear arguments, both on the Fifth Amendment issue—the legality of the marijuana tax—and on our argument that the Government is wrong in its automatic presumption that any grass seized in the United States was smuggled. Much to our disappointment, our claims that the First Amendment protects the right to use drugs in religious practice—as sacramental aids to prayer, meditation and higher union—were refused a hearing.

This means that reversal of conviction in the case will knock out the Federal grass laws as incompetent, without facing the basic issue. A more clever Congress will still have the right to formulate laws prohibiting Americans from getting high for God or pleasure (if the two can be separated).

On December 12, 1968, again in Washington, the appeal was argued before the Supreme Court. The Government had a bad day. Bob Haft and his assistants came out smiling. "Nine to nothing. We think we shut them out."

Rosemary and I retired to our desert mountain retreat and started waiting out the decision. We lived in an 18-foot Sioux tepee, with Cheyenne smoke flaps made of sailcloth translucent to the moonlight. We watched the stars very carefully every night, planted seeds, milked the cows, made butter, and stayed high.

Every Monday morning at nine o'clock Pacific time (traditionally, the time for Supreme Court decisions), I'd walk down to the nearest brother's house and listen to the news on a battery-operated radio. When the weekly decisions were reported, I'd walk back to the tepee.

"Well, we've been given another week."

And then we'd stay high for the next seven days.

May 19, 1969, was a sunny day, with bees buzzing and apple-blossom pollen scenting the mountain air.

We looked down the valley and saw two city sedans approaching. The road to the ranch is left deliberately rough, to discourage city visitors. All mountain people know that city cars bring nothing but trouble.

"Do you think it's a bust?"

We watched with pagan wariness as the white men in short hair and business suits cautiously picked their way up the hill.

They were friendly. ABC and NBC-TV. This was the first Monday morning in months that I had not listened to the news. "The Supreme Court has cut you loose. Unanimous decision. The Federal marijuana prohibition is repealed."

Rosemary and I asked the newsmen to make themselves at home on the grassy hillside and we joined our tribal brothers in the tepee and felt, *Oh, happy day.*

Then Rosemary and I were arranged in good camera angle of the tepee and were interviewed by the networks.

"How do you feel?"

"High and happy for ourselves and for the thousands of young people who are imprisoned for psychedelic crimes."

"What is your estimate of the number of people now in jail for marijuana possession?"

"In the state of California alone, fifty thousand kids will be arrested this year for psychedelic-drug possession."

"What are you going to do about it?"

"Run for the highest office in the state. Pleasure is now a political issue."

"What are you going to do when you're governor?"

"As little as possible. The state is best governed which is least governed."

"What are you going to do about student protests?"

"Turn all state colleges and universities back to private enterprise. The state has no business supporting or interfering in trade-union squabbles among students and professors."

"Will it be a grass-roots campaign?"

"You're hired as speechwriter."

"What about crime?"

"There is only one crime, and that is violence to another creature. The violent should be therapeutically isolated. All other illegal behaviors fall under two headings: financial dishonesty and differences in moral preferences. The state cannot legislate or forcibly enforce laws about moral differences. And financial criminals should be offered the chance to avoid prison and pay off their dishonest gamble. We are also going to eliminate taxes for the sober, industrious, conventional person."

"Eliminate taxes! What have you been smoking?"

"We'll institute a thousand-dollar-a-year license fee for any activity that is considered to be unhealthy, asocial, frivolous. To be specific, the following actions will be legal in California upon payment of the annual Frivolity Tax: abortion, divorce, bigamy, drinking hard liquor (beer and wine become tax-free), gun possession, killing fish for sport, frivolous purchase of a new smog-producing car more often than once every five years (ditto smog-producing motorboats) and smoking marijuana or nicotine cigarettes (cigars and pipes are tax-free). The following activities will be available to license holders in restricted areas and neighborhoods: prostitution, gambling, public nudity, homosexual courting, and the use of LSD and heroin."

"What will you do for the blacks?"

"Mainly get the whites rewarded, high, happy, healthy, and off the black's back."

"What do you want people to do for your campaign?"

"Rosemary has come up with our first political slogan. COME TOGETHER, JOIN THE PARTY."

The Supreme Court decision did more than launch my political career, of course. It also meant that Congress will now have to come up with a whole new set of marijuana laws if it wants to regulate our happiness—and it surely does. The Nixon Administration has already entered the field, with a law that classifies marijuana and LSD with heroin and that makes possession of any of them, even without intent to sell, punishable by imprisonment for not less than two years nor more than ten and/or a fine of not more than $20,000. The law also includes a neat, patently unconstitutional provision to the effect that any cop can bust into your pad to get the stuff without a search warrant.

One can only hope that liberal politicians will counter with bills specifically allowing possession of grass. Right, Senator McGovern? Right, Senator Cranston? In any case, there will be hearings and lobbying. These should be accompanied by smoke-ins—peaceable, jolly outdoor gatherings. The Gallup Poll will certainly join the fun. The nationwide samplings will show that 50 percent of the American public thinks the weed law should be toughened. ("Hanging's too good for dope addicts.") And half will want the new laws liberalized. Mr. Gallup's age and race breakdowns will be carefully studied by Ted Kennedy's staff of alert advisors. Ninety percent of those over 50 will be shown to vote no on grass, but 90 percent of those between 15 and 30 (come on, George, you've got to include the teeny-boppers in your survey) will vote *si* on tea. Sixty percent of white will vote no, 80 percent of blacks, browns and redskins will vote to turn on. Certainly, most of Gene McCarthy's constituency can be rallied to the hemp camp.

It is an interesting characteristic of democratic pendulum politics that as soon as an issue moves from the state of unmentionable taboo and attains the status of a debatable difference of opinion—that is, as soon as it moves to the bumper-sticker stage—its eventual social acceptance is assured. In the past 30 years, we have seen Negritude, formerly a dark evolutionary taint, become an issue of personal choice. ("My God, while I wasn't looking, my sister *did* marry one!") Sexual behavior and pornography have similarly moved from a matter of hushed depravity to a matter of taste. Recently, we have seen the celibacy of priests become debated by Catholics. The idea of parish curates happily and righteously balling their wives after Saturday-night confessions, a notion unthinkable five years ago, is now enthusiastically discussed by young seminarians and lay Catholics alike.

A taboo defended by the aging and under skeptical attack by youngsters has little chance of surviving. In a democracy, that is. I make the flat prediction that the Democratic Party convention in 1972 (if you can consider that unmentionable inevitability) will debate and vote on proposals to legalize marijuana. Of the many proposed plans to control and distribute psychedelic drugs, there is one that recommends itself by Spartan simplicity and economy. Every American citizen will be allowed to grow enough grass to supply the erotic-spiritual needs of himself and his family. You won't be allowed to transport it or sell it, but you will be able to grow your own. God must have had this in mind when he made marijuana one of the hardiest, most peripatetic plants on this green planet. Anyone can grow it in his garden. The only problem is fencing; most animals seem to love the weed. City dwellers who have a view to the sun can harvest their window boxes; city dwellers who *don't* have any sunlight will prefer whiskey, anyway.

Peyote, the hardy desert cactus, will become legal and popular (Sophisticated acidheads are already switching to this pure, natural herb of the Indians.) LSD? Anyone desiring to take the big mind-blowing trip will obtain a card entitling him to purchase a dose each week of Sandoz Blue or Owsley White Lightning from his local druggist. If he shouts too loudly in the street about God and love, take his card away from him.

Sure, there'll be some problems. Some people will take too

much and most people won't take enough. Fools will continue to be foolish and the uptight will continue to worry. And jet-set connoisseurs will demand special imported and domestic brands. In any case, if this bill passes, there will be less abuse and reckless use of LSD that there is right now. In spite of the army of narcs and informers patrolling the campuses, the new prohibition hasn't worked. More LSD is being released on the black market every month. Six new underground laboratories that I know about were built in one three-week period by alchemists in the suburbs of just one large and swinging city.

Another interesting by-product of repeal will be the delightful discovery by millions of grass smokers that what they have come to love and love *with* is incredibly low-quality weed. Friends who have devoted their professional lives to the subject inform us that only one in a hundred pot smokers has ever tasted high-grade, high-resin hemp. A generation of prohibition kids brought up on the limited pleasures of bathtub gin will suddenly discover the gaseous equivalent of quality-controlled, bonded, 20-year-old cognac. Someday, I am sure, the political battles will be won, here in California and in Washington. Then Rosemary and I will be able to pack the same blue station wagon (we had to buy it from the rental agency after its year in the Laredo government garage) and head back to the land of hemp and honey from whence we were so rudely detoured.

FRANK BARDACKE

On Trial With The Oakland Seven

This is a story about the trial of the Oakland Seven. It contains some hitherto unrevealed dirt, a few laughs, a smattering of politics, and a confession or two. I have been an Oakland Seven for some time now, and if you read on, you will learn a lot about me. But this is not a story of my life. Some things just don't belong in the newspapers.

Alameda County District Attorney J. Frank Coakley created the Oakland Seven a year and a half ago. He indicted seven leaders of October 1967's Stop the Draft Week for conspiracy to commit three misdemeanors—resisting arrest, trespass, and creating a public nuisance. Conspiracy to commit a misdemeanor is a felony. It carries a three year prison term.

An American court of justice is a mysterious institution, perhaps impossible to understand. It is the enforcer of the State's rules; the place where a man comes up against "thou shalt not." We live under thousands, perhaps millions, of thou shalt nots. A few are reasonable rules that help us live together, like the laws against murder and drunk driving. But the vast majority are designed to serve, consolidate, and perpetuate power. That is the purpose of all the laws that make it illegal to rip off property, just as it is the purpose of the law that prohibits young men from interfering with the Selective Service System. If you fight people who have power, almost by definition, you will violate the law.

The Law, the Judge, the District Attorney, and the police (represented in the courtroom by the bailiffs) form an enormous protective association that has at its command the legal authority to take away part or all of a man's life. This protective agency of the State serves in the name of the people, and does protect some people—those with power and money.

All sorts of men serve in this giant organization. They are not all villainous men. Often they are just doing their duty as they see it, and they always believe that they are protecting all the people. No judge, no D.A., no cop believes that he serves only the rich and the powerful.

Allow me to introduce the Honorable Judge George W. Phillips, Assistant District Attorney Lowell Jensen, Special Assistant to the D.A. Chick Harrison, and bailiffs Sigler and Lindstrom.

Judge Phillips is a little man, barely over five feet tall, with only one finger on his right hand, and the face of a fat bird. Very much a liberal, he voted for Eugene McCarthy, is against the war, and was all smiles to the defendants. His liberalism is tempered by an enormous fear—a fear that befits a man of his size and deformity. He let prosecutor Jensen push him around, he let defense attorney Garry push him around. The only people he was not afraid of were his assigned inferiors: the court clerk, the court recorder, and the bailiffs. To them he was demanding and rude.

Whenever he made a decision he explained that he had no other choice. "I have to follow the law, and I don't like many of them any more than you do." When he said that he was looking down at his desk afraid to look up at the court. This pretense of simply following the rules is a favorite trick of petty bureaucrats. It helps Phillips soften the psychological damage caused by the clash between his nicy-nice liberalism and the reality of his role—punishing the victims of the State.

On the first morning of the trial we went into the Judge's chambers. A plush carpet, big, rather cluttered desk, and a TV set in the corner. It was not an extravagant office, but right there on the wall was the perfect symbol of this man George W. Phillips: a series of idealized photographs of very expensive racing yachts next to a photograph of poor Oakies. Phillips believes he can have it both ways. Lead a life of casual luxury and be a friend of the poor.

But he has a heavy conscience. He has to make countless decisions. Take our case. Basically sympathetic to the defense he had to be careful not to displease the District Attorney. "You see," he explained to anyone who would listen, "the D.A. might do to me what he is doing to Judge Avakian." Judge Avakian is another liberal whose decisions angered D.A. Coakley and now the D.A. challenges him every time a criminal case comes before his court. Avakian has probably presided over his last criminal case in Alameda County. Phillips does not want the same thing to happen to him.

Phillips knows well the basic calculus of the liberal: is it more important to do good here and now or should I save myself so I can do good later? Trapped into such a calculus by their very existence in ruling institutions, liberals live on — oppressing, exploiting, managing, and killing — sure that they are doing as much good as possible. This calculus could have been used by liberal guards at Nazi concentration camps. It will be used at the American ones.

Phillips used the liberal calculus perfectly in the trial of the Oakland Seven. One of the strongest legal arguments was that the charges against us represented selective prosecution. District Attorney Coakley had made the case of selective prosecution when he said, "Technically we could have indicted thousands, but we took the most militant leaders." California courts have recently ruled such political discrimination unconstitutional. But Phillips would not allow us even to introduce the question of selective prosecution. If he had, we would have put Coakley on the witness stand. Coakley surely would have punished Phillips for that.

But ultimately the threat of Coakley's reprisal was not as great as the threat to Phillips' own image of himself as a liberal. At the end of the trial, under the intense prodding of one of our attorneys, Mal Burnstein, Phillips went out of his way to give good instructions to the jury. Without those instructions we might not have been acquitted.

The one regret I have about our acquittal is how satisfied the Honorable Judge George W. Phillips must be with his perfect display of liberalism.

District Attorney Lowell Jensen is a man who deserves to be

taken seriously. Here is a descripton of him taken from my notes early in the trial:

Jensen is a cop's lawyer. He stands 6'4" and is very much a big man. Dark scowl, might say he has a ruddy complexion, but to me it just looks like he had very bad acne as a kid. He is a brilliant no nonsense straight talking man. In court is is very economical with words, never saying more than necessary. He always starts with his strongest points and shows a very forceful logical mind. I often end up agreeing with him when there is a legal dispute between him and our lawyers. Very impatient with stupidity. He has great contempt for Garry's showmanship. Contempt is his emotion. His face is built for it. He rolls, raises, purses his lips—they seem to travel half way up his face—in a beautiful expression of total contempt when Phillips goes through his shuffle. His smile is somewhat similiar—just a slight protruding of the lips. He sits up straight, stands up straight, and has the tightest asshole west of the Rockies. He considers himself a liberal.

During the course of the trial I developed some affection for him. Outside the context of the law he is capable of decency, kindness, and genuine emotion. When Charlie Garry had a stomach seizure that we all were afraid was a heart attack, Lowell was one of the most concerned men in the courtroom. He walked around nervously, tried to call an ambulance, made Charlie sit down, and touched him affectionately. Jensen once accidently knocked down my son, who was playing behind a swinging door, and he was embarrassed and concerned. He laughs with shaking shoulders and a lot of teeth.

But within the context of the law, Lowell Jensen is capable of murder. He worked hard to send Huey Newton to the gas chamber and he stands behind the pigs who murdered Bobby Hutton.

While waiting for the verdict, I was reminded of the evil that Lowell Jensen has given his life to. Warren Wells, a Black Panther, who was involved in the Eldridge Cleaver-Bobby Hutton shoot-out, is in jail at the Alameda County Court House where our trial was held. His first trial ended in a hung jury (10–2 for acquittal) and the pigs are keeping him in jail until the new trial. For some reason the Alameda County Sheriffs threw Warren into solitary confinement in a strip cell. While he was waiting for our verdict to come in, Charlie went before a Superior Court Judge to get Warren out of that cell. He was opposed by Lowell Jensen.

The strip cell, which is located on the 10th floor directly over Judge Phillips' courtroom, is slightly over six feet long and 4½ feet wide. It has four concrete walls and one small window which is opened for only 15 minutes a day. There is no running water. A round hole in the floor, four inches in diameter, is supposed to take care of defecation and urination. But that is difficult to manage. The cell is not cleaned until the prisoner leaves and then it is not cleaned very well. The prisoner is stripped bare and put in the cell. All he gets is a peanut butter sandwich and half quart of water three times a day. The cell also has a small blanket. Nothing else.

Lowell Jensen, an intelligent and in some respects decent man, found himself defending the existence of that hole and protecting the men who use it to destroy other men.

Lowell Jensen has given himself up to the law. That law is capable of leading him anywhere. But why such total devotion? To answer that we have to go back to Lowell's most obvious peculiarity—his obsessive neatness. Lowell Jensen is a very clean man. His notes are always well organized and filed smartly in large manila envelopes. He was disgusted at the end of a day if we recessed too early and lost even five minutes of court time. He brushed away invisible dirt from his desk throughout the trial. His cross-examination was detailed and meticulous to the edge of insanity.

Some will argue that all of this is due to unfortunate toilet training and has nothing to do with politics. Perhaps. I think it is at the very root of his politics and helps to understand his enslavement to the law. Lowell Jensen is terrified of confusion. He has organized his life so as to avoid chaos. The mere hint of a mess threatens to rip apart his careful organization. The law is a necessary system of rules that stands between society and anarchy. Any disrespect for the law, any slight weakening of it, will bring about total cataclysmic breakdown. The danger of living without law is so great, nothing but complete devotion to law will protect us. If we don't formally and rigidly organize ourselves there will be shit everywhere. Lenny Bruce had a routine about the law that went something like this. At first a bunch of people were just lying around being together. Then one man got up and threw some shit at somebody else. The other guy threw some shit back. Pretty soon everybody was throwing shit. And then they had to make rules about just when and where you could throw your shit.

Without sounding like a psychoanalytic nut, I would like to suggest that Lenny Bruce has given away the whole secret. The first experience a person has with the law is the rules of his toilet training. That training colors his attitude toward law for the rest of his life. The fear that without law there would be anarchy and chaos is rooted in the parents' fear that without rigid, inflexible rules the kid would shit all over the place.

If you want to understand why so many in our generation have a casual attitude toward law you must start with Dr. Spock's *Baby and Child Care*. One of the main purposes of the book was to relax parents and to break down the system of rigid, inflexible rules that dominated the child. It was a revolutionary book when it came out in the early 1940s, and it helped to raise a revolutionary generation. Those right wing nuts who blame everything on Spock are not far wrong.

As the clincher, think back to Warren Wells' strip cell. It is a detention cell for convicts. It provides discipline for people who are already being disciplined. And the primary horror of that cell is the tiny hole in the floor through which it is almost impossible to defecate or urinate. The appropriate punishment for the lawless man is to force him to live in his own shit.

Special Assistant to the D.A. Chick Harrison is my favorite cop. A big round man with a friendly baby face, part of Chick's job is to spot political agitators at rallies, demonstrations, and riots. (He told me that Marvin Garson is his favorite agitator.) He goes in plain clothes and aids whatever police department is around. He is one of the men who identified and arrested Jerry Rubin, Steve Hamilton, Stew Albert, Mike Smith, and Bill Miller at the 1966 U.C. sit-in. He does all this in good humor and without rancor. Mid-way through the trial the Oakland Seven jokingly proposed a deal to him: We will not point him out to the demonstrators as a plain clothes cop if he doesn't point us out as agitators.

I first noticed Chick a couple of days into the trial. We were seated at opposite ends of the courtroom looking right at each other. Jensen was making a good point and Chick raised his eyebrows at me and smiled. I looked away. Later Charlie was making a good point. I looked at Chick, gave him a wink and smiled.

From then on it was a fine relationship. We would make faces at each other, feign sleep when the trial was particularly boring, and roll our eyes at the weakness of the judge. At breaks we often talked about sports together—he told me that he had read my sports columns in the *Express Times*. I think that our affection was cemented when I bumped into him as we were both leaving an Oakland Seal hockey game late in the trial. The Seals lost 9-0. He did a triple take when he saw me. I walked right up to him, patted him on the shoulder, and said, "Man, *we* sure played some lousy hockey tonight."

Chick Harrison is into the game of cops and robbers. He enjoys it as a game, and I believe he has a comic distance from himself. I am sure that he is physically fearless and that he would give his life to protect his friends — most of whom are cops. He will continue to be a cop — and although he is incapable of any colossal evil — he will do almost anything that is asked of him. If there ever were a showdown, however, and he discovered a way to preserve the integrity of his physical courage, I think Chick Harrison just might cross over.

I don't think there will be many more cops like Chick Harrison. Any man who now becomes a cop must know that he is going to kill blacks and bust hippie heads. That means that the naive, nice guy jocks, like Chick, simply will not join the force.

This is not just my fantasy. Every metropolitan police force is having difficulty recruiting. Not many people want to be pigs. Those who sign up definitely hate us, and don't care what we call them. It is a good development. In a few years we can be confident that all the cops are both objectively *and* subjectively our enemies.

(Stew Albert read these paragraphs about Chick and blushed with embarrassment for me. Stew says that Chick once kicked a woman demonstrator in the head and slapped someone who was handcuffed. Stew cannot understand how I could be so wrong about a pig. "Jesus, Frank, all sorts of people like sports.")

The two baliffs, Mr. Sigler and Mr. Lindstrom, were sad cases. Mr. Sigler, a heavy sullen man, seemed to sleep through most of the trial. His main function was to run around doing the judge's chores. Although Sig didn't seem to like anyone, he liked the judge least of all. I would guess that Mr. Sigler has a lot of violence in him. I don't want to be in the way when it all comes out.

Mr. Lindstrom, or Lindy as he liked to be called, was the darling of the judge. A big, curly-headed, sunny-faced Swede, Lindy had a smile for everyone. Phillips believes that he is the model cop. I think he is a pig.

Lindy ran the seating arrangements in the courtroom. This was a postion of some power, because often there were more spectators than seats. And Lindy was sure to exercise whatever power he had. He made the spectators feel that the seats were his own personal property, that that he was letting people sit in them out of the goodness of his heart. Spectators had to line up in front of the courtroom door and then Lindy would let them in one by one.

Often when there were empty seats in the courtroom, and people were waiting outside, Lindy would make those people wait for 45 minutes until the next recess. And all the time that he was fucking people over in this extremely petty way, he wanted everyone to love him. He often came up to some spectator and said, "How do you like your seat, pretty good, huh?" His manic friendliness and desire to be loved (even by people he was mistreating) made Phillips think Lindy was the perfect cop.

Once a woman reporter and I were sitting in the hallway outside the courtroom. Lindy came over and told me that it was against the rules to sit down in the hallway with your feet out. I was furious and told him that he should mind his own business and stop telling people the exact manner that he wants them to live. He was shocked. He pointed to Emma and said, "See, she is sitting O.K. She has her legs folded under her." I told him he would have to physically move me if he wanted me to change my position. He said he was going to tell the judge on me. And he did.

Lindy gave himself away during the Warren Wells strip cell controversy. Most of us were outraged about the strip cell, and someone mentioned it to Lindy, who always came on as The Humane Cop. Lindy looked genuinely confused. "What is Wells complaining about? He's been in the hole before. He can do it standing on his head."

For bailiff Lindstrom the world is neatly divided into two kinds of people. The ones who go to jail and the ones who don't. Those who go to jail are some other kind of species — and although you might show a little kindness to that species and want it to like you just as you would want a dog to like you, basically it is subhuman. We humans, thinks Lindy, can do most anything to those others. They are used to it.

The courtroom was designed to intimidate the poor bastards who come before it. The judge sits behind a huge desk, peering out over his dominion. Behind him is an enormous American flag, perhaps 10 feet wide and 25 feet long. The people are reduced to spectators, bullied by the bailiff, and forced to sit in the back. They are under totalitarian control. More than once Judge Phillips told them, "There will be no laughter in this courtroom unless it is *absolutely* justified."

Much of the language of the Judge, the D.A., and the lawyers is incomprehensible to any defendant. People on trial are supposed to be confused observers, not allowed to speak or display emotion. At the beginning of the trial the Judge pulled me aside and told me affectionately, "Mr. Bardacke, your face is much too expressive. You are just hurting yourself with the jury." The perfect defendant, like the perfect high school student, should come to court wasted on smack.

The conspiracy law was the strongest part of Lowell Jensen's case. The law is so broad and vague that it seems to make the planning of any militant demonstration illegal. One conspires when he adopts, along with others, a common design to commit an unlawful act—or a lawful act in an unlawful manner. You don't even have to know your fellow conspirators. All you have to do is to "adopt a common design."

Confident that the law was with him, Lowell Jensen put on his case. His two undercover agents—young recruits taken right out of Junior College police science classes—identified all of us as leaders of Stop the Draft Week. Some grown-up pigs testified that they ordered the crowd to disperse and they didn't, forcing the cops to clear them out.

A few other witnesses testified that we hired buses, opened bank accounts, passed out leaflets, all in the name of Stop the Draft Week. One pig said brother Bob Mandel had hit him. And finally Jensen read from our leaflets which advocated shutting down the induction center, freeing people from the police, and blocking the inductee buses.

The prosecution's star witness was undercover agent Bruce Coleman. A young man whose face seemed to disappear under close scrutiny, Coleman was terrified on the witness stand. The muscles in his face went a hundred miles an hour. When Jensen asked him to identify us, he slowly rose, crossed the room and carefully looking away from our stares, pointed us out. He deserved to be hated, but I only pitied him.

Our lawyers cut up these witnesses pretty bad. But we did not really dispute anything they said (except the lie about Bob hitting the cop). We helped organize Stop the Draft Week. We were proud of it, and not about to deny it. In cross-examination we simply tried to bring out the cop witnesses and let them display themselves to the jury. A few were pigs, a few were mechanical men, and a few were liars. We hoped the jury would notice.

Our defense was managed by three lawyers: Charlie Garry, Dick Hodge, and Mal Burnstein. These three entirely dissimilar men worked beautifully together and pulled off the miraculous. At the beginning of the trial they told us that an acquittal was impossible and the most we could hope for was a hung jury. Their skill as political lawyers far surpassed their talent as prophets.

I first met Charles R. (R for Rasputin, says Charlie) Garry three years ago. Stew Albert, Marvin Garson, Pete Camejo, Mike Smith, Jack Weinberg, and I were charged with several misdemeanors, stemming from a Berkeley street demonstration in support of Buddhist demonstrations in South Vietnam. We knew nothing about Garry, and he knew nothing about us. We just dropped by his office to see if he would take our case. He let us talk for a little while and then interrupted, "OK, what are your politics?" Stew, in the great P.L. tradition he then followed, puffed out his chest and announced in a large voice, "I am a communist." Charlie answered, "Big fucking deal."

Toward the end of the "interview" we still did not know if he would take the case. We had asked him a few times, but we never got a straight answer. Then Charlie noticed that one of the soles of Stew's shoes was almost worn away. Charlie casually asked him his shoe size. "I don't know, it's so long since I bought a pair." Charlie pulled out from under his desk a fifty dollar pair of shoes, "Here, see if these fit you." Stew tried them on, they fit, and he began thanking Charlie. He was cut off. "Listen, I can't have my clients going without shoes—it might give me a bad name."

There are a million Charlie Garry stories, but they don't capture all of him. He surprised us, right up to the last day of the trial. An hour before the jury brought down the verdict, Charlie stood on his head for ten minutes in the middle of the courtroom. All I can do is lay down some disconnected impressions, all of which, I should warn you, are highly colored by my love for the man.

Charlie lives for the courtroom. During our trial he often ate a quick lunch and returned to court an hour early to study his notes. The year he took our Berkeley street demonstration case he handled 50 trials. Since the Huey Newton case he has given full time to the Panthers, the Oakland Seven, and now the Chicago Conspiracy.

He finished the Warren Wells case on a Friday. Then, the day before Christmas, he called up all us defendants. "I have been studying your case over the weekend. Let's talk about it. Can you make it to my office in a couple of hours?" When I got there he was running all over the office, answering the phone, and trying to cement an alliance between us and the Black Panthers. I think it was then that he jumped up and screamed, "Hell, they should pin a medal on you guys, not charge you with conspiracy." It was a terrific Christmas present.

In court Charlie is aggressive and dramatic. It is not an act. He is always aggressive and dramatic. At first his aggressiveness puts people off. During jury selection he screamed at some of the jurors. He even asked one woman if her constant twitching meant that she was too nervous to be a fair juror. His manner shocked the jury and infuriated the judge. But he got away with it. He screams, but he also jokes. He gets angry, but he also gets sad, hurt, embarrassed, and happy. He hides none of it.

But the reason juries love him is that he cuts through the pretensions of the court. He has little education—he never went to college—and he speaks plain old American. He cannot pronounce any of the court Latin, and he cannot spell. During the trial he wrote Hap Hazard on the board. He loved the jokes that ensued. He is incapable of a pompous act, and if the jury is made up of working-class Americans they know immediately that they have at least one friend in the courtroom.

His great virtues as a lawyer are setting the proper political tone and cross-examination. Rather than taking the politics out of a case—as most lawyers do—he emphasizes the politics. He claims that in a political trial you must explain your politics to the jury. What happens is that *Charlie* explains the defendant's politics to the jury—that is not always the same as the defendant's politics—but it is pretty damn good. He turned the Huey Newton trial into a teach-in on racism and self-defense. He turned the Oakland Seven trial into a teach-in on free speech, police brutality, and the war in Vietnam.

Charlie is a master at cross-examination. He showed his stuff on the very first prosecution witness, Deputy Chief Brown. A tall, smooth middle-class cop, Brown is a professional witness. He testified with a practiced look of confused innocence. When Charlie was done with him he looked more confused and not at all innocent.

Charlie's technique with Brown was simple and direct. While he was cross-examining him he held a copy of Brown's earlier testimony about Stop The Draft Week before the Grand Jury. Brown had given that testimony over a year ago. There would be a long pause (Charlie is not afraid of a 3-minute silence while he prepares a question) as he read the testimony to himself, sure that Brown could see what he was doing. Then a burst. "Mr. Witness, is it your testimony *now* that you gave three dispersal orders? Remember you are under oath." The cop was terrified that he would be caught in a lie. Real quick he had to try to remember what happened, what he said had happened a year ago, and what he should say now. That was simply too much to ask, even of a Deputy Chief.

Charlie's cross-examination was filled with shotgun questions which kept witnesses off balance. "Do you know what a fink rat is?" "You are a man with a tremendous temper, aren't you?" "Is that a baseball bat in your hand?" he asked a cop looking at a picture of himself with a billy club. He also staged a battle with a cop, tricking the poor sucker into manhandling him in front of the jury.

The last Charlie Garry story I will lay on you displays his own favorite skill: the quip under pressure. Several Black Panthers were interviewing Charlie before he was hired to defend Huey Newton. Some Panthers were reluctant to have Huey defended by a white man. They were putting this 60-year-old man through his paces, acting tough, and throwing questions at him. Finally someone said, "You think you are so good—are you as good as Perry Mason?" Charlie shot back: "I'm better. Both of us get all our clients off; but Mason's clients are innocent." Ain't nobody going to fuck with Charles Rasputin Garry.

But as great as Charlie Garry is, the Oakland Seven case was not his victory. We were defended by a team of three lawyers, and it was the team that won. Richard Hodge is a good looking young man with a constant smile and the demeanor of a swinger. He has all the tools to be a highly successful establishment lawyer. Good looks, intelligence, an easygoing manner, and a straight background. He studied to be a Methodist Minister and he has worked in a District Attorney's office. But somewhere along the line he picked up a nagging conscience. He is now sacrificing a potentially lucrative practice to become a Movement lawyer. That is a mark of the Movement's health.

Dick played a crucial role in the trial. Charlie's cursive cross-examination was often sloppy and Dick unfailingly cleaned it up. He prepared most of the defense witnesses and always brought the best out of them. His summation was magnificent—a beautiful mixture of political plain talk, common sense discussion of the evidence, and passion. Everyone congratulated him afterward, but Chick Harrison gave him the greatest compliment. Chick looked very worried.

Our third lawyer, Malcolm Burnstein, was the legal expert in the case. He had at his command all the legal arguments against the war and a forceful argument showing the relevance of the Nuremburg judgment. Mal claimed our attempt to close down the Induction Center was legal because the war in Vietnam is illegal and a crime against humanity. During the trial he constantly pressed this view whenever it conceivably could be introduced. Phillips turned him back at every turn, but Mal's arguments were so good that Phillips could never say why he was turning them down. He would just apologize and rule against us. Once he pointed out that the issues had not been introduced in other cases and said, "I am sorry, Mr. Burnstein, but I am just a Superior Court Judge."

Poor Mal suffered, as he is wont to do. A man committed to the intellect, Mal could not stand to have his arguments turned down without being answered. He would stand before the judge and die a little. But all this suffering was rewarded. Phillips brought Nuremberg into the instructions. He told the jury that they could take into account any evidence that indicated that we believed we were upholding the law and not breaking it.

The instructions were Mal's triumph. He argued for a day and a half in defense of his suggested instructions. Not only did the judge grant the Nuremberg instruction, he also gave several good First Amendment instructions. He even told the jury that the First Amendment protects the advocacy of illegal acts in the absence of immediate danger. After all those losses, Mal scored the single most important victory of the case. Legally it was now possible for the jury to consider our attitude toward the war, and how the conspiracy law measures up against the First Amendment. That was an important wedge.

We had a simple defense strategy. We attempted to focus attention on the war in Vietnam, police brutality, and the First Amendment. We tried to force the jury to vote not on our guilt or innocence, but rather for or against the war, for or against the police, and for or against free speech.

The war and the cops are straightforward issues, but the First Amendment is weird. We did try to shut down the Oakland Induction Center. Our lawyers could argue that this was just an ordinary demonstration, but it was not. We said at the time that it was a new kind of militant demonstration. The First Amendment does not protect those who close down government agencies. Some day a Movement lawyer is going to argue that blowing up a police station is protected by the First Amendment because it is symbolic speech.

But the Federal Government did not indict us for interfering with the Selective Service System. Instead they left it up to Alameda County to punish us. In order to pin felonies on us Alameda County charged us with conspiracy to commit misdemeanors. Organizing almost any demonstration involves planning to break misdemeanors. And the conspiracy law makes such plans a felony. That is unfair and unjust, but I don't believe it is a violation of the First Amendment.

All of this is very hairy and quickly becomes impossible to understand. But don't worry. You are not supposed to be able to understand the law. That is for judges and lawyers. Just remember, if you fight people who have power you will surely do something illegal. But when you get into court you may discover that you can convince the jury that the people with power are evil and wrong—and you are right. The jury will then try to find a legal excuse to let you off.

We tried to show the righteousness of our cause through 47 defense witnesses. They were supposed to represent the Movement to the jury. Primarily young, they ranged from McCarthy kids to Crazies. All of them had been at the demonstration. We did include some respectable types—doctors, ministers, and even a probation officer. But we did not attempt to represent ourselves as any more respectable than we actually are.

Each witness tried to get across our three major political points. The first question to every witness was, why did you attend the demonstration? This allowed the witness to give a short speech against the war. In some cases the witnesses gave long speeches against the war — Phillips allowed that because the witness supposedly was only reporting what he earlier had said to a defendant. Then the typical witness said that he was not under orders from any of the defendants and that the demonstration was organized just like any other demonstration. Finally the witness reported incidents of police brutality.

Although the majority of the testimony fit this simple pattern, it was highly varied and usually exciting. The defense witnesses stood as strong contrast to the mechanical testimony of the prosecution witnesses. None of our people were professional witnesses. Some got mad and yelled at Jensen, some wept, and most were open and obviously telling the truth.

Their testimony was so successful that we no longer considered our own testimony crucial. And all the lawyers felt that if we testified, Jensen would be able to build up his weak case through cross-examination. All of us had written articles which tied together all the loose ends of Jensen's case. These articles could not be introduced unless we testified. So in a move that dropped Jensen's jaw we rested our case without taking the stand.

And the whole mess went to the jury. The jury was a wondrous mystery. We gave them our constant attention, always guessing and arguing about where they were at. This reached an insane level when the jury returned to re-hear testimony. We sat there staring at them, trying to interpret a raised eyebrow or a tightening mouth.

When they left to deliberate Charlie called a conference, and we discussed our impressions. "Mrs. Wood looks very tired, she is being put through a wringer." "I am sure she is against us." "Why?" "She takes notes whenever there is a good prosecution point." "So does Salazar, and he supports us." We actually had some bad-tempered arguments about how the jury lined up.

This attempt to guess the position of the jurors was particularly difficult because the jury was picked for their lack of obvious feelings. American courts are committed to the ignorance theory of objectivity. Supposedly, the less you know about a subject the more objective you can be. During jury selection anyone who voiced a strong opinion about the war or the draft or demonstrations was sure to be rejected. Mrs. Daws, juror No. 11, is the perfect juror. She does not read a newspaper. She doesn't watch TV news or listen to the radio. She has no opinions. She is one of those women who thinks that ignorance is attractive.

Anyone who had any direct knowledge of the demonstration was automatically rejected. Judge Phillips put it best: "Eyewitnesses, of course, would have a hard time judging the evidence." If there were a general uprising, would it be impossible to bring the leaders to trial because there would be no objective jurors? I understand the Chicago Eight asking for a 25-year continuance on just those grounds.

More goes on during jury selection than just trying to find people who have no opinions. Both the prosecution and the defense try to figure out which jurors do have opinions and are trying to hide them. It is an exciting game. Jensen, assuming that all blacks would be anti-cop, kicked them off the jury. He finally accepted one, Ulysses Peters, who said that he had a son in Vietnam who disapproved of anti-war demonstrations. That and the man's polite demeanor encouraged Lowell to believe he had found a Tom.

We tried to keep on workers with trade union affiliations, any third world people, young people, and those who we guessed were against the war but hiding it. After more than two weeks the game grew very tiring and we accepted a jury.

The jury had two secretaries, 39 and 49 years old; two housewives, 44 and 38; a carpenter, 51; two post office clerks, 43 and 54; an assembly line worker in a Ford plant, 28; a tool and die maker who works for Defense Technology Laboratory and has a security clearance, 48; a supply manager for Lawrence Radiation Laboratory also with a security clearance, 40; an accountant for Smith Corona, 34; and a retired Marine colonel, 62.

Who knows how to categorize this jury? Should we call them average Americans? Working class? New working class? Old working class? Lower middle class? Upper lower class? Liberals? Protofascists? Neopopulists? I don't know. Ask some of your friends who are expert in such matters.

This collection of Americans acquitted us in a situation where the law allowed them to find us guilty. They chose the Movement over the police. Mrs. Reitsma, the lone Republican juror, is now reading *Soul on Ice* "to find out why the Oakland Seven supports Huey Newton." She told a reporter that "I have been a sitter my whole life, but I now realize I was just playing into the hands of the power structure."

The whole experience must have been quite special. One of the jurors told us that the jury plans to have a reunion every month. That won't last, but it is easy to see why they want it.

How many Americans have an opportunity to make a decision of the highest public importance? Americans are hungry for politics. These lucky twelve, chosen because they were apolitical, were thrust into a situation where politics was forced upon them. They loved it.

A special experience for the jurors, the trial was an extraordinary experience for us. At first we were afraid our trial might go the way of the Spock trial. The Spock conspirators never got together. They each had separate lawyers running separate defenses. I am told that their lawyers did not even sit together in court. The defendants lived through their trial separately, afraid for their individual safety and suffering private pain.

But we were too young to do that. The Spock conspirators had fully-developed private lives they felt they had to protect. Most of us were kids, still in the street, trying to decide how to live. We had little to protect; the indictment eventually shook us away from our private lives and threw us together as brothers.

The trial and our defense forced us to work together on a single project for an extended period. That is a blessing for a New Left activist. It is probably the only way to get anything done in politics. It is certainly the only way to live.

We worked together, rode to court together, got high together, shared our "personal" problems with each other, fought viciously among ourselves, and finally looked at each other and said, "OK, brother, I see who you are, I respect it, and you are good enough for me."

Now that the trial is over it will be impossible to keep all that. The Oakland Seven was created by D.A. J. Frank Coakley. We cannot artificially hold it together. We are not a revolutionary party, we cannot find a single political project to unite us, and eventually we will go our separate ways. We will still be friends, of course, but brothers and sisters, no. We won't achieve that until we meet on the barricades.

MICHAEL ZWERIN

One Of 'Them'

"Inside, the situation was such that I was worried about the safety of my wife and child. But there were a lot of cops outside, so I knew it wasn't safe there either."

— Fred Powledge

The horny courts grind away . . . day after day . . . while you and I . . . you anyway . . . go oblivious about business . . . out in so-called normal society.

Drunks with scabby faces named McCabe, Jones, Kelly, and Washington weave their way to the bench:

"Ten days, suspend execution."

"Five days, suspend execution."

"You've had nine suspended sentences . . . ten days." Who cares?

Then there are the breakers and enterers, the armed robbers, the car thieves, the disturbers of our peace, the alimony welchers.

Relatives, friends, witnesses, and accused sit quietly in the chock gallery, blank, submissive, terribly sad, resigned, mostly black. Lenny Bruce knew what the law does to these people.

The court will come to boredom . . . boredom, please, boredom in the court. The Sixth Circuit Court of New Haven is now in session. I am charged: breach of the peace, resisting arrest, and interfering with a police officer.

This is my case. Fred Powledge was writing a story on rock for *Life*, Yvonne Chabrier his reporter, Tim Page the photographer. I went with them to hear The Doors in the New Haven Arena. Jim Morrison was taken into custody on stage for alleged obscenities. A small riot ensued. Only slightly oversimplifying. Tim was arrested for taking pictures of cops enjoying their work perhaps a bit too much. Yvonne asked the poleaseman—thank you John Lennon—if she could have Tim's car keys, cameras, and film. She was arrested. I went over to inquire after the situation. "Excuse me, officer, but I'm with these people. Can you tell me . . .?"

"He's one of them . . . You're under arrest too.

Patrolman Legrand is right, of course. I am indeed one of "them." I just don't look right. A guy like me must be doing something wrong.

You ought to know Patrolman Legrand, badge 480. His cheeks are cherubic, dimpled, his dark hair crew-cut. He probably loves his children, if he has any, but his eyes are not paternal, they are cold, dull, shifty—all cop. He is formidable in his uniform. I suggest you stay out of his way. His hand shook and his face twitched arresting me. Maybe it was nervousness or tension, but the word "orgasm" crossed my mind.

We were booked. They took our belts and put us in the tank about 12:30. Fred Powledge arrived with a lawyer, a bail bondsman, and Yvonne, just sprung from the women's pen, and Tim and I were out on $300 bail at dawn. Morrison, who had been in the same tank, was already on his way to L.A. by then, his bond of $1500 having been posted in case four hours earlier. As Sophie Tucker said, "I've been rich and I've been poor. Rich is better."

Back in New Haven two weeks later, *Life* hired a member of the Connecticut bar to defend the three of us. I was paying my own third. The New Haven courthouse is right out of Dickens, a Victorian monstrosity, patched, peeling, dimly lit, and smelly. An empty pint of BonCore white port wine—"Pure California, alcohol 20 per cent by volume"—stood by the courtroom door. Crooked, weathered shades cover the dirty windows. The ceiling is at least 60 feet high, and neon lighting fixtures hang from it on 40-foot unpainted chains. Green paint peels off the wall near a clock, which is slow. There are no slowly turning hanging fans.

On the other side of the barrier: the boys. The courthouse gang. Bailiffs, clerks, bondsmen, stenographers, assistant D.A.s, cops, detectives—you know, the guys. Jack Ruby was like that. They took the little woman and the kids out for a pizza last night, and they talk about it. The conversation moves along to dirty jokes and bowling scores while they're waiting for their scene to start. And there isn't much doubt that it is their scene. You are uncomfortable, they are not. You don't know correct procedure, they do. You have no idea how long you will have to wait, they don't care. We know who the courthouse in-crowd is.

"Everybody stand." Justice creaks to the bench, a very old and not wise looking man with an extremely sour red face. Thank God we were there only to plead.

That week we learned that Jim Morrison paid the city of New Haven $1500 for having violated his constitutional right of free speech. The deal: "Tell ya what, fella—you agree to drop da ball and we just forget about da whole ting. Dat way we save each udder a lotta trouble."

The flower people in L.A. said O.K. A practical decision. Morrison can afford it, particularly in view of all the concerts and record dates he'd have to cancel to come back. Besides, the judge takes one look at that freaky-looking kid and he's guilty in front anyway.

Still paying for my own defense, and worried about it (*Life* had hired a high-powered firm), I was tempted to take the same escape route when the prosecution suggested we plead guilty to breach of peace, pay a $25 fine, and they would drop the other charges. But the legal lawyers, as my friend Harry calls them, decided that a unilateral action like this on my part would damage Tim and Yvonne. They offered to pay for my case too. Thanks to *Life's* money, I was still not guilty in the eyes of the law. Did you hear that, Sophie?

And how, rich is better! If you make, say, $100 a week and are supporting a wife and kid, you won't qualify for Legal Aid.

But you also can't afford the time and expense for your defense. You'll probably be just one more, and end up paying the $25, or more, anyhow. Better plead guilty. There's only one drawback: you'll have a record.

Two weeks later we were up at 6:30 again, on the turnpike by 7:30, in the lawyer's office by 9, in court at 10 for the trial. Fred Powledge was there as a witness for the defense. So was Steve Burbank, a senior at Harvard who had been to the concert, observed the busts, and volunteered his name and address to Fred. Joan Rubin came as my character witness. David Hubbard, a lawyer and old friend of Yvonne's family, came for her.

We waited while justice plodded, impotent as ever. First the drunks came out of a padlocked door, some going back in, others suspended. Everything is processed, documents are shifted from one pile to another, cases come and go, solving nothing. Set bail, change plea, recess, wait and smoke outside, some continuances, lunch at a greasy spoon, wait some more. At 2 o'clock case number 60, your honor: Sam Thompson. Is Sam Thompson in the court? Sam Thompson steps forward in need of a shave. His white Legal Aid pleads extenuating circumstances and the judge gives him 30 days suspended.

Another judge this time: Judge Rottman. Do I have to describe him? He looks just like his name. We were called before him, but instead of a trial we got the word that Patrolman Legrand had phoned in with laryngitis early that morning and, without its witness, the State needed a continuance. Our lawyer pleaded extreme inconvenience: "Your honor, these people are from out of town." He requested that the charges be dropped. His honor stared—bored—and denied. A new date was set, two weeks later, at which time we went through the same thing all over again, except without Tim. On assignment somewhere, he had left instructions to forfeit his bond. The power of the State was beginning to take its toll; we were suffering casualties. And the prosecution kept the initiative. They refused to try us without Tim, on the ground that the lawyer had not moved to separate the cases. The fact that Tim would never be tried did not stop the judge from agreeing that to proceed without him would be an "undue hardship on the State."

Judge Rottman was a pillar, his face a study of the fix. Not a pay-off graft or anything as minor as that—a bigger fix, accepted, legal, permanent, and hopeless. "Give me your tired, your poor, your huddled masses yearning to breathe free, the wretched refuse of your teeming shore, send these, the homeless, tempest tost to me . . ."—fuck all of you forever.

This case was a nuisance. Neither prosecutor nor judge wanted it. Any technicality on which to base a postponement was
208

welcome. Under normal circumstances, people like us busted like that would have made our deal and quit long ago. We were, according to our lawyer, Bill Egan, a rather special case.

The fourth time up, we finally had our trial. The scene in the courtroom was the same. Only the judge had changed and, it was apparent from the beginning, for the better. Judge Philip Dwyer could play Joseph Welch: extremely short, bald with a small grey fringe and a pixyish face, his clip-on bow tie completes the picture. His face was bright, always ready to smile, handling the inevitable morning lineup with some degree of compassion and humanity — about as much, I'd say, as that futile scene allows.

The prosecutor, Herb Scott, is a busy man who must keep the mill going. We had many briefings and strategy sessions. Our witnesses were substantial people, lucid and sure of their veracity. All Herb Scott had was Patrolman Legrand, a shifty-eyed witness who did not tell the truth, although I couldn't say whether it was a matter of lying or forgetfulness. The tables were turning in any case.

The trial lasted a total of four hours and was worthy of Perry Mason. Witnesses were cross-examined, exhibits — some of Tim's photos — were introduced, objections were allowed and overruled. Judge Dwyer took notes, diligently and continually. He ruled carefully and asked questions often. From his attitude, you would have thought it was a manslaughter case at least.

Legrand said I had interfered along with Page and that we had been arrested together. He related how Yvonne had leaped on his back and scratched his neck, bringing blood with her nails. We had independent witnesses to testify otherwise.

In his summing-up, Bill Egan pointed out that Patrolman Legrand had been wearing an overcoat, the collar of which covered his neck. He pointed this out on one of Tim's pictures and proceeded to spell out why the other charges should be dismissed. I half expected a commercial when he sat down.

Judge Dwyer retired to his rather funky chambers to study his thick sheaf of notes, remaining there fifteen minutes. Then, settling back on the bench, he gave his opinion, which was a monument to lucidity, logic, and the law. He spoke quietly, formal but not without humor. And the courtroom no longer seemed so dismal.

He dismissed the charges one by one until only interfering with a police officer against Yvonne remained. Carefully considering his words, and with no grammatical lapses, he said: "I suppose, technically, Miss Chabrier could be found guilty of interfering . . . She did hold up an officer in his duty of executing an arrest and removing the suspect expeditiously from the scene so that the arrest would not prompt more trouble. But I think it

209

was an impetuous act and she did not intend to interfere . . . and I see no purpose being served in finding her guilty. We certainly don't need her money and the fine would be nominal in any case. She is only 24. Next year she will be 25. Someday she will be 50 and possibly look back on all of this with some degree of humor . . . and I imagine she has learned a lesson by now anyway . . . I find her not guilty."

All along the way he was careful with Legrand, complimenting him and stating that he was not implying the officer had lied, only that the State had not proved its case beyond any reasonable doubt, which is its obligation.

In the hall, Judge Dwyer stopped to chat with us. He had enjoyed this case, he said. "All morning, during the usual hub-bub, I was thinking of my afternoon with the Ivy League."

Nothing had changed, I remembered. We had been acquitted not so much because we were innocent, but because our economic situation had permitted us the luxury of seeing the thing through to trial, to pay transportation for our witnesses, to have a good lawyer from a name firm. Without *Life* magazine's money behind us, both Yvonne and I would almost certainly have pleaded guilty to something long before. I'm no expert, but there is clearly something wrong with that.

I thank Judge Dwyer, not so much for finding me innocent, but for giving me a little hope for justice in America. As long as there are men like him presiding, it's not all lost. But I can't forget the continuing "hub-bub of the morning" in the Sixth Circuit Court of New Haven. I can't forget Judge Rottman's face, or the expression on Legrand's when we were acquitted. We got away with something only because we are "them." Next time he will be rougher.

This is not a happy ending.

EPILOGUE
ABBIE HOFFMAN

Testimony:
United States of America, Plaintiff, vs. David T. Dellinger, et al

December 23, 1969

Direct examination of Defendant Abbott H. Hoffman by Defense Attorney Weinglass.

Q: Will you please identify yourself for the record.

A: My name is Abbie. I am an orphan of America.

Q: Where do you reside?

A: I live in Woodstock Nation.

Q: Will you tell the Court and jury where it is.

A: Yes. It is a nation of alienated young people. We carry it around with us as a state of mind in the same way the Sioux Indians carried the Sioux nation around with them. It is a nation dedicated to cooperation versus competition, to the idea that people should have better means of exchange than property or money, that there should be some other basis for human interaction. It is a nation dedicated to—

THE COURT: Excuse me, sir.

Read the question to the witness, please.

(Question read.)

THE COURT: Just where it is, that is all.

THE WITNESS: It is in my mind and in the minds of my brothers and sisters. We carry it aound with us in the same way that the Sioux Indians carried around the Sioux nation. It does not consist of property or material but, rather, of ideas and certain values, those values being cooperation versus competition, and that we believe in a society—

MR. SCHULTZ: This doesn't say where Woodstock Nation, whatever that is, is.

MR. WEINGLASS: Your Honor, the witness has identified it as being a state of mind and he has, I think, a right to define that state of mind.

THE COURT: No, we want the place of residence, if he has one, place of doing business, if you have a business, or both if you desire to tell them both. One address will be sufficient. Nothing about philosophy or India, sir. Just where you live, if you have a place to live.

Now, you said Woodstock. In what state is Woodstock?

THE WITNESS: It is in the state of mind, in the mind of myself and my brothers and sisters. It is a conspiracy.

Q: Can you tell the Court and jury your present age?

A: My age is 33. I am a child of the 60's.

Q: When were you born?

A: Psychologically, 1960.

Q: Can you tell the Court and jury what is your present occupation?

A. I am a cultural revolutionary. Well, I am really a defendant—

Q: What do you mean?

A: —full time.

THE COURT: . . . Will you remain quiet while I am making a ruling? I know you have no respect for me.

MR. KUNSTLER: Your Honor, that is totally unwarranted.

MR. SCHULTZ: That is not unwarranted. Mr. Kunstler here in the presence of the jury the other day said the Defendant Hoffman had changed his name from Hoffman because it was the same name, indicating it was the same name. Mr. Kunstler is the one who initiated this, and now he takes great offense that your Honor—

THE COURT: I am mindful of that.

MR. KUNSTLER: I think your remarks call for a motion for a mistrial.

THE COURT: And your motion calls for a denial of the motion. Mr. Weinglass, continue with your examination.

MR. KUNSTLER: You denied my motion? I hadn't even started to argue it.

THE COURT: I don't need any argument on that one.

THE COURT: The witness turned his back on me while he was on the witness stand.

MR. KUNSTLER: Oh, your Honor, aren't—

MR. SCHULTZ: Mr. Kunstler went out of his way, out of his way the other day to explain to the jury that the Defendant Hoffman had eliminated his last name.

THE COURT: I will have no further argument on your motion. I will ask you to sit down.

THE WITNESS: I was just looking at the pictures of the long-hairs up on the wall.

Q: During the year 1967, were you living a totally private life?

MR. SCHULTZ: Objection to the form of the question.

THE WITNESS: I understand that one.

THE COURT: I sustain the objection.

THE WITNESS: I didn't understand the other one, but I understand that question.

THE COURT: I heard the objection. I sustain the objection. I relieve you of the obligation of answering it.

THE WITNESS: Oh, thanks. Gee.

Testimony by Defendant HOFFMAN *regarding previous Yippie activity.*

A: The money that I got from that job two weeks later I threw it out in the Stock Exchange in New York City on Wall Street, meaning to the other people who were in the money, we wanted to make a statement that we weren't doing it for money, and that, in fact, money should be abolished. We didn't believe in a society that people had to interact with money and property, but should be on more humanitarian bases. That was what the community was about.

MR. WEINGLASS: Now, in exorcising the Pentagon, were there any plans for the building to raise up off the ground?

A: Yes. When we were arrested they asked us what we were doing. We said it was to measure the Pentagon and we wanted a permit to raise it 300 feet in the air, and they said "How about 10?" So we said "O.K." And they threw us out of the Pentagon and we went back to New York and had a press conference, told them what it was about.

MR. SCHULTZ: I would ask Mr. Weinglass please get on with the trial of this case and stop playing around with raising the Pentagon 10 or 300 feet off the ground.

THE WITNESS: They are going to bring it up.

MR. SCHULTZ: There are serious issues here and if we could get to them so that he can examine the witness, I can cross-examine the witness and we can move on.

MR. KUNSTLER: Your Honor, this is not playing around. This is a deadly serious business. The whole issue in this case is language, what is meant by —

MR. SCHULTZ: This is not —

THE COURT: Let Mr. Weinglass defend himself.

MR. WEINGLASS: Your Honor, I am glad to see Mr. Schultz finally concedes that things like levitating the Pentagon building, putting LSD in the water, 10,000 people walking nude on Lake Michigan, a $200,000 bribe attempt are all playing around. I am willing to concede that fact, that was all playing around, it was a play idea of the witness, and if he is willing to concede it, we can all go home.

THE COURT: I sustain—

MR. WEINGLASS: Because he is treating all these things as deadly serious.

Q: What equipment, if any, did you personally plan to use in the exorcism of the Pentagon?

A: I brought a number of noisemakers—

MR. SCHULTZ: Objection if the Court please.

THE COURT: I sustain the objection.

Testimony by Defendant HOFFMAN *concerning remarks made by* JERRY RUBIN *at a pre-Convention meeting.*

A: Jerry Rubin, I believe, said that it would be a good idea to call it the Festival of Life in contrast to the Convention of Death, and to have it in some kind of public area, like a park or something, in Chicago. . . .

At one point, I believe it was Mr. Krassner, when we were talking about the Hippie community, Mr. Rubin asked how come we are called Hippies when we never called each other that, but we look in the papers and read day and night about this thing, and we are called Hippie, and I said that was a myth, that myths are created by media, by people communicating to each other, but it wasn't an accurate description of the phenomenon that was taking place, and the phenomenon had to be experienced itself, and I described to Mr. Rubin my attitude about communication.

December 24, 1969

Colloquy between JUDGE HOFFMAN *and* MR. KUNSTLER.

MR. KUNSTLER: . . . [I]n the years I have practiced in both federal and state courts, I have never accused, if I can recall at all, either judge or prosecutor of using intimidating tactics on me. This is my first time.

THE COURT: This may come as a surprise to you. In all the years I have sat on both benches, no lawyer, no lawyer has ever charged me with intimidation.

MR. KUNSTLER: Well, your Honor, this is an unusual case. There have been unusual things done and said by many people.

THE COURT: In many respects, it is unusual.

MR KUNSTLER: Your Honor has for the first time found lawyers in contempt.

THE COURT: I didn't ask for this case to be assigned to my

214

calendar, and if you think that I recommend it to any other judge for a summer vacation, you are mistaken.

MR. KUNSTLER: I think we all agree on that.

Colloquy concerning absence of Defendant HOFFMAN.

MR. WEINGLASS: . . . I ask the Court to adjourn to Room 406A of Michael Reese [Hospital] where your Honor could for yourself talk to Abbie and see his condition with doctors present and make a determination right at that point.

THE COURT: You know despite the complaints that have been made by representatives of the defendants about the size of this courtroom, I find it pretty nice. I don't feel that I am living in squalor here. I think I will refrain from going to Michael Reese. It is really very depressing, hospitals are depressing, especially in their crowded conditions now.

Present my compliments to Mr. Hoffman and thank him for the invitation. Tell him that I decline it with regrets.

December 29, 1969

Continued direct examination of Defendant HOFFMAN. *Testimony by* A. HOFFMAN *about founding of Yippies.*

A: . . . Anita said at that time that although "Yippie" would be understood by our generation, that straight newspapers like the *New York Times* and the U.S. Government and the courts and everything wouldn't take it seriously unless it had a kind of formal name, so she came up with the name of the "Youth International Party." She said that we could play a lot of jokes on the concept of party because everybody would think that we were this huge international conspiracy, but that in actuality we were a party that you had fun at.

Colloquy concerning admission of "flyer" as evidence.

MR. SCHULTZ: . . . The identical sheet is already in evidence. It was put in by the Government. It is marked Government Exhibit C-2.

I don't see any reason for there being two of them.

MR. RUBIN: Ours is in color.

MR. WEINGLASS (*speaking to* JUDGE HOFFMAN): We have attempted to lay a foundation that the Festival of Life was a further conceptualization of guerrilla theater and to give an idea of what their intent was in coming to Chicago to have a festival, you have to go back and see how the Yippie concept developed and grew through these guerrilla theater activities, starting with the money at the Stock Exchange and coming through this mock raid at Stony Brook, right up through Grand Central Station and Central Park be-in and on to Chicago. It's part and parcel of the whole history and pattern of why and how the Yippies came to Chicago and what they had in mind when they came here, so I think it is essential and critical to an understanding of precisely what's on trial, and what is their intent in coming here.

MR. WEINGLASS: Directing your attention to Sunday, May 13, which is Mother's Day, 1968, where were you on that day?

A: I was in Lincoln Park in Chicago.

Q: What was occurring in the park at that time?

A: There was what we might call a mini festival of life, a rock concert, I believe. Rev. Tuttle was marrying people. There were marriages taking place and there was a preparation—everybody had pies, apple pies and cherry pies and were going to march to the 18th—there was the beginning of a march to the police station to present the police who were on duty that Sunday, Mother's Day, with pies, apple pies.

Q: Do you know that this was done?

A: There were about 300 people—

MR. SCHULTZ: Objection. Marching to the police station on Mother's Day with pies is irrelevant.

MR. WEINGLASS: It is irrelevant by Government standards. If they went to the police station carrying bombs, they would say that was relevant.

December 30, 1969

Continued direct examination of Defendant A. HOFFMAN.

THE COURT: Bring in the jury, please, Mr. Marshal.

DEFENDANT HOFFMAN: Wait a second. We have a matter—

THE COURT: Who was that waving and talking at me, one of the lawyers?

MR. SCHULTZ: He is acting as his own lawyer, I think, your Honor. Abbie Hoffman. He is doing a pretty good job of it. He shows Mr. Weinglass up.

DEFENDANT HOFFMAN: Wait until you get your chance.

Q: Could you relate to the Court and to the jury the substance of your conversation with David Stahl [Deputy Mayor of Chicago] at that time.

A: Well, I said, "Hi, Dave. How's it going?" I said, "Your

police got to be the dumbest—the dumbest and the most brutal in the country," that the decision to drive people out of the park in order to protect the city was about the dumbest military tactic since the Trojans first let the Trojan horse inside the gate and that there was nothing that compared with that stupidity. I again pleaded with him to let people stay in the park the following night. I said that there were more people coming to Chicago. There would be more people coming Monday, Tuesday, and subsequently Wednesday night, and that they should be allowed to sleep, that there was no place to sleep, that the hotels are all booked up, that people were getting thrown out of hotels, that they were getting thrown out of restaurants, and that he ought to intercede with the police department. I told him that the city officials, in particular his boss, Daley, were totally out of their minds, that I had read in the paper the day before that they had 2,000 troops surrounding the reservoirs in order to protect against the Yippie plot to dump LSD in the drinking water. I said that there wasn't a kid in the country, never mind a Yippie, who thought that such a thing could even be done, that why didn't he check with all the scientists at the University of Chicago—he owned them all. I said that it couldn't in fact be done.

He said that he knew it couldn't be done, but they weren't taking any chances anyway. I thought it was about the weirdest thing I had ever heard. I said, "Well, it was good advice, that he could withdraw those troops, that that couldn't be done, but maybe Mayor Daley was taking a little acid," and I told him—I told him that he could get in touch with me through the Seed office but that really if he just wanted to contact me, he knew where to reach me any minute since there were two policemen and sometimes four from the Chicago Intelligence office following me all day . . .

MR. WEINGLASS: Did you speak for an hour, Abbie, on this speech?

MR. SCHULTZ: It isn't Abbie, it is a 33-year-old man. His name is Mr. Hoffman.

THE COURT: Oh, yes, but that has been gone into. If a lawyer persists in that, there is nothing very much I can do about it at this time.

MR. WEINGLASS: Could you relate to the Court as much as you can of your speech?

A: I think I can, Len.

THE COURT: What did he call you?

THE WITNESS: Len.

MR. WEINGLASS: Len. It is the appropriate name.

Defendant HOFFMAN *testifying about his arrest.*

A: They grabbed me by the jacket and pulled me across the bacon and eggs and Anita over the table, threw me on the floor and out the door and threw me against the car, and they handcuffed me. I was just eating the bacon and going, "Oink, oink."

Q: Did they tell you why you were arrested?

A: They said they arrested me because I had the word "fuck" on my forehead.

Q: Now, will you explain—

A: They called it an "obscenary," they said it was an "obscenary."

Q: Can you explain to the court and the jury how that word got on your forehead that day.

A: I had it put on with this magic marker before we left the house.

Q: And why did you do that?

A: Well, there were a couple of reasons. One was that I was tired of seeing my picture in the paper and having newsmen come around, and I know if you got that word, they aren't going to print your picture in the paper, and secondly, it sort of summed up my attitude about the whole—what was going on in Chicago. It was a four-letter word for which—I liked that four-letter word. I thought it was kind of holy, actually.

Testimony describing a speech in Grant Park.

Q: Do you recall what you said to the group that had gathered there at that time?

A: I described to them the experience that had happened to me in the jails of Chicago. I said that there were young people in the jails being beaten up, that they weren't being allowed to have their lawyers. I said it was typical of what took place in jails all around the country. I described the experience in the courtroom and the attitude of the Judge and I said it was particularly common among judges in this country. I said that Lenny Bruce had once said, "In the halls of justice the only justice is in the halls." And I said that the judicial system was as corrupt as the political system.

THE COURT (*answering* MR. WEINGLASS.): . . . I have ruled on that, Mr. Weinramer—Weinglass, rather.

MR. WEINGLASS: Prior to coming to Chicago, from April 12, 1968, on to the week of the convention, did you enter into an agreement with David Dellinger, John Froines, Tom Hayden, Jerry Rubin, Lee Weiner, or Rennie Davis to come to the city of Chicago for the purpose of encouraging and promoting violence during the Convention Week?

A: An agreement?

Q: Yes.

A: We couldn't agree on lunch.

Cross-examination of Defendant HOFFMAN *by Government* ATTORNEY SCHULTZ. *Colloquy concerning a book written by Defendant* HOFFMAN.

MR. WEINGLASS: I will have fourteen copies of the book for the jury in the morning, and they can read the entire book. We are not ashamed of a word in this book.

THE COURT: No, you will not. You may have fourteen copies, but they will not go to the jury.

MR. WEINGLASS: Mr. Schultz is indicating to the jury that we are afraid of this book, and—

THE COURT: If you will listen to me, sir, I am the one who determines what the jury sees. Those books are not in evidence.

MR. WEINGLASS: Then you should admonish the U.S. Attorney not to say that we are afraid of this book.

THE COURT: I will admonish the jury—the United States Attorney—

THE WITNESS: Wait until you see the movie.

THE COURT: . . . if it is required that he be admonished.

THE WITNESS: Wait until you see the movie.

THE COURT: And you be quiet.

THE WITNESS: Well—the movie's going to be better.

MR. SCHULTZ: Did you see some people urinate on the Pentagon?

A: On the Pentagon itself?

Q: Or at the Pentagon?

A: In that general area in Washington?

Q: Yes.

A: There were in all over 100,000 people. That is, people have that biological habit.

Q: And did you?

A: Yes.

Q: Did you symbolically—

A: Did I go and look?

Q: Did you symbolically and did you—did you symbolically urinate on the Pentagon, Mr. Hoffman?

A: I symbolically urinate on the Pentagon?

Q: Yes.

A: Nearby yes, in the bushes, there, maybe 3,000 feet away from the Pentagon. I didn't get that close. Pee on the walls of the Pentagon?

You are getting to be out of sight actually. You think there is a law against it?

Q: Are you done, Mr. Hoffman?

A: I am done when you are.

Q: Did you ever on a prior occasion state that a sense of integration possesses you and comes from pissing on the Pentagon?

A: I said from combining political attitudes with biological necessity, there is a sense of integration, yes. I think I said it that way, not the way you said it, but—

Q: You had a good time at the Pentagon, didn't you, Mr. Hoffman?

A: Yes, I did. I am having a good time now.

Could I—I feel that biological necessity now. Could I be excused for a slight recess?

THE COURT: We will take a brief recess, ladies and gentlemen of the jury.

Ladies and gentlemen of the jury, we will take a brief recess.

THE WITNESS: Just a brief—

THE COURT: We will take a brief recess with my usual orders. The Court will be in recess for a brief period.

Brief recess.

Q: At this meeting on the evening of August 7, you told Mr. Stahl that you were going to have nude-ins in your liberated zone, didn't you?

A: A nude-in? I don't believe I would use that phrase, no.

Q: You told him you were going to have public fornication?

A: I might have told him that ten thousand people were going to walk naked on the waters of Lake Michigan, something like that.

Q: No, you told him specifically, didn't you, Mr. Hoffman, that you were going to have nude-ins, didn't you?

A: No. I don't—No, I don't recall using that phrase or that I ever used it. I do now. It's—I don't think it's very poetic, frankly.

Q: You told him, did you not, Mr. Hoffman, that in your liberated zone you would have—

A: I'm not even sure what it is, a nude-in.

Q: Public fornication?

A: If it means ten thousand people, naked people, walking on Lake Michigan, yes.

MR. KUNSTLER: I object to this because Mr. Schultz is acting like a dirty old man.

MR. SCHULTZ: We are not going into dirty old men. If they wanted to have 500,000 people in the park and are telling the city officials they going to have nude-ins and public fornication, the city officials react to that, and I am establishing through this witness that that's what he did, that and many more things.

THE COURT: There is no objection. Do you object?

MR. KUNSTLER: I am just remarking, your Honor, that a young man can be a dirty old man.

THE WITNESS: I don't mind talking—

THE COURT: I could make an observation. I have seen some exhibits here that are not exactly exemplary documents.

MR. KUNSTLER: But they are, from your point of view, your Honor—making a dirty word of something that can be beautiful and lovely, and that's what's being done.

THE COURT: I don't know that they have been written by the United States Attorney.

MR. SCHULTZ: We are not litigating here, your Honor, whether sexual intercourse is beautiful or not. We are litigating whether or not the city could permit tens of thousands of people to come in and do in their parks what this man said they were going to do.

THE COURT: Oh, you needn't argue that.

MR. SCHULTZ: Yes, your Honor.

MR. KUNSTLER: The city permitted them to do it in trees, your Honor, as I recall some of the testimony. The policeman was right under the tree.

THE COURT: The last observation of Mr. Kunstler may be stricken from the record.

Q: By the way, was there any acid in Lincoln Park in Chicago?

A: In the reservoir, in the lake?

Q: No, among the people.

A. Among the people was there LSD? Well, there might have been. I don't know. It is colorless, odorless, and tasteless. One can never tell.

Q: What about the honey, was there anything special about any honey in Lincoln Park?

A: There was honey, there was—I was told there was honey, that there was—I was getting stoned eating brownies. Honey, yes. Lots of people were—

Q: There was LSD to your knowledge in both the honey and in some brownies? Isn't that right?

A: I would have to be a chemist to know that for a fact. It is colorless, odorless, and tasteless.

Q: Didn't you state on a prior occasion that Ed Sanders passed out from too much honey?

A: Yes. People passed out.

THE COURT: You have answered the question.

THE WITNESS: Yes. Passed out from honey? Sure. Is that illegal?

MR. SCHULTZ: And that a man named Spade passed out on honey?

A: Yes. I made up that name. Frankie Spade, wasn't it? It must have been the strong honey.

221

THE COURT: The last observation of the witness may go out and the jury is directed to disregard it and the witness is directed again not to make gratuitous observations.

Q: It was part of your myth in getting people to Chicago, Mr. Hoffman, that it was announced that the Yippies would block traffic, isn't that right?

A: That I said that people would block traffic?

Q: No, not what you said but that it was part of the Yippie myth created early in 1968, a statement that they would block traffic?

A: Yes, I believe I heard it from Sheriff Joseph Woods.

Q: Now, prior to the beginning of the convention, Mr. Hoffman, that is, on August 22 at about five in the morning, do you recall having coffee with some police officers? I think August 22 was the day that you later went into court before Judge Lynch, so that it would be that morning, if that helps you.

A: With the policemen that were trailing me from the Chicago Red Squad? Yes. They bought me breakfast every morning and drove me around. It could have been—yes. Do you want to go further and then maybe I can recall what was said?

Q: Do you recall while having coffee with—

A: I don't drink coffee so—I haven't drank coffee for three years, so—

Q: While having breakfast—

A: It is one of the drugs I refrain from using.

Q: It was your Yippie myth, Mr. Hoffman, was it not, that people will among other things in Chicago smoke dope and fuck and fight cops?

A: Yes. I wrote that as a prediction. So did Normal Mailer, I might add.

December 31, 1969

Continued cross-examination of Defendant A. HOFFMAN *by Government* ATTORNEY SCHULTZ.

Q: In fact, you thought it was a great boon to you that your case [requesting a permit to use city park] had been assigned to Judge Lynch because you could make a lot of hay out of it, isn't that right, Mr. Hoffman?

A: No. No, I had learned at that time that they had turned down the McCarthy people's request for a permit, and I thought if they weren't going to get it, we sure as hell weren't, either, and that was one of the decisions.

THE COURT: Mr. Witness, we don't allow profanity from the witness stand.

THE WITNESS: Well, I wouldn't want—all right.

MR. SCHULTZ: When did you prepare, Mr. Hoffman, your—

THE COURT: And I don't like being laughed at by the witness —by a witness in this court, sir.

THE WITNESS: I know that laughing is a crime. I already—

THE COURT: I direct you not to laugh at an observation by the Court. I don't laugh at you.

THE WITNESS: Are you sure?

THE COURT: I should?

THE WITNESS: I said, "Are you sure?"

THE COURT: I haven't laughed at you during all of the many weeks and months of this trial.

THE WITNESS: Well—

MR. SCHULTZ: May I proceed, your Honor?

THE COURT: Yes, you may.

MR. KUNSTLER: I am not sure, your Honor, "hell" is classified as profanity, and I think from what has been circulated in this courtroom it's hardly profane language.

THE COURT: Oh, I will concede that it is a lesser degree of—

MR. KUNSTLER: I am not even sure it is classified as profanity.

THE COURT: You don't think so.

MR. KUNSTLER: I don't think—

THE COURT: Well, probably not among your clients, but I—

MR. KUNSTLER: I take it among your friends, too, Judge, and I would say you have used it and everyone else has used it.

THE COURT: I don't allow a witness to testify that way on the witness stand, if you don't mind, sir.

MR. KUNSTLER: I object to the dictionary—

THE COURT: We strive here to conduct this Court in the traditional—

MR. KUNSTLER: You say my clients are habituated to using "hell," you know, which is a categorization of my clients. My clients use lots of words, and your friends use lots of words—

THE COURT: I don't think you know any of my friends.

MR. KUNSTLER: You'd be surprised, your Honor.

THE COURT: Please don't—

MR. KUNSTLER: The father of one of our staff men is a close friend of yours.

THE COURT: If they know you, they haven't told me about it.

MR. SCHULTZ: Your Honor, may we proceed?

THE COURT: Yes.

THE WITNESS: I know your chauffeur.

MR. SCHULTZ: Mr. Hoffman, when did you prepare your original—I'll wait until you're finished laughing, Mr. Hoffman.

A: I was just laughing at your profanity.

Q: Are you ready, Mr. Hoffman?

A: Yes, ready.

Q: Are you finished, Mr. Hoffman?

A: Yes, I'm finished.

Q: Do you want to do any headstands for us?

A: No, but I think I might like to go to the bathroom, if I could.

MR. SCHULTZ: Your Honor, we only have about ten more minutes. I'd like very much to get this finished.

THE WITNESS: Ten more minutes?

MR. SCHULTZ: Can you wait ten more minutes, Mr. Hoffman? Your Honor, can we go for ten more minutes?

THE WITNESS: Yes. Yes, I'll wait.

MR. SCHULTZ: Did you hear Davis say that on the last day of the—on the last day of the Democratic National Convention there was going to be a march if there was anybody left? Did you hear him say that?

A: Was the last question—Did you ask me to do a headstand?

THE COURT: Answer this question, please.

THE WITNESS: Oh. I was going to oblige.

THE COURT: If you can.

THE WITNESS: Go ahead.

MR. SCHULTZ: Did you hear the question?

A: No, sorry. I was thinking about the last one.

THE COURT: Read it to the witness.

MR. WEINGLASS: Your Honor, he is indicating he would like to answer the question before. Mr. Schultz has expressed a request that he do a headstand, and I think he should have, in answer, an opportunity to comply with that request if that is what the witness wants to do.

THE COURT: I don't think that was put in the form of a question.

MR. SCHULTZ: I didn't intend it to be.

MR. WEINGLASS: He is stating—

MR. SCHULTZ: He is clowning for us, and I thought maybe in his clowning he would want to do a headstand or a cartwheel or something.

THE COURT: You don't want to do that, do you. You don't, do you?

THE WITNESS: I want to comply with Mr. Schultz' request, if he wants to see such a thing.

THE COURT: You want to answer the question. All right. He says no, in effect.

THE WITNESS: I think it might start a riot.

THE COURT: That question has been answered.

THE WITNESS: Could you hurry it up a little? O.K. Sorry.

MR. SCHULTZ: Mr. Hoffman—Well, maybe we ought to take a break now, Mr. Hoffman is uncomfortable.

THE WITNESS: Well, is it five more minutes?

THE COURT: Well, I don't know whether "uncomfortable" is the proper characterization.

THE WITNESS: Just two minutes.

The Court then recessed.

Concerning JUDGE'S *ruling that Witness* HOFFMAN *must answer a prosecution question.*

THE WITNESS: I consider that an unfair ruling and I am not going to answer. I can't answer.

THE COURT: I direct you to answer.

THE WITNESS: Well, I take the Fifth Amendment, then.

MR. SCHULTZ: Your Honor, the witness has taken the stand to defend the charges here. He has testified on direct examination and he has waived his Fifth Amendment right.

THE COURT: I order you to answer, sir.

THE WITNESS: What does that mean?

THE COURT: I order you to answer the question, sir. You are required to under the law. . . . I order you to answer the question. Do you refuse?

MR. WEINGLASS: Your Honor, could we have a recess.

THE COURT: No, no. We just had a recess for that purpose.

MR. WEINGLASS: For another question —

THE COURT: No, no. No further recesses. And I ask you to sit down.

MR. SCHULTZ: Your Honor, may the court reporter repeat the question.

THE COURT: Yes. Read the question to the witness. *(Question read.)* You may answer. I order you to answer.

THE WITNESS: I just get yes or no, huh? Yes. I was there. All my years on the witness stand, I never heard anything like that ruling.

January 2, 1970

Continued cross-examination of Defendant A. HOFFMAN *by Government* ATTORNEY SCHULTZ.

Q: I show you Government's Exhibit 18 for identification, which is a photograph. Do you recognize the photograph?

A: Do I recognize the general scene?

Q: Yes.

A: Yes.

Q: Do you see yourself in the photograph?

A: Well, we all look alike. . . .

MR. WEINGLASS: When we were cross-examining on grand jury testimony —

THE COURT: Mr. Weingrass, I must caution you again when there is a ruling, the argument ceases. That is good courtroom procedure.

THE WITNESS: Weingrass?

Q: Mr. Hoffman, isn't it a fact that one of the reasons why you came to Chicago was simply to wreck American society?

A: No.

Q: Isn't it a fact, Mr. Hoffman, that —

A: Do you consider the Democratic Party part of American society?

THE COURT: Mr. Witness, you are not interrogating the lawyer; he is asking you questions.

MR. SCHULTZ: As you watched on Thursday, you knew you had won the battle of Chicago. You knew you had smashed the Democrats' chances and destroyed the two party system in this country and perhaps with it electoral politics, isn't that a fact?

A: I knew it had destroyed itself and that the whole world would see, and that was the sense of the victory.

PRISON

PROLOGUE
TIME
INSIDE
LOOKING OUT
DEATH ROW
EPILOGUE

PROLOGUE
JOHNNY CASH

Folsom Prison Blues

The culture of a thousand years is shattered with the clanging of the cell door behind you. Life outside, behind you, immediately becomes unreal. You begin to not care that it exists. All you have with you in the cell is your bare animal instincts.

I speak partly from experience. I have been behind bars a few times. Sometimes of my own volition—sometimes involuntarily. Each time, I felt the same feeling of kinship with my fellow prisoners.

Behind the bars, locked out from "society," you're being rehabilitated, corrected, re-briefed, re-educated on life itself, without your having the opportunity of really reliving it. You're the object of a widely planned program combining isolation, punishment, training, briefing, etc., designed to make you sorry for your mistakes, to re-enlighten you on what you should and shouldn't do outside, so that when you're released, if you ever are, you can come out clean, to a world that's supposed to welcome you and forgive you.

Can it work??? "Hell no," you say. How could this torment possibly do anybody any good. . . . But then, why else are you locked in?

You sit on your cold steel mattressless bunk and watch a cockroach crawl out from under the filthy commode, and you don't kill it. You envy the roach as you watch it crawl out under the cell door.

Down the cell block you hear a steel door open, then close. Like every other man that hears it, your first unconscious thought reaction is that it's someone coming to let you out, but you know it isn't.

You count the steel bars on the door so many times that you hate yourself for it. Your big accomplishment for the day is a mathematical deduction. You are positive of this, and only this: There are nine vertical, and sixteen horizontal, bars on your door.

Down the hall another door opens and closes, then a guard walks by without looking at you, and on out another door.

"The son of a. . . ."

You'd like to say that you are waiting for something, but nothing ever happens. There is nothing to look forward to.

You make friends in the prison. You become one in a "clique," whose purpose is nothing. Nobody is richer or poorer than the other. The only way wealth is measured is by the amount of tobacco a man has, or "Duffy's Hay" as tobacco is called. All of you have had the same things snuffed out of your lives. Everything it seems that makes a man a man—women, money, a family, a job, the open road, the city, the country, ambition, power, success, failure—a million things.

Outside your cellblock is a wall. Outside that wall is another wall. It's twenty feet high, and its granite blocks go down another eight feet in the ground. You know you're here to stay, and for some reason you'd like to stay alive—and not rot.

TIME
JOHN ROSEVEAR

The Fourth Mad Wall

Going to jail has become rather fashionable. Of course, it is more fashionable if the goer has a cause; but then again, being thrown in jail overnight for some preposterous charge isn't so bad either. The main thing about the jail business is that the drama is losing its social curse, and circles of friends can nowadays easily find one of their members who has been at least in a county or city jail. Further, there is nothing wrong with it, and whomever it might be cannot expect undue sympathy. He was simply out of circulation for a while. Civil rights, civil disobedience, and disturbing the peace are in the process of changing their outward posture.

It is upon this presumption that the following article takes form, for as we are going to go to jail, it might be wise to find out some things about the place.

City and county jails are fugitive. They accommodate immediate offenders—those pending bond, those who are drunk although drunkenness is not a crime, those who constitute an immediate threat to the safety and welfare of society. With rare exceptions, terms in these places are seldom over a few months. AWOL soldiers, habitual drunks, overzealous demonstrators, and the rank and file of the unsavories are thrown into jail. One cannot, therefore, expect comfortable accommodations. The toilet, for instance, is often a porcelainized hole with running water. There may be a shower (cold water predominating). There are no mattresses on the bunks because some of the tenants have crabs, lice, and/or fleas, and metal racks are less likely to provide a home for these insects than is a mattress.

Did you ever drive past a prison? Or visit someone who was living there? If so, you saw nothing of prison. Nothing at all. You have to go there, be locked in it, meet and live with the people there to know what the place is like. There is nothing romantic about a prison, except walking away from it.

Upon entering, the inmate is first dusted for lice and/or vermin, and then given clean clothes, and then photographed. Variations, of course, are accepted. But in the main he is made to realize that the thick iron door has closed behind him, and he is entering a life that, if this is his first visit, holds a number of surprises. Immediate preliminaries done with, the inmate will prob-

ably live in a transient society for a month or so that will ana-
lyze, test, evaluate, interview and otherwise peer into the new
arrival's statistics and decide what to do with him. Naturally,
there are a series of physical examinations. When these things
have run their course, which takes about a month and a half, his
destination is decided upon. Most states have satellites other
than the Walls to accommodate their new members: work camps
that maintain public parks, schools that accept peaceful offenders and provide them with the facilities to finish their high school
education, vocational units, factories that supply the rest of the
facilities with non-expert commodities such as soap, clothes,
mattresses, furniture and so on.

The first exposure to prison usually takes place within the
diagnostic area, where the new arrival lives in a cell, as do all
the others within the walls, eats the same kind of food, and lives
the same kind of life that the others might live (except he has no
assignment); but he is segregated from the others because he is
innocent of the prison's activities and language and society.

First impressions are the most lasting. Everything is either
bolted down or painted or both. There are no gay colors. The
noises are fierce: cell doors slam, chairs screech and clatter on
the concrete floors; the guards are tired of seeing your kind, and
don't like to repeat themselves. Therefore they yell, and you can
hardly mistake their command. And if the sounds are not dramatic enough, the smells certainly run a close second. Depending on locale and sanitation practices, urine is the most prevalent
odor, followed closely by pine oil soap. One never, never forgets
the smell of pine oil. At night, when the lights go out in the cell
block, the smell of sleep and the anonymous sounds of farting
descend like an abysmal curse.

Adjusting to the routine of living in a cell is not difficult, for
there is nothing else you can do. Each cell has a sink and toilet,
but there is seldom a wooden seat to the latter. Cells can be one,
two or three-man places. You learn to live together. If a man is
to live alone in the same cell for a long period of time, he will,
depending on local restrictions, decorate it to suit his tempera-
ment. He cannot repaint the pale, mint green walls or the egg-
shell ceiling, or put tile on the floor, but he can add paintings to
the walls, install a cabinet to house his meagre property, and
throw a rug on the concrete. Rules usually prevent a man from
putting curtains over the bars that form the end walls of his
domain. Many of the decorations are original and attractive.

Except for death row and maximum confinement, men leave
their cells to eat. This thrice-daily function takes place in a large,
rather somber dining hall. One always tries to get in the chow
line with a friend to have company for the meal. The men get a

232

stainless steel tray and spoon, and are ladled food into compartments. The food is bland and starchy but adequate. It used to be that one had to eat everything on the tray, but that rule is now more lax. One drinks from plastic, not tin cups. Chow halls are areas of high tension, and occasionally a riot starts there—just like a James Cagney movie—with men pounding their plates and trays and cups on the table, demanding better food or more dancing girls or something. Recently, I was told a man stood on the table and yelled that the warden was no good, and had no sooner said it but was shot dead. True or not, it indicates that the halls are surveyed by armed guards.

When the routine has lost its drama and begins to become a regular thing, some of the more painful discoveries appear. Possibly the first reality might be that you're going to be in these surroundings for quite a while, and you're going to have to make the best of it. Anger is, naturally, absolutely useless. If you have a battalion of attorneys and unlimited finances, you can probably get out on an appeal. If you have neither, you may as well adjust to the future.

Perhaps the first and most painful realism will be the fact that a prisoner has absolutely no rights. Well, he has the right to worship at the faith of his choice, but there his privileges end. He cannot vote, pay taxes, have any say in local or foreign affairs, has his mail censored, and has no say about anything that the warden cannot overrule. If a prisoner doesn't completely obey all the rules he can be thrown into the hole. Every prison (and jail) has a hole.

There is an additional right that a prisoner is denied, and it might take him quite a while to become aware of it. It is, as the book puts it, the right of Territorial Imperative. A prisoner has no territory. His area is not his own and even when he leaves prison the parole officers exercise an extension of the rule when they visit his home. The prisoner's cell is not his own, even though no other prisoners are allowed in it. He is periodically inspected, and his locker or drawer is peered into by the guard. He has no private property. Anything he may write can be read and examined and confiscated.

And what is so despairing about the situation is that the inmate can say nothing about it. He has no grounds for objecting. He has no right of protest. No right at all.

Is there ever a murder in prison? Yes, by a variety of methods. Because such occurances are expected, and because older men sometimes fail to outlive their twenty-year sentence, prisons usually come equipped with a graveyard. Murder is infrequent, but one might say that out of ten thousand prisoners per year there is at least one killing. The most dramatic is burning. When the chosen is locked in his cell, men walk past it squirting either lighter fluid or fuel oil into the cell, and onto the man. Then the "murderer" arrives with a book of matches (the guard is conveniently absent), utters a few last words of sadistic pleasure, and throws some flame into the cell. A soft puff, and the place is an inferno. There is no escape from the cell, and the trickle of water from his sink or toilet is inadequate. The victim is usually charred beyond recognition.

But aside from such dramas as murder, the place is hopelessly dreary. Life has little variety, and the Buddhist concept of useless conversation is abused daily. Laughter is infrequent, and usually forced. One's stomach never aches from too much of it. When a joke is told, and most concern sex, the teller can be assured he will get some laughs—perhaps more than he might get in a tavern. One TRIES to laugh in prison; it seldom comes out without some effort.

In prison, time accumulates a new dimension. You try to eat it away, rather than enjoy it. If a prisoner is having difficulty with his station, if the days are hopelessly long, he is doing "hard time." Instead of asking why another is making life difficult, one asks. "Why are you cutting into my time?" And a frequent answer when one tells of his trouble is "Do your own time," or "Don't press my time."

The language of prison Negroes is peculiar. They talk about a "hoe" back on the street, but finding a hoe or discovering a use for a hoe on asphalt appears difficult. Then one realizes that the word is really "whore." All women who have had intercourse with more than one male, apparently, are evermore known as hoes. Another word, "beech," is equally puzzling. It is, nonetheless, used interchangeably with hoe. Beech means "bitch." "Close the doe." "Don't walk on the wet flow." "She a hoe." And we have but scraped the surface.

There is very little dramatic change in prison routine or programming. The places are run by the state, and the employees are civil servants. As such, they lose their dynamics in a common desire for "security," which is a favorite word of theirs that continually crops up in job discussions. They have lost their dynamics because the system won't tolerate any, and the upper administration is rich in conservativeness.

And to condense statistics, it is no special encore to point out that the system doesn't work: those who once enter prison usually return.

Further, one must remember that people in the capacity of state prison employees are not the sharpest people in the world. Signs of their inefficiency are easy to spot, and after they have been so employed they seem to lose sight of the fact that they deal with human destiny daily. Do not dismiss them with a sigh. The whole system is so turbulent, so many people come and go, that the good ones (both prisoner and civil servant) have left their marks.

The mail routine is an excellent example. Severe restrictions used to be imposed on mailing privileges. Not only were the number of addresses limited, but the inmate could receive no mail other than from those on his list. All mail, both incoming and outgoing, used to be rigidly censored. But now things are different. In many prisons the inmate may write to whomever he pleases. He can send out as many letters as he can write, providing he can afford the postage. Usually after a letter is written, it is placed in a mailbox unsealed. However, unless there is reason to suspect the prisoner of writing undesirable things (obscene letters occasionally are sent to movie stars) the correspondence is simply charged for postage and sealed by the prison censors. In some camps the restrictions are very few: outgoing letters can be sealed, incoming mail is uncensored (but opened), and one would hardly know he was in prison, mailwise.

It may be difficult for the newcomer to understand how the system operates, run by these highly inefficient guards and directors, and one can easily find that the operation is hopelessly inefficient. Yet somehow it works, and has been working for quite a while. It has gotten rid of flogging and leg irons, and now capital punishment is slowly being dissolved as the body might purge a poison.

Have there been other improvements? Certainly. Convicts no longer wear striped suits, nor is the ball and chain in effect. The dungeon-like holes of the Bastille and Inquisition times have become a bit more refined, and criminals are no longer chained to the wall. In the field of conservation, particularly forest conservation, many camps provide facilities for prisoners to bring seedlings and plant them with free rein. Arizona has a separate facility for their senior citizen criminals, and there is a large variety of vocational training facilities in most states.

Still, the prison system is designed so that a newcomer is expected to fit into a prepared niche and stay in that niche for the term of his confinement. If he leaves the niche additional problems are immediately created. Individuality is not, one might guess, encouraged. What is the niche like? It is governed by regulation, fed by routine, denuded of fun, and the pace is slow—ever so slow. Anything can be done later because there's plenty of time. Dangling in front of the prisoner are various rewards that make him want to stay out of trouble, for if he does, some additional time may be taken from his sentence. That is, although the prison year is only nine months, it can, under special circumstances, be reduced to eight or seven months if the inmate not only steers clear of trouble but performs an extra role that might enhance his reputation. For instance, some institutions have a book-tape program. Prisoners who can read fluently are called upon to read aloud either a book or current magazine onto tape, and the tape is sent to a home for the blind or to a blind library. And along that line, some institutions have braille typewriters operated by inmates.

These programs tend to instill a sense of righteousness in a prisoner, but they also afford him the means to learn, contribute, and escape from the dreary routine of regular prison life. But above that, the fear principle guides more movement than does the reward system. Since bad behavior is expected, measures to counter it have been instilled and installed, and fear remains today, as it has been for all ages, the one certain catch-all preventative. If you're caught doing something against the regulations, you will be punished. If you're discovered doing something good (such as helping an illiterate write a letter home) then you're simply not doing bad. There is no reward for good in prison, except good itself.

There is no book of instructions that can supply the answers to all the questions a newcomer might have about prison life, or prison routine, or prison itself. The only way to get along there is to keep your mouth shut, remind yourself frequently that the ordeal cannot go on forever, that you aren't going to change it, no matter what you do, and you might as well make the best of it—without giving aid and comfort to the enemy. It might be relative fun, but it can be miserable. You will certainly meet a variety of people there. Play a game. Decide which one of them you'd like to see after your term is over. See if your guess holds true throughout your confinement. Write letters to the government inquiring about things you've wanted to know about all your life. Read books you've put off for years. Try your hand at poetry.

The goddamn time will pass, you can grow a cock again, and rediscover the world.

DONN PEARCE

Life-styles:
Building Time

You build one day at a time. You let the years build themselves.
And those days pass by like slimy worms which you swallow
very, very slowly.

You lie here in one of the bullpens on G-Floor, listening to
the snores; the guy doing life for murder who has already been
in for seventeen years but hopes to get a special pardon any day
because he is going blind; the soft-spoken guy who just got a
brand-new fifteen-spot on 157 counts of daylight burglary and
who knows he will never get a parole because this is his third
fall; the snarling, genuine gangster-type hood from Boston; the
deeply tanned kid with the scars on his head who mumbles in his
sleep about bloodhounds and about son-of-a-bitch and about I-
ain't-gonna-do-it. There are reflections on the ceiling from the
searchlights aimed along the triple fences from the gun towers.
The bars on the door and the windows cast a gridwork of shadows on the walls and on the bunks and on the one open toilet
bowl which has no seat, gleaming over there all white and porce-
lain and all-knowing. You are locked up. And you will stay here
until they let you out in the morning and put you to work. And
tomorrow night and the next you will lie here staring at the lights
and the shadows and listening to the snores, and realizing, finally, that the whole world hates your guts. Because you broke the
Law and committed a Crime. And you know damn well that no
matter how old you ever get or what you ever become or what
you do, the whole world will always hate your guts. Yet you still
don't know if you really should be sorry that you committed that
Crime. Caught? Oh, yes. Hell, yes. But beyond that? And now
they're going to rehabilitate you. Man, they're going to rehabilitate the living shit out of you.

So you lie here and you think about what would happen if the
moon suddenly came too close to the earth and a monstrous tid-
al wave washed over the whole joint and flooded this very cell
that you're in. They would never get you out in time. They
wouldn't try. But with luck, maybe, the water wouldn't reach the
ceiling. If you held out long enough, if you put you nose up
against the ceiling and kept treading water. . . .

In the morning you hear a key being dragged across the radiator and across the bars. The cowboy boots are clicking and the hoosier Turnkey is growling his monotonous chant.

Aw right. Rise and shine. Let's shake'em.

The light goes on. Sixteen pairs of feet hit the floor. Lockers are dragged and banged open and closed. The toilet flushes continuously. Beds are arranged. Water from different pocket combs is splattering different faces as three men at the same time try to use the one small mirror. The handle is pulled and the long, complicated mechanism moves across the door. The convict Cellwalker dances swiftly from lock to lock. The handle is pulled again and the cell doors bang open and the corridor is filled with grey, wrinkled shapes shuffling and murmuring, clinking and rattling through the darkness and through the courtyard and into the line and into the mess hall, where you get your watery grits and a stale cat head and a piece of sowbelly with a few bristles left on the rind and sometimes even a teat all for your very own.

When it is light enough so a guard could take aim, the gate is opened and the mob drifts out into the yard to form into little groups or pairs or singles slowly walking around the path worn into the sand. And you hear the dull, rattling sound which comes from the back of every man's belt where he hangs his spoon and the cup made out of a tin can. And here and there is a Chain Man, some tough guy who was naughty and now has thirteen links of chain connecting two heavy rings riveted around his ankles.

The guards begin walking between the fences, headed toward the River Gate. They are dressed in dungarees and khaki shirts, cowboy hats, straw hats, beat-up, shapeless felt hats, a dirty white tropical helmet. Their faces are tanned and leathery and creased and wrinkled, their shotguns and rifles languid across their lean, hunched Cracker shoulders; Jack in the Bush; Peeping Tom; Lard Ass; Frank Buck; Mahatma Kane Jeeves; honest Free Men, one and all, too lazy to work and too scared to steal.

The squads begin to form in a double line, men who work in the tag plant, the tobacco factory, the grist mill, the shovel squads, and the grubbing-hoe squads. They are counted off and march toward the West Gate, which opens mysteriously, controlled and commanded by invisible hands, by hidden mirrors and secret eyes, opening like the front door at the supermarket. And as the squads come out, the prison band begins. They sit in one of the pavilions in the Visitors' Park, pounding their enthusiasms into your heart. The feet shuffle, the tin cups rattle, the hopes are stiffened. A cigarette dangles from the lips of the drummer, the Lifer on the sousaphone red in the face, the trombonist with his shirt unbuttoned. You shuffle and stagger and swagger past Freeheart, the Supply Officer and the Captain of the Guards, who wears an overcoat whenever the temperature drops below eighty. Further down the road is Pappy West with his snarl and his moustache, his cigar and Panama hat, his potbelly and underslung belt, the Director of Education who swears at the illiterates in his school and ships them to the Flattop for a week on Bread Row if they fail their examinations or otherwise misbehave.

The band finishes up the last few scattered bars and always, without fail, that one extra, accidental clarinet note makes its escape after the last beat. Like the wooden cuckoo it marks your days with a ridiculous chirp.

. . . *ta, ta, ta, boom, da, boom, da, BOOM . . . (peep).*

And then it is noon. The whole pageant rewinds in reverse. The population drifts back to the Rock from the plants and shops and fields. The last man passes in, gets checked, counted, and herded inside the closing gate. There is that one great, prolonged blast of the steam whistle on top of the power plant screaming out its earsplitting exclamation mark, reverberating through the fences and among the pine trees and over the fields and down those three black asphalt roads.

Then it's slimy, unseasoned army beans and a soggy brick of cornbread and a puddle of blackstrap molasses. Afterward it's out into the yard to make a few more laps of the circle in the sand. The Chain Men tinkle out their Te Deums. In the distance a pipe smoker leaves a trail of wispy cloud behind him. From the baseball dugout comes the singing of four Negroes who gather every day to practice their harmony. There is excitement from the volleyball court. A softball bat cracks when it hits the ball.

Or it's back to the cell for a quick nap until that chant begins somewhere within the walls of the Rock. It is repeated and echoed and carried to the Nigger Rock. And then up to the Second Floor and the Third Floor.

OUTSIDE!   (Outside)   —everybody out*SIDE.*

Iron bangs against iron. Doors slam and feet scrape. Cups and spoons and chains begin to rattle. The Turnkeys and the Cell-walkers singsong their chants up and down the corridors, prompting you, luring you, ordering you out of your cell and back to the yard and through the gate to limp, to jig, to skip out and away as the band plays on and on:

Oh, the monkey wrapped his tail around a flagpole. . . .

And then supper again, the mess hall again, turnip greens and boiled potatoes and those same wieners that emit a greenish liquid when you cut into them. But tonight there is milk, a special treat. Provided you are on the milk list. But you can't be on the milk list two months in succession.

However. Do not forget. You were the one who broke the Law and committed a Crime. And now you are going to get your mind right. And that means: *right*.

The checkers tally up their counts and report to the Captain. The clarinet peeps. The whistle toots. The band carries in its instruments. Inside the Rock there are shouts and curses. There is laughter. Cell doors slam. Locker boxes scrape. The chanting cry goes out.

In your HOLE. Check time. Everybody in YOUR HOLE!

When the cells are filled the handle is pulled and the long flat bars slide over the edge of each door. The Cellwalker comes by, counts the faces and marks his sheet. In a moment the bars clank open and a yell goes out:

Wash 'em up!

The doors are thrown open and the corridors are filled with naked men swarming toward the shower room with slapping bare feet, an occasional chain sliding in spasmodic tinkles over the concrete. The nude paraplegic goes by, walking on his hands, his withered legs held up by his cell mate. Like kids playing wheelbarrow, he maneuvers through the parting, acquiescing crowd, padding swiftly on huge gorilla arms as the naked chimpanzee behind him hops up and down and giggles.

The shower room is jammed with bodies which softly jostle and nudge and press to get wet, to step aside and lather, to rinse off, to make way back through the crowd. As each man comes out another goes in, entering the befogged cube of steam and spray and lather and mud, the line outside eager and anxious because the hot water lasts only fifteen minutes.

In yer HOLE! IN YER *HOLE!*

The Cellwalker dances from cell to cell and from lock to lock. The handle is pulled, the flat bars closing with a dull clank. There is a faint buzz from the cells. The toilets flush. Your cell partners relax, lying on their bunks, leaning over the edge to look up or to look down, to talk, to argue, to explain how it was. You sit on a footlocker by the door, staring out through the bars at the canteen, the Visitors' Park, the hospital, the gun towers, and the fences, at the walls of the Flattop which houses Bread Row, Feed Row, Forgotten Row, and Death Row. Just outside the Rock is a small asphalt drive, a sidewalk, a row of live oak trees and a few date palms. A Trustee is sitting on the curb smoking a pipe and watching the sunset.

Hey, Newcock. You got the Black Ass already?

You turn and try to grin. As nonchalant as possible, you climb up to your third-tier bunk and look at the ceiling, thinking of nothing at all. The man beneath you rolls over, the bunks swaying, the cups and spoons hooked to the springs rattling and tinkling. A voice yells out and a big bell rings.

First bell. *First* bell.

There is a scurry of movement in G-15. The one, narrow, inadequate sheet is rearranged. The extra blanket is rolled up to make a pillow. The toilet flushes again and again. At the sink next to it, two men are brushing their teeth.

Last bell—pull your lights out.

From every tier, every floor, every section of the Rock and the Nigger Rock come the different accents and tones, the different emphasis and volume as the bell tolls out the tempo.

—Pull 'em out. PULL 'EM *OUT*! (Pull your lights out.)—ding—ding—ding—LAST BELL! (Lights *out*.)

In a moment it is dark. But again you are aware of the reflections from the gun towers. Cigarettes brighten and dim, lighting up the cupped hands and the gaunt faces. The snores begin. The kid with the scars on his head starts to mumble. Far away, you can hear the caterwauling of the big black cat that lives in the Newcock Court and the patrolling heels of the Turnkey. And later the bunks begin to creak with a sly, careful vibration, fists all aflutter as each of you flies off alone into that wild, secret dream. Oh, girls! Girls! The loving that is going to waste in this place; the youth, the muscle, slipping away in the furtive gloom of this barred and shackled night.

The weekend:

Clean clothes, haircuts, volleyball. Find Satchel Ass or one of the other boys from G-5. Visit a buddy in another cell. Get into a crap game while the lookout rolls a smoke with State tobacco and watches for Peeping Tom.

Saturday you can go shopping among the rows and rows of cells, seeking someone In-The-Know, searching for a merchant, a *contrabandista*, haggling, wheedling, buying a few strips of soft material taken from the inside of a smuggled nose inhaler. The strips are saturated with a crude, unrefined benzedrine. A quarter strip is all it takes to get you started, swallowing it down with some canteen coffee.

Sometimes there are late-Saturday-night parties. There is a certain way of winding a long strip of toilet paper around your fingers. You can fold the ends over and light the inside and it burns with a slow, controlled flame that is very hot and very blue. Locker boxes are dragged over to shield the glare. You hold a tin cup over the stove and when the water is hot enough, you drink it down to lubricate your mouth and shrunken stomach and to get rid of some of the taste of tar and vaseline.

There is a marathon of whispers hissing from every corner of the cell, once again going over the details of your cases, the complications of your lives (oh man, if only—but get this now—and not only that), explaining, lying, questioning, yet always skirting the edge of that raw, throbbing truth as you desperately convince each other that you are not ordinary men.

The portable radio is tuned very low. Your heads are closely circled as you eavesdrop on the Free World, yet scarcely listening to that background of music and news items and commercial advertising, taken up instead by those eternal tales of how you robbed that other world, how you bamboozled it and murdered it and then escaped with truly magnificent ingenuity.

Two men are posted at the windows with pocket mirrors carefully angling through the bars to left and to right. There is a low hiss. The toilet bowl is briefly ignited until it is simultaneously flushed and straddled. The radio clicks. Bare feet rub and slide. Snores begin. A bunk spring squeaks and bends as spoons and cups tinkle out pastoral melodies. Very slowly there is the approaching click of heels. There is the jangling of keys. A flashlight flickers and glares and nervously inspects, exposes and withdraws. You wait. A match is struck. The flame brightens and turns blue. The radio clicks. There are tinkles, scrapes and whispers. A voice begins:

What we'll do is. We'll strip 'em naked. Then tie their hands behind their backs. And stick a piece of dynamite up their ass. With a string tied to it. We got two posts set up in the ground. As far apart as the string. And the fuse is timed. If they can run to the second post fast enough the string will yank the dynamite out. Man! Man, can't you see it? The band is playin' and the cons are cheerin' and this hoosier is huffin' and puffin'. And *then*. He's near the post. He's gonna make it. And *then*. You reach down and cut the string.

On Sunday you go to church. You go because there is an attendance book at the rear of the auditorium and the Parole Board goes over those names to see who is keeping a Good Record. The chorus starts singing the doxology in four-part discord, the band practicing its ingenuity in hitting sour notes with the greatest amount of innocence. Jones leads the choir with vigorous arms, one foot off the floor and behind him, in a mincing step so artful and revealing that he himself is the only one left who really thinks he is an alcoholic instead of a repressed homosexual.

The choir moves up the aisle wearing robes of all colors and all sizes, blasting away or mumbling into a hymnbook, the Chaplain at the pulpit, singing out of the side of his mouth the way Edward G. Robinson would sing if he were impersonating a

242

prison Chaplain. He is wearing a Roman Catholic collar, although he himself is a Baptist. During extracurricular meetings such as the Forum of Faith or Alcoholics Anonymous, he also wears riding boots. Ceremoniously, he ends each monthly meeting of the Sea Scouts by standing up and imitating a bugle, solemnly blowing taps on the back of his clenched fist.

So there you are. It is Sunday and you are in church. The walls are decorated with a series of large murals copied from picture postcards. It is said the job took several years and earned the artist a parole. So now you look at his legacy; a full moon above a tropical beach, a flock of flamingos, a sunset, a lake filled with water lilies. And the Chaplain tells you to get your mind right, to get yourself rehabilitated. Meanwhile, every week, right in the middle of it all, somebody always has to go to the john. He moves down the aisle and across and then up front to the corner. He is wearing shackles and walks with a slow, pigeon-footed step, trying not to let the chain rattle too much as the congregation holds its breath and rolls its eyes and again hears all about those Ten Commandments.

But on Sunday there is also the movie. The band is dressed in its special best, white dress shirts and starched white Trustee pants. Every one of them is chewing gum, his face benny-red, his eyes wide and eager. And tonight they can really play. Tonight they are hot, hysterical, belting out their jazz with stamping feet and convulsive shoulders, with puffed cheeks and elongated lips, with closed eyes and spidery fingers. The Free Man stands there at the head of the stairs. He raises his hand and drops it. And then they start. Rising up from the depths of the Rock, from the bullpens and from the two-man cells and from the Trustee Floor in an uneven, sloppy line, they move up the aisles to the benches and folding chairs dressed in State-issue clothes straight from the laundry in a mass of tangled wrinkles or dressed in Free World shirts and ties and shoes with their prison pants privately altered to fit and then carefully starched and ironed by personal Laundry Boys.

Up they come: cripples, lunatics, fairies, killers, thieves, cheats, beggars, drunks, addicts, and rapists; sauntering, shuffling, prancing up from their cages and their tombs, smiling, scowling, sulking.

There's a guy with three years for mayhem—sat with a girl on a park bench and bit off the nipple of her breast. There's Chicken who is dying of paresis of the brain—five years of sodomy with a chicken. There's John and his brother, both of them young, neat, quiet and well-dressed—fifteen years for armed robbery. Herby is a short-timer with only one month to go. Herby is a con man extraordinary who once organized a veterans' parade to raise a subscription to build a war memorial and then skipped with the donations while the town cops were still directing traffic and holding back the cheering crowds.

Da, da, da, DAA*AAAA!* Here they come; your rap partners, your cell partners, your work partners, your buddies; pimps, punks, forgers; the seniles and the adolescents, frivolous, crafty, mean, wild-eyed, silly, sad.

There are the two boys from Texas—one year for stealing a quart of milk off a front porch while driving by in an old jalopy looking for work. One of them has a shriveled arm that had once been caught in a threshing machine. He threw an epileptic fit in G-15 one night. But he hasn't had to worry about women anymore since the night he was hit in the balls by a shotgun while stealing watermelons.

The jazz is building up into a frenzy. The convicts continue to pour up the stairs and into the auditorium, shuffling their feet, snapping their fingers, nodding at guys they know, stumbling, dancing, their faces inspired:

Da, da, da, DAA*AAAA!*

There's Satchel Ass. He has no teeth. No teeth at all. For the greater glory of Love, they say. There's "Molly' with her lisping speech impediment, sandals, and loud socks. "Gail" is wearing a trace of powder and lipstick. Diaz—cut off his wife's head and put it on a meat platter under a glass cover. He weighs about ninety pounds, his face a dry leather mask of wrinkles. He smokes incessantly. He has been here twenty-one years. A Chain Man goes by. The paraplegic comes up the stairs on his hands, someone carrying his legs, someone else carrying his crutches. Time and again he wrote bad checks and his father always made them good. Until something went wrong. Someone got mad and prosecuted and he got three years. There's Percy—collector of sticks and string who totters about the yard with a scarred golf ball and a rusty, warped club, playing the holes he has dug in the sand and keeping his score in a little notebook. Percy is over seventy. He already finished his ten years for embezzlement. But he has no family, no friends, no home and so he kept breaking the rules until they took away his Good Time. But before long his Time will be finished flat and then he will be forced to leave.

Da, da, da, DAA*AAAAA!*

Tommy—life for murder plus five years for escape. Over twenty years ago he chopped off his left hand with an ax in order to evade the brutality of a Chain Gang camp and get sent back to the Rock. Here come several men from the TB isolation ward and behind them the hophead whose wife finished her six-month sentence in the Women's Ward and got home just in time for her baby to be born. Booger Red, the ex-pug. He was in jail for stealing a car and knew he could beat the rap if he had some money for a lawyer. So he thought he could collect the reward that was out by showing them where that missing body was. The cops wanted to quit digging after seven feet but Booger Red made them go on.

Da, da, da. DAAA*AAAA!*

The Senator—who used to be a state senator. He says it was a political frame but the records say he was found guilty of molesting an eight-year-old girl. The Judge—who used to be a Justice of the Peace. Rector—who used to be the principal of a grammar school. There's the big-city cop who went into the drunk tank to quiet down a seventeen-year-old kid, but beat him to death with a blackjack and got twenty years. After six months he went before the Parole Board and got his work papers. He is soon due to be released. There, that one over there. That's the guy who's in for blowing a dog. And that one raped a sixty-seven-year-old woman. And that one has ten years for the statutory rape of a fifteen-year-old whore. That one didn't pay his alimony. And that little, funny-looking guy with half of one arm missing and the limp and the scars—he's a German lion tamer with five years for stealing a cow after a local yokel convinced him the thin, mangy cattle wandering loose over the highway were wild and he could load one up on his truck and feed it to his cats. There's your buddy, Greene—twenty years on four counts of armed robbery. He has two children. He went hysterical when they told him his wife had filed suit for divorce and they had to carry him back from the office of the Captain of the Guards. Greene is twenty-two. There's the nervous kid with the freckles and the very deep, deliberate voice, caught hanging paper all over town while dressed up as an Army officer. He and two others did a week on Bread Row recently for trying to rape a punk who had been giving it away to everyone else in the cell but them. And there's the crazy kid with the ecstatic face of a visionary who stood in the courtyard one foggy morning laughing and snickering out loud about how last night he had killed both his parents. A quiet circle of cons stood around him, their faces wrinkled and tanned and hard, their clothes dirty and grey, their hands calloused, their heads bowed.

Da, da, da, DAAAA*AAAA!*

The jazz is violent now as the population fills up section after section of seats. They are cheering and yelling as the band gets hotter, the trumpets competing, the drums crashing until with one big cacophonous smash, there is—*silence.*

A knot of Free Men gather at the head of the stairs. There is an absolute hush. The last stragglers have taken their seats. The aisles are empty. The Captain raises his arm and drops it. The band starts playing *In a Persian Garden.* The music is muted and voluptuous. Never has it been played so dirty. Never has it been so sentimental. Every American boy knows the words:

> There's a place in France
> Where the women wear no pants —

On that signal the inmates of the Women's Ward come up the stairs, whores, shills, killers, shoplifters, accomplices, molls, lesbians. They are dressed in starched blue uniforms, each one with additions of embroidery on collars and cuffs. Or a handkerchief, a flower. They have feminized their imprisonment with high heels and nylons, a necklace, earrings, cosmetics. As they come in, some of them jiggle their shoulders and sway their hips in time with the music. But who is that sly wink for? That smile? That nod?

The music has segued back into jazz again, shrieking out with a musical whinny of lust and frustration. And then that yell begins, that tolerated, weekly breach of discipline. Once a week you may stand up and scream. You may drown out the music with one prolonged roar of defiance, of hate, of passion. One thousand men let out their feelings. One thousand voices vent their lust and their rage at an authority so implacable that it even dares to stand there unarmed and unflinching, that it even permits you to break its own rules, that grants every man the right to demonstrate in his own way his own helplessness.

The lights go out. The music stops. The sound track and the flickering images begin, reminding you for two hours how it really used to be way out there in the mythical, forgotten land; there in that full-colored, synchronized, softly focused land; the Free World.

JAAKOV KOHN

Time: Two Interviews

ONE

A man who barely two years ago played, with his cool, a steady relentless game of Russian Roulette, has returned from a two year jail exile serene and centered.

Whose actionmania turned into clear purpose and whose old

*tightrope balancing act became a steady affirmation of all that
is positive, loving and laughable in the precarious prison we so
wistfully call freedom.*

Survival under penal oppression—A talk with a FREE MAN.

Q: What was the charge against you?

A: Felonious possession of marijuana with intent to sell.

Q: What was the sentence?

A: 3-5 years in State Prison.

Q: How long were you in?

A: Two years, almost to the day.

Q: How long were you in the Tombs?

A: Five months.

Q: Any comments?

A: I think the name speaks for itself. The place definitely lives up to it.

Q: Where did you go from there?

A: I was sent to Sing Sing, which is the reception center for the southern part of New York State. It is the orientation center where all those sentenced in the southern part of the State are received, processed, checked over, and put through the shots and medical test routine.

Q: It sounds like the Fort Dix of the Penal System.

A: Yes, and they even ask you to which prison you wish to be sent.

Q: Do you really have your choice of prisons? Do they furnish catalogs and brochures like resort hotels?

A: Well, they do. It's all part of orientation. They bring you into a classroom and explain to you the different prisons. Auburn prison, for instance, is known for its "high educational standards." They have the "best, finest, newest, most modern" school. In Auburn one can make money too. They have the license plate factory where all the license plates for New York State are made. The wages for that are 10¢-20¢ per hour. If a guy works on a double shift, he can make on a 12-hour day up to $2.40. Very hard labor on big plate-cutting machines that imprint the numbers too. The guys that work there have to slip in each number by hand and thus risk having their fingers cut off.

Q: Do you remember the supposed merits of the other prisons?

A: Clinton Prison, which is in Donnamora near the Canadian border, is known for its cold winters. Skiing is the big thing there. They have a hill inside the prison for skiing and tobogganing. Clinton is also known for its "Hobo Jungle." They have stone stoves in the yard with lockers, tables and benches. Guys go out in the middle of the winter and cook home meals on those wood-burning stoves. It's like 20 below zero, and those cats are out

247

there cooking "home meals." Then there is Attica — that's where Willie Sutton is doing time.

Q: Has Willie Sutton become a legendary figure in prison circles?

A: He is not known so much for his thievery as for his fantastic escapes. He was the greatest escape artist since Houdini. Sutton managed to escape from every major prison in New York State except Attica. Attica has the highest degree of security and regimentation. It's all uptight. Then there is Green Haven. Really a bad place. Nobody ever wanted to go there. The food is bad, and the hacks are worse than anywhere else.

Q: Is there a tradition of badness in Green Haven that is being carried over from one generation of hacks to another?

A: The administration of each place sets the tone of the general atmosphere. If the warden is an easy going guy who isn't looking for trouble and perhaps has even heard about modern penology and maybe even believes in some basic reform measures, a place can be, comparatively speaking, pretty nice. On the other hand, if you have a guy who was a career man in the army and when he gets out he works his way up the ladder of the penal establishment, he believes in carrying through his military way of doing things. For the wardens, the alternatives are either keeping people in line through fear or keeping them relatively cool by making it comfortable for them.

Q: Where did you end up?

A: In Auburn, which happened to have been my original choice.

Q: What was the situation there?

A: When I arrived, the warden wasn't too good, but that really didn't matter because he wasn't around too much. The guy who took care of everything was his assistant — the P.K. — the Principal Keeper. His job is to deal directly with the prisoners and their problems, and he presides over the prisoners' disciplinary trials. He is also in charge of the hacks.

Q: How many inmates did Auburn have during your stay there?

A: 1,800 – 2,000.

Q: What is the ethnic makeup of the prison population?

A: About 60% are black. The remaining 40% is a mixture of Puerto Ricans, Cubans, Upstate Anglo Saxon hillbillies, country music types who listen to the "Hayride" on the radio. Then there are small enclaves of Jews and Italians, small time Mafia *apparacci* that always stick together.

Auburn itself is pretty interesting. It is the site of the first electric chair in the world. Prisonwise, it has a long history. It is one of the oldest in the State. The original wall around the prison was built in 1838. Do you know the term "being sent up the river"? That's exactly what they meant, literally. First they sent the guys up the Hudson River to Sing Sing and from there right up to Auburn. As you can see—right up the river.

The prison is a pretty large place. The school's supposed academic atmosphere is naturally not what it is supposed to be. It's just a front. A showpiece for the visitors in to look at this nice, clean, shiny, brand new plastic school with all those phony teachers that couldn't make it in the public school system. They are being shlepped into these jobs, and they are naturally half hearted at best about their jobs. They all have a basically negative attitude toward the prisoners.

Q: Are they scared?

A: No, not scared. There is so much security around them that being scared simply doesn't enter their minds because the atmosphere in Auburn is comparatively relaxed.

Q: What work did you do?

A: Upon arriving, I asked for the library. Clerking and classifying. The initial position of the prison administration is to fuck around with you. When you first enter, they give you the exact opposite of what you ask for. If you are cool doing that job for a while, then you may get transferred to the job you originally asked for. If you fuck up, they make you keep on doing whatever you are doing or even shift you to a worse job.

I applied for the library and got the cabinet shop instead. Cutting boards to make institutional furniture. It was a draggy place with a draggy atmosphere, a real bum trip job. They marched us out there under guard in single file, counting us ten times going out and coming back just to make sure everybody was really there. One really can't split. I don't know how Willie Sutton ever got out of there because Auburn has class security with 40 ft. high walls.

Q: How did you spend your free time?

A: Since I landed a job in the yard library, which was only open for 20 minutes after lunch and for about an hour during the afternoon, I had a lot of free time which I could spend in the yard or in my cell. When the weather was nice, I would be in the yard and the rest of the time in the cell. I spent quite some time there.

Q: What was your routine? Were you the master of your time?

A: The situation I got myself into was just perfect for me. For a long time prior to getting busted, I lived a very hectic life. Running around like crazy trying to make a lot of money and do a lot of things. Just getting involved in too many things at one time. The value that I got out of living that way was a lot of good empirical experience. What I needed and what I always was aware of needing was some literary enrichment. A little more wisdom

249

and knowledge through the written word. I never had time for the classics. I only read a little bit on and off. Little Ouspensky, some Allan Watts.

After coming to Auburn, I started right from the beginning and went through the Myths, the Greek Classics and everything else from Cervantes to Dostoyevsky, Tolstoi, and Balzac. A lot of things just kept coming along because there were a couple of very literary cats in there. One guy who is serving a 14-year term and with whom I became friendly was very literary. He had thousands of books, and he turned me on a lot.

Q: Were you allowed to keep books in your cell?

A: Yes, I had stacks of books all over.

Q: Bearing all this in mind, wouldn't you say that, in this respect, those years were well spent?

A: I think that any reasonable jail term—that is, no more than 5 years—can be very beneficial to an individual if he can put his head in the right place to do this thing. This is something not many do, and even less are aware of the possibility of doing this thing.

Q: Did you come to this realization right at the beginning, or did you undergo a period of adjustment before you saw the light?

A: This has been the story of my life. Changes and adjustments and trying to make the most out of every negative and oppressive experience situation. Jail is, after all, the most oppressive experience imaginable. There is nothing more harmful to a person than oppression and repression of feelings. You are being oppressed and in turn have to repress your own feelings toward the oppression because it in turn will clamp down on you mercilessly.

Q: When you say that Auburn was relaxed, in prison terms, what would you consider a relaxed atmosphere?

A: Like guards not being uptight in respect to where they build up little personal hatreds and vengeance toward inmates.

Q: How many hacks are there in Auburn?

A: About 400. The trouble is that these guys don't live up to their titles. They are supposed to be correctional officers, yet they don't do any correcting. Those guys should have at least some knowledge in psychology. They should be able to relate to these prisoners and help and enlighten them. Instead they are a bunch of slobs. These people have one job to do, one thing on their minds and that is keeping YOU inside. Security is the foremost thing on their minds. It's the only thing they have been instructed to do, and they don't vary. There is absolutely no flexibility.

Q: From what you told me, you must have had it considerably

easier than the average Joe Shmoe. This points to a certain degree of flexibility on their part.

A: No, I made it easy for myself. Due to my job I was able to spend a lot of time in my cell reading. Once I was in that cell and the doors closed, nobody could bother or bug me. That was my own world, my own life, and I could turn it on and off at will. I also kept my food there. There was a commissary where you could buy all sorts of food. You can also have 15 lb. food packages mailed to you once a month by friends or relatives that are on your mailing list.

Q: If one doesn't have money or friends — what happens then?

A: If you don't have money or a job where you make money — 10¢ an hour in the plate shop, 10¢ a day elsewhere — you subsist on prison fare in the messhall.

Q: Could you give me a sample menu?

A: Breakfast: a bowl of milk with oatmeal, a sticky bun and a cup of chicory coffee. Lunch: one canned boiled vegetable, boiled potatoes, some sort of meat. Dessert would be a watered down, tasteless, and elastic pudding made out of powdered milk. For me whatever they served was totally inedible. Completely processed, devitalized, adulterated food. Starch with hardly any fresh vegetables. Dinner was equally inedible.

Q: Could hacks be bribed?

A: There are always some hacks that are corruptible to a certain degree. Like smuggling *Playboy*.

Q: What's the price of a night's possession of *Playboy*?

A: "A pack a night" — the going rate. For many it is a regular business. Some have up to 20 pieces of material out. At 40¢ per pack of cigarettes — you figure it out. Other guys are in the numbers racket, and others have baseball pools.

Q: Is all this organized? Is there an infrastructure that regulates it all?

A: They set up a structure like a guy would set up a numbers operation in Harlem. Bankers, runners, everything. They get the daily number from the *Daily News*. The *News* is a good paper according to the administration.

Q: You had some problems with some periodicals which you subscribed to?

A: They wouldn't let me have the *Nation* and the *New Republic*. They saw a story on Che Guevara, and the name alone freaked them out. They drew the warden's attention to this, and he deemed both too liberal for his institution. It all smacked of outright communism.

Q: What happened to you with the *East Village Other*?

A: They made a big thing out of EVO. They considered it

obscene and therefore not fit for prisoners' reading. The hacks always got a big charge out of the paper. It completely freaked them out. Those guys are complete idiots.

Q: Do you have any further thoughts about the prison environment?

A: It is definitely a very pernicious environment. For most people it's just a place to get together and figure out what to do when they get out. The whole experience makes people more cynical and more negative. For most it is a dulling experience. Theirs is a fantasy trip to begin with. Once they are in prison they fantasize about the street in order to evade the situation they are in. This naturally does not hold true for everybody. Quite a few are generally pretty happy in there. Their situation in the street was even less comfortable than in jail. They were strung out and living in misery. In jail they don't have to think for themselves. The guards tell you what to do, and that's it. You just get into this horrible groove—monotony, tedium, and total banality.

Q: Was this your first incarceration?

A: No, but the longest.

Q: Did the sudden lack of superimposed tyranny cause you any problem after your release?

A: No, because I had been preparing myself for months to get out and fall in with the streams of things. I am trying to take up where I left off, only from a different starting point. I also try to carry through some of the ideas that I have been mulling over in my mind during my time in prison. Ideas that came from things that I have read and become interested in. I am now pursuing these things.

Q: For you, then, it was a very necessary breather.

A: It was also harmful to me. Oppression is harmful to everybody. No matter how aware you are of the mechanics of it. It works on you, and you can't escape it. Even when you understand it, you can't stop it from being done unto you. It just hangs over your head. It is also tragi-comic because your oppressors are really funny cats right out of a cartoon strip. They are the biggest stooges going. You have to keep smiling and laughing, and I used to put these cats uptight just by smiling at them and giving them the love thing. They couldn't understand how a guy in prison could smile so much. They think that if you smile a lot you must have something up your sleeve.

Q: How did they react?

A: They thought I was a nut freaked out on marijuana. In their minds I "got involved with *that* marijuana and got off the deep end," and now I was just a nut smiling away.

Q: Do you experience any after-effects of the oppression?

A: I had no problems adjusting, but I feel that had I been

much longer in prison, it would have affected me considerably more. It would have made me much more uptight. Because that's exactly what oppression does to one—it makes you UP-TIGHT. Just look at the average person who is living under oppressive conditions that he has created for himself out of obligation to the American way of life. Even in prison I considered myself freer than all the hacks put together. Those guys—their life was really fucked up. Their eight hours in jail was happiness as compared to their homelife. That was for them the real jail, with a lot of bullshit thrown in for good measure. For them to bullshit with some prisoner was a hell of a lot better than putting up with their old lady's shit. That's why it was so tragi-comic. And so for that matter is life on the outside.

TWO

Fear, paranoia and general uptightness have become the leit-motif of our time.

The fear of ultimate punishment, i.e., imprisonment, has driven us into a lifestyle of impossible pirouettes that all too often land us flat on our collective asses. It renders us listless and therefore useless.

Time has come to clear up the musty cobwebs of fear so that what to many may seem to be the ultimate in oppression—i.e. detention—will be just another life-giving experience. It is possible. It works, and my friend is a living, breathing case in point.

Not only was he unscathed by the two years behind bars. He emerged a bigger, more conscious and therefore wiser man. The power of positive thinking—or how to beat the MAN at his own game—a primer in jail survival.

Q: Many good people are in or about to enter prison. Their understandable apprehensions are primarily due to a lack of knowhow regarding life on the inside. You have spent a number of years in Federal Prison as a pot offender. Having known you for a long time before that interlude, I find you now in exceptional shape. How did that happen?

A: The thing you have to realize about the prison system—I am talking about the Federal Prison System—is that it is a part of the federal bureaucracy. It's just like the Army. Same kinds of rules and regulations. Pass the buck and so on. Naturally it is very easy to feel maligned by the guards and realize what a bunch of fuckpigs they are. As in the Army, the most important thing is to survive it with a sane head. The weird thing about prison is that it's like some weird kind of family. You have to realize that the guards are there doing time just like the inmates.

I remember asking a guard how long he had been in Sandstone. "Twelve years." "Do you think that you will be doing all your TIME here?" "No, Ill finish up in Leavenworth." It blew my mind. He was talking about the next twelve years, which he has to serve in order to be eligible for retirement. I thought to myself—Wow, I am going home in a year, and this guy has twelve more years of this stuff.

As I said, just like the Army, and therefore many of the guards come from the Army. They are mainly career men who wanted to get into something else and still have their thing intact. They come to the system already regimented as hell. The thing that attracts them is the chance for promotion. Guards start as junior officers. Then become senior officers. Eventually they make lieutenant and the captain of the guard. If a guy is on the ball, he can then transfer to the administration, become assistant warden and perhaps even WARDEN. The interesting thing is that a guard cannot advance from one position to a higher one at the same institution. If one wants to advance, one has to move about. They have an interinstitutional newspaper, like a trade magazine, where one can find want ads like "WANTED—a Warden." If guys buck for promotion, and most of them do, they move from one institution to another. As always, the government, being BIG BROTHER, pays for all their expenses. Upon transfer, nothing changes much. The guy is again in a small town, just like the place he left, with the same rules and regulations, the same uniforms, and the same people. That's why the Federal bureaucracy is full of these square cornball people.

Q: Aren't different institutions famous or infamous for their own individual patterns of functioning?

A: In the Federal system there are the Federal Correctional Institutions and the Penitentiaries, which means absolute maximum security, with machine guns on the walls.

In the F.C.I. they primarily keep people that are doing minimum terms. They try to keep the age level above 25. Many of the inmates there began with long terms in penitentiaries. They usually spent 5–6 years there. If they were on good behavior, they were eventually sent to the country clubs—the F.C.I.s.

Q: Is there really such a difference between the two?

A: It is really a joke. Even though the F.C.I.s are less secure, they are in the middle of nowhere, and one really can't escape.

If you do, all the farmers in the area hear the sirens, and they are all out, with their shotguns, for the $50 bounty that is set on your head. Because of the lack of privacy, they know about your escape the minute you split. Therefore the concept of minimal security, like the guards not carrying arms, is strictly a psychological thing. In contrast to penitentiaries, the monotony factor is there simply because most of the people there are on good behavior. You couldn't get a food riot going if you fed shit. Everybody is bucking for parole, and for the most part they are a bunch of bootlickers. It is indeed a very bland place with a very bland atmosphere.

It is easy to complain that you can't get the books you want, that you can't write, or that this or that can't be done. I say this is a lot of selfdefeating bullshit. When you are sent to an institution, try to go through the few weeks of orientation with a strong, positive attitude. You have to come to terms with the fact that you are THERE. You have to be at times brave in adjusting. If you do that, you have, in reality made it because after that you can fuck up all you want. All you have to do is to get the people on your side in the beginning. You don't have to lick ass. You can be what you are and do what you want. Then, if you encounter trouble, you just write to the Bureau of Prisons in Washington, and, man, they come right down, and in most cases it really works. If you raise the stink in the right places, it usually works.

Q: Does that mean that only by working through the established channels does one get what one wants?

A: Yes. In many ways it is a drag, but remember that you end up beating the system and fucking with the people more than if you have a temper tantrum. To blow one's cool is just a waste of time and energy, because as long as the prison system is going to function, it is going to function pretty much the same way as it has been functioning until now. I was certainly not there for the mere purpose of changing it. I was there because of an illegal bust, an illegal trial which was so adjudged by the Court of Appeals. I was nevertheless THERE, as an observer of a part of the American way of DOING THINGS.

Anybody going in there should dig this attitude and use the time as a creative, positive period to get things done. To read, to write, to communicate and dig what's happening. You should also dig a class of people whom you might not snub in real life — yet you would never have the chance to be so close with, to eat, sleep, and play with on such equal terms. In prison everybody is as one. Everybody is wearing the same clothes, eating the same food, and living the same existence. Everybody looks the same, and you can't tell a maligned innocent apart from the greasiest token pigs. It is certainly an interesting experience.

Q: Fear of incarceration plays a big part in the chemistry of our paranoia. How does that relate to prison reality?

A: You don't have to have any real fear of prison and its system, because it is like going away to camp. Nobody is going to whale on you, and you would be surprised how much you are respected for taking a stand against the government. Everybody in prison hates the government. Everyone believes in his innocence and firmly believes that he was framed by the government. If you come in with a positive attitude, you are not being looked down upon. To roll with the system does not mean that you have got to kiss ass. All you have got to do is to dig the vibes. Asslickers do not get paroled, because even the system does not like them. They use stool pigeons to get information and in turn make promises to them. But they are considered incapable of getting along with their fellow human beings and therefore unparolable. Besides, why parole anyone that is so useful to the system? If you aren't what they want, they are eager to get rid of you as soon as possible.

Q: There is much talk about rehabilitation. How do you feel about that?

A: It is all sheer bullshit. Just bear in mind that up to 75 percent of their budget goes for custodial expenditure — not rehabilitation. It is a catch phrase which doesn't mean much. To REHABILITATE suggests that you have been habilitated once and now they are going to rehabilitate you once more. It is a ridiculous concept.

Q: You mentioned to me your preparation for prison. You mentioned Gurdjieff, Ouspensky, and Hatha Yoga.

A: I mentioned these only in terms of the positive aspects of their philosophies, which always did appeal to me. It all came into play when I found myself in a jungle called Cook County Jail. My positive attitude was the thing that kept me going. To be negative puts you in a black mood and prevents you from functioning. On the other hand, while focusing on the positive you say to yourself: "I fucked up, I've got to do three years. I'll probably get out after two, and if I am lucky I'll make it even sooner."

Look, where else would you have a chance just to lie back, not worry about food, clothing, or housing and be able to read all the books you may want to read, do all the thinking, and just dig what's happening? How many people do you know that wouldn't want to knock off for a year and be able to do just that?

Therefore I think that all those who have to go in and are uptight about it, are fools. It *is* a drag, but the positive aspects of prison life can elevate it from a level of negativism and make it a very lifegiving experience. I think this is one of the ways to take the government, which is out to make you pay for something, and say to them in return, "You haven't hurt me. You have just given me more strength by showing me that you can't do a thing to hurt me."

Q: I have spoken to a number of people that, like you, have served time. Basically they substantiated what you have said. The only thing that seemed to have gotten them was the element of oppression—the oppressiveness of incarceration.

A: Right—boredom and regimentation. But they aren't your real concern. They are just an insignificant detail. To get hung up on it is to defeat yourself. The days that I got hung up behind one thing or another made the nights black and unbearable. Boredom is the biggest problem, and the woman thing is a complete drag. The homosexual thing is practically nonexistent in the Federal system. All this may boil down to is handholding and an occasional coy glance. Due to a lack of privacy, it is almost impossible to beat off, let alone fuck. The sex thing is something that necessitates sublimation, otherwise you drive yourself up the wall.

In the long run, all these are details that you learn to deal with. The anticipation of them is considerably worse than the actual thing. Remember that there is always a tomorrow.

INSIDE
BUSBY CROCKETT

The Prison Trip

1. DOING WEIRD TIME: WALL TO WALL BLUES

So you're going to prison. Maybe you are out on bail living in that strange never-never world, just wandering and reaching new heights of aimlessness. If you are a draft resister you are waiting for the war heat to lessen. If you are a drug (soft) offender you hope the judge's son will soon try some of that fantastic kettle weed and hip his old man to where the danger really lies.

But in case none of these events occur, chances are that "time" is imminent. Now Baden Powell had with him a little too much of a fondness of uprights and uniforms, but he did say "be prepared," and so as with Girl Scouts it is with prison. If you are able, try to square up loose ends that you may have let yourself dangle into. I thought of it as a long trip, most of it internal . . . kind of a sojourn of the mind, resembling a Hesse-like "Journey to the East." Don't pack a lunch or take books (they can be sent in later). Try to get into a habit of deriving enjoyment out of your mind. I see a lot of people doing weird time. I can't put down weird time but all these people have the most painful look in their eyes.

I haven't found any of the real physical rigors that I had pictured. There isn't any of the run, run, wait, wait, that the military is so fond of. I find it to be more of an atmosphere of wait, wait. And it is easy to get into a wait-wait groove. I was waiting and dreaming, which was nice, but after a while I developed strange pains in the back of my head. Camus once said that part of becoming a man is spending time in prison. Now I can't really at this time define what being a man or becoming a man means. I do know the experience is total and that my head is changing toward a feeling of togetherness. The experience is also long—which tends to make the situation one of making it or breaking it. There is no more wafting around on little rafts of unreality (no matter which side you're on). Every morning I wake up and I see me standing stark naked in front of myself. If I didn't like what I saw, or if I don't like what I see, the pains are on the way. I've seen me on that wondrous cell-opening, eye-opening chemical, but that is sort of like seeing me from the third power and there are all those nice feely things too. I don't find that to be very here and now down in the joint.

If you expect nonsense, you will find it stacked wall to wall. All I can say is that the people running this place are people. Some of them suck. Some play very high quality head games. I think that the goal of the captains of this ship is to make this place resemble a little America (the flag can be seen from anywhere on the compound): the machine may be slow and say goshucks, but it is very well oiled and running smoothly, thank you. The people resemble robots or any other non-human label you might apply, but I find it very difficult to use labels any more. I've learned that performing superficial robot games keeps my keepers satisfied. I don't argue about who is right. MAN, I KNOW who is right and who is crazy, but I also know where I am. I threw my pride out the window of the marshal's car somewhere along the turnpike.

Most white inmates still live in a honkytonk paradise of the girls who would or wouldn't and the girls who do it for money, and dying must be groovy because look at all the people who are killed. Born to lose tattoos, yeah, that's part of it. And so I cop out to this place and its outer-space nonsense but I can't see how some people can cop out to Elvis Presley being King of EVERY-THING. I don't see how they can have wet dreams about a woman they will never touch. Some tell me they want to get out so they can join the Pepsi generation.

The television schedule is set up by one man somewhere in the Education Department. Controlled environment. Beautiful. Everything is an hallucination.

The black inmates tend to be of a different order. The Muslims are given a room every Sunday to meet. The local authorities resent this, I think; but Washington blew one of its strange liberal winds in the direction of free assembly and so the Muslims are kept above ground. Due to the strictness of the order, only a few are fulltime members. A lot of fringies are to be found. The remaining black population perfects the bugaloo and does a kind of laughdance to pass the time. Those mud flats seem real and of good quality. The Black Is Beautiful thing is getting hold now and the laughing is coming more at the expense of the honkytonks. Still, I guess that some wouldn't mind getting hold of some of that white Pepsi generation pussy for a laugh, at least. And oh, white America, they're all going to get out some day.

I've heard people describe this place as a college, penitentiary, kids' joint, and a joke. Lately, I've seen it as an English garden because of the flowers that grow in abundance along the walks, and because the grounds are super-neatly manicured by the overly supervised inside maintenance crew. Flowers are flowers. Walls and fences have no real power over them. It's along the lines of LBJ versus the Beatles—Who Wins?

Now I live in an honor dormitory. I have a pay-toilet-like cubicle all to myself, to live a little private life and I suppose to play with my privates if I do it quietly. The dormitory has no bars and resembles a Route 128 electronics firm. All draft resisters would eventually live in this dorm if, of course, their games are well played and they don't get too many dirty room demerits. I even have a lamp of my own that was made in Norway. The building overlooks the English garden with its multi-colored benches.

Homosexual scenes are big. Undercover, overcover, punk-boys, hiding out, hanging out, playing the good games, the bad games, and the non-games. If you're all-American with the right color blood it's natural to be attracted to the sweeties. And everybody knows who's sweet and who isn't and the sweets are surely to be made sweeter and, of course, the guards like to watch. And you better win at all costs-if you don't win you got to be a loser and everybody knows where losers are at.

Right about now the sun is setting and the bugs are wailing and the papas are wooing present and future mamas and the real down druggies talk about those outasight times of yesterday and tomorrow, and the birds and the color of the sky make the whole thing seem somehow insane, and I sit here watching a Hank Williams movie.

2. JAMMING ON VEGETABLES: A SOLOIST ON THE DICER

DATELINE: PRISON MESS HALL. Does anybody care? Busby got caught trying to get two portions of pork grease steaks, I think it was. Caught cold duck with the pork that previously had been graciously bathed in some of its own mother's juice. ''ve heard it said that you are what you eat and my greaser stage was kind of stunted in high school. So why not, I thought, become a greaser when you're locked in a farm with a bunch of guys who got their chance to become full flown greasers. Back to the point. Apprehended by a pig for having an extra portion of pig that was considered by the whole pig with grey pants and jingly-jangly keys to be contraband (God forbid). I was convicted immediately and sentenced to four hours duty in the vegetable room. The word vegetable always made me shake a little. I had an aunt once who was a vegetable, and at one time I ate some celery and I swear I heard it scream. Confidentially, a head of cabbage defeated me (squashed?) in a debate on migrant labor, a few years back, and since I've been on bad terms with all kinds of heads.

All these happenings I could have put together as forewarnings of my cosmic demise when I reached the room itself. I had various schemes bubbling through my head like having my sentence commuted to the pot room, but pot put me here in the first place. I also had heard rumors from the compound wire to the effect that the kettles controlled the pots and some very strange people stir those kettles.

I baked a cake once on the street (spice) which stuck to the pan and burned a little on the outside, but then a cake is a cake and I knew I had one last chance in the bakery room. In the nick of time, though, Baker Goose came by and put me straight to the bakers and their whims and ways. Seems that every time a big batch of bread is baked — every day — the cooks knead the dough until it resembles the texture of flesh (preferably female), puncture the dough with broomstick turned dildo, and proceed to unload their kicks into the dough, now turned skinny-legged tv goddess (eyes closed, of course). This has started me thinking where Wonder Bread got its name. The now fully enriched dough is baked and sliced and served to the unhip and hungry alike. "No thanks," I told Goose, cause just the night before I had transformed my right hand into this eight-foot-two-inch blonde Pan Am stewardess I had met on an Istanbul-New York run. Goose mumbled something about all bread being the same to him and shuffled away.

Leaving the carnival-like atmosphere of the bakers, I found my way to the green door of the vegetable room. I open the door and am greeted by fantastic organic smells coming from somewhere. What's this? Duffbo Bums is waiting by the potato-peeling machine, and California Mountain Man is sorting lettuce. Some guy who looks like he should be elected to the Catfish Hall of Fame is giving carrots the business in the dicing machine. It's starting to hit me that these lions are jamming on just plain plants. I get to quarter the peeled potatoes, sort of a second chair potato man. Actually, I like to think in terms of boss potato man, but that's spacing things a bit.

Duffbo appears to be the leader of the session and instructs me in the art of quartering the spuds and pitchem in the garbage can turned potato pail. Duffbo says to quarter the rotten ones too as that adds spice.

Mountain Man and the lettuce are talking about this gassy iceberg lettuce he met on this last bit in Chino. The lettuce just scrunched and let Mountain cut her all he wished. Man said he always like good listeners, and under his knife the sheaves and shums gave in green surrender.

All the while Catfish is dicing and dicing, I can see that Duff and Mountain Man don't like him cause he can't get rapport with the dicer. He'd cut the stems and feed the dicer OK, but the dicer only chopped the carrots and fed them back to him, making sly noises in the process. Now even Catfish is hip that the dicer is trying to ruin his cool, so old Catfish smacks the dicer, whonck. Gumbo is the first to see that Cat is trying to do dirt to the dicer, and he also knows that the old dice doesn't work without some respect. Real easy-like he says, "Catfish, cut the dicer a break and she'll make it mellow for you." But Catfish takes Duffbo for a jive, little knowing that the Gum was once a soloist on the dicer himself. So this time he smacks the dicer twice. This brings Mountain out of his lettuce riff cause Mountain too knows the dicer has feelings. "You better dig yourself, Catfish, for just like me and this lettuce can sing, you and that dicer could put out some fine little squares if you and her could become one." The Fish won't buy any of this. He runs down how he has been dicing and peeling and cutting in two state joints and a county jail and nobody but nobody could talk any shit about him not being tight with his dicer. "OK," says Gums, "but I know that the true test of a real dice man is if he can run the carrots through the dicer, still keeping hold of the stems that are still keeping hold of the carrots." Catfish gets kind of a shaky look in his eyes but agrees, "Man, that's nothing." By now I've filled an entire pail with quartered potatoes, so I feel about ready for a smoke break, and besides, I'd like to get a good position to view the Fish's carrot test. Mountain gives the dicer a final inspection and wipe job while Gumbo meticulously chooses which pack of carrots Catfish will use for his performance. Things are getting quiet now and I see the Cat eyeing the door. Mountain counters the eye move by getting hold of the stem knife and puts Cat back to his test. Gums switches on the machine and hands the carrots to Fish. Fish is shaking all over now but starts easing in the carrots. Everything is going pretty well till the machine starts shaking in kind of a funny way and pulls the carrots, stems, and well—old Fish's hand. Gums and Mountain both crack up, but I feel kind of sick. I switch off the machine seeing that the test is over and ask Gums what to do with the hand. Throw it in the potatoes. Should anybody care?

BOB KAUFMAN

Jail Poem

I am sitting in a cell with a view of evil parallels,
Waiting thunder to splinter me into a thousand me's.
It is not enough to be in one cage with one self;
I want to sit opposite every prisoner in every hole.
Doors roll and bang, every slam a finality, bang!
The junkie disappeared into a red noise, stoning out his
    hell.
The odored wino congratulaes himself on not smoking,
Fingergrints left lying on black inky gravestones,
Noises of pain seeping through steel walls crashing
Reach my own hurt. I become part of someone forever.
Wild accents of criminals are sweeter to me than hum of
    cops,
Busy battening down hatches of human souls; cargo
Destined for ports of accusations, harbors of guilt.
What do policemen eat, Socrates, still prisoner, old one?

MICHAEL ROSSMAN

Notes From The Country Jail

*On December 2, 1964, 800 Berkeley students were arrested in
the big sit-in that climaxed the Free Speech Movement. Two
and a half years later, the Supreme Court refused to review our
case. So a number of us went to the county jail, for having
(successfully) fought the university's attempt to prohibit our
advocacy on campus of actions—like burning draft cards or
trying to shut down the Induction Centers or signing complicity
statements or smoking pot or being black, though at the time we
were thinking more of Civil Rights sit-ins—which might prove to
be illegal.*

    *These notes were written, then, during last year's summer
vacation, nine weeks in the Santa Rita Rehabilitation Center.*

264

*They were written to my friends, who know their longer original
form as "The Adventures of Garbageman Under the Gentle
Thumb of the Authority Complex." I wish I were certain of their
relevance to the many more who are going in soon, and for far
longer.*

They locked us in messhall again, to wait through a recount
and a recount and a recount outside. Shadowboxing, the black
kids singing. "Hey, sport, you're kinda crazy," said my new side-
kick on the garbage crew. A Mexican kid with a sour expression, he pulled his toothbrush out and combed his mustache.
You see it on most of them, that bent-over plastic handle
hooked over their shirt pocket. Sideburns and beards are verbo-
ten, a mustache is all you can nurse. "Grows out all kinky if you
don't keep after it," explained the kid who married a virgin. It
really gave me a start, the first time I saw someone pull out his
toothbrush and use it, casual as a comb through greaser hair.
   "You're kinda crazy, sport," said my partner—he does the
kitchen head, I keep after the cans. "I know," I said, idly. "No
. . . you act kinda crazy most of the time." "Yeah, I know."
"No, I really mean it, you do." "Man, I *know*," I said, "it's
cool." "You like acid, dontcha," he stated. I cracked up and
eyed him for a moment, doing that little widening motion so the
pupil floats like a blue yolk in its innocent white. "Man, I was
crazy *before* I took acid," I said, "but yeah, I do." He was the
fourth one to tell me I like acid; they all say it with the positive
relief of a bird-watcher hitting the right page in his manual. No
one asks about grass. It's taken for granted: everyone here
smokes shit on the outside. But—even though a number of the
spades have tried acid and dig it, and some of us haven't—LSD
is taken as a kind of dividing line. We are the hippies. Even
though we stalk around with books in our hands all the time,
that's our identification: not college kids, or "professor" (as it
was when I used to dig ditches, that traditional tag), but hippies.
No question about it. The other inmates are friendly, curious,
josh us. There's a goodly amount of respect for us as a group: we
have status, an identity. Hippies.
   "They don't understand you guys," said the wiseacre kid who
tools the messhall truck around and jokes with the guards.
"Whaddaya mean?" I asked him. "Like, what went on between
you'n the officer inside, it really put him up tight. He was about
ready to roll you up and send you off to Greystone, thought you
were some kinda fruit." We were sitting behind the messhall,
waiting for the count-clear siren. Earlier I'd walked into the little
glassed-off office in the kitchen, to get the duty officer to clear
my work so I could go. Four of the mess crew were clustered

265

around his desk. "Whaddaya want?" An antic impulse: I answered, "Love." "What?" "Love, man, and I'm happy. Also you could check my work." He gave me a very odd look, and said to wait a bit; cleared me later without mentioning the incident, which I thought no more of till the kid brought it up.

He went on. "A lot of the officers, they don't like you guys. I mean, they're cops, you know, and you guys fought City Hall, and got away with it. Now with us, that's cool, we understand and dig you, know what I mean? But you made the cops look foolish then, and a lot still have it in for you even if it was a couple years ago. They look for you to be troublemakers, and when you aren't, well, that bugs 'em too. You gotta be careful with them, because they don't understand you."

But aside from not letting our books through, there's been remarkably little hard-timing. Partly this is because, almost to a man, we're easy with being here. (Today at lunch I remembered how bristling with hostility we'd been on our first visit, the night of the arrest, and we all had a good laugh at the contrast. "But," said Mario, "there were reasons then, you know, like getting dragged down stairs and all that.") But also it's because we've violated their expectations. We're open and friendly and curious, and we work hard. That counts for a lot. Garson, Lustig, and Saslow are on Bakery crew, up at 4:00 in the morning; now Mario has joined them. At first the ex-service guy who runs that show was down on them, riding them. Now he treats them with open friendliness, so much so that it's getting to be a bit of a distraction. "He keeps trying to father me," says Mario. Word has leaked back from the Booking Office, Santa Rita's nerve center: he keeps talking about us. "Get me nine more like them . . . hell, I'll have this place so changed. . . ." There has been a bit of trouble: a couple of kids have wound up in the Hole for four days, for refusing to work. But the work was painting Army barracks, the objection moral rather than lazy. All in all, our stock is sound and rising. But still no books.

Everyone's curious about Mario. "Which one he, where he, he you leader? Say man, point him out to me." Sitting around behind the mess hall, waiting for the count siren to sound all-clear: a dozen of us, all but two black. They talked about Mohammed Ali, about the fighters he admires, then about us. "Mario, he the leader of them hippies." "Shit, he had like a million people following him, that dude. And why? Man, because he spoke *freely* what he thought, that why. . . ."

A bird flew into the garbage compound. Some wanted to kill it: three of us went in. One heaved a brush as it flew, missed.

I climbed the mountain of boxed empty tins, retrieved it, jumped down. Outside someone took it gently from my hand. "Look here"—to no one—"here's how you hold it, see so he free in you hand." Then chucked it into the sky, underhand and up. *Away*. The tension broke, and suddenly a tall black kid did a spot routine. "Ho, when he get home. . . ." The circle acted it out: the girl birds hanging around twittering, testing his muscles. "There they was, hundreds of them, two of 'em had me by the wings and one by the legs, oh, but I faked 'em all out. Shit, they was *all* over me, man, they was gonna roast me . . . you got any idea what they smell like?" "Tell it, man, tell it. . . ."

Rehabilitation—with a vengeance. This place is so middle class I can't believe it. Dig: we get up at 6:15 every morning; our lights are out by 9:30, though we get till 10 on Saturdays (that's our big day). Make your bed, sweep up, keep your area clean. Or Else. I shave and shower every other day, and change clothes on the day in between. Three square meals a day, perforce, nutritionally adequate and sometimes even good (with respect to regularity, bulk, and nutrition, I eat better than I do at home. Karen's mad at my spreading that about). We work five or seven days a week. No beards permitted, hair to be kept neatly trimmed. My mother would love it.

Me, I'm the Garbageman: three times a day I keep after the mess in the messhall, so to speak, cleaning and jerking 150-lb. cans full of slop, again so to speak. "You gonna have some muscles when you get out of her I bet, man." (The slop goes to the hog farm, where Jack is working.) "How long you in for?" asked the messguard when I reported. "90 days." "What for?" "Sit-in." "Garbage!" I still don't know if he was for or against me: I dig the job. My hidden advantage, of course, is that I can't smell: but if I keep after the stuff, even that doesn't make much of a difference.

My day is criss-crossed by counts, meals at the odd hours of Messmen's Schedule, and having to sling garbage after each regular meal (which runs me two to three hours a day of welcome work). I am left with seven clear segments of one-to-two hours. Mornings and afternoons I read or write; evenings now, volleyball, or an occasional game of chess or dominoes. That's an idyllic picture, actually; unless I go off and hide to write, people are constantly falling on to me, and I get into conversations with them—or, more often, listening and watching. I've begun mild calisthenics morning and evening (many of us, and a few of the regulars, go through some such counting ritual). All in all, there's much more freedom than I'd expected.

Taking a page from Cassius Clay, when he still used that name, I cultivate a somewhat antic air: careening down the tile corridors with an endlessly varied wail of "Gaaaaarbage, make way for de gaaahbudge . . . " like a London street-cry. And at other times, endlessly with a book and writing pad in my hand. "I'm conditioning the guards," I told the kid who asked why. If they think you're slightly mad, you can get away with a lot.

Many of us are looking on this imprisonment as our only possible live rehearsal for what draft-resistance might bring. A county jail isn't much like a federal prison, nor is a month or two like three to five years, but that's the best we can do. I have been cheered both because I adapt easily to the life and people here, and also because I've had no trouble at all in launching and sustaining a mind-project: the essay I'm working on, about the generation gap. For the month before I came in, I was working my ass off to finish another manuscript: I expected to need an (involuntary) vacation. Instead, my desires to talk with people and to plug away on the essay are constantly fighting each other.

Paradoxically, even as maintaining an independent mental and emotional life here is much more practical than I'd expected, the idea of spending a long time in jail becomes even less appealing. I'm not sure why. Weinberg points out that Santa Rita is oppressive precisely because it's relatively humane, a model county jail (he likens it to the ideal socialist state). I dig what he means; it confuses me even more about doing federal time, behind bars. S——, W——, a couple of others have already decided to split for Canada; their stay here has had little impact on that decision. I have begun thinking about it seriously, for the first time. Barely.

Visiting days are a mixed blessing, mail call also, "You have to be where you are to make it," points out Steve, "and news or touch of the outside pulls you back, between two worlds." There are other reminders, besides the papers, to keep our thoughts ambivalent. Last Sunday's flick was a World War II romance, set in S.E. Asia: jungle warfare, the whole bit. We have been well-conditioned: we cheered when Sinatra and his faithful handful of natives wiped out the Jap jungle airstrip with its planes near the end, in a sneak attack, and then penetrated the Chinese border and executed a couple of hundred captives taken there, in retaliation for their attack on the supply convoy that was supposed to support our boys. Back in the barracks, the papers describe Westmoreland's request for 140,000 more men. How many of us lay awake that night, trying to pick apart that snarl of feelings generated by the flick: exhilaration, regret, detachment, anger, and fear?

Saslow has built a microscope: an improvement on the Leeu-wenoek model, with a carefully formed drop of Karo syrup held in a pierced thin metal plate for its optics. A rock, string, twigs, glue, paper, pencil pulleys for focusing, tongue-depressor slide platforms, the chrome blade from fingernail clippers as reflector, etc. The prisoners have been very attentive and helpful, scrounging things he needs. They all agree on the one ground rule: no contraband material to be used in its construction. His first slide is onion-skin tissue, stained with beet-juice to bring out cell walls and nuclei. I overheard some of them discussing it—they use "telescope," "microscope" and "magnifying glass" indiscriminately, but no confusion results. "Mario showed him how," said one, "he smart, that dude, he the leader."

College kids in jail. We learn quickly the patient shuffle that the random cloddy shoes enforce, the perfect complement to the floppy prison blues we wear. "Too fast to be standing still," as one inmate put it, or to be yelled at by The Man; slow enough not to raise a sweat in the sky-covered roaster of Valley summer. For those of us who have lived in dormitories, this *in loco parentis* scene is basically familiar, and—save for the frequent recall-to-barracks-and-count, which I imagine the girls recognize—scarcely exaggerated. The food, in fact, is better than that at most college dorms. The barracks scene may look like Army; but the pace of our lives and the general atmosphere are much closer to the Academy.

At night, after lights-out, we visit other bunks and swap stories about backgrounds and travels, and—again like a college dorm—talk a great deal about our past sexual exploits, in boastful detail, and how we wish we were getting some pussy, and what we'll do when we get it. Under the constant glare of the blue bulbs in the tall ceiling, the young spades in their corner chatter like jaybirds for hours, punctuating it occasionally with horse-play yelps. The quiet longtimer from the end of the barracks sits on the john with the light on, fighting a compound interest prob-lem The old drunk blows silent insomnia smoke, as Al and I crouch at the foot of Dennis's bunk listening to him tell of burglaries in Berkeley: a life of smashed windows, snatched TV sets and suits, and careening 3 A.M. chases down the quiet streets of the city we know so differently.

Still slightly sweaty from pushups—the silent spade across the way looked up from Richard Wright, said not to do them just before bed, didn't do no good—we listen to the lanky kid from Tennessee dissect the lives and loves of the small California town where he was sent up for moonshining. Al, knowing the town and some of its citizens—yeah, I remember her, tall skinny girl well-hung, she was half Piyute Indian and half Scandinavian—is particularly tickled. "So there they was, going at it on the mountain, and him sitting down there with this fifty-power sniper scope, everyone in town come have a looksee. Whoo-*ee*!" Vern, the gentle old alky who taught me to tap out the mop deftly in the morning, allowed as how if they legalized pot it would be the salvation of him and a lot of others. But Tennessee's never touched grass, "no, nor bennies nor H nor none of that stuff." We try to straighten him out on drug categories, tell him of hiking on acid at 11,000 feet and swimming on grass, balling on both; invite him to Berkeley. The door to the barracks slams open and an officer lurches through with flashlight waving— "Bull session, uh?" We swallow our start of guilt and fear. He's looking for someone to butcher a deer just brought in, leaves for another barracks. This morning the carcass hangs behind the messhall, someone is at it. The meat will grace officer's mess, we'll never see it.

Bananas for lunch. Their fragments will reappear the next day, encased in jello as the beans turn to soup: the principles of cooking here are few and predictable. They saunter out of the messhall, sly pockets full of peels: "mellow-yellow" they whisper, with a knowing wink. Later that afternoon: "Hey, hippie, what you guys know about how to fix these? there a special way or sumpin?" We are in demand for certain minor specialized functions: "Hey, what kind of complex you call it when a guy keeps coming on like he knows everything?" Since we haven't been singled out for any special kind of treatment—good or bad—by the guards (or inmates), we are left to define our own identity as a group. We aren't overly clannish, though a few stick to their own devices and with most the book or writing-pad in hand has become a near trademark. Except among ourselves, we listen much more than we talk—though sometimes art or politics will flare in a tight knot for an hour on the street in front of the library, and some of our new friends or strangers will hang around the edges, curious to hear us at our own game.

The dormitory atmosphere of the place is partly due to the age-distribution: a good half of the inmates are twenty-five or under (many of the rest are old alkies: their numbers rise after the weekend, you can tell them in messline Monday morning by their shaking hands). Most of them are here for trivia: driving with a suspended license, dodging child support, burglary. A few for heavier things: manslaughter, slugging a cop, and so on: the county jail. "Shit, most of them are just kids, nothing serious," said the officer who confessed to having read *Walden* five times, after I complained to him that we were disappointed because we'd expected to be locked up with criminals.

There is very little sense of being among criminals here. The kids in the kitchen constantly mimic the "crank" (methedrine) rituals, going through the motions of tying up and shooting—but with exactly the same good humor with which we noisily inhale the last drag on a handrolled cigarette ("square"), holding the roach delicately between thumb and forefinger. To have a candybar and a pack disappear from my drawer came as a surprise. "Hide your stuff in your pillow," advised the queen trusty, "remember, you among thieves here."

It's hard to believe, as I lie here stripped to the waist on the beach of the volleyball court (five days in the Hole for stripping to shorts). Sounds of argument drift from the open doors of the barracks. There are always arguments going—most discussions get there quickly, on any subject—but they seldom flare into real anger. Al points out the high aggressive quotient, the many overlapping pecking orders: everything becomes a vehicle for proof, in this arena of constant enforced contact. Yet strangely, there is no pressure: and much of that appearance is deceptive. You are in the pecking order only if you choose to be. (None of us does.) To opt out is simple, and nobody bugs you to get in. And so organized or permanent competition is totally absent. There is no barracks chess champ, no constant volleyball team, scant interest in the ping-pong table.

Low key and easy is the word. Almost everyone's out to do easy time— those who aren't soon get on the guards' wrong side and wind up in Greystone. (But generally, hostility between guards and inmates is almost completely absent; and there has been only one fight that I know of in our first three weeks, plus a few punches quickly concealed after a flick.) Such action as takes place is lined with good humor, mostly: the eternal games of men-against-the-System. Two kids come furtive, zip! out of the messhall, with a twenty-pound tin of coffee under an army blanket. Guard at the barracks gate, they split it up in the john into paper bags to stash it, and crushed the can's carcass, hid it in the garbage. They boosted it on commission, so to speak: for packs (of cigarettes, the standard currency) plus grass if it came through. (There *is* grass here, but it's pretty far under the surface.) Needles zip out of messhall clothing, to be embedded in toothbrush handles and wound with black thread, as a tattooing device. Slippers disappear from Little Greystone, to be hidden under mattresses, worn at night, and turned up among protestations of innocence in occasional shakedowns. All things considered, the atmosphere is pretty familiar. As Mario points out, this place is no great shucks as a deterrent. If they'd let our women in on the weekend—as they do in Mexico and Russia—pass through our books and make a decent cup of coffee now and then, I'd be nearly contented.

Most of the people here are black; and of the remainder, most are Mexican. There seems to be no active discrimination, though colors have a way of hanging together to chatter. The reading room, with its stock of tattered journals, has no black magazines, like *Ebony* or *Jet*, nor any in Spanish; the library has a handful of books in Spanish and a double handful of black books—Malcolm X's autobiography being conspicuously absent—balanced by a magnificent collection of mysteries, a fair one of science-fiction and westerns, a lot of old novels, and little else. (Our boys are rediscovering the classics—Zola Dostoevsky, Flaubert—mainly because the books are old and worn enough to have found their way here.) As in the Haight-A., there is much tolerance for deviant behavior. Nobody comes on—or, rather, coming on is so clearly that, that it makes no difference.

A week ago, a dozen of our thirty clustered rapping after every meal. Now more than four in a knot is unusual. One by one they are leaving; after this weekend, almost all of the short-timers will be gone, and a week later we'll be down to five, two of whom I dislike. It'll be a bit lonely. Partly for this reason, I've kept more to myself than I usually would, not wanting to build a dependence. Aside from talking with Mario—we fall into instant intricate dialogue on any trivial or major detail—I've spent time only with S—— and W——, neither of whom I knew before and both of whom I dig immensely. (Within a few months both will probably be out of the country to begin the long exile.) Today the mess officers offered me a new job, leaderman of the mop crew. I blew their minds by refusing—they kept coming back out to make sure I understood. "No, man, I'm comfortable at it," I told them—not sure that *they* understood how one programs even days full of life into a mechanical pattern, so as to make the time pass quickly and unnoticed, without disturbance.

Behind messhall, gathered waiting for the all-clear, a gem of a scene, Dennis is jiving, and somehow this other kid brings in pimping, and they build a contrast. You got to have a hustle, says Dennis. Don't get one, the kid says; can shoot a little pool, but got beat out of $20 last time I tried so can't really do that; but you really gotta work at a hustle like pimping. Big money in it, says Dennis. I pimp too, says the kid, for Ford. It bring me $127 a week, she do; I drive to work and back with the heater on, don't have to get out in the rain and make them broads work.

Same thing every day, says Dennis, today and tomorrow, you get home and go to bed, too tired to do anything: you hustle, you c'n work when you choose. Got a car but not one of them fine, fine Caddies, says the kid, and a little in the bank, about to get married, save up for a down payment on a house. A stoniness invades Dennis's face; the kid goes on, sure would like some of that money, though, but I'm too strung out behind my woman to put her on the street. Get home too tired to do anything, repeats Dennis. That's right; this here's my vacation, two weeks, that 127 keep coming in; if I had the kinda money you make hustling I'd sure use it to bail out. How much? I asked. $59 or 9 days he gave me, tickets, didn't have the money so here I am; I'd say to one of them broads, hey, go out and get me the money. I c'n dig it, Dennis keeps repeating, meaning I understand or you're right or I'm cool with what I'm doing or I'm hurting, depending on how you read the look in his voice; and against this background the kid goes on. "Where I made my mistake, I learned to do something"—he's a welder for Ford—"got stuck in it, went in the Army, took two years at school, got an Associate of Arts degree in Criminology; sure wish I had a hustle, still owe $300 on 5 suits that've almost wore out now; but when I want I can go down to the bank and say, 'give me some bread. . . .'"
"And they'll suck your blood," chime in Al and me, enthusiastically. We've been listening with total absorption, providing a running third voice about not digging work or the things money can buy; fill in the antiphony yourself. Abruptly, at some point—precisely when doesn't matter—Dennis gets up without a word, takes his milk box, moves it twenty feet away into the sun, sits down on it. The circle reforms, talk shifts to unfaithful lovers (wives). "I didn't know whether to cry or beat the shit out of the dude or beat the shit out of her." "So she asked him for five dollars." "Cheap." "Wait, you ain't heard what he did. He nailed the bill over the doorway. Whenever anyone came over he'd take out his .38 and say: 'Honey, tell 'em what that five dollars for.' And she knew he meant it, and she'd say, 'my husband caught me fucking with another man.'"

Scarlatti this morning, over the barracks radio that shakes us from sleep each 6:15. Like fresh water, that crystal streamflow of melody. I have forgotten what real water tastes like, I no longer notice the flat mineral-thick taste of the hydrant and bathroom streams. Only the coffee reminds me. Once a week I try a sip, recoil. And the Beatles and Stones tonight, just before lights-out. Real music: what a treat!
Usually the mornings are breakfast-club chatter and song, bright and false as yellow formica in an L.A. motel; and at eve-

ning either a talk-back program or cocktail-music, denatured mush to drown us to sleep. All too loud, you never quite get used to it. And even when the radio's silent the speaker is still live, so that the morse machinegun of the mad telegraphist, frantically punching his key somewhere beyond the hills in Pleasanton (we presume), can catch your soul at any moment: unaware, floating free of your body.

For a time it was KJAZ—good jazz—twice a week, rock once, some rhythm and blues. The spades and everyone else dug it. Then mush. No explanation. Eventually they got up a petition: can we have our music back? No—the answer came down from the Olympia of the Detail Office—because the petition was a demand, an attempt to pressure.

Well, mood control, that's the secret to making it here. At first I was genuinely, perpetually cheerful, because I'd imagined a constant boot-camp attempt to grind us down that didn't materialize. So I made the mistake of relaxing, of letting my guard down—and all of a sudden it looks like a jail with cops, and I feel somehow reassured, vigilant again. Like the food: initial hosannahs because it was edible; but now that the menu begins to repeat its weekly cycle for the fourth time, we realize that you don't need teeth for any of it, that everything is full of pepper for a reason; that. . . .

A chorus of groans goes up from outside, in the dark main room. The radio has just snapped off for the night, after the first bars of a good song. An inflexible rule: if the last song is slop, it plays through to the end; good songs get cut in the middle. That's how this place is, no kidding. Seeing that I wasn't dismayed by the garbage detail, the mess officer started also putting me on the short line to serve in the mornings. Innocent, I asked why. "Standard practice." And suddenly I found myself promoted to long line: an hour and a half sometimes serving food, before I can eat. I got the message. Then, gratuitously or to make sure, he sent me to get my second haircut in three weeks, at the butcher-barber's. I now have the shortest hair of any Anglo or Mex in the whole Mess Barracks. That was the guard who'd read *Walden* five times; I don't smile at him any more.

The blond, sallow one with the big ears and the hard voice did the pre-mail call count last night. (Our main recreation is getting counted, at least six times a day.) He caught me with a book in my hand, Dennis with a paper, Fast Black slouching; pulled us outside; gave us what-for, with words that slapped like dominoes. You will *stand* up *straight*, having *nothing* in your *hands*, five *days* in the *Hole*. Our faces were rock. I wanted to kill him. Literally. We blew it off inside, horseplay, yelling. Dennis slugged the wall. Most of the guards just whiz through, counting; but you can never tell who'll play ego-games like that, or who will get the two bakery men up at 4 a.m. for the early shift by standing in the middle of the barracks and yelling their names until they dress (though their names and bunk numbers hang together on the wall by the door).

So mood control is the word. The cheap bit with the second haircut cost me two days of rage; my head was sheerly scrambled, I couldn't write a word, all those intricate lovely thoughts scattered like trout when the wind rises. I read science-fiction furiously, five books, a drug. Finally I pulled up to a real smile, by thinking what a joke it was to have let the *Walden* bit shape my expectations so deeply. The sallow-faced guard only cost me three hours; I'm learning. Mood control.

And you've got to make *genuine* changes. There's no burying anger, not here: it builds up and blows at any unforeseen order—and the place, oddly enough, is full or orders, many with no point. The kids who can't work the magic of transmutation on their emotions wind up in the Hole, almost to a man.

All yesterday the Beatles were singing, "All you need is love." I think maybe we also need fewer cops, no cops . . . I am not sure if it comes to the same thing. But people who enjoy having power over others are a stone drag; and the matter is worse when it is cloaked in a social sanction. They offered me leaderman of the mop-crew, the guards who still seem sympathetic did. No, I said, I'm cool with being garbageman—no one knows I can't smell—"and besides, I don't like to be nobody's boss." Nor, but this silent, to have nobody boss over me. Benevolent or not. Not even the Beatles.

Reading this last rap, Mario is worried lest I give an unbalanced view of the guards. I don't mean to: the place is not vicious, just erratically petty. Yesterday I actually got some books, after three weeks trying. There's one compound officer who's overtly friendly to us—and hides out most of the time, seems completely ineffectual in the officer pecking-order. He has a good reputation with the inmates; such is the fate of good guys here, his goodness has become an ego-crutch in a losing battle: how lovely, how common, how sad. He felt guilty because I'd searched all over for him for six days running, asked him each time to get a paper from my box so I could revise it; took my name each time, forgot. So when I bumped into him with a note from the history teacher okaying my getting books, he escorted me up to the front office, glaring around with a bluff protectiveness made safe by the note, and let me take out Keniston's *The Uncommitted*, Friedenberg's *Coming of Age in America,* and

Ulysses. "*Ulysses*," he mused, "I flunked that book once. . . ." His voice trailed off. "Tough book," I responded glibly, "my chick's flippy about it, been after me three years to read it, promised her I'd get through it while I was in. You know . . . Gee, thanksamillion for helping me to get these," enthusiastically, scrammed. Not daring to meet his eyes or ask through the excuse of literature what lies beneath his lonely and passionless decency.

The history etcetera teacher was most obliging when I showed him the book list, even though he didn't understand quite why I wanted them; wrote me a note only the second time I saw him. "Hey, Mac," he called over to the accounting etcetera teacher, in his high, piping voice, "how do you spell 'taking'? T-a-k-e-i-n-g or . . . ?" Mac told him, while I stood respectfully by, and as he finished the note in his childish scrawl I looked down on his bald head, worn as the once-linen backing on the ancient texts, and thanked him very much and honestly; left him to his two occasional students, wandering toward the front office thinking of model jails. "It's a model jail," said the guard in the office, "known all over the state." "It's a model jail," said the old-timer in the mess-hall, "why, at San Bruno you can get a steak out of the officers' mess for a pack, and pussy now and then. And they don't hardly have no commissary."

Commissary here is run by an old codger named Dyke, who is subject to unpredictable fits of temper in which he imagines he hears talking in the line and closes it down for the day; those outside are out of luck, for he's an officer and can do what he wants to, right? He also arbitrarily decides what and how much may be bought each day. Not surprisingly, the regulars here speculate endlessly and cynically about where the commissary take goes. But he has his kind side. The twenty-seven-sheet tablet I'm writing on *says* 25 cents on its cover, but he lets the prisoners have it for 20 cents. All in all, it seems to be a much straighter operation than the one the old junkie doctor runs.

I was thinking about the haircut incident, which happened well over a week ago, while hustling garbage after dinner today. It was probably not malicious, but gratuitous, I decided: meant as a sort of benign amusement. And so my account of my reactions probably says a lot about my hairtrigger feelings about authority, pun intended.

That being so, and me being in jail, I've decided there's a definite advantage to my college background, despite the way the high-school dropouts in the officers' mess tease me, with their oranges and corned beef. For what is jail but a primitive form of the Authority Complex, cast in locks, alarms,and barbed wire? And what sort of problem does *that* present to a young man trained for nine years in the most Prestigious Multiversity in the land? Despite my touchiness about personal integrity, my dislike of stupid orders, and so on, I get along just fine: doing easy time, an exemplary prisoner: *my* suntan will never pale from days spent in the Hole, and if they gave Extra-Good Time I'd get that too and be out of here the sooner. For if there's anything being in college teaches you, it's how to relate to authority: even more than being black does, though the techniques are similar.

For here I am, the friendly Garbageman. With an antic smile and an off-key wail of "Gaaarbaaage . . . ," like a London street-cry. (Establish a distinct but non-threatening identity.) My cleaned cans upside-down on the cart so the imprisoned steam can *puff*! impressively as I upend them back in their places. (Pick a symbol of excellence in your subject; accentuate it.) Clanging the cans with great zeal, even risking an occasional caution about too much noise when the officers are eating. (Be passionately dedicated to the pursuit of Truth; venture a daringly unorthodox hypothesis whose subtle flaw the instructor can point out.) Candidly confessing—when nothing could be proved—that the carbon paper found among the empty cans was mine, hastily thrust there after someone I'd asked idly for a sheet brought me a sheaf, swiped from the office. (Admit an evident mistake gracefully; show yourself open to instruction and able to profit by it.) Wheeling the cart like a madman past others leaning indolently on their mops; cleaning up someone else's mess silently and for free—but in public—once in a while. (Invite favorable comparison, but let others provide it.) Changing clothes at best every other day, and not trying too hard to keep clean—it goes with the role. (Be a bit of an eccentric—you *must* be bright.) Hosing the whole garbage-room down on Mondays; asking innocently if this wasn't standard practice before. (Establish a minor but admirable innovation in the System's procedures; undervalue it.)

I could go on, but fuck it. The truth of the matter is that I *do* hustle—partly because I simply dig hustling and doing a good job, partly because being a political prisoner is or seems to be like what being a Jew and short was for my old man *in situ* thirty years ago: "You've got to be twice as good as anyone else to come out even," he reasoned or felt, and he may have been right, who knows? But over all this, as a surface gilding long since learned into instinct (Woodrow Wilson Fellowship, '63), is the complex of little actions, attitudes, and details that constitute my way of relating to—of "handling"—the Authority Complex. They are as involuntary as the deep anger, whose possible consequences they so nicely avert, even as they disguise and are fueled by that anger. I learned my lesson well, in a thorough school.

Strolling through the litter of porkchop bones that graces the barracks yard—which is always decorated on the rare morning-after something decent and portable appears for dinner—a puzzle came clear to me. Before I came here I phoned all over the country to get quotes for an article I was writing. This gave me a chance to hear some dear voices again and apologize for my absence and silence. But there was an awkward air about some of the conversations, which I only now understand.

One friend confessed shyly—to my complete surprise, though I knew him for a long and ardent student and admirer of Gandhi and King—that he envied me deeply and would take my place if he could: that he felt keenly, as a lack in his own life, never having gone to jail for his beliefs. Another friend was terribly agitated because no one was making a fuss over our finally going in, or seemed even to remember why. Somehow a proper response was absent: we, and what we meant, were unheralded, unsung. "Surely someone must say something publicly," he cried to me over the phone.

I was taken off-balance and touched by their real concern, and responded to both with the embarrassed careless callousness I so often face emotion with: toss it off, downplay it, trying badly to be gentle. And my own closure is so familiar that I didn't realize till now that something else confused my response—and what it was. One of these men is a college president; the other—generally one of the two most perceptive observers of my generation I know—was offered a presidency and refused it. I love them both; but neither can afford such romantic innocence about the contemporary young. For it is dangerous to lose track of which revolution you're watching—especially if you'd like to help it—or you'll find yourself responding inappropriately.

My grandfather, whose eyes were also blue, was a Bolshevik: prison and exile. I too had certain time-honored feelings when my friends and unknown beloved peers were beaten and bailless in Southern jails. But we are freedom *trippers*, not riders. And there is nothing romantic, nor inspiring, nor unduly grubby, about being this kind of political prisoner. It is a dull and practical necessity, and will not be emulated or repeated. For FSM was a signal beacon which started much, both locally and nationally; but its message was sounded and heard, and there's no need to do certain parts of it again. Eight hundred kids should never again need to choose arrest to spite a college administration that doesn't deserve so much respect. The small price of our current

278

jailing (and the $100,000 in fines) is not even a symbol: merely the tangible mark of a learning experience, a necessary experiment. And so our own kids know better than to waste inappropriate or sloppy sentiment on us. Though FSM and our jailings are in some senses inseparable, their warm feelings about the one and their indifferent practicality about the nuisance of the other are the best indication that the connection is only operational. Being here accrues me no capital save the (considerable) writing I'm doing and some insight. Grandfather or not, if I could buy out, I would.

Granted, I had those nice warm feelings too when we were busted, as much as anyone did; and the martyr's pride did not entirely evaporate in the disgusting tedium of that hot spring's trial. I have traded on it since, for which I somewhat dislike myself, and will again; and a residue accompanies me here, probably making jail a bit more bearable, spice in the stew of my feelings. But by far my main emotion is simple and sheer irritation: *What a drag!* I've better things to do with my time—not only making love, but building what I was arrested for and have pursued since, in forms which have changed with my understanding. For FSM, in retrospect, was the first clear signal that America was involved in not one but two revolutions; and the rapid events since have brought the newer one out from under the shadow of the Civil Rights Movement and an old politics. Our problem now, and mine, is to learn, by doing, what feelings and actions are proper to being observers and shapers of this other revolution, of which we have no choice but to be a part even as it outdistances our understanding of it. The emotions of the older one, which include familiar forms of martyrdom, give us no clue. But, though I struggle uncertainly with their residue, I don't mean to put them down: they are simply inappropriate.

For us, that is. The spades who are going to jail for the flaming cities are quite a different story, as it will be if—no, when—they try to frame Stokely and Rap Brown for that. And those brave kids who are choosing, quietly, calmly and without hope, four years in a federal pen rather than play the System's death-games or run out on what they know of their souls—they are also a different story, partly because Vietnam and the spades are slices off the same overdue hunk of my grandfather's flesh. But the steadily growing pool of kids in jail across the country for grass and acid and "street-blocking" are political prisoners just as surely as we are—I think of beautiful Michael Solomon with his black flame halo, busted in the Haight on a trumped-up charge: forty-five days in San Bruno, off light compared to the kids here doing six or nine months—and, because they are movers in the same other revolution as we are, as little deserve to be romanticized. (Though that is not meant to inveigh against feeling or action for the human cost involved in their imprisonment, which is considerable.)

No, a new trip demands new guideposts; and jail simply is not our thing. Not that we too are not romantic — though I think we will ultimately prove less so than our elders, because we are more willing to abandon our foothold on what we have known. But the voices on the telephone wished me well with the expectations of my own past, which will no longer serve. We cannot inherit even the form of our symbols now: which leaves us nothing but trial-and-error to find or build them.

LAWRENCE FERLINGHETTI

Santa Rita Journal

SANTA RITA REHABILITATION CENTER, JANUARY 4, 1968 — what are we doing here in this dank tank? Probing the limits of legitimate political dissent in this unenlightened country? Nonviolent gesture of blocking the entrance to war at Oakland Army Induction Center hereby judged beyond that limit. Rehabilitate us, please . . . First rough impressions of anybody's first time in jail: suddenly realizing what "incarcerated" really means. Paranoid fear of the unknown, fear of not knowing what's going to happen to your body, fear of getting thrown in The Hole. . . . Routine of being booked, fingerprinted, mugged, shunted from bullpen to bullpen itself a shock for any "first offender." . . . Naive vestigial illusions about the inherent goodness of man fly out the barred window. . . . From Oakland jail, shunted through a series of sealed boxes, the first on wheels — long gray bus, windows blinded, 50 inmates behind locked grate, the freeway where yesterday we rode free now visible only through holes in grate. . . . Prison sighted half hour later on a forlorn plain at Pleasanton. . . . Barbed wire fences and watchtowers. Poor man's concentration camp? . . . Shunted through another series of holding cells, several more hours of not knowing one's immediate fate, just as likely you'll be put in "Graystone" maximum security pen as in General Compound. . . . I take the easier way out: I don't refuse to shave or work. Reforming the prison system is another issue. Rather have a pen than a beard (and so keep this journal). Pen mightier than beard. Opportunity to infiltrate general prison population with nonviolent ideas? Another naive liberal illusion!

The prison is about two-thirds black, and the other third is Mexican, Pachuco, and white North American. They've got their own problems and their own enemies, and they've no use for "nonviolence." The jungle is full of felons and, as for the war, most of them have the attitudes of their jailers and think what we're doing in Vietnam is great, violence being one way of life they fully understand. This sure deflates the myth promoted by Our President equating anti-war demonstrations with "crime in the streets" and with ghetto wars. If there were any blacks busted this time at the Oakland Induction Center, I didn't see them. (And if I were black, in Oakland, I'd stay away too). . . .

JANUARY 5 — There's not a political prisoner in my barracks. The most "uncooperative" of the demonstrators are in Graystone, two in a cell in The Hole on bread and skimmed milk. A larger group is in Compound 8 with no privileges and a meal and-a-half a day. A little incident happened today when they were marching back from the mess hall. The last in the line suddenly went limp and sat down in the middle of the Compound street. He was a kid of about 20 with medium-long hair he'd refused to cut. One officer ran up to him and tried to make him get up. He would not. The officer made a signal and four other officers wearing black leather gloves came at the double up the center of the street from the gate. They had no guns or nightsticks. Each took an arm or a leg of the boy and started dragging him. He was a big kid, and they couldn't get his tail off the ground. They got him out of sight in a hurry. When I got back to barracks, someone had an Oakland Tribune with a photo of four Marines carrying a dead Marine buddy away from a Vietnam battlefield in the same style. . . .

JANUARY 6 — I told them I had printing experience, and they put me stencilling pants! *Santa Rita* in pure white on every pair. "Gives us something to aim at!" the deputy told me, laughing, sighting his fingers at the stencil marks. Very funny. Holy prison, named for a Spanish saint. . . . Goya should have seen a place like this. He did, he did. Goya faces in the morning chowline, a thousand of them sticking out of blue denims, out of Goya's "Disasters of War." These are the disasters of peace. Down rows and rows of long wooden tables, half of skid row mixed with Oakland ghettos and the backwash of various nearby penitentiaries, long-term cons now here hung up on short-term crimes — petty boosters, bad check artists, child molesters, freeway drag-racers, car thieves, armed robbers, mail frauds, sex-freaks, winos, hypes, pushers, you name it. And political prisoners. . . . Sit swine-like at the trough, gobbling the chow from metal trays. Great place to keep from getting too refined; dig these myriad beat faces. . . . Here comes "Orfeo" — very handsome young Negro dude with a fine great black beard. Walked out of a Genet prison novel. Just stood there smiling like a black angel without wings when they told him to shave or get thrown in The Hole. They came back later and took him away. Now he shows up again in the mess hall, looking as wild and gentle as ever. I believe he is truly mad and they know it. I don't believe he understood anything they told him. They let him keep his beard. He'll fly away over the rooftops one day, to a shack on a hillside above Rio and live with a beautiful mulatto and tend goats, blowing a wreathed horn. And the horn full of grass. . . .

Another face in the gallery across the table from me: enormous ragged gray head, with hogshead snout, on a 200-pound body in ragged jeans. Great hams of white hands. But the face, the face: white stubble from shaggy hair to throat, rum-pot eyes. Small pig-eyes, but not mean looking. Just dumb and staring. This is what has become of "The Man with the Hoe." Long, heavy jaw with great protruding rows of white teeth. Grunted and snuffled as he slurped his pancakes. When he called for the coffee pitcher, his voice came out in a thin squeal. Man, what have you done to this man? Man, who made you like that? Man, has Mother ever seen you, seen what has become of you? Man, you still alive inside? (I hear your stentor breath.) Man, are you to be born again? Live again, love again? Man. Who is there to redeem you. Fidel Castro? The true revolutionary, Fidel said, is one whose first concern is the *redemption* of mankind. . . . Faces fallen out of wombs somewhere, long ago. Now rolled down streets and come to rest among writhing bodies in a painting by Bosch, Garden of Paradise. . . . Feed and shuffle out, doubles of models Goya used in a Toledo madhouse. "By Graystone's foetid walls." . . . One doesn't eat here to consume food; one eats to consume time. And time is life. . . .

JANUARY 7 — Sunday in the Compound, and "religious services": let them explain away the existence of evil here. The older one gets, the more one learns to believe in the very real existence of evil. This place proves it. The making of criminals. The redemption of mankind? The rehabilitation of man? They put 19-year-old Judith Bloomberg and Joan Baez on bread and milk for three days. (On the men's side, Gary Lisman fasted for 12 days.) These kids are the greatest. They are busted for disturbing the "peace" and are hauled away. They plead *nolo conten-*

dere. They do not wish to contend. They are telling their elders they can have it. They are telling the Establishment that they want nothing to do with its power structure and refuse even to dispute the legal terms of that evil. . . . As long as there are guns, they will shoot, telescopically. . . . At the weekly movie tonight, the inmates spy Joan Baez through a crack in the curtain hiding the balcony where the women prisoners sit. A hundred felons turn and raise their hands in the Peace Sign and shout, "We love you, Joan!"

JANUARY 8—The Enormous Room of my barracks: a black inmate is reading "Synanon" (the place is full of junkies). He doesn't realize what an elite place Synanon may be. Diedrich, the founder, must have read Hermann Hesse's *Magister Ludi (The Bead Game)* and seized upon the conception of an elite world-within-a-world depicted by Hesse in Germany—Castallia being the name of the German intellectual elite created to govern society with its own special *esprit de corps*, its own hierarchy, its own pecking order—a self-contained world of its own—Synanon also having developed its own cadre of first leaders framed on the wall, approval and status in its society dependent on length of residence, etc., the drug user rejected by the outside straight world here able to reject that society himself in favor of Synanon's own hierarchy: the Bead Game on its own level. And the prison system with its own Bead Game. . . . Shigeyoshi Murao comes to see me during visiting hours and tells me it looks just like the prisoner-of-war camps they kept Nisei in during World War Two.

JANUARY 9—Obscenity: violation of the Penal Code: today in the Commissary line when I tried to exchange a word with Dr. Lee Rather (a political prisoner), Officer Dykes hollered at me: "Get your fucking ass out of here, you motherfucker!"

JANUARY 10—Back in the barracks, the sealed life goes on. We are on some blind ship, all portholes sealed. Siren sounds and loudspeaker barks. Up for the count. Then down again, felon shipmates stretched in their bunks, staring at the overhead. . . . You spend a lot of time staring at nothing in a place like this. Great place to develop the Tragic Sense of Life. "Lucy in the Sky with Diamonds" comes over the barracks radio, and I picture myself in a boat on a river, where newspaper taxis await on the shore, waiting to take me away. . . .

JANUARY 11—Awakened at exactly three a.m. by a guard with a flashlight and told to get up and stand by my bunk.

"You're going to court today." From three to eight a.m. I wait in a bullpen with over 50 other inmates going to court. The cell is 20 by 20, and over half the inmates have to stand up all that time. I talk to one black felon who has been gotten up like this three days in a row, and if he wants to fight his case this is the way he can do it. . . . Life goes on at Santa Rita. Or death. . . . I got the Santa Rita blues. . . .

Afterthoughts and vituperations: Really realize how a hole like this literally makes criminals: 18-year-old first-offender thrown in for disturbing society's deep sleep now making his first hard connection with hard drugs (they are shooting it up in the john!) and enforced homosexuality (bend over, buddy!). . . .

Guards with hard-edge voices careful not to show any human feelings for inmates, on the watch for the slightest lack of obsequiousness on the part of prisoners, now and then goading them a bit with a choice obscenity . . . a slip of the tongue in return, and you're in The Hole with your tongue hanging out. . . .

Plus mail officers with German names withholding mail and books at will, first class letters opened and censored. . . . Working in the mailroom I note two books (sent directly to an inmate from City Lights Bookstore) withheld: Debray's *Revolution in the Revolution?* and *Black Power*. . . . Burn, baby, burn — but in here, baby, it's you who'll be burning. . . .

Unhappy Dehabilitation Center, man-made excrescence befouling the once-beautiful landscape in the shadow of distant Mount Diablo: Devil's mount!

If only revolution can blot out such scenes, let there be revolution; but not a revolution of hate leading in the end to just another super-state. . . .

JOAN BAEZ

Notes From Santa Rita

". . . That's cool, baby, you in here for your reasons and I in here for mine. We both believe in them just as strong. Soon as I git out I go back, do my thing. I guess you do the same . . ."

". . . They wouldn't give me no medicine, wouldn't let me see no doctor. See, I got this cerbicle here, in my neck. An' there three discs have been took out. So at times I gets this turrible headache where I can't see or nothing, and I was s'posed to go to court in the morning. I was cryin' and pleadin' for my medicine, they had it right there in my purse, but they jus' told me to shet-up. They got me up at five and I couldn't hardly walk. They drag me down to the holding room and my lawyer were sitting there. They act real nice when they bring me in to where he's at, figurin' I'm too scared to say anything, but the minute I saw my lawyer I started in sayin' how they pratilly kill me . . . I cried an' wailed. My whole leff side were numb, and it looked like it might be permanent . . . That was the city jail. This place ain't so bad. But I'm tellin' you, I wanna get out. I wanna see my kids . . ."

". . . Me, I came in here for a rest. I bin in an' out of jail for so many years I can't count 'em. This time I was sick, man. I was shootin' up five times a day, and that was costin' me a hundred and forty dollars a day . . . Shit. I was real tired. I took the rap for my little sister. We was in a store lookin' at this suit. I was real nice, an before I knew it my sister had it under her coat and she was sayin', 'Shit, man, let's blow this place.' I couldn't believe it. When we reach the front door there was the cops. I was relieved. I just said, 'Take me, man,' and they let my little sister go. I was tired, man, an I was sick . . ."

". . . You axin' me what's she in here for? I don' know. I bin tight with her for three months now an I ain't never ast. That's somethin' I never do. Ain't cause there's anything wrong with it, baby, don' worry 'bout that. It's just that I don' give a damn. It just don' interest me. At first it did, always goin' round all nuts to find out who done what. It's bin too many years. I'm twenty-five. Jail's been a part of my life long as I can remember. It ain't bad. You jus' be straight, baby, that's all that matters. I judges a person on what she's like. If I like her, fine. If I don', that's fine too. Know what a friend is? It's easy. I'll tell ya. A friend is someone who accepts you for what you are and don' try to change you. Simple as that. You OK, baby. You got more soul than I thought . . ."

". . . There's two things I know. Dope and women. A little about men, too, but when you're in here you get to likin' women. It's nice. I got a husband on the outside. I got kids. Sometimes I need a man, and then I go to my husband. He's nice guy. He's doin' time in L.A. right now. He's got his life, too, like I got mine. We respect each other. Last time I seen him was just when I got out of Corona. I'd bin in for ten months. Boy, it was good to get out, man! He says to me, 'What do you wanna do first, wanna go see the kids, or you wanna fix?' I says, 'Let's fix first, man . . .'"

". . . Hey, baby, come an' talk to me. What you do on the outside, side from make records and sit-in? Tell me sumthin' 'bout yourself . . ."

". . . Hey, you the one bin drawin' all the pictures? Do me. Which side is my good side? Git my hair like it is . . . hey. You ever make it with a broad?"

". . . Oh, well, into each life a little rain—That's all my life has bin. Jus' one big storm! I think I'm gone git me a new boy-friend."
"What about your husband?"
"SICK of my husband. Anyway I got a crush on Teddy. Think I mon take her home wit me. Oooo, have you ever seen anything like that? She has a entire Adam's apple. An' men's arms. An' she jus hates that dress. I swear, there's something *wrong* with Teddy. I feels *funny* calling Teddy a she . . ."

". . . Whatsa matter, Virginia?"
"Got my feelins hurt."
"How?"
"Just got my feelins hurt. I don' know. I don' know. I just don' know . . ."

". . . They tol' us you was a bunch of hippies an' weirds and communists, and they wanted to keep us seperate so's you wouldn't pervert us . . ."

". . . She the one fastin'? What the hell she doin' that for? She ain't eat nothin' for eight days."
"She's fasting to show her disapproval of the jail system."
"Yeah, well she got a point there. It stinks. Don' know why they call this place a re-habilitation center. It's just somewhere you go to rest up fore you go out and git busted agin. It don't ever change no one. What she gone prove by fastin'? Woo whee, shit! Lawd. I'd be dead by now. She amazin' walkin' aroun' like that. Some you guys somethin' else . . ."

". . . Yeah, well, I'm glad I listen to all you talkin' with that psychologist. Because what he said about it's pointless for you dimonstrators to be in jail? Well . . . He's full of shit. I mean . . . well, I think I beginning to understand the word 'pacifist,' you know? I jus' listen. Lot of times I wanted to say something, but I jus' listen, so's I can learn, you know what I mean? An it makes sense, what you guys doin'. And jail, you know what I mean, jail the BEST place to be. Because it's the only real grapevine. There ain't *no* one in here won't know what you guys doin', and then when we get out, there ain't no one on the outside won't know. It's like a underground, you know what I mean?"

And there was a poem I found on the back of a notebook which said,

> *My little star that shine so bright in the sky at*
> *night,*
> *My little heart that wanders through the night.*
> *I wonder if you ever think to yourself what the*
> *world would be like if there was no love*
> *If there was only evil among the stars and hate*
> *among the hearts.*
> *Is this just a thought, or a wonder that shine so*
> *bright in the stars at night.*

BARBARA DEMING

Prison Notes

Our cage in Albany is seven by seven by seven. Three bolted steel walls, a steel ceiling, a cement floor. For bunks, four metal shelves slung by chains—two on one wall, double-decker, two on the wall opposite. Thin filthy mattresses. No sheets, no blankets, but, very recently, muslin mattress covers have been added. The chief expects publicity, perhaps. Against the third wall, a tiny washbasin. Cold water. Next to it, a toilet without a lid. The mattress of the lower bunk rests against the toilet. The upper bunk is so close above the lower that one can only situp on the lower bunk with a curved spine. The floor space allows one to pace one short step—if there are not too many inhabitants. We are six at the moment, but we'll be more. Other cells are more crowded. It is not by stretching out that the prisoner here will recover himself.

The fourth wall is made of bars and a thick barred door, cen tered in it. In the corridor outside, guards and plainclothesmen come and go, day or night. If one is sleeping, a sudden knock at the bars: "Hey!" Or a little tug at the hair of the sleeper's head: "What's this one?" No corner of privacy in which to gather oneself together again.

The dirty windows in the corridor look out upon an alley and a brick wall. (They are very dirty. A prisoner long ago had flung a plate of spaghetti against one of them. Shriveled tatters of it still hang there. On the window next to it a shrunken condom hangs.) A little weak sunlight filters through to us at certain hours, but there is no real day.

And no real night. Our only other lighting is a naked bulb hanging in the corridor out of reach, and this burns around the clock.

Not enough space. No real time.

From the cage behind us, around the corridor, a man calls to his wife in the cage next to us: "Are you still there?" She grunts for answer. He calls to her: "I'm still here!"

Laboriously scratched in the metallic gray with which our walls and ceiling have been painted are name after name. RUFUS WAS HERE — was "still here." THE MELTON BROTHERS (sic) WAS HERE. BOB WIMBERLY. JACKIE TURLEY. "SUPER" NORMON. Was here, was still here. HAWK, to remind himself, has uttered his name seven times, has flown from wall to wall to ceiling to wall.

The cops read the names with irritation. It is cheating for the prisoners to assert in this way that they do exist.

"We hardly get it painted fresh when it's covered over again." FREEDOM! LULAMAE. The names appear where they oughtn't, as cries might issue from under the earth.

We have scratched our names, too: QUEBEC-WASHINGTON-GUANTANAMO WALK FOR PEACE AND FREEDOM. EDIE, YVONNE, KIT, MICHELE, ERICA, BARBARA. Later, CANDY and MARY will appear.

The man calls to his wife again. She doesn't answer. He calls again. She doesn't answer. He calls again.

"Yeah."

"Do you love me?"

Very low, very tired, "No. You're no good."

I remember suddenly the first prison cell I ever entered — twenty-six years ago. I entered that day out of curiosity an abandoned New England small-town jail, attached to the old courthouse friends and I were turning into a summer theater. The few cells were like low caves, windowless; the walls were whitewashed rock. In one, I noticed on the uneven plaster of the ceil-

288

ing, scrawled in candle smoke—or cigarette smoke—the declaration I AM A JOLLY GOOD FELLOW. I tried, that day, imagining myself the prisoner—tried and failed. But the words have recurred to me over the years. Today I think of them again.

Hard work, in here, to feel like a jolly good fellow; and so pride almost requires a man to feel he is the very opposite.

From one cell to another an old man calls to a pair of teen-age boys, just arrived. We have heard a detective talking with them; they're in for breaking into a store. "Who are you?" the old man calls. His voice is slurred with drink.

"I know who I am!" one of the youths shouts.

"I'll show you who you ain't," the old man teases.

"You want me to come over there and whip your ass?" one of them asks.

"I bet you're tough," says the old man.

"You're goddam right."

"You think you're bad, don't you?"

"Bad, bad!" asserts the boy.

A little later, "What are you in for?" the old man calls. There is a pause.

"Murder!" one of them suddenly shouts.

"What are your names?"

One of them starts to answer and the other cuts in: "The Sizemores," he decides. (Later we'll find that name scratched on the wall of their cell—dated months earlier.) "We're the Sizemores. Ed and my brother Dan and my brother Richard. He's not here. Ed is. I mean I am. And Dan. Don't you know the Sizemores? The Sizemores, man—the meanest motherfuckers in town!" He elaborates upon the theme.

The old man is full of words, half incoherent. Somebody yells at him, "Shut up, Pop, shut up!"

The two boys take it up: "Shut up, Pop!" He begins to beat against the bars.

"Only baboons beat on the bars," one of them yells. "And queers. He's a queer, ain't he?"

And now they launch into an endless obscene tirade against him. Pop returns the compliments. The voices rise in hysterical crescendo. "Talk to my ass awhile; my head hurts."

Both sides tire; there is a lull. I hear the two boys tossing on their mattresses. One of them groans to himself, "Oh God, oh God."

Then it begins again. "I'm the motherfucking superior of you!" the old man suddenly insists. "I'm here because I want to be!" He begins to beat again upon the bars.

They taunt him: "Keep a-beatin', keep a-beatin', beat on, beat on!" The voices swell again, in flood.

Silence. They have tired again. I doze a little; wake. They are calling again. My companions are awake, too, and we stare at one another. The voices are quieter now and contain a different note?"

The old man is asking, "Did you mean those names you called me?"

"I did at the time," one of the boys replies.

"How about now?"

A pause. "Give me some reason not to and I'll withdraw them."

Pop relapses. "You're a no-good sonofabitch."

Silence.

And then we hear the young man call out again in a voice suddenly as frail as a child's: "You want to be friends? Heh—you want to be friends?"

"I'd rather be friends than enemies," the old man mumbles—then abruptly declares, "I'm friends with everybody."

Another night: We hear the familiar scuffling, cursing, the slam of the metal door. A drunken officer from the nearby air base has been brought in. "Don't put me in here with that goddam drunk!" he commands. "Get me out of here! Cop, come here! Open this door! Open this door!" A fellow prisoner makes a comment. The officer yells, "Shut that goddam sonofabitch up or he's dead!" His voice shifts to a growl: "I'm going to kick the everloving shit out of you." He screams, "Open the door!" Then suddenly, "Leave it locked, you sonofabitches! Shut up, you're dead." He begins to sob. Then again: "Anybody who moves is dead!" His voice mounts in hysteria.

Somebody calls, "I know you're tough-assed, but take it easy."

The officer breaks into quavering song, to the tune of "Bye Bye Blackbird":

> *"You can kiss my ass, ya ya!*
> *You can kiss my ass, la la!"*

Somebody calls to him, "How long have you been in service?"

"Thirteen everloving goddam years."

"What are you in—I mean, besides jail? The goddam Air Force?"

"The Peace Corps," he growls. "Shut up, you're dead!" He resumes, "Open the door, open the door!" Then very very quietly, "Open the door!" Then in a yell.

And then suddenly, almost eerily—we stare at one another again—there issues out of the midst of all this clamor that other voice we have heard, frail, childlike: "Heh friend, heh friend," the officer calls. "You think they'll let us out of here tomorrow?"

It is another night—scuffling of feet again, the clanging to of the steel door. Curses. Groans. More curses. A fellow prisoner calls out, "You're a bad-ass, aren't you?" "Yes, I'm a bad-ass," the new man confirms loudly. The familiar exchange of obscenities begins. The voices mount in the familiar rhythm. But in the very midst of it—we have learned now to expect it—the voice alters; he calls: "Say—we're friends now, O.K.?"

KEN KESEY

Jail Diary

Aug 4, Friday—Allow me to introduce one of our prime heroes;

The patrol picks him up somewhere in Redwood City! In one side of the car out the other! "Catch him!" Hard to do, he's small, muscled like a wolverine, shifty as a fox and a road-runner topnot on his head indicates the boy is fast!!!

They get him hog tied and finally into the jail—"We got a unidentified flying object here. What'll we do with him."

"You kees my bleenking light," say the UFO.

He's Puerto Rican, neat little moustacho a black roadrunner shock of hair and fast!!! *A fireball crink shooter. "I never come down, man. I jess shoot crink and fuck, shoot crink and fuck. Can you deeg it?"*

He bunks next to me. Cant sleep for five nights. Prowls the dark barracks with a walk like a 200 pounder (he's many inches shy of five feet but muscled like a sonofabitch.)

("I never fucked my sister," Sweet confesses to Fullum, "A man gotta draw the line somewhere.")

Anyway, Speedy Lopez is our hero's name and shooting crink is his fame. And a good man to have in the barracks like a P. R. Cassidy. "I don' hurt nobody; I just shoot crink . . . can you deeg it."

Maybe one of the best liked guys in camp. Good heart and most important, you soon learn, much style. The Prankster reigns supreme in jail. And you dont never let nobody pull your covers. Man gets his covers pulled—no fucking class a-tall. (Yet, weird thing, the man with all cover, a young punk named talley, never let his covers be pulled yet was least liked of all. It was that thing in his eyes that said to you *"I'm* scared *to* death *under these blankets.")*

Not so with speedy. Littlest man here but no fear in his face. Just joy and dance when he's coming back from Redwood today with that prick (Cox forgive me for straying from the Teaching) Glick who is the transportation man they don't make a corner and Ka Zomb into the ditch upside down maybe bad maybe dead but when Speedy finally scrambles out from under, what?

"Can you deeg it, man?"

Did you ever figure out what it was that she and Billie Joe tossed off the Tallahatchie Bridge?

My first visitor appeared across the table from me, with very little hocus pocus or showmanship . . . simply was there, glowing like a bar of Dial soap and speaking to me as though we'd been interrupted only moments before

You young Americans . . . of course I understand the necessity of the force and I'm not complaining mind you . . . but such impatience at the beginning of such a show . . . shook his head in benevolent disgust over a ream of papers and vanished.

Tired dead sniff time.

With all the fucking deputies suspecting me of being loaded because I'm taking kalium, some kind of middle mind tranquilizer and my clothes are dirty and I'm hot and pissed and the paper is even splotchy and I cant sleep because I've got TIME is 455 turn in tolls *And I damn near climb the wall with guilt— oh mosquito, fuck off will you*

Aug 12—Today I am re-assigned to the Bushy crew, which means out on the road which means work (I've heard how often a bastard Bushy is) which means again "Something is happening and you don't know what it is."

Well what it is not going to be is the tailor shop.

Dismissed for the same reason I was dismissed from the VA . . not showing enough interest in the organization and inmates.

Or because material was tacked to the walls.

Lots of bus talk. What it means is maybe it can't happen there.

Oh bittah, bittah is the sweet of the honey somebody aint got. Can you deeg it, man?

"Don't sit there,"

They tell me—

"That doors about to
open in a couple minutes."

A Tank

how rent—
"How come you
leave camp—
how *come* you
leave camp,
it being the
best of all
possible jails.

coming going
overflowing
cons old
cons learning
bloods keeping quiet

and Knowing.

"That sounds like Mr' K."
"What we're you doing staying in Tank A.
"I was hitted by a tree. Now I'm in to have an X Ray to show I'm a nut. I been going like a washing machine for the last two days.
"Hey Deputy Dawg," somebody hollers from somewhere. "They just snuffed a dude in T2."

"But, dig!
I mean
eatin' crabs?

And I
Just developed
a strong
suspicioun
of crabs

scratch
scratch

Them motherfuckers is *good*! Specially in a good gumbo with some shrimp."
Not *that* kind of Crabs.
But listen: I dont have any habit. I mean you dont see me running round telling up sawdust in a piece of paper.

THE HIPPY in the TANK NEXT DOOR:

I just moved in playing my stereo at moderate volume and this motherfucker comes banging in the door . . . "You gonna play that motherfuckin radio that loud every night."
"Mercy, now, most nights I'm gonna really turn it up."
And from tank T3 down the way "THIS DUDE BEEN DEAD TOO LONG HE STINKIN'"

Gossip from the camp:
70-1/2 gallons of milk came into the kitchen on Wednesday, 5 left on Thursday. Who is the Culprit of this dire deed,.? Write

293

wants to know. And finds an emptied milk bottle on the back porch of C barracks. also an empty cornflakes box. "We was framed," says C barracks. "We'll see about that," says Write. "We're taking prints on that bottle and checking with Redwood. And the men with it hanging over them better get ready to ride a burglary beef.

Two deputies walking past: "yeah, I broke it." "Scope and all—and right after I saw a forked harn in a 3 point area."

(Some days are just pure bad luck)

Anyway the milk is finally hung on Fruit, the paranoid Tomcat that lives under our barracks.

Then who else is in Redwood this very night but Henry, the very man that fullum split camp to avoid. Seems that Henry took offense to having Grooms sit in the car with his wife's sister during visiting day while Henry's wife visited. I'd watched some of it. Grooms a good looking acid head blood with slender blue shades and a habit of walking head tipped back to peer out from under the blue shades and purring "Man Man" under his breath . . . he's just spent the last couple full moon nights in A tank with a bunch of other Homier-sort bloods and has a lot of juice buzzing around in him.

"he don't smoke but he likes ZuZu's, anything sweet—snickers, lollypops, sugarcubes, and he don't sing the familiar sides with the other bloods like the Myracles and the Temptations— just watches quiet and cool out from under his thin blue specs— a sort of big black flower child and noplace to plant his roots"

So when Samuri Henry, the bad dude of the whole camp, says "you stay out of my wife's car," and slings little Grooms don't quake a quivver but says instead "man, you don't know who you're talking to like that." it kinda makes the fellas wonder just who exactly is this wierd blue dude that Henry is talking to like that.

But Henry press it on. And Grooms keeps coming back smart-ass weird cool and saying "you don't know what I got for you," in his "Man Man" purr, and the fellas saying "Hit him, Henry, bust him Henry" until Henry hits him and they go to rassling and some how Henry gets his finger hung in Grooms shirt and spins away and tells Henry "I hope you busted the motherfucking thing!"

And Henry, looking in amazement at his pinky which is jammed all the way back into his big Samuri hand says, "It looks like I did bust the motherfucking thing."

And comes into see the doctor with Chandler, who is having his blood drycleaned as a result of a dirty needle.

Morning—
The limeliters tell us about

This land is your land
this land is my land
and
glory Hollehelaria.
and
this old dude tells about how his wife used to be a good thief a
good *thief until she started shooting chrystal.*

This land was made for you a me reach an apocolyptic cly-
max on station KPEN — and the morning sun comes rattling
through the bars like a high caliber repeater while we wait for
our morning mush — still in A tank, still waiting unshaven and
forlorn to have my head X-rayed — (a tree hit me on the head,
um lets see, it must have been Tuesday a week — "Zip a dee doo
da" cause I took a lay in the the following day and was supposed
to go to the doctor the next day but didn't because Glick so late
that I fucking got sucked into the thursday group meeting —
shoulda known after a knock on the head — and just like a pearl
in a slimey old oyster there I were and Molinoui aimed it at me
and I layed it back at them. Told them what it was where it was
and even spun a Tobasco bottle to prove it. "Chug-a-lug, Chug-
a-lug." So Glick didn't wait around. So I didn't come in friday
either not wishing to miss visit. So I came in Monday morning.
So I saw the doctor Tuesday and he scheduled an X ray — So
here it fucking is Friday and If I dont get it this morning I miss
Visit and I languish, I suffer the weekend away in old tank A —
but our mush as arrived, at least.

ABIODUN

Silent Tears And Prison Noises

POEM

Have you ever been
in jail waking
up in the morning to
the sound of a steel door
knocking against a steel wall
waiting for a meal that
you wouldn't feed your enemy

the dingy gray, the dirty brown
the pissed up mattress
where your ass and your head
lay trying to forget what they
could do together while your
sun hungry eyes gaze
through the bars searching
for a visitor, a friend, a pardon
anything that will set you
free but you know the
outside you know the slaves
that sing the monotonous song
calling you a criminal running
from you in the street and you're
wearing hand cuffs being escorted
by a 30.30 There's no
where to go outside now you're
inside a four walled cell
60 ft. by 40 ft. and
the memories of the outside world
are Fantastic all the
pretty little girls big girls
a living garden walking through
the streets of the city
clothes teasing, eyes leading
smile deceiving and then there's
your baby sweet as the sugar cane
they chopped down on the road camps
bright as the sun you see once
and a while as beautiful as
life is bad, your baby gone
after you've had the powdered eggs
mixed with spoiled ham grits and
liver gravy you take your tin
cup and tray up to the steel door
rinse your aged mouth out and
sing the blues silently
thinking about today this moment
and how forever it is right
now.

JAIL FATIGUE

I'm so tired of thinking
thinking about the freedom
I ain't got and the love I
can't have
All I do is sit here on this
prison bunk bed waiting for
the Man to call my name tell
me to pack my gear it's time
to go home. Sometimes I get
so scared when the Man comes to
the door with a list of names in
his hand and some go to court
some go home and some join the
chain gang the chain gang
I'm so tired of thinking about
the stories I've heard of the
chain gang the fly little sissys
with soap in their asses touching
the floor with their hands while
pussy boys get on the pony and
ride all through the night in
corner of a shower Then there's
the hole were you eat shit piss and
sleep all in a tiny little cell
with no light a monotonous diet
they say grits with liver and gravy
comes in a can the bloodhounds
won't eat but the convicts do cause
they get hungry they get real hungry
after ten to thirty days in the hole
I'm so goddam tired of hearing them
say it'll be alright I'll get you out
and I wait I wait and listen to the siren
screeching after another victim of
American justice then there's the
preacher telling you about sinners and
how they must repent telling you to
give your soul to Jesus and you got
thirty years on life in the name of
God and If you don't believe in Jesus
you go to the hole nigger sinner
wickedness corruption in the world
evil doing and am I to believe that I am

the sick that has spread my disease
throughout the world when I have
problems moving from town to town
Am I to believe that I am a sinner
Am I to believe that this little
old white man that looks like my
jailer is the messenger from heaven
Am I to believe in something other
than myself and the things in my
image
I'm tired so tired go away fatigue go
away let me die in peace please
let me die in peace please let me
die in peace in peace in peace peace

37 DAYS IN WAKE COUNTY JAIL

37 days in Wake County jail
How much pressure can one man take
The mind is the motor for all feelings
Inner and outer
In jail all feelings turn inward
To define each other
Each muscle, each twitch, each word,
Each heartbeat
And all memories frighten you
For they make you think you're dead
I who have stood on the soap box
Rapping about slavery
Making noises about the system
Writing poems about jail
Telling my brothers and sisters
To dig themselves
I knew nothing
Of the endless pounds of pressure
A man could take
I knew nothing
Of the silent pain
A man could endure
I knew nothing
Of life
Until now
Now I can see
The trees in the forest

And the forest on the earth
I can see for real
Every breath I take
Must become a reproductive life force
So that I may save
Someone who is not as strong as I
And I am not strong
I am growing stronger
Each minute
The job to be done is so great
Only a few will survive
At times I thought we all would survive
I know better now
At times I thought we'd shake ourselves loose
Dancing away from the flames
With laughter in our hearts
And a beautiful smile on our face
At times I thought we'd win
Easily with more joy than sorrow
Now I know
Blood will flow
And the rain will wash the dead into the gutters
And more blood will flow
Until the sun shines
Everywhere all at once
OH GODS OF AFRICA
PLEASE GIVE ME STRENGTH AND
    COURAGE
TO FIGHT WISELY AND REIGN
    SUPREMELY
OVER THE GRAVES OF MY ENEMIES
IN THE BEGINNING
WE SHALL FEAST
A GREAT FEAST
AND REJOICE
TO THE GODS
THAT WE SHALL ONE DAY BECOME

PIRI THOMAS

Sex In The Can

Everyone talked about it, most of us indulged in it solo, and some guys took their kicks with each other.

The talk was almost always reminiscences. One of the best of the bullshitters was a big con we called Ching. He had a very vivid memory. "Now dig this," he would say, biting his lower lip and inhaling a long, shuddering breath of jailhouse passion, "this broad's name was Dolores, and she was real fine," and he would paint a dream picture for us. Each of us would get a different picture of Dolores. She would be a blonde, or dark, or Puerto Rican, or whatever we wanted.

But the real action was between men. If you weren't careful, if you didn't stand up for yourself and say, "Hands off, motherfucker," you became a piece of ass. And if you got by this hassle, there always was the temptation of wanting to cop some ass. I had a Negro named Claude after me to make him my steady. "Look, why won't you be my man?" he asked me. "I'll give you the moon, the stars, the world, the uni—"

"Shove it," I hissed out. "Cut the shit out. Stop making like you was a for-real broad and get your black ass from here."

"I'll give you cigarettes, anything, baby; I'll keep you real good," he insisted.

I looked past the green bars at Claude and saw a woman's pleading, tormented face. *He wants to buy a daddy-o*, I thought. *But I ain't gonna break. One time. That's all I have to do it. Just one time and it's gone time. I'll be screwing faggots as fast as I can get them. I'm not gonna get institutionalized. I don't want to lose my hatred of this damn place. Once you lose the hatred, then the can's got you. You can do all the time in the world and it doesn't bug you. You go outside and you make it; you return to prison and you make it there, too. No sweat, no pain. No. Outside is real; inside is a lie. Outside is one kind of life, inside is another. And you make them the same if you lose your hate of prison.* "Claude," I said, "if I gotta break your fuckin' jaw, I will. They've put a wall around me for fifteen years, but I've got something real outside, and it makes no difference when I get out, married or not, she's mine, and there'll be no past for the two of us, just a stone present and a cool future. Meanwhile, I'll jack off if I gotta, but I ain't gonna marry you, faggot, no matter what."

Claude got the message and peddled his ass elsewhere. About two weeks later, he found a taker, Big Jules, a stud who was doing life for cutting somebody up into little pieces. There was a formal wedding, complete with preacher, best man, and attendants. I dug the whole scene. It was held outdoors in a corner of the yard. The sun was shining and the birds were singing. A few tables were pulled together to make a long table and all the guests were seated. The bride and groom sat behind a big cake, the bride in a clean white blouse (or was it a shirt?), the bridegroom cool and attentive. Across from them sat the preacher, a con who on the outside probably played a cool racket as a phony minister.

I looked around and thought, *Do the hacks think it's a birthday party, or do they know what's shaking and are making like they don't see it?* I heard the preacher man say, "Do you, Claude, take this man to be your lawful wedded husband, to love, cherish, honor and obey . . . ?"

"I do," Claude said softly, just like any bride anywhere. *My God, what an unreal world. Look at Big Jules' face, he really is serious. This faggot is gonna be his wife, for better or for worse, until death do them part.* And it came to me, scared and hard, that this was what I had to fight against. This farce was for Claude and Big Jules their real life, the whole of existence. *Look, they see each other as Romeo and Juliet, as though the world were a part of them and not the other way around.*

The groom slipped a ring on the bride's finger and the minister siad, "I now pronounce you man and wife," and the guests offered them congratulations and best of luck. It made me sick inside. *Where to now, wedded couple? Niagara Falls, Bermuda, Europe for a blissful honeymoon? Great. Where you gonna get your break? Where will you consummate your vows? Behind the cell-hall blocks, in a corner of the workshop, during idle time?* "Oh, yesss, he's mah man now," purred Claude to a well-wisher.

A few days later I got another love problem dumped in my lap. I had been playing handball in the yard and was in the middle of a break, sitting against the great gray wall, when Little came up to me, scrunched down beside me, and asked me if I had a cousin called Tico. I didn't, but I said, "Maybe, why?"

Well, there's a kid on the new shipment from Elmira, and he sez he's your cousin. Know him? His real name is Ricardo, and he's about eighteen years old."

"Yeah, I know him." *Hell,* I thought, *can it really be Tico, Little Red's kid brother? I wonder why he's pushing himself off as my cousin?*

Later, when I saw him, I knew why. A baby-faced, small-framed, good-looking kid who looked about fourteen years old, he was perfect prey for the jailhouse wolves. He was scared, too, though he tried not to show it. He needed a friend or a "cousin" who was established in jail, who had a rep as a down guy. I watched him huddle in a corner of the yard with all the green mickies. They were laughing loud and making talk, putting on fronts and looking blasé, like being in jail was a daily kick. I walked toward the huddled bunch of citizens and Tico saw me. He moved toward me with jerky, twitchy moves, smiling the biggest, happiest smile I ever dug. He threw his arms around me and said, "Piri, I'm glad, man, I'm glad to see you."

"So am I Tico. How did you know I was here?"

"Oh, my brother let me know from time to time how you wuz, and where. When I heard I was on a boat to Comstock, I knew you'd be here."

"Come on over here," I said, "and we'll set."

Tico turned from me and loudly called over to his huddled buddies, for them and for the whole yard to hear, "Hey, guys, this is my cousin I wuz tellin' you about." He looked surer of himself for that identification, and his huddled buddies looked envious of him for having established residence.

I sat down on my snag bag (a cloth bag with whatever junk you carried around) and he squatted next to me. I said nothing. I took out a bag of rollies (Bull Durham) and rolled one and offered it to him. He took it and in turn took out a pack of tailor-made smokes and offered me one. I took it and we lit up, inhaled and exhaled, and then he let it out. "Piri, I hope you ain't mad about me saying you were my cousin," he said, and he looked down at the barren concrete walk.

I looked at him and thought, *Baby, don't you know I know how you feel? Don't you dig I was like you a million years ago? With a brave front and a* cara-palo *defense? Shit, my little her-mano, if we were anywhere else, I'd take you in my arms and hold you close and tell you the facts of prison life.* I broke my own thoughts and said, "Tico, we're more than cousins, kid, we're brothers. Just handle yourself right, don't make fast friends, and act cool. Don't play and joke too much, and baby, don't, just don't, accept candy or smokes from stranger cons. You might end up paying for it with your ass."

He kept on looking at the concrete walk and his face grew red and the corners of his mouth got a little too white. "Piri, I've been hit already," he said.

I thought, *My God, he's got a jailhouse gorilla reception already.* "Yeah," I prompted, "and . . ."

"Well, I got friendly with this guy named Rube."

Rube was a muscle-bound degenerate whose sole ambition in life was to cop young kids' behinds. "Yeah," I said, "and so . . ."

"Well, this cat has come through with smokes and food and candy and, well, he's a spic like me and he talked about the street outside and about guys we know outside and he helped me out with favors, you know, real friendly."

"Yeah," I said, "and so . . ."

"So this," Tico said, pulling from his pocket a folded piece of paper and handing it to me. I knew what it was, but I opened it and read:

> Dear Tico,
>   Since the first moment I saw you, I knew you were for me. I fell in love with your young red lips and the hair to match it. I would like to keep on doing things for you and to take care of you and not let anybody mess with you. I promise not to let no one know about you being my old lady and you don't have to worry none, because I won't hurt you at all. I know you might think it's gonna be bad, but it's not at all. I could meet you in the back part of the tier cell hall and nobody's going to know what's happening. I've been doing a lot for you and I never felt like this about no girl. If you let me cop you, I'll do it real easy to you. I'll use some hair oil and it will go in easy. You better not let me down 'cause I got it bad for you, I'd hate to mess you all up.
>
> Love and Kisses XXX
You know who
R.
>
> P.S. Tear this up and flush it down the shit bowl.

My God, I thought, *what can I tell him?* Tico had to show man or he was finished. Rube would use that first time to hold him by threatening to tell everybody that he screwed him. And if anybody found out, every wolf in the joint would want to cop. The hacks would hear about it and they would put Tico on A-1 tier where all the faggots were, and he'd be a jailhouse punk. "What do you owe him, Tico?" I asked.

"About three cartons of smokes, fourteen candy bars, some canned food, and a couple of undershirts."

"You damn fool," I said, "couldn't you see what was happening? That lousy shit was courting you, making time with you, like you've done on the outside with broads. You appealed to him 'cause you're to him like a virgin would be on the outside, a first cop."

"What am I gonna do, Piri?"

"Look, I'll get the stuff he gave you and—"

"No, that won't work. I already told him I'd give him back his stuff, and no dice; that motherjumper wants to punk me and he said if I didn't punk out, him and his boys would jack me up. So what do I do?"

"Look, Tico," I said, gazing down at the concrete walk, "there's only two things you can do. One, you can punk out and become a girl." I felt him get stiff and I knew he was looking at me, or maybe into me. "Or, you can get him off your back. Does he work in your shop?"

"Yeah, he does."

"Well, the first time he says something to you or looks wrong at you, have a piece of pipe or a good heavy piece of two-by-four. Don't say a damn thing to him, just get that heavy wasting material and walk right up to him and bash his face in and keep bashing him till he's down and out, and yell loud and clear for all the other cons to hear you, 'Motherfucker, I'm a man. I came in here a motherfucking man and I'm going out a motherfucking man. Next time I'll kill you.'"

"And?" Tico said softly.

"And nuttin', baby. You'll be free, an accepted man—part of this jailhouse scene. All the weight will be off your back. The word will get around you ain't to be messed with 'cause you got heart and you ain't afraid to deal." Ba-ra-ta-ta-ta-ta, the bugle sounded, and I said, "Let's go, cousin," and our eyes met for the first time since we had sat down on the concrete walk and he said "Thanks" with his and I said, "You're welcome," with mine. As he walked away, he didn't seem so nervous, so twitchy. I figured that even if he didn't get a chance to hurt Rube, even if Rube took that wasting stick from him and messed him up, everybody would know he had heart to stand up to muscle-bound Rube; and it was better to get hurt outside where it could be seen and attended to than inside, where it would stay all his life.

Two days later I learned that Tico was locked up in isolation. The news traveled fast: Rube had approached Tico with a "gonna-punk-out-kid" smile on his face. Tico hadn't said a word, but before Rube knew what was happening, Tico had bashed him with an iron bar. If he had caught Rube flush on the head, his brains would have been all over the place; as it was, he had caught him a glancing blow on the shoulder and the hack had jumped in before Tico could swing again. Tico had screamed out hate at Rube and anybody else that had funny ideas about trying anything with him. Now he was in, but he was gonna pay with a week of bread and water and one meal a day.

I passed the isolation cell block the next day and whispered to Tico, "How you doing, kid?"

"Great," he said, "but I'm hungry."

"Cheap price, kid, to keep your ass," I answered. I looked around fast and let a pack of tailor-mades fall to the floor. I couldn't get next to the cell; a heavy wire screen kept everyone about five feet away. But there was a little space at the bottom of the screen, and I gave a fast hard kick to the pack of smokes and it slid right into his cell. Then I kept walking.

RAY BREMSER

Penal Madness

. . . and I feel like Nellie Lutcher,
want to sing and fornicate in sheer
suggestion—most/
I want to sit
on a stool, that's all—just sit and sit
and try to dig the drags
who go by in their stocking-feet.
. . . deserve their pair of legs . . . to
go their nowhere . . . knees grown together, they
cannot see great stride to the gutter . . . cannot
see me satisfied . . . they call me nigger
lover . . . evil . . . jazzhead
fuzzy is the dissonance
of their wrath!
out of the Hudson County Jail
I am taken while idiots laugh.

Great edible crotch full of hermitage lore
and excusable gloom!
Great predying tomb of innumerable black and
white negros, crazy and hip
and uproarious laughter-laid
pure cherry nights!

Great basketball court of the Harlemite ref,
full of human and brown breaking balls!
Great trolly-car terminal corridor track
And the pitiful fish
who are new to it all are amazed!

At the womb they call Center!
Chief-Deputy squats—or captain
fatly abides in the mother-tongue
chair at the lip—at the sperm
that is gathered lieutenantly into the vat
where the keys to the kingdom
prevail!
where the morbid machine
INTERCOM

        has its source
In the wide teethless mouths of the little
alternative lords!

O Mammon, invisible indian-chief of the stalls
in successive uncomfort called rooms—
Pall Mall is you highest ascension!
Converse of the world!
Its recto extreme!
At arm's-length's impotent reach—
do not touch!
            do not come!
                    do not learn!
only read me in beautiful tears,
for then you will have what is vision,
and tremble your whole and unreasonable
penitent years!
. . . and of love?
I would rather be cool
and consider your ends
and then, maybe—
unleash myself full
of immediate needs—
too much stock-market sex—
too much pressure today!
Do you guess how I want
and desire your great explosion of not?

Do you know for how many
unnumbering days
I have waited
and waited, immobile?
Insane with the brawn
of oppression, the bane
of a thousand and radical hardons.
lusty with dream!

Do you think I might finally
end in the wakening
wet of your thighs?
The stocky ineloquent odor
profuse in its fish-fetid
lubricant fumes!

Argh!
        What desires!
Unconscionable dews!

I would rather be cool
and consider your tough
and your thick
and your tonnage
of crazy.

Nights in the slop-bucket house
of the morbid and boredom
                            sweet flesh
get the better and sent me out hunting
a boy!
          Love! You are always precise
and penultimate tears. Yet, the horror
converts to the physical digging
                         the boy
and the girl and the somehow
                       duality!
illegal love of illusory black listless night,
praise to your coolness and noninterference
beatitude lighting my brain fever dark
with a harmony flash
in the otherwise idiot's music!

You are delicate, yet, an unbreakable diamond
of Solomon's taciturn mine!

Only poetry now, in a quick whisp, going!
No heroes nor marvel-magicians nor witches
nor conjurers—brothers nor beautiful laggards
stuffing unanimous hearts stripped clear of the
    lead
and insensitive refuge—
                    The creation of NATURE
projected by poetic eyes,
                    whose condition of soft
and affection for life
has been characterized as the sickness
today . . . but
is neither
the sick
nor the rot
nor the stunted unscrupulous growth . . .

but the wild
and the breath
and the rage
and the cure . . .

HERBERT HUNCKE

Cuba

Cuba is what is known in present prison jargon as a peddler. He is a real hustler in the sense that if there is anything in the way of contraband to be obtained within the prison—such as eggs, meat, grease, winter overshoes, coats, shirts, tailor made pants, special hair preparations, after shave lotions, etc.—he is the man to see. When any new young boys or fags or potential broads appear on the scene Cuba is the first to know and loses no time making contact.

At present he is serving out the last year of a 10-year sentence. He was paroled on one occasion and deported back to Cuba. He refused to remain and through some manner or other succeeded in returning to New York where he immediately became a dope pusher. He operated fairly effectively until he was caught and returned to prison.

I don't recall a great deal of his past history, although I became friendly with him and he spent much time telling me of himself.

The first time I saw him he was coming across the prison yard. It was summer and he was without a shirt. The entire upper part of his body is a mass of scars—from the shoulders to the waist—and once seeing him in the shower I noticed a continuation of these scars on his legs. He obtained these scars—which are like shrimp pink colored welts—by lacerating himself on numerous occasions with razor blades. Whenever he becomes enraged or has a fight or does something of which he is deeply ashamed he afterwards slashes himself. Just a short while before I left he went into his cell after an episode in which he had beaten a man severely in a fight and had been punished with 60 days keep-lock—60 days which meant almost solitary confinement—and cut himself so that something like 172 stitches were required to staunch the flow of blood.

He is short of stature with a well proportioned body. He is of light tan color with—other than the scars—smooth, almost delicate appearing skin quite free of chest hair and nearly beardless. He has pleasantly symmetrical facial features with a large brown mole on his left cheek. His eyes are a deep innocent brown. He wears at all times a thin gold chain with a large—nearly the size of a quarter—medallion, given him by his mother, and a thin red silk cord with a tiny rose-shaped knot in it—of which he is quite secretive, refusing to explain and resenting having anyone touching it—around his neck.

He considers himself a great lover and is always in the midst of a passionate affair with one of his fellow inmates. He constantly speaks of the size and shape of everybody's ass and will exclaim in positive terms—"Man—I got to cop" each time he sees an ass which especially appeals to him. He goes to great lengths arranging meetings in the yard with his most recent desires and will entice them up to his court where he surreptitiously feels them, all the time trying to convince them they should try and get a job in the messhall where he is working and that all he wants to do is kiss them on the ass. He will say—"Man—I no want—fuck you—just love you. Man—I like your ass. Come in the messhall—we turn steam on in the shower—nobody see—I cop lots times that way. You let me love your ass—I jerk off." Sometimes he is successful and he then goes around beaming at everybody and telling his friends all about how this time he has a lover that really loves him and that this time he is not only going to kiss ass but he's going to get in. He keeps himself well supplied with cigarettes from his peddling activities and sees to it his current interest is never without smokes.

He is a very kind person and is always doing unexpected favors for people he likes. He gambles a great deal and if he wins something gives all his winnings away to people he knows haven't anything of their own.

About a week before I left the prison someone turned a note in to the Principal Keeper about him. Just what it was supposed to contain no one was quite sure, but whatever it said apparently caused the P. K. to refer Cuba's name to the prison psychiatrist, who promptly called Cuba up for an interview, the result being —Cuba was sent over the wall to the State Hospital for the Insane.

When prisoners are transferred from the main prison to the State Hospital they are, if violent, placed in strait-jackets (restraining jackets they call them) and, if not violent, are handcuffed and ankle-shackled.

When we last saw Cuba he was being literally draggged into the waiting station wagon wearing a restraining jacket.

Dancing In Prison

I have been in prison—they don't dance in prison—nobody dances unless
> perhaps, in the cell alone—
> snapping fingers and wearing
> earphones—and of course in dreams.

And there are good sounds in the prison I was in because it is close to Canada—Montreal—and they like fine sound and many of their programs are dedicated to young jazz musicians and it is not always commercial and some of these cats come on. And then there is some crazy stuff too, right here—that occasionally reaches there. Also, in the yard, groups with horns, guitars, and anything to drum—let go and clap hands and beat and I've heard it great—in fact there was one wayout man on a sax who blew all the time alone or with others—in the cell alone and sometimes with a guy two cells away who would pick on a guitar and listen to Jap and these guys would really let go till 7:00 o'clock, when the bell would ring for no more talking.

They sometimes talk about dancing, remembering past experiences with social chicks—"who could dance their ass off, man"—or going to the Palladium and even sometimes the old Savoy and innumerable other spots specially when name bands were on the scene—Basie—Ellington—Kenton—all of them. Of course names are mentioned like Miles Davis—Yardbird Parker—and Shearing—and Sarah Vaughan—Anita O'Day—Keely Smith—Dakota Staton and I could go on naming a while yet—but most of these are for hearing only—I don't suppose that is actually true because one can dance to any sound.

Anyway, I danced last night and it made me very happy. I am not a clever dancer—that is, I don't ever know what I am doing—particularly with my feet—but I always sort of let go—and wow I get some great kicks. And I did last night.

LOOKING OUT
MALCOLM X

Satan

One day in 1948, after I had been transferred to Concord Pris
on, my brother Philbert, who was forever joining something,
wrote me this time that he had discovered the "natural religion
for the black man." He belonged now, he said, to something
called "the Nation of Islam." He said I should "pray to Allah
for deliverance." I wrote Philbert a letter which, although in
improved English, was worse than my earlier reply to his news
that I was being prayed for by his "holiness" church.

When a letter from Reginald arrived, I never dreamed of associating the two letters, although I knew that Reginald had been
spending a lot of time with Wilfred, Hilda, and Philbert in Detroit. Reginald's letter was newsy, and also it contained this instruction: "Malcolm, don't eat any more pork, and don't smoke
any more cigarettes. I'll show you how to get out of prison."

My automatic response was to think he had come upon some
way I could work a hype on the penal authorities. I went to
sleep — and woke up — trying to figure what kind of a hype it
could be. Something psychological, such as my act with the
New York draft board? Could I, after going without pork and
smoking no cigarettes for a while, claim some physical trouble
that could bring about my release?

"Get out of prison." The words hung in the air around me, I
wanted out so badly.

I wanted, in the worst way, to consult with Bimbi about it.
But something big, instinct said, you spilled to nobody.

Quitting cigarettes wasn't going to be too difficult. I had been
conditioned by days in solitary without cigarettes. Whatever this
chance was, I wasn't going to fluff it. After I read that letter, I
finished the pack I then had open. I haven't smoked another cigarette to this day, since 1948.

It was about three or four days later when pork was served for
the noon meal.

I wasn't even thinking about pork when I took my seat at the
long table. Sit-grab-gobble-stand-file out; that was the Emily
Post in prison eating. When the meat platter was passed to me, I
didn't even know what the meat was; usually, you couldn't tell,
anyway — but it was suddenly as though *don't eat any more pork*
flashed on a screen before me.

I hesitated, with the platter in mid-air; then I passed it along to the inmate waiting next to me. He began serving himself; abruptly, he stopped. I remember him turning, looking surprised at me.

I said to him, "I don't eat pork."

The platter then kept on down the table.

It was the funniest thing, the reaction, and the way that it spread. In prison, where so little breaks the monotonous routine, the smallest thing causes a commotion of talk. It was being mentioned all over the cell block by night that Satan didn't eat pork.

It made me very proud, in some odd way. One of the universal images of the Negro, in prison and out, was that he couldn't do without pork. It made me feel good to see that my not eating it had especially startled the white convicts.

Later I would learn, when I had read and studied Islam a good deal, that, unconsciously, my first pre-Islamic submission had been manifested. I had experienced, for the first time, the Muslim teaching, "If you will take one step toward Allah — Allah will take two steps toward you."

My brothers and sisters in Detroit and Chicago had all become converted to what they were being taught was the "natural religion for the black man" of which Philbert had written to me. They all prayed for me to become converted while I was in prison. But after Philbert reported my vicious reply, they discussed what was the best thing to do. They had decided that Reginald, the latest convert, the one to whom I felt closest, would best know how to approach me, since he knew me so well in the street life.

Independently of all this, my sister Ella had been steadily working to ge me transferred to the Norfolk, Massachusetts, Prison Colony, which was an experimental rehabilitation jail. In other prisons, convicts often said that if you had the right money, or connections, you could get transferred to this Colony whose penal policies sounded almost too good to be true. Somehow, Ella's efforts in my behalf were successful in late 1948, and I was transferred to Norfolk.

The Colony was, comparatively, a heaven, in many respects. It had flushing toilets; there were no bars, only walls — and within the walls, you had far more freedom. There was plenty of fresh air to breathe; it was not in a city.

There were twenty-four "house" units, fifty men living in each unit, if memory serves me correctly. This would mean that the Colony had a total of around 1200 inmates. Each "house" had three floors and, greatest blessing of all, each inmate had his own room.

About fifteen per cent of the inmates were Negroes, distributed about five to nine Negroes in each house.

Norfolk Prison Colony represented the most enlightened form of prison that I have ever head of. In place of the atmosphere of malicious gossip, perversion, grafting. hateful guards, there was more relative "culture," as "culture" is interpreted in prisons. A high percentage of the Norfolk Prison Colony inmates went in for "intellectual" things, group discussions, debates, and such. Instructors for the educational rehabilitation programs came from Harvard, Boston University, and other educational institutions in the area. The visiting rules, far more lenient than other prisons', permitted visitors almost every day, and allowed them to stay two hours. You had your choice of sitting alongside your visitor, or facing each other.

Norfolk Prison Colony's library was one of its outstanding features. A millionaire named Parkhurst had willed his library there; he had probably been interested in the rehabilitation program. History and religions were his special interests. Thousands of his books were on the shelves, and in the back were boxes and crates full, for which there wasn't space on the shelves. At Norfolk, we could actually go into the library, with permission—walk up and down the shelves, pick books. There were hundreds of old volumes, some of them probably quite rare. I read aimlessly, until I learned to read selectively, with a purpose.

I hadn't heard from Reginald in a good while after I got to Norfolk Prison Colony. But I had come in there not smoking cigarettes, or eating pork when it was served. That caused a bit of eyebrow-raising. Then a letter from Reginald telling me when he was coming to see me. By the time he came, I was really keyed up to hear the hype he was going to explain.

Reginald knew how my street-hustler mind operated. That's why his approach was so effective.

He had always dressed well, and now, when he came to visit, was carefully groomed. I was aching with wanting the "no pork and cigarettes" riddle answered. But he talked about the family, what was happening in Detroit, Harlem the last time he was there. I have never pushed anyone to tell me anything before he is ready. The offhand way Reginald talked and acted made me know that something big was coming.

He said, finally, as though it had just happened to come into his mind, "Malcolm, if a man knew every imaginable thing that there is to know, who would he be?"

Back in Harlem, he had often liked to get at something through this kind of indirection. It had often irritated me, because my way had always been direct. I looked at him. "Well, he would have to be some kind of a god—"

Reginald said, "There's a *man* who knows everything."

I asked, "Who is that?"

"God is a man," Reginald said. "His real name is Allah."

Allah. That word came back to me from Philbert's letter; it was my first hint of any connection. But Reginald went on. He said that God had 360 degrees of knowledge. He said that 360 degrees represented "the sum total of knowledge."

To say I was confused is an understatement. I don't have to remind you of the background against which I sat hearing my brother Reginald talk like this. I just listened, knowing he was taking his time in putting me onto something. And if somebody is trying to put you onto something, you need to listen.

"The devil has only thirty-three degrees of knowledge—known as Masonry." Reginald said. I can so specifically remember the exact phrases since, later, I was going to teach them so many times to others. "The devil uses his Masonry to rule other people."

He told me that this God had come to America, and that he had made himself known to a man named Elijah—"a black man, just like us." This God had let Elijah know, Reginald said, that the devil's "time was up."

I didn't know what to think. I just listened.

"The devil is also a man," Reginald said.

"What do you mean?"

With a slight movement of his head, Reginald indicated some white inmates with their visitors talking, as we were, across the room.

"Them," he said. "The white man is the devil."

He told me that all whites knew they were devils—"especially Masons."

I never will forget: my mind was involuntarily flashing across the entire spectrum of white people I had ever known; and for some reason it stopped upon Hymie, the Jew, who had been so good to me.

Reginald, a couple of times, had gone out with me to that Long Island bootlegging operation to buy and bottle up the bootleg liquor for Hymie.

I said, "Without any exception?"

"Without any exception."

"What about Hymie?"

"What is it if I let you make five hundred dollars to let me make ten thousand?"

After Reginald left, I thought. I thought. Thought.

I couldn't make of it head, or tail, or middle.

The white people I had known marched before my mind's

eye. From the start of my life. The state white people always in our house after the other whites I didn't know had killed my father . . . the white people who kept calling my mother "crazy" to her face and before me and my brothers and sisters, until she finally was taken off by white people to the Kalamazoo asylum . . . the white judge and others who had split up the children . . . the Swerlins, the other whites around Mason . . . white youngsters I was in school there with, and the teachers—the one who told me in the eighth grade to "be a carpenter" because thinking of being a lawyer was foolish for a Negro. . . .

My head swam with the parading faces of white people. The ones in Boston, in the white-only dances at the Roseland Ballroom where I shined their shoes . . . at the Parker House where I took their dirty plates back to the kitchen . . . the railroad crewmen and passengers . . . Sophia. . . .

The whites in New York City— the cops, the white criminals I'd dealt with . . . the whites who piled into the Negro speakeasies for a taste of Negro *soul* . . . the white women who wanted Negro men . . . the men I'd steered to the black, "specialty sex" they wanted. . . .

The fence back in Boston, and his ex-con representative . . . Boston cops . . . Sophia's husband's friend, and her husband, whom I'd never seen, but knew so much about . . . Sophia's sister . . . the Jew jeweler who'd helped trap me . . . the social workers . . . the Middlesex County Court people . . . the judge who gave me ten years . . . the prisoners I'd known, the guards and the officials. . . .

A celebrity among the Norfolk Prison Colony inmates was a rich, older fellow, a paralytic, called John. He had killed his baby, one of those "mercy" killings. He was a proud, big-shot type; always reminding everyone that he was a 33rd-degree Mason, and what powers Masons had—that only Masons ever had been U.S. Presidents, that Masons in distress could secretly signal to judges and other Masons in powerful positions.

I kept thinking about what Reginald had said. I wanted to test it with John. He worked in a soft job in the prison's school. I went over there.

"John," I said, "how many degrees in a circle?"

He said, "Three hundred and sixty."

I drew a square. "How many degrees in that?" He said three hundred and sixty.

I asked him was three hundred and sixty degrees, then, the maximum of degrees in anything?

He said "Yes."

I said, "Well, why is it that Masons go only to thirty-three degrees?"

He had no satisfactory answer. But for me, the answer was that Masonry, actually, is only thirty-three degrees of the religion of Islam, which is the full projection, forever denied to Masons, although they know it exists.

Reginald, when he came to visit me again in a few days, could gauge from my attitude the effect that his talking had had upon me. He seemed very pleased. Then, very seriously, he talked for two solid hours about "the devil white man" and "the brainwashed black man."

When Reginald left, he left me rocking with some of the first serious thoughts I had ever had in my life: that the white man was fast losing his power to oppress and exploit the dark world; that the dark world was starting to rise to rule the world again, as it had before; that the white man's world was on the way down, it was on the way out.

"You don't even know who you are," Reginald had said. "You don't even know, the white devil has hidden it from you, that you are of a race of people of ancient civilizations, and riches in gold and kings. You don't even know your true family name, you wouldn't recognize your true language if you heard it. You have been cut off by the devil white man from all true knowledge of your own kind. You have been a victim of the evil of the devil white man ever since he murdered and raped and stole you from your native land in the seeds of your forefathers. . . ."

I began to receive at least two letters every day from my brothers and sisters in Detroit. My oldest brother, Wilfred, wrote, and his first wife, Bertha, the mother of his two children (since her death, Wilfred has met and married his present wife, Ruth). Philbert wrote, and my sister Hilda. And Reginald visited, staying in Boston awhile before he went back to Detroit, where he had been the most recent of them to be converted. They were all Muslims, followers of a man they described to me as "The Honorable Elijah Muhammad," a small, gentle man, whom they sometimes referred to as "The Messenger of Allah." He was, they said, "a black man, like us." He had been born in America on a farm in Georgia. He had moved with his family to Detroit, and there had met a Mr. Wallace D. Fard who he claimed was "God in person." Mr. Wallace D. Fard had given to Elijah Muhammad Allah's message for the black people who were "the Lost-Found Nation of Islam here in this wilderness of North America."

All of them urged me to "accept the teachings of The Honorable Elijah Muhammad." Reginald explained that pork was not eaten by those who worshiped in the religion of Islam, and not smoking cigarettes was a rule of the followers of The Honorable Elijah Muhammad, because they did not take injurious things such as narcotics, tobacco, or liquor into their bodies. Over and over, I read, and heard, "The key to a Muslim is submission, the attunement of one toward Allah."

And what they termed "the true knowledge of the black man" that was possessed by the followers of The Honorable Elijah Muhammad was given shape for me in their lengthy letters, sometimes containing printed literature.

"The true knowledge," reconstructed much more briefly than I received it, was that history had been "whitened" in the white man's history books, and that the black man had been "brainwashed for hundreds of years." Original Man was black, in the continent called Africa where the human race had emerged on the planet Earth.

The black man, original man, built great empires and civilizations and cultures while the white man was still living on all fours in caves. "The devil white man," down through history, out of his devilish nature, had pillaged, murdered, raped, and exploited every race of man not white.

Human history's greatest crime was the traffic in black flesh when the devil white man went into Africa and murdered and kidnapped to bring to the West in chains, in slave ships, millions of black men, women, and children, who were worked and beaten and tortured as slaves.

The devil white man cut these black people off from all knowledge of their own kind, and cut them off from any knowledge of their own language, religion, and past culture, until the black man in America was the earth's only race of people who had absolutely no knowledge of his true identity.

In one generation, the black slave women in America had been raped by the slavemaster white man until there had begun to emerge a homemade, handmade, brainwashed race that was no longer even of its true color, that no longer even knew its true family names. The slavemaster forced his family name upon this rape-mixed race, which the slavemaster began to call "the Negro."

This "Negro" was taught of his native Africa that it was peopled by heathen, black savages, swinging like monkeys from trees. This "Negro" accepted this along with every other teaching of the slavemaster that was designed to make him accept and obey and worship the white man.

And where the religion of every other people on earth taught its believers of a God with whom they could identify, a God who at least looked like one of their own kind, the slavemaster injected his Christian religion into this "Negro." This "Negro" was taught to worship an alien God having the same blond hair, pale skin, and blue eyes as the slavemaster.

This religion taught the "Negro" that black was a curse. It taught him to hate everything black, including himself. It taught him that everything white was good, to be admired, respected, and loved. It brainwashed this "Negro" to think he was superior if his complexion showed more of the white pollution of the slavemaster. This white man's Christian religion further deceived and brainwashed this "Negro" to always turn the other cheek, and grin, and scrape, and bow, and be humble, and to sing, and to pray, and to take whatever was dished out by the devilish white man; and to look for his pie in the sky, and for his heaven in the hereafter, while right here on earth the slavemaster white man enjoyed *his* heaven.

Many a time, I have looked back, trying to assess, just for myself, my first reactions to all this. Every instinct of the ghetto jungle streets, every hustling fox and criminal wolf instinct in me, which would have scoffed at and rejected anything else, was struck numb. It was as though all of that life merely was back there, without any remaining effect, or influence. I remember how, some time later, reading the Bible in the Norfolk Prison Colony library, I came upon, then I read, over and over, how Paul on the road to Damascus, upon hearing the voice of Christ, was so smitten that he was knocked off his horse, in a daze. I do not now, and I did not then, liken myself to Paul. But I do understand his experience.

I have since learned—helping me to understand what then began to happen within me—that the truth can be quickly received, or received at all, only by the sinner who knows and admits that he is guilty of having sinned much. Stated another way: only guilt admitted accepts truth. The Bible again: the one people whom Jesus could not help were the Pharisees; they didn't feel they needed any help.

The very enormity of my previous life's guilt prepared me to accept the truth.

Not for weeks yet would I deal with the direct, personal application to myself, as a black man, of the truth. It still was like a blinding light.

Reginald left Boston and went back to Detroit. I would sit in my room and stare. At the dining-room table, I would hardly eat, only drink the water. I nearly starved. Fellow inmates, concerned, and guards, apprehensive, asked what was wrong with me. It was suggested that I visit the doctor, and I didn't. The doctor, advised, visited me. I don't know what his diagnosis was, probably that I was working on some act.

I was going through the hardest thing, also the greatest thing, for any human being to do; to accept that which is already within you, and around you.

318

JULIAN BECK

Thoughts on the Theater from Jail: Three Letters To A Friend

Jan. 28, 1965.

Dear Karl,

Thoughts on the theater from jail. Remember that our two greatest successes, *The Connection* and *The Brig*, came out of our jail experience, Judith's and mine. Judith dedicated the production of *The Connection* to "Thelma Gadsden, dead of an overdose of heroin . . . and to all other junkies, dead and alive, in the Women's House of Detention."

She had known Thelma in jail; we both met many addicts there and had come to respect them as individuals. In jail you get very close to your companions in a way that you don't "on the street." There is a candor, an honesty, that prevails in the talk; and the close living breeds understanding and affection. In doing *The Connection* we wanted to show these people not as degenerates, but as individuals worthy of our respect, such as we had felt when we had come to know them.

When you leave jail you don't leave altogether. Anyone who has ever been in is in some ways forever tied to it hrough a bond of sympathy coupled with the hope that some day everyone will be free. Jail gives you new ideas about freedom. We felt compelled to do *The Connection*, not only because of our great admiration for Jack Gelber's accomplishments, but also because we were still somehow bound to jail and the junkies there and hoped, naively, that a play might help set them free.

The connection between *The Brig* and our jail experience is obvious. When we did *The Brig* we wanted to bring to the production all of the facts, without any faking, as we knew them. That, for instance, is why we made the play so loud. Jail is loud and we wanted the audience to feel the affliction of the noise, the reverberation of sound in steel and concrete buildings. Audiences complained, but we insisted on keeping the sound level, because that's the way it is. And again, by showing facts, we hoped, in our usual naive way, that the theater might bring freedom, at least from the abuses of authoritarian discipline.

It is interesting that in here my chief thoughts about everything, theater and life, revolve around the concepts of freedom and honesty. And when I dream of a theater of the future I dream of a theater that will be honest and free. Now my chief criticism of the contemporary theater is that it is neither honest nor free.

Honesty. I'm not even talking about truth; that's less accessible; the truth is so holy, so related to abstract values, I think, that it would be asking too much to ask for that. I am, however, asking for the simple presentation of things as they are; and I ask this of actors, directors, designers, and producers. Just give us a chance to see what things are really like, then maybe the theater can lead to real understanding.

But the theater, like life today, is so drenched in attitudes and phony concepts; it labors, like life, under the weight of so much propaganda from advertising, newpapers, public agencies like the F.B.I. and the Narcotics Bureau, Senatorial committees, campaign speeches, and classroom information molded by the morals of school boards that we hardly know any longer how to think honestly.

I am not putting down imagination or fantasy or symbolism. The imagination of the poet is not dishonest; it is the real factual statement of his imagining. I do put down what masquerades as imagination: when writers are only dishing out pre-conceived notions of what's supposed to be imaginative.

I think if we will look at this world as it really is we will find that even what is most ugly has within it the sparks of life, and is therefore moving and worthy of our attention. And I think we go to the theater to glimpse those sparks. That's why we get so excited with anticipation before we go to the theater. It's because we're looking for light in a very dark world.

As I write this I am sitting in a very ugly room in this jail but I find it, strangely, more beautiful than most of the settings I've seen in the past year on the stages of London, Paris, Berlin and New York. Because stage designers are more concerned with dramatic effects, sentimental lighting, tricks, and imitation of both art and life, rather than with art and life themselves. Life is very dramatic, you don't have to fancy it up. Art does not simply dispose of charm, which seems to be the constant effort of contemporary stage design.

Life in jail is very real. No one has to fake. I hear real speech all the time, and how I wish I could hear more of this kind of speech in the theater. Actors don't have to speak better than people. Nothing is better than people. We have to get rid of the idea that elocution constitutes good speech; I think elocution and the throaty way even our best actors often speak is related to some kind of respect for royalty, 1965. We ought to be beyond that.

I want actors to stop posing, I'm talking to Method actors,

too, to stop trying to create effects and to break through into the representation of honest life. It would be thrilling to hear Shakespeare spoken honestly, and Brecht. I think it would be startling. We might be so moved that we might begin to respect ourselves, and, instead of accepting substitutes for life in the theater and "on the street," we might find that what is real surpasses all our foolish notions.

Faithfully,
Julian.

January 30, 1965.

Dear Karl,

I got so hung up on honesty in the last letter that I left out freedom, a common fault. Am I overwhelming you with polemic? I'm guilty of that all the time, but jail makes you want to rail and yell. I often think that if the people on the street would realize how the world we live in is a prison, they'd do more yelling and railing, too. The sad, perhaps tragic, thing is that people do not realize they're not free. How thoroughly we have lulled ourselves with our pride into our brand of limited liberty.

There's liberty here, too, within the rules of the institution. There are books, lectures, classes, movies, television, though the programing is table d'hôte; pretty good food, air, trees, clean clothes, cleanliness in fact almost to the point of sterilization, much as modern American life upholds cleanliness so much that we have become enslaved to the process of keeping clean. But here we know we're not free.

Outside, people delude themselves because they don't see the bars, I dream of a theater that is free. What do I mean by that? To begin with, let us recognize the fact that everyone is not free to go to the theater; it costs too much. And then, there are the production costs that are so great that even the plays many people might want to do they are not free to do. But the public is also guilty. We applaud too easily expensive productions, which leads me to believe that we are enchained by the notion that only wealth can give us something worth major attention. In the theater we aren't free to speak freely about sex, or politics, nor are we a free enough thinking public to permit the theater to criticize all but our obvious frailties without becoming irate.

Nor are we free to fail. That's the great fear. We are so much the slaves of the success-pattern idea, that we regard failure as killing. And it is often psychologically killing. Directors and actors aren't even free to work in this so-called free society of ours. You have to plot, scheme, deceive, and dissemble to get a job. Or spend months, or even years, of your life waiting for the opportunity to work. And when, finally, you do work, you are not free to act, you have to be realistic the way, let us say, so much sculpture is realistic. No pubic hair. And when finally you do work, the pressures of time and money are so severe that you are rarely free to see your work through to completion.

What remedy do I suggest? I guess I am recommending complete social restructure. Just changing a few conditions in the theater won't help. That's an illusion. How? No answer. But if enough people start thinking about the state of things we're in, we might find a solution, an action, together.

> Faithfully,
> Julian.

Jan. 31, 1965.

Dear Karl,

Will try to make this letter less gloomy than the others. Fortunately you know me, as, at least, occasionally cheerful. A fellow inmate remarked, "You know, there are two kinds of guys in jail, the guys that are hip and the nondescripts." "How do I classify?" I asked. "You? Why, man," he replied, "you're entertainment."

Entertainment. My high-priest act tends to cover the fact that I'm an ardent admirer of entertainment, of the theater of music and dance. I think even the Hasidim regarded the delights of the flesh, and their cultivation, as ways of celebrating the lavish world created by God. But I think entertainment loses its purity and joy when it tries to put itself over as an art and becomes arty.

Genet adores popular songs because of the lush words they put in the mouths of common men who otherwise might never utter such phrases as "I adore you." Bring on dancing girls, pretty boys, music, color. Swing. But too often the true spirit is destroyed by the falsehood of artistic pleasure.

Repertory. Its chief virtue is that it provides a chance for artists to work together on many plays over an extended period of time, and therefore there is the chance to develop the craft of communal work and to develop as men working communally. Repertory theaters will fail when they keep working competitively and will succeed, at least in their work, as they develop communally and as the public develops its admiration for art made by unified groups as opposed to that of lone star individuals only.

The Theater of Cruelty. The only prediction I venture: More and more will be seen and heard of and about this kind of theater, named by a Frenchman, Antonin Artaud, who envisaged a theater which did not numb us with ideas for the intellect, but stirred us to feeling by stirring up pain. We are a feelingless people (consider all the suffering we permit in this world as we go about our business); and if we could at least feel pain, we might turn towards becoming men again instead of turning more and more into callous automata.

Black Theater. The theater is a mirror of the world. In the West, especially in the United States, the more it avoids the presence and problems and world of the Negro, the more distorted it is. More black writers and actors are only part of the problem; the other part is that the whites, who control most theater, if they want to see the truth, will find ways of bringing black into the theater. And to do that we must learn to communicate, black and white, each learning about what goes on in the others' heads and lives. We don't know now. That's part of the work. Love is the measure of the degree of communication. When I love someone I want to be with them.

I look forward to being with you soon.

Faithfully,
Julian

DICK GREGORY

Nigger

It's a great thing to go to jail for right, but whether you're there for right or wrong, when you hear that big steel door close and that key turn, you know you're there. That was Birmingham, May of 1963. Martin Luther King asked me to come down. I arrived at 11:30 A.M. on a Monday, and an hour and a half later I went to jail with more than 800 other demonstrators. It was my first time in jail to stay.

"You Dick Gregory?"

"I'm Mister Gregory."

Somebody snatched my collar and my feet didn't hit the floor again until I was in solitary confinement.

Later in the afternoon I was brought downstairs and put in a cell built for twenty-five people. There must have been 500 of us in there. When they moved us out to eat, the corridors were so crowded you couldn't walk. Just stand still and let the crowd move you along. The last one back in the cell didn't have a place to lie down and sleep.

There was a little boy, maybe four years old, standing in the corner of the cell sucking his thumb. I felt sorry for him. He didn't even have someone his age to play with. I kind of rubbed his head and asked him how he was.

"All right," he said.

"What are you here for?"

"Teedom," he said. Couldn't even say Freedom but he was in jail for it.

The older kids sang church songs, sitting and waiting for the night to pass away. None of us knew how long we were going to be in jail. We were hoping new people would come in with information about the movement outside. We didn't really know, squatting there in that Birmingham jail, that the first really great battle of the revolution was going on outside. That a man named Bull Connor was becoming a symbol to the world of how low and vicious and stupid one American could be to another. That an Alabama city was becoming a symbol to the world of the cancer eating away at our country. On the other side of that wall were dogs and fire hoses and guns and clubs, and the blood of black men and white men, good men and bad men of both colors, and children and women and old people. We were in the battle, but the rest of the world, outside that jail, saw more than we did. Bombs and soldiers and killings. And some of them outside were horrified that Martin Luther King used little children, and some of them understood that Freedom was for little black children, too, that in an all-out war for survival there are no civilians. There were little children in Hiroshima.

The jailers fed us in the morning, and it tasted good because some of us hadn't eaten in twenty-four hours. They harassed us, too, and that second day they opened the cell door and tried to reach in and pull some of the kids out. The kids wouldn't go, and we were trying to close the door while the guards were trying to open it. Part of my arm was hanging outside the bars, and one of the guards slammed down on it with his billy club. Before I could remember about nonviolence I threw the door open and jumped out after him. Right into the arms of five guards.

It was the first really good beating I ever had in my life, a professional job. End to end, up and down, they didn't miss a spot. It didn't really start hurting until about midnight when I tried to touch my face, and I couldn't get my arm up that high. What the hell, if you're willing to die for Freedom, you have to be willing to take a beating. For a couple of days, though, I thought that dying was probably easier.

It was just body pain, though. The Negro has a callus growing on his soul and it's getting harder and harder to hurt him there.

That's a simple law of nature. Like a callus on a foot in a shoe that's too tight. The foot is nature's, and that shoe was put on by man. That tight shoe will pinch your foot and make you holler and scream. But sooner or later, if you don't take the shoe off, a callus will form on the foot and begin to wear out the shoe.

It's the same with the Negro in America today. That shoe — the white man's system — has pinched and rubbed and squeezed his soul until it almost destroyed him. But it didn't. And now a callus has formed on his soul, and unless that system is adjusted to fit him, too, that callus is going to wear out that system.

I thought about that for five days in the Birmingham jail while Martin Luther King was waking up America.

JERRY RUBIN

To My Brothers and Sisters

I am at this writing locked in a tiny cell in Cook County Jail — a cell which I share with too many friendly cockroaches. I can't get out except to go to court — I can't see any other people but I hear their screams — the hysterical cries of people going mad because they are treated like caged animals —

The man in the cell next to me talks aloud to himself all through the night and I find it hard to sleep. Prisoners satisfy their frustration by cursing at each other. "Suck my dick!" Every man feels crushed by the Machinery of injustice — One man vs. the State. What chance do you have? Cynicism! Anger! Desperation!

Inmates in Jail have little to look forward to — You wish that time would fly, that the hours would rip off. Tomorrow brings more boredom, loneliness, isolation —

Yes, this is a Hell. This is it.

I entered Santa Rita Rehabilitation Center in Oakland, California on Monday, Sept. 8 on an all-expense-paid trip to backstage into the nightmare of America's dark soul — My 45-day sentence was for a 1966 sit-in on the Berkeley Campus — if the officials were really trying to "rehabilitate" me, they did everything backwards — I wish everybody could be sentenced to spend some time in any jail in America. If you do not come out a determined revolutionary, it's because the system has smashed your capacity for compassion, love, and hope.

Santa Rita Rehabilitation Center tries to "rehabilitate" by destroying one's individuality, ego, self-respect. We are given numbers, identical clothing, counted and recounted five times a day, degraded by 1001 rules and regulations, and placed at the total mercy of non-merciful cops. You don't call a cop a "pig" while in jail. You jump to attention when the "Bull" approaches. Any slight show of disrespect means automatic banishment to the "hole"—the jail within the jail.

My brother Stew Albert was ordered from a sick bed in the hospital and sent to the Hole for 10 days because he dared to question the word of a prison bull.

The first thing that happened to me at Santa Rita was that I was ordered to get a haircut. Jail regulations demand that every inmate have a 1½ inch standard haircut. I was turned from a beautiful, long-haired, bearded beast to a crew-cut, bare-chinned ugly pig by the Murderers of Santa Rita.

Cultural Genocide!

You can cut off my long hair but you cannot cut off long hair. The pigs think that if they shear our hair, they will destroy us. They know that long hair represents our new community's sense of identification. As part of the brainwashing in jail, they try to destroy our identity by cutting our hair. But—surprise! hair grows back! They can cut our hair, but they cannot cut our soul.

As an act of solidarity with a scalped long hair, yippies from all over America are symbolically snipping a lock of their hair and donating that lock to a wig which I will wear when I get out of jail. Mail your lock to: Jerry Rubin's Wig. Federal Court Building, Conspiracy Trial, Chicago, Illinois 60604. My wig will therefore be tribal, community hair, reflecting our solidarity against those who try to destroy us. (If you have any locks left over, happy Judge Julius is also badly lacking in hair.)

On Wednesday September 16 I was sleeping in my bunk when at 2 A.M. cops threw a flashlight in my face and told me to get dressed. I was then locked in a packed bullpen with a couple hundred other prisoners until 9 A.M., when two federal marshals put me into a 1969 Rambler and told me they were taking me to Chicago. BY CAR. I asked the logical question: "Why don't we fly?" They said they would not fly because they feared a hijacking to Cuba.

They refused to let me notify my lawyer, family, wife, brothers or friends. For five days I was held incommunicado. I was told that until I got to Chicago "in a week or so" I could maintain contact with no one!

To enforce their kidnap and prevent any attempted escape, I was double-handcuffed, chains were put around my stomach and hands, shackles were placed on both my legs. Handcuffed, chained, and shackled from San Francisco to Chicago! There were two other prisoners in the car. One was on a 5 years-to life sentence in San Quentin for armed robbery. The other, Art, was one of the FBI's Ten Most Wanted Men, a bank robber going to prison for a 45 year jail sentence. I was chained to Art.

The two federal marshals sat in the front seat. Don, the driver, packed a gun, played the radio occasionally, and kept asking me questions about "The revolution." The other marshal, Percy(?), spent his time dropping gum drops and eyeing us with hate.

As the trip rolled on, I learned that two years earlier, in a similar trip across the country, Art unlocked his handcuffs and chains, grabbed the marshal's gun and said: "Now you'll take orders from me." He handcuffed, chained, and shackled both marshals to a tree in the woods and drove off with their car, guns, and money. He was caught in a shoot-out with cops in Hayward, California, after a bank robbery two years later.

The marshals drove every day from 7 A.M. to 4 P.M. At lunch hour our leg shackles were removed and we entered small truck stops for lunch, eating with our handcuffs on. At night we were placed for "safe keeping" in different jails along the route. I spent my nights in the county jails of Reno, Salt Lake City, Cheyenne, Wy. and Council Bluffs, Iowa.

When I finally arrived at Cook County I was met personally by the Warden, who warned me: "We allow no organizing here—jail is for the forgotten." (Just as I was removed from Santa Rita, Stew, a number of other prisoners and I were starting to circulate a petition in the jail for humane treatment). The warden then placed me in maximum security.

Inmates are the most oppressed class in society. A prisoner has NO rights—"No matter what *they* want", is the way the cook at Santa Rita put it, referring to the long, long lines of prisoners lining up for the pure starch slop that ought to be flushed down the toilet.

In Cook County Jail, prisoners are stripped and searched every time they move. "O.K., everything off, including your drawers. Spread your cheeks." Last time I was in Cook County Jail, during the Democratic Convention, a guard put a rubber hose on his finger and stuck it up our rectum, looking for what? That medical practice has apparently been dropped. The stripping and searching is part of the process of dehumanization.

Justice, justice, what a can of worms! Prisoners must be grateful for the simplest human decency—a smile, politeness, a bit of information. We are constantly told: "You are shit. Who are you to ask for anything? You are a dirty pod of urine".

Malcolm X said that no man "reforms" when he is behind bars. I agree. I've met hundred of prisoners in jails across the country and I have never met one who regretted what he did or did not do. When you meet a prisoner you begin by asking: "What's your beef?" Never, ever, ever, ever have I met a prisoner who was ashamed to say. It's a standard question and everyone answers proudly. We all know the real criminals are the pigs who put us in jails like these. The criminals have the keys.

One of the most frightening things about jails is how quickly you are forgotten. The convicts will make the revolution—but prisoners cannot move until they get support from the outside. We must relate at all times to those behind bars—we must throw America's death jails into her smiling Sunday School face.

In Cook County Jail I am with Bobby Seale, National Chairman of the Black Panther Party, who is the subject of the most severe repression you can imagine. Bobby is being railroaded with us in the Conspiracy Trial, and has been jailed without bail on the framed up ridiculous charge of conspiracy to murder, based on the lying testimony of a police agent. Bobby is in high spirits. He realizes that it is the revolutionary power of the Panthers that has forced the power structure to expose dirty hand. Bobby is an inspiration to anyone who meets him in jail.

Anyone who's heard anything about the Conspiracy Trial so far sees that the government has ripped off its "liberal" face and is determined to jail us—whatever the cost. The trial has become the symbolic attempt by the government to turn back the New Left, the movement and the hippies and yippies. It is a "show-trial"—the 74 year old post-menopausal judge belongs in a mental hospital. We have been denied our attorney, Charles Garry, and two of the other lawyers have been jailed. Every motion we make is denied. The FBI has tampered with the jury. The government controls the courts—but we, the people, can stop the trial if we move in the streets.

WE DEMAND IMMEDIATE FREEDOM FOR JOHN SINCLAIR JAILED FOR 10 YEARS IN MICHIGAN FOR POSSESSION OF TWO JOINTS. FREE ALL PRISONERS! JAIL THE JUDGES! JAIL JULIUS HOFFMAN! SOLIDARITY! WE ARE ALL ONE! GIVE ME SOME HAIR! LOVE FROM HELL,

Jerry Rubin

JOHN SINCLAIR

A Letter to Leni

Dear Leni;

Every day it gets weirder, huh? Today, when I was walking out to lunch a dude came up and told me that he'd heard on the radio that I was being arraigned in Detroit next week for conspiracy to blow up the CIA building last year. That's pretty far out, but it's right on as far as I'm concerned. They might as well arraign me on that—the only crime I'll ever admit to is the only one I ever committed—the assassination of President McKinley in 1901! They'll never pin it on me! Never! Those punks . . .

I can't wait to get on the stand and tell the real story of those bombings—How Valler got the dynamite and told everybody about it and got all those young kids involved in Detroit and now is the government's witness so he can get special parole. I don't know how the fuck he ever got me into his paper conspiracy, and that's pretty wierd, too, since I didn't even know who he was or that he existed until after he was arrested with Valler. But the *police* and the papers and the courts don't care who really did it anyway, as long as they get somebody and have somebody to lie for them. What's really the funniest thing about the whole deal is that I didn't even know there *was* a CIA building in Ann Arbor until I read in the paper that somebody had blown it up, and then I figured that Valler and them had done it. Now I read in the papers that *I* was the one. Far out. It's quite an honor, I guess, and it would certainly go to prove that the dope bust was political after all, despite all their protestations to the contrary, and now they prove our point by sticking me with a political arrest pure and simple. I confess! I started the Cold War too! I'm responsible for inflation and the trial of the Green Berets too! I'm the reason Howdy Doody isn't on the air anymore, too! What else do you want me to say? I read a book by Che Guevara once! I jack off at night sometimes! I'm a real crook, buddy, and don't try to cross me or I'll eat your Wheaties! What the fuck . . .

I'll see you soon enough, if I make it, and wouldn't you know, the indictment comes down on the 2nd anniversary of the CIA offing Che! All power to the People! Off the Pig!

Love,
John
Political Criminal and Criminal Conspirator

329

DEATH ROW
TRUMAN CAPOTE

Eight Interviews with The Condemned

"Today, I was scheduled to die . . . but I got my sixth stay of execution. This was the closest time. I came within one week. When they say that this is Friday and on next Friday you're scheduled to die, it just doesn't register on you because you can't comprehend no longer existing. Actually, a condemned man is a vortex of a hurricane, but he is the calm part. And all the drama, the tension is not really with him. It's with his family and his attorneys and the administration and the court personnel who are involved with it, because these are the ones that the thing really affects most. When a person is executed he loses any sense of punishment because you have to have him afterwards to say, 'We had to punish you and now you're not supposed to do this no more.' And when they use capital punishment, they can't do that. The only people that can benefit from it are the ones that carries out the execution. We can't accept it as even being punishment because we can't comprehend the actual act of losing our lives."

> **MICHAEL JOHN BELL**
> Death Row
> Colorado State Penitentiary.

FRED BASSETT, *twenty-two, has been on San Quentin's Death Row since February, 1967, convicted of fatally shooting his mother and father. He had been planning the crime since he was eight years old and succeeded when he was eighteen, a college freshman and editor of a college literary magazine. He was in a state hospital for the insane for two years after the shootings, then was released as legally sane, and tried. He spends his hours on Death Row writing stories and poetry.*

"I warned them. I said I was going to do it. But nobody paid any attention. Then the time came. And I did it. There's no way of telling when or whether I'll go down to the chamber. You never know how they decide who goes and who doesn't. Sometimes I think they decide on a dart board.

"I never get to keep my writing. As soon as I finish a story the guards take it away and tear it up. The people here don't like anybody writing anything—not since the experience they had with Caryl Chessman. Literature is out."

WILLIAM MICHAEL NOAH *has been described as a "life-long incorrigible"—in and out of correctional institutions most of the twenty-one years he has lived. He owes his present confinement on Death Row to a number of violent assaults against prison guards and fellow inmates: in one instance he stabbed his victim more than fifty times, then dragged him to a cell so that the prisoner within could stab him as well; other prisoners stabbed him an additional fifty or sixty times.*

"But the guy lived. So you can't say I actually ever killed anybody. I don't belong on Death Row. Nobody does. This is supposed to be the modern world. But it's more like ancient Rome. Tossing people to the lions. Why don't they just cart us off to the lions every Friday?"

SYLVESTER LEE GARRISON *was convicted of first-degree murder in 1959 in Denver, Colorado. He has been on Death Row in Colorado State Penitentiary for more than eight years.*

"I just can't sleep here. I can't get accustomed to it. I don't care how long I've been here, I'm never going to get accustomed to it. And I drives myself away from it. I can't relax. I don't want to relax. I want always to go out. I don't want to get institutionalized. If I have to do the rest of my natural life here, I'm never going to like it. I'm going to find some fault. The bunk is too hard, I'm too close to the wall, or something. I don't want to fall in love with this place.

"We got two TV channels and if you don't want to watch you can read or do what you're going to do, or you can take a trip. I can go anyplace I want to go, you know, make-believe. Tripping is not like you probably think. It's not a question of going back over your childhood where you've been. It's a question of looking ahead. I starts off tripping about six or six-thirty. I can talk to you and still be on a trip at the same time. And when I quit tripping, then I stop. Then I fool around, fool around. I want to get back on that trip. I start all the way over the beginning, come all the way up, and I changes it as I go along. I might go to New York or maybe I'll go to California this time. And that's the way the trip is. And it takes me six, seven months sometimes to get off one.

"They're real people with me. Could be people that I know

or people that I would like to know like the Kennedys, Johnson—people like that. And I'm in a position that I can throw my weight around too. I can get my two cents in. I'm not a prisoner, you see. I'm a free man. And that's my power.

"The death penalty, it don't serve no purpose. You've got thirteen states that've done away with it. In ten years we won't have it in this country. And if I have to go, I hope I'm the last one going—they don't do nobody else that way. No, it just isn't right."

JOSEPH MORSE, *twenty-four, is a multiple murderer who has been sent to San Quentin's Death Row on two separate occasions. He was first sentenced to death for slaying his mother and crippled sister (in a second trial, held to establish punishment, he was re-sentenced to life). During the retrial period, however, he killed a fellow prisoner in the jail where he was being confined.*

"I was always a lost kid—on my own and out on the streets since I was twelve. Filled with wanderlust. Not running away so much as running to something. Something I never found. Love, maybe. I never was in love. Though I guess I've been loved. Yes, I'm sure I have. But my problem is I'm a case afflicted with severe sociopathy. I can't change because I can't benefit by experience. Experience teaches me nothing. If I were to get out of here tomorrow, I'd probably kill again. Do it without any thought of the death penalty. Even though I've already spent five years on Death Row and know full well what it means."

RICHARD B. SCHWENSON *was convicted of first-degree murder in 1962 and spent two years on Death Row in Oregon State Penitentiary. Then he was re-tried for murder on appeal and was acquitted. Previously he had been convicted of violent assault for a near-fatal beating of a woman and is now serving out that sentence.*

"September of 1961 I was in a bar in Portland and met this woman. After the bar closed we left in her car and she drove me out to my home. We parked in front of the house and during intercourse, she passed out. And rather than just leave her in the car—I couldn't wake her up at the time—I drove about thirty or forty miles out to the highway, and she still hadn't awakened. I had the windows open and it was beginning to rain and this was the point where I discovered she was dead. I drove back to Portland. Hindsight says I should have gone to a hospital or to the police, but I didn't. I panicked, parked the car, and left it. The body wasn't discovered for a week and when they finally did perform an autopsy they listed the cause of death as an air embolism. And when we finally got to trial they had a pathologist from Tacoma come in who was supposed to be one of the authorities on impact of embolism. He said that according to this autopsy there was no way that they could have established any cause of death. The main arguments in the trial were medical, and I think to this day that most of the jury didn't understand one way or another what the doctors were talking about.

The death penalty almost never seems to affect anyone with money. It's still the poor slob that's going out the back door. We had several cases here in Oregon where a good attorney and a lot of money laid around resulted in, if not acquittal, at least a life sentence. Life is a tough sentence to live down in this state. It doesn't have the indeterminate sentence, but it's better than death. There is a future to it somewhere. The death penalty is a final thing, any way you look at it. It is a deterent to the particular individual executed, but it doesn't help society as a whole. And it's still killing, no matter how you justify it."

ERNEST SHEPARD III, *twenty-three, was sentenced to death for the muder of a fifty-two-year-old man during a robbery. He has been at San Quentin for eighteen months and claims to have found a certain salvation in his fate.*

"The death sentence, that matured me, helped me to see life clearly—now that I live so closely to death. Before I was just more or less skating around. Trying to survive. To exist. But what has happened has given me time to think and grow. To read and study and learn. Of course I'm not saying Death Row is a 'Rehabilitation Center.' For most of us it's just the opposite. This place is nothing but a warehouse of death. All the same, this has been a good thing for me. It has given me a spark mentally, and even if the end is death I will have progressed up until that time. It's unfortunate if I have to go before my potential has been tapped. But I've come to grips with the aspect of dying— most men in my situation do. We're not scared the way people think. My happiness radiates from within. If I go I'll go like a man. Otherwise my manhood will have been a fraud."

ROBERT LEE MASSIE, *twenty-six, is the product of a broken home and has been a delinquent since the age of eight, finally resulting in the murder of a California housewife whom he was*

334

attempting to rob. He has been on Death Row at San Quentin
for three years. But, unlike virtually all other condemned men,
he adamantly claims his right to execution and has instructed
his court-appointed attorneys to cease their appeals.

"I'm sick of the whole mess. Life never gave anything to me.
It was always just drugs and alcohol and misery. And I never
gave anything to life. I always knew it would end up like this—
killing people. That's why I tried to join the Army. At least that
way it would have been legal. But they didn't want me. Nobody
ever has. So let's get it over with. All I have to say is, see you in
the next world."

CARYL CHESSMAN

Ex Ungue Leonem

Who are the doomed? What are they really like?

Entertainment almost invariably and news media too often
depict them as: (a) snarling and low-browed anthropoidal types
ready to leap out of their cages at their keepers' throats if given
half a chance; (b) unregenerate, sly, vile and vicious incarnations
of inhuman evil of the sort so admirably portrayed by Peter
Lorre; or (c) cringing, subhuman creatures, leading a foreshort-
ened and tormented existence in a kind of spiritual vacuum.

This, of course, is a grossly distorted picture, overdrawn and
oversimplified—but it's the picture the public gets foisted upon it
repeatedly. Too, it's one jerked from context. So before individ-
ualizing, let's look briefly at what the doomed man—no matter
who or what he is—faces, and the stark awareness that comes to
him after a few days or weeks on the Row that he is here—to
die!

Often his anxiety causes him to overlook the fact that all the
other men around him are here for the same reason and he will
want to discuss his case over and over with anyone who will listen, as though what has happened to him is unique. To his listen-
er, it isn't. "Hell, Mac," he'll be told, "I got a death sentence,
too." Here condemnation is an everyday thing, and he, this new
arrival, is just one more on the count sheet. This is unsettling.
He has been suddenly snatched from the public eye and confined in an isolated place. The marked contrast disturbs him.

During his trial time and events moved so swiftly that what was happening to him didn't quite seem real, and there was a reassuring warmth even in the stern gaze of the public. There he was surrounded by life — not death.

Then, coming to the Row, he encounters the cold and unnatural reality of a place where men are held suspended between two worlds, for weeks and months and years. It's then as well as subsequently that he must be wary. Naked fear will make repeated attempts to capture and subjugate his mind. If successful, such a fear is capable of deluding him into believing he cannot die, that for "reasons" he is unwilling to explore critically, he is too important to die. It can make him useless to himself, hated by others. It can kill him, slowly, or drive him insane. It can transform him into a human vegetable.

Should he sidestep this first and continuing psychical trap (and many do), he will encounter others. He knows, or soon learns, that he has an appeal; but the word "appeal" has only a vague meaning. Moreover, it will be handled for him by an attorney, either one he has hired, or, if he is without funds, one the court will appoint for him. Since, almost without exception, he has but the haziest of notions, often wishfully erroneous, of the mechanics and purpose of the appellate process, he is a man waiting alone in a dark room, while other men in some remote place wrangle over his life. The executioner meanwhile waits confidently just outside his cell door.

Death, seeking permission to foreclose the claim it has upon him, is simply too inexorable and elusive an opponent. So death becomes Death, no longer an act but an actor. Death becomes "Digger," the guy to beat.

A stay is granted. Its recipient may shout: "Digger ain't nowhere!"

There's an argument. One of the man may want to fight, but the other will brush him off with: "Man, I ain't gonna mess with ya, I'm gonna let *Digger* get you!"

The doomed man is galled by the months of waiting and the infernal uncertainty. Instinctively, as the tension generates inside him, he wants to fight back. Not able to do battle with Digger, he may take a poke at his neighbor. He may fight himself.

Discovering he lacks a sword and a sword arm to combat his tormentor, he may attempt, with characteristic fervor, to forget him. He may seek out a hiding place from the reality of his situation. He may become submissive, subconsciously operating on the theory that Death surely would not take advantage of such a helpless being. This is his way of entering a plea of *nolo contendere* — no contest. Or, without being fully aware of his purpose, he may be trying to frighten Digger off when he roars through the bars at his neighbors.

Unable to save himself, he may suddenly believe he can save mankind. Here pansophists spring up like toadstools, as do marvelous kinds of religionists and soul-searchers. It is not an uncommon thing to be assured by an indignant speaker that he is the victim of the machinations of his society and its cynical servants.

And, seeing and hearing all this, you begin to wonder if this parody called Death Row is really what society wants after all.

Here there is no norm to guide the condemned man because here there is nothing normal. Properly speaking, there is no right way or wrong way for him to adapt to this mocking milieu. There is only a positive and a negative way.

Positive in the sense that the doomed man can take a reasonably knowledgeable look at what confronts him both immediately and ultimately. He can, to the limit of his resources, take all the steps available to avoid execution. He can get along to the best of his ability while awaiting the outcome of his appeal or appeals. Then, if execution proves unavoidable, he can calmly go to his death with a philosophical shrug.

Negative in the sense that he can irrationally refuse to face up to the twin realities of Death Row and death in the gas chamber. He can distract his subconsciously tormented mind by frenzied self-deceptions. He can turn desperately inward or outward in seeking to blind himself to the fact the executioner is waiting for him. He can woo or feign insanity or a destructive mania. And, when the Grim Reaper finally claims him, he can whimper or scream or curse.

In most cases it doesn't make the least difference how the condemned man reacts to the Row or how he acts while on it. However exemplary his conduct while waiting to die, when the judicial and executive mills stop grinding he usually is just as thoroughly dead.

A few months ago the death sentences of two doomed men were commuted to life imprisonment without possibility of parole. One had been in constant conflict from the time he was brought to the Row. While serving an earlier sentence, he had killed a man in prison and was convicted of manslaughter. The other had been sent to prison originally for murder. A couple of years after his arrival at San Quentin he had stabbed another prisoner and freely admitted he had intended to kill him. Only a surgical miracle saved his victim's life. Tried and convicted under the state's "assault by a life-term convict" law, a capital offense, he thanked the jury. During his trial he had demanded the death penalty and said he would kill again if not given it.

The day these two men were transferred from the Row a third man was executed. Dull mentally, quiet and resigned, this farm worker in his fifties had spent his time here reading the Bible

337

and preparing for death. In a moment of emotional chaos, he had shot and killed a young girl with whom he had become infatuated in a non-sexual way. "I deserve to die," he told me. His execution rated six lines in the back pages of the newspapers. The commutation of the other two men was front-page stuff.

Theoretically, punishment for the condemned man's penal act does not begin until he is strapped into a chair in the gas cell. Actually, it begins the day he comes to the Row.

Sixty men have taken that last walk by my cell. One was an old dodderer with a persecution complex. Another was a frightened youngster with a harelip who was executed before he really had to shave. They were tall and short and in between; thin and fat; young and old; religious and irreligious; bright and dull; brave and not brave; some distinguished looking, some nondescript. Among them were men of Indian, African, Irish, Spanish, Jewish, Polish, French, Scandinavian, and English blood.

Each different, they had only their grim fate in common, and the fact that they were convicted murderers. With gun, club, poison, knife, hatchet or bare hands they had snuffed out another human life. For that the law had demanded their lives, and while waiting to exact payment had held them together here on Death Row. The time they waited for the executioner ranged from eight months to over six years. A majority of them were put to death on the first date fixed for execution following affirmance of their appeals. Others received one or more stays before taking that final walk. One of them dodged death twelve times; the thirteenth time his luck ran out.

Those are the dead.

When one left, another came to take his place; and when he leaves there will be yet another to replace him. The population during my "tenure" has varied radically, from a low of nine to a record high of thirty-one; but, on the whole, it remains rather proportionately constant. At the time of writing (late 1954), the number of men held on the Row under death sentence is twenty-one; while nineteen plus has been the average population over the last six and a half years. Row population continues to rise in direct ratio to the growing population of the state. Dividing the number of people living within the state who are eighteen years of age and over—the age at which you become legally eligible to be executed—by the number of persons under death sentence, I learned that approximately one man (or woman, a rarity) out of five hundred thousand is condemned each year.

If you live in California and are eighteen or over, the odds are roughly only one out of five thousand you will be charged with homicide and only one out of fifty that you will be sentenced to death if convicted. But once the death penalty is assessed, the odds are almost hopelessly against you. All you have left then is what gamblers aptly call sucker's odds—and a cell on Death Row.

EDGAR SMITH

Life in the Death House

A new death house was opened in December 1966. The old building, in which I had spent nine and a half years under sentence of death, could not be enlarged; and since all eighteen cells were occupied by the fall of 1966, with no executions scheduled, new quarters had to be found. The authorities, always hampered by limited funds, hit upon the idea of erecting a wall across the interior of one of the larger wings in the main section of the prison, thereby creating two small wings. The wing finally selected for alteration had been used for many years to house the prison's honor inmates.

When we moved to our new quarters on December 28, it was necessary for us to walk a hundred yards or so across the prison's inner courtyard. It was a memorable occasion for me: the first time in nine and a half years that I had not had a roof over my head and four walls closely surrounding me, and I was temporarily blinded as I stepped through the door into the sunlight. It was as if I were emerging from a dungeon, or Plato's cave. Gradually, however, my eyes became accustomed to the glare, and as looked up and saw nothing above me but the limitless expanse of cloudless winter sky, I was gripped by a sudden feeling of insecurity, reminiscent of the initial seconds of my first parachute jump. For one fleeting moment I yearned for the familiar surrounding of my old cell, just as fourteen years earlier I had wanted to climb back into the airplane from which I had jumped. Sunlight, sky, snow remaining from a pre-Christmas storm: these things were completely foreign to me, as if I were seeing them for the first time.

The new Death House is no longer a Death House, or so the official fiction proclaims. Someone, probably a bright young bureaucrat with an Alice in Wonderland complex, came up with the notion that something—the image?—would be improved, and that someone—the inmates? the authorities?—would feel better if the Death House were discarded and the designation

"Three Wing" substituted. But to the inmates, none of whom are in here for stealing hubcaps, this name-changing is just another example of official gobbledy-gook, part of the state's let's-pretend-we-aren't-killing-people fiction. As Gertrude Stein might have put it: A Death House is a Death House is a Death House.

Our new quarters consist of twenty-seven cells on three tiers. It is a much brighter place, with fluorescent lighting and twenty floor-to-ceiling windows. The outer wall of the prison is only forty feet from the windows, four of which are directly opposite my cell on the second tier, and through them I can see both the sky and the Norway maples lining the street in front of the prison. Even the sun has ceased to be a stranger. The windows face east, so that as the sun rises above the wall each morning, my cell is filled with light. A far cry from the old building.

Between the Death House and the outer wall is a 40-by-200-foot recreation yard, formerly the exclusive playground of the honor inmates. Access to the area is through a door from the Death House. Each day an inmate-gardener from the prison's general population goes into the yard to tend the walks, mow the lawns, and care for the hundreds of flowers he has planted — zinnias, petunias, marigolds, pansies, lilies, snap-dragons, and begonias. At one end of the area is a small handball court, and alongside that is an inmate-constructed miniature golf course. Completing the scene are several concrete benches, and an always crowded birdbath.

The honor inmates are no longer permitted to use their private yard, for fear, one supposes, that they might approach too close to the Death House. Nor is the yard destined to be used by the inmates under death sentence. An effort would be made, we were most solemnly assured shortly after moving, to provide us with daily recreational periods. In this regard, the warden, Howard Yeager, has stated that "there is no reason why the condemned men should not be allowed out of their cells for exercise."[1] But the assurances proved empty.

The excuse for not permitting us to use the yard is that another officer (a guard) would have to be hired to maintain order among the inmates — a sensible precaution — and that the state officials refuse to allocate funds for this purpose. When it is suggested that one of the two officers always on duty in the Death House could handle the job, since there would be nothing for either officer to do inside if all of the inmates were outside, the authorities respond by shrugging their shoulders. This sort of logic tends to befuddle them. Hence, the recreation yard re-

[1]*Sunday Press*, Asbury Park, N.J., July 16, 1967, p. 30.

mains unused, and the Death House inmates remain in their cells twenty-four hours a day.

Life in the Death House—an oxymoronic phrase—is not as difficult as the uninitiated might imagine, but certainly, and unnecessarily, far more difficult than it should be, as the unused recreation yard indicates. One would assume, quite naturally, it seems to me, that the prison authorities would prefer to have the inmates keep themselves occupied in some relatively harmless fashion, but that is not the case. Unlike the situation in other parts of the prison, where hobby work of every sort is encouraged. Death House inmates are not permitted to engage in any of a number of harmless pastimes. Not even oil painting, a patently inoffensive method of passing the long hours of confinement, is permitted, though there are some indications that the idiocy of this restriction is becoming apparent to those in authority.

Model building, including the assembly of those pre-molded plastic models, another excellent time-killer, is strictly prohibited. Card playing is also taboo, and the game of checkers, because of the construction of the cells, is virtually impossible. Chess was popular for a while, each player in turn calling his move to the other, but the shouting back and forth soon got on the nerves of the other inmates, and it was discontinued.

A number of the inmates, of whom I am one, have felt the urge to write—as a creative outlet and to raise money to pay legal bills—but typewriters are not permitted in the Death House, though they are in every other part of the prison. The logic behind this restriction is difficult to grasp. We have been told that it is a security matter, that we might do something "inappropriate" with the metal components of the machine; but when it is pointed out that our cells abound in metal—there are enough readily detachable, high-grade spring steel parts in my bedstring to build two typewriters,—the authorities mumble excuses about "security" and "policy." Because of the restriction on the use of a typewriter, every word of this book has been written, revised, and edited entirely by hand.

There is an interesting legal implication involved in the denial of the use of a typewriter, aside from all of the other considerations. At one point, while without an attorney, I had three days over a weekend to prepare and mail to the United States Supreme Court a supplemental petition regarding a petition for reconsideration of an appeal then before the Court. In addition to those copies required by the Court, a certified copy had to be served upon the prosecutor. With a typewriter, I could have prepared the petition and all the necessary carbon copies at one time, and all within a few hours. It was impossible to do so by hand, however; as the filing deadline passed, I had, both in effect and in fact, been denied the right of appeal.

Inmate-guard relations, and inmate morale, reached such a low ebb in February 1966 that the inmates went on a hunger strike, a fact not generally known outside the prison—officialdom at every level is loath to admit that things are ever anything but "normal." Tensions had been growing for many months, but the spark igniting the trouble was the decision by one of the guards to attempt to eliminate some of our privileges—and at the same time give himself more time to loaf. One of the privileges was to have hot coffee available at all times, a not unreasonable compensation for the privileges—motion pictures (the latest), recreation yard, monthly food packages from home—that are accorded all prisoners except those in the Death House.

After several days, when it became apparent that the inmates were serious in their resolve not to eat until the issue was settled, and when news of the affair reached the officials in charge of state institutions, some of the withdrawn privileges were restored. Other compensatory privileges were promised, among them the assurance that we would be permitted to use the recreation yard. That promise, obviously, was a joke. The root causes of the trouble—boredom, restlessness, and deteriorating guard-inmate relationships—were left unsettled.

One of the things most resented by the men under sentence of death has been the recent practice of putting men in "the Hole"—a dank, totally dark, indescribably filthy dungeon-like cell in another part of the prison. There, clad only in thin pajamas, the inmate is confined on a bread-and-water diet. There is no water for washing; he is not permitted a toothbrush; and in the wintertime, an open window turns the cell into a frozen-food locker.

During my first nine and a half years in the Death House, no inmate was put in "the Hole." Arguments with officers were usually forgotten five minutes after they ended. Since moving to our new quarters, however, an argument with an officer is a sure-fire ticket to five days in "the Hole," as a number of men have learned. And as in so many other things, a degree of discrimination against Death House inmates is apparent. Every inmate of this prison, when charged with an offense, has the right to appear before a court composed of three senior officials, who hear his side of the story before punishment can be imposed. Those under sentence of death, however, have no such right. Death House inmates charged with offenses are told simply: "You've got five days in the Hole, beginning tomorrow." So arbitrary is the system that one inmate received five days in the

342

hole for calling an officer a liar, while another inmate who attacked and injured an officer went unpunished.[2]

In all fairness, I must state that there are some excellent guards working in the Death House, men with whom the inmates get along well. There is no great secret to their success: when they come to work, they leave their personal problems at home; and if the inmates treat them decently, they do not go out of their way to make confinement more difficult for the inmates. It is a very simple formula. Some of the other guards should try it.

We do have some light moments in this abominable establishment, moments which often have been connected with the rather inept attempts of the prison psychiatrists to interview us. As they appear to most people, I think, psychiatrists appear to me to be but one step, two dried toads, a handful of powdered chicken bones, and sixteen hairs plucked from a bat's belly removed from being witch doctors—and quite ineffectual witch doctors at that.

I recall one occasion when a psychiatrist asked an inmate to draw a picture of a family. He would return to examine the drawing the next day, he said. That night, from a clothing advertisement in a newspaper, the inmate traced what must have been a Madison Avenue adman's dream of the ideal American family—mother, father, little girl, little boy—tall, slender, each exuding a vitamin-enriched health, and all with Pepsodent smiles revealing perfect, pearly white teeth. Only the family puppy was missing. The psychiatrist was beside himself with praise for the inmate's artistic abilities, and after studying the drawing, seemed convinced that he had found an incredibly well-adjusted human being. It was beautiful.

On another occasion, a psychiatrist-psychologist team arrived in the Death House to give an inmate a Rorschach test, the test in which the subject interprets so-called "ink blots." Unknown to these doctors, who had drawn their chairs up to the bars of the inmate's cell—they are not allowed to enter the cells—the escort officer standing behind them was signaling the inmate, telling him what to say. As each of the hand-painted, colored ink blots was flashed to the prisoner, he would study it for a moment, then turn his eyes upward and bite his lower lip in an attitude of deep thought, seemingly searching his mind for just the right description of the design on the card. In reality, he was watching for the guard's signal. Alas, to this day, the doctors do not know that they once spent an entire morning administering a

[2]Lest the reader think that I am crying sour grapes, I wish to say that I have never been involved in infractions of rules—a state of affairs subject to change after publication of this book.

Rorschach test to a prison guard. It would be interesting to know how he made out.

The wildest incident of all, however, and one I am always being asked to recount to new inmates, involved me. It began when a psychiatrist, a Ukrainian, who became terribly upset whenever anyone called him a Russian, came into the Death House several years ago and went around asking the inmates what they saw in the various pictures he pulled from a paper shopping bag. All went well for him until he came to me.

The picture the doctor pulled from his bag depicted, as I recall it, a log cabin set in a snow-covered forest on the side of a mountain. Above the cabin, against an overcast sky, white smoke rising from the chimney had formed a cloud the shape of a ghost, or at least a child's Halloween version of a bedsheet ghost, complete with eye holes. It was pure Freud.

"Vot is dot?" the headshrinker asked.

"Vot is vot?" I asked, mimicking him.

"Dot," he said, pointing to the ghost figure. "Vot is dot?"

"Oh, *that*. That's a spook."

"Spook? Vot is spook?"

"*That's* a spook. It's a beauty, too."

"You mean is ghost?"

"No, I mean is spook."

"Explain. Vot is spook?"

"Gee, Doc, it's pretty hard to explain. If you were an American you'd know. You see, Doc, there are ghosts and there are spooks. I'm pretty square when it comes to ghosts, but I dig spooks pretty well. Man, I can spot one every time, and that there sure is a spook. Yes, sir, no doubt about it. No ghost could ever go up a chimney like that. Down maybe, but not up."

The poor doctor stared at me for a few seconds, then put his pictures back in his shopping bag and walked away mumbling to himself. I would love to have been in the office when he returned to tell his colleagues that what they had thought for years was a ghost was really a spook.

Incidentally, or perhaps not so incidentally, my Ukrainian friend was the last psychiatrist to interview me. Since that time, they have been avoiding me. I wonder why.

Given the restrictive policies cited in this chapter, the question arises: How *does* one pass the time in the Death House? For most inmates, the answer is reading and television, the latter having come to the Death House three years ago. I am not, myself, too much of a television fan, though I do make it a point to watch all three of the network news programs each night, and most of the news specials. Also, like other inmates, I regularly watch the talk shows: Johnny Carson, Joey Bishop, David Susskind, Merv Griffin, Alan Burke, and Joe Pyne—and, lately, William F. Buckley, Jr., on *Firing Line*. But the entertainment programs, generally, have an inane sameness that repels me.

Reading takes up most of my time. Having found myself unable to continue my formal education after exhausting my savings, I turned to reading as the next best form of self-education. I have developed a particular interest in politics and world affairs, and keeping abreast of them requires an enormous amount of reading. Fortunately, with twenty-three men in the Death House, many of whom subscribe to one or more newspapers and magazines, a great variety of these are available to me. My day begins with *The New York Times*, which I read from first page to last, including the financial section. In December 1966, just before our move to new quarters, I had the privilege of meeting Mr. Edwin Roth, the distinguished British newspaper columnist, who was being given a tour of the prison. He was in this country to attend the United Nations session called to deal with the Rhodesian problem, and our conversation naturally gravitated to that subject. Mr. Roth left the Death House slightly shaken by having met a man under death sentence who 1) understood the issues involved in the Rhodesian matter; 2) could quote the previous day's closing price of the pound sterling; and 3) could relate the latter to the former. He also left convinced, I think, that because I was sympathetic to the Rhodesian position, I must therefore be a confirmed racist, colonialist, fascist—or all three.

The Times is usually followed by the *New York Daily News*, the *Philadelphia Inquirer*, the *Bergen County Record*; and two Newark, New Jersey, newspapers—the *Evening News* and the *Star-Ledger*. In addition, I am a member of the Reader's World Press Club, which every second week supplies me with an English-language newspaper published in a foreign country. Through this service I receive such disparate publications as the *London Times*, the *Manchester Guardian*, the *Jerusalem Post*, the *Baghdad News*, the *Beirut Journal*, the *Malay Echo*, the *Borneo Bulletin*, the *Saigon Daily News*, the *Calcutta Statesman*, and the *South China Morning Mail*.

Then there are the magazines: *Time, Newsweek, National Review, New Republic, Atlantic Monthly, Commentary, Life, Look, Esquire, National Geographic* (I am a society member), and *Ebony*. I also read three Communist publications: the Russian *Moscow News* and *New Times*; and the Chinese *Peking Review*.

Finally, there are books. A sample of my reading over the past several months includes: Santo Mazzarino's *The End of the Ancient World*; Ortega y Gasset's *The Revolt of the Masses*;

John King Fairbank's *The United States and China*; David Caute's *The Decline of the West*; Edgar Snow's *The Battle for Asia*; Senator Fulbright's *The Arrogance of Power*; Anthony Eden's *Foreign Affairs*; Karl Mannheim's *Ideology and Utopia*; and Herman Kahn's *On Thermonuclear War*.

I realize that the above may appear at first glance to be a tremendous amount of reading, but I do have twenty-four hours a day, seven days a week, week after week, month after month, with little else to do. Then, too, reading serves three distinct purposes: 1) It keeps me informed of, and in contact with, the world from which I have been banished—temporarily, I hope; 2) It helps me to pass the time, so that the long hours of confinement are more bearable; 3) The need to maintain a regular reading schedule, even while writing this book—if I fell behind I would never catch up—instills in me a discipline I have lacked in the past.

Still, I am often asked: Why bother reading all of that heavy stuff, rather than some pleasant light fiction, or just watch television? Why knock myself out when the odds against me are so formidable? My reply could be that I have found there is personal satisfaction to be gained in learning for the sake of learning, and that would be true. Or I could reply that the acquisition of knowledge, however esoteric, is never a waste of time, and that also would be true. But perhaps most compelling is the simple fact is that I read and study because I have wearied of being a half-educated lout in a world in which education is a parochial necessity. There is perhaps nothing more frightening to me than the prospect of finding myself stuck for the rest of my life in some dreary small town, working in some gas station or hardware store for sixty dollars a week. That would be going from one prison to another, from a cell to a cage, and I have had enough of prisons and cages.

EPILOGUE
ETHRIDGE KNIGHT

He Sees Through Stone

He sees through stone
he has the secret
eyes this old black one
who sits under prison skies
sits pressed by the sun
against the western wall
his pipe between purple gums

the years fall
like over-ripe plums
bursting red flesh
on the dark earth

his time is not my time
but I have known him
In a time now gone

he led me trembling cold
into the dark forest
taught me the secret rites
to take a woman
to be true to my brothers
to make my spear drink
the blood
of my enemies

now black cats circle him
flash white teeth
snarl at the air
mashing green grass beneath
shining muscles
ears peeling his words
he smiles
he knows

the hunt
the enemy
he has the secret eyes
he sees through stone